HOW TO
BE A
LIBERAL

Ian Dunt

First published by Canbury Press 2020
This edition published 2020

Canbury Press
Kingston upon Thames, Surrey, United Kingdom
www.canburypress.com

Printed and bound in Great Britain by CPI Group (UK) Ltd, Croydon
Typeset in Mrs Eaves/Avenir
Cover: Alice Marwick

This is a work of non-fiction

ISBN
Hardback: 978-1-912454-41-9
Ebook: 978-1-912454-42-6
PDF: 978-1-912454-44-0
Audiobook: 978-1-912454-43-3

HOW TO
BE A
LIBERAL

Ian Dunt

CONTENTS

To mum and dad,
who gave me the two most important gifts of all:
To be loved, and to be free

TODAY

Nationalism is marching across the world.

Nowhere is immune to its advance. Everywhere must come to terms with the threat it poses.

In the last few years, nationalism has become the driving force behind the Republican party in the United States, the Conservative party in Great Britain, the Bharatiya Janata party in India, Likud in Israel, the Alliance for Brazil in Brazil and PDP–Laban in the Philippines. It conquered Hungary under Fidesz and Poland under Law and Justice. It dominated political debate in Italy through the Lega, Austria through the Freedom Party, Bulgaria through Attack and Estonia through the EKRE.

Sometimes it loses a battle. Sometimes it wins. In some countries, it takes over the government in its entirety. In others, it acts as a junior partner in a coalition. Often it does not even need power. It simply dictates the political narrative from opposition.

Wherever nationalism establishes a position, it transmits its narrative, which consists of six lies, or a combination of them.

The first lie is that you do not exist as an individual. Nationalism claims that society is composed of two groups, who are in a perpetual conflict with one another: the people and the elite.

In reality, neither of these groups exist. There is no such thing as the people. Individuals do not compose a homogeneous mass. They do not speak with one voice. They have different values, interests and eccentricities. They are not singular, but plural.

The elite is also a fiction. There is no one centre of power, not in politics, economics, culture or anywhere else. The world is composed of distinct clusters of power, which sometimes flow together and sometimes apart.

The notion of the people versus the elite sounds like a challenge to power, but that is a misdirection. In fact, it consolidates power. It does this by creating a moral through-line, a fairy story, by which the nationalists can claim unchallengeable legitimacy on the basis of those they claim to represent. In their eyes, only the votes of the people who agree with them count as democracy. The rest of the population is ignored.

This process warps and diminishes what it is possible for humanity to be. Nationalism pretends that we have only one identity, that we cannot be more than one thing at once. It makes us uniform and categorised, a part of the mass: an undifferentiated component of the whole.

The second lie is that the world is simple. This lie proceeds logically from the first. If the world is split between two groups, instead of being a vast and diffuse network of individual and organisational interests, it follows that all that is wrong is the result of the elite and all that is right is the result of the people.

The notion of complexity is thereby eradicated from existence. The great ecosystems of the world – from trading networks, to law, finance and sovereignty – are wiped away. They are replaced by childish assessments of problems and infantile proposals for their solution.

These solutions never work, because they do not address the real-world circumstances which caused them. But when they fail, as they invariably do, the blame is not placed on nationalism. It is placed on a conspiracy of the elite. Nationalism therefore works as its own intellectual consolidation and enforcement program. The things which disprove it are used to justify it. The events which go against it are taken as evidence of its necessity.

The third lie is that you must not question. To speak out, to interrogate, to inquire, is to reject the purity of the people. It is to place yourself above them.

Independent minds are a threat to power. Their mere existence disproves nationalism's world view and their conclusions undermine its policy platform. They are a living refutation of the notion of a binary class system of the people and the elite. It is therefore necessary that they should be denigrated and abused. They are branded enemies of the people.

The fourth lie is that institutions are engaged in a conspiracy against the public. On a national level, these institutions include the courts, the parliament or Congress, the press, charities and research institutes. On an international level, they include the United Nations, the European Union, the World Health Organisation, and the World Trade Organisation.

By their nature, institutions limit the power of government. They scrutinise it, balance it, separate it, hold it to account, block it from taking illegal actions and force it to abide by democratic standards. Internationally, they solve problems countries cannot handle on their own, demonstrating the capacity of humankind to co-operate across national borders.

The narrative of the people versus the elite does not allow for that degree of organisation. If the people are pure and the nationalists represent them, then there can be no legitimate restrictions on their expression. So the institutions are attacked, at all levels, at all times. First they are discredited. Then they are disabled. Then they are destroyed.

The fifth lie is that difference is bad. This applies to people from other countries, or with different coloured skin, or sexuality, or clothing, or language. This view is entailed by the concept of the people as a singular, virtuous body. All outside entities are, by definition, a challenge to its purity.

Nationalism asserts that you should be afraid of those who are not like you. Minorities are treated as a threat to the integrity of the people, rather than proof of the richness of human experience. The language it speaks is of uniformity, conformity – the machine over the organism.

The sixth lie is that there is no such thing as truth. A commitment to objective fact is treated as the mewling of the elite. Evidence and reason, the qualities that allow humanity to aspire towards certainty, are dismissed as plots against the people. Statistical authorities, academics, economic analysts, trading experts and investigative journalists are categorised as political opponents. This is because truth is a challenge to power. If voters base their views on verifiable data, the nationalist narrative can be contradicted. Those who live under its shadow are therefore encouraged to process information according to their tribal identity rather than its veracity, to close themselves off from anything that might challenge their faith.

The lies of the nationalist movement range from the gigantic to the trivial, from the systemic to the opportunistic. This disinformation is not just a means to an end. It is an end itself. It serves two distinct agendas. Firstly it attempts to redefine day-to-day events in whichever way most suits the nationalist narrative. Secondly it works to degrade the entire notion of empirical reality. If nationalists can lie without consequence, the concepts of truth and falsity fall into irrelevance. And then there will be no checks on their power whatsoever.

There is a system of thought which understands what is happening to us and offers the means to resist it. Its name is liberalism. It is the single most radical political programme in the history of humankind.

This is not because of its conclusions or its tactics. It is certainly not because of the political parties that bear its name. It is because of its unit of analysis.

Liberalism is the struggle for the freedom of the individual. When it is truly followed, it can never be the tool of the powerful. It can never be used to oppress. It can only liberate.

It rejects the false choice of the people versus the elite. It is committed to empirical reality. It stands up for institutions, and diversity, and, chief among all values, the liberty of every person to engage in their own act of self-creation. To be who they want to be. To live where they want to live. To love who they want to love. To do as they please, with the only restraints on their actions entailed by the protection of liberty for others.

It pursues freedom, because freedom makes all other values possible.

Liberalism does not have a party line. It does not worship leaders. It is a living, breathing thing, a constantly evolving set of questions and answers. It is the rebel thought. The view of the world which springs from within – rather than the one imposed from above.

There are countless ways to fight back against what is happening to us, but they all start with this one moment: of understanding what liberalism is. Of knowing what we fight for and why.

This book tells the story of liberalism, from its birth in the age of science to its new status as a resistance movement against nationalism.

It is a story of war, romance, economics, eccentricity and struggle. It is the story of a single idea, which grew more complex and daring over the centuries, and of the dangers and tragedies that followed from its articulation. It is the story of some deeply unusual, stubborn, free-thinking people, who lived life on their own terms and devised a system that would allow others to do likewise.

It is also an account of how it faltered – how a combination of economics, culture and technology weakened it and brought us to the situation we are in today. It's through understanding that process that we can repair liberalism, gather ourselves and undo the damage that is being inflicted upon us.

This is how we fight back. Not by compromising with nationalism. Not by respecting it or getting so lost in our ideological confusion that we allow it to prosper. We fight back by rediscovering our principles. And that means going right back, to the dawn of science, to see where the dream of liberty first took hold.

1. BIRTH

On 10th November 1619, René Descartes had a nightmare. He was walking down a road in a violent storm and shadowy figures were following him. He couldn't keep a straight line. A weakness was affecting his right side and driving him constantly to the left. Strong gusts of wind kept spinning him around and preventing him from getting a sure footing.

Ahead of him he could make out some gates and beyond that a church where he could flee the storm. But even when he went in the courtyard, the wind kept throwing him off balance. He saw a man he recognised and tried to say something to him. It was impossible. He couldn't stand upright. Then, slowly, other figures began to appear, all of them steady on their feet, unaffected by the weather. And they stared down at him as he scrambled in the dirt.

He woke up. It was the dead of night. A fire crackled in the corner of the room. Descartes was inexplicably terrified. For hours he lay in bed and there in the darkness, half-mad with anxiety, he started to develop a terrible thought: what if there was an evil demon watching him, putting these nightmares in his head?

He prayed. And then, finally, he fell asleep again.

As soon as he lost consciousness there was a loud explosion. He snapped back awake and stared at the fire. Had it crackled loudly? Or did that just happen in his mind? He felt more terror, more of the anxiety of the night-time, and then eventually drifted off again.

He was standing by a table with two books on it. He opened one of them and saw the line: '*Quod vitae sectabor iter*?' – what path in life shall I follow? A man appeared and they discussed the books for a while. Then the books and the man faded.

But Descartes did not wake up. He stood there, by the table, and realised something. He was dreaming. And then he started to interpret the dream, to think it through, while he was still in it. When the analysis ended, he woke up.

These dreams would come to define Descartes' life. He became concerned with the gap between dream and reality, the thin line between being awake – existing in a real physical space with ordered thoughts – and the crazed world of dreaming, where everything is bizarre and volatile.

The aspect of dreams which seems to have disturbed Descartes was how life-like they felt. If dreams seemed so real at the time, he thought, then who was to say that the things we thought or perceived when we were awake were any more reliable? For all he knew, the evil demon he imagined that night was real. It could be putting thoughts into his mind when he was awake as easily as it could while he was asleep.

Descartes didn't believe there was an evil demon. What concerned him was that he could not prove – utterly, without any trace of doubt – that there wasn't. And if he couldn't prove that, then he couldn't really prove anything. Perhaps green was red. Perhaps two plus two equalled five. Perhaps the bed he slept in wasn't real. If you followed this line of reasoning far enough, the world fell down: maths, geometry, physics, politics, religion, civilisation. Everything was built on shaky foundations.

Descartes, an aimless 23-year-old Frenchman, decided to dedicate his life to finding certainty. He roamed the world, speaking with scientists and theologians, trying to find bits of knowledge, priceless slivers of certainty, which he could be absolutely sure were true. He was engaged in an act of existential quarantine: finding and isolating facts that someone could believe without any shadow of doubt.

'During the following nine years I did nothing other than wander around the world trying to be a spectator rather than an actor in the dramas that unfold there,' he wrote. 'I rooted out of my mind all the errors that could have slipped into it.' Then, eventually, he settled down and started to write philosophy. It was not until he was 45, in a work called *Meditations on First Philosophy*, that he properly grappled with the dream and its implications. It is arguably the most important book ever written, but not for the reason Descartes thought. He intended for it to be an affirmation of religious faith. He wanted to protect belief in God from the relentless doubt he had experienced, from nagging questions of scepticism. But instead of finding certainty in God, he found it somewhere else entirely. He found it in the individual.

This idea would go on to destroy the old world and create a new one, based on rights, reason and liberty. It was the birth of liberalism. And it happened by accident.

Descartes was a hard man to like. He combined haughty arrogance about the brilliance of his writing with extreme sensitivity to criticism and a disregard for the work of almost everyone else.

He dismissed even great thinkers and seemed completely uninterested in any book, by any author, on any subject. 'Although when one publishes a book one is always very anxious to know what readers say about it,' he once wrote, 'I can assure you that it concerns me very little. Indeed, I think I know the ability of most of those who pass for learned so well that I would think little of my views if they approved them.'

He was no more interested in people's company than their writing. When he returned from his early travels, he lived like a recluse, moving constantly from house to house, town to town, in a bid to be left alone.

In the end, he started to conceal his location from even trusted friends and put misleading return addresses on his correspondence. His acquaintances, such as they were, began referring to him as *Monsieur d'Escartes*: Mr Evasion. His few friendships almost always ended in bitterness and recrimination.

Insofar as he kept contact with anyone, it was Marin Mersenne, a French mathematician who acted as an intellectual hub for the scientific minds of Europe. As Descartes became more and more reclusive, Mersenne served, to all intents and purposes, as his emissary on earth. He forwarded his correspondence, told him of the current debates among learned men in France, and helped him publish his books.

They were living through a period of great change, where rationality was starting to challenge the old authority structures.

Since around the end of the 12th Century, the ideas of the ancient Greek philosopher Aristotle had begun to meld with Catholicism and fossilise into dogma. Subjects like epistemology, the study of knowledge, and metaphysics, the study of reality, had narrowed into unchallengeable truisms. Those who questioned them too forcefully were accused of heresy. Religious authorities used torture and execution to keep people in line.

Then something broke. It started with the work of Nicolaus Copernicus, a Polish polymath. His book in 1543, *On the Revolutions of the Celestial Spheres*, rejected the idea that Earth was the centre of the universe. In fact, the Earth was just a part of a solar system. The other planets in the sky were not circling around it. They, like the Earth, were circling the sun.

Copernicus was reducing the stature of humankind. He was implying that we were just one part of a greater story, perhaps just a minor part, rather than the centre of existence. The theory contradicted several passages in the Bible, including I Chronicle 16:30, which stated that 'the world also shall be stable, it be not moved.' The more confident scientific thought became, the more it challenged religion's monopoly on knowledge.

In 1593, Giordano Bruno, an Italian friar who claimed that the universe was infinite and had no centre at all, was tried for heresy by the Inquisition, the Catholic Church's religious courts. He was found guilty and burned at the stake in Rome. By 1615, the Inquisition had found Copernicus' theory to be 'formally heretical.' Later, it would persecute the Italian astronomer Galileo Galilei. He was dragged to Rome, threatened with torture and put under house arrest.

Descartes spent his life worrying about these controversies and what they might mean for his own writing. He was wise to do so. His work strongly implied – but never explicitly stated – that Copernicus' theory was correct. And there was something else, something deeper. While Descartes was a committed Christian, his thinking, when you got down to it, was fundamentally heretical. In an age of rigid religious belief, his life's work was premised on the idea that it was hard to establish certainty.

'I shall say nothing about philosophy,' he wrote in 1637, 'except that it has been practised by the best minds that have appeared over many centuries, and yet it still contains nothing that is not disputed and consequently doubtful.'

To write his first book, *The World*, Descartes retreated alone to Amsterdam between 1630 and 1633. He wrote in the opening sentence: 'In proposing to treat here of light, the first thing I want to make clear to you is that there can be a difference between our sensation of light and what is in the objects that produce that sensation in us.'

It's hard to put yourself in the mind of someone who would need to be told that light and our perception of it are different. We know that light exists and that our visual and mental apparatus – our eyes and brain – translate that phenomenon for us to experience. But in Descartes' time the orthodox view of the world was entirely human-centric. Objects were thought to contain the qualities people saw in them: blood, for instance had the quality 'red' in it. Fire had the quality of 'heat.'

Descartes was saying something completely different: an object existed independently of our experience of it. Our sensory apparatus did not tell us the truth about reality, but only what we perceived.

rule out ever being branded heretical or atheistic. This would set him free to get on with his broader study of doubt without constantly looking over his shoulder.

It turned out to be a terrible misjudgement. Descartes had become too good at what he did. He was a master of prising things apart and exposing their inner flaws. By turning his focus on God, he would end up breaking the entire composition of human knowledge. And worst of all, he would do so by accident.

In 1637, Descartes finally published his first book, a series of three essays on optics, geometry, and meteorology, with an accompanying note called *Discourse on the Method* to introduce them. The three essays are now barely remembered, but *The Discourse* has become part of the canon of western philosophy. It was where he first laid out his system for rigorous, systematic doubt – an unflinching critical gaze one could apply to any problem.

It had four sequences: First, separate out what you know to be true from the parts you can doubt. Second, break down the remaining problems into smaller units. Third, solve the simple ones first and work your way up. Finally, review the work and assess if anything has been left out.

Today it seems like a perfectly normal approach to problem-solving. At the time, it was a deeply subversive system. It didn't matter how Descartes tried to dress it up. The method implied that reality was open to the human intellect. Anyone who was prepared to sit and think could evaluate the evidence for themself. It left no room for authority, unless it had something to contribute in the search for truth, which in most cases it did not.

Descartes took care to protect himself. He published *The Discourse* anonymously. He inserted a chapter titled 'morals and maxims of conducting the method' which explicitly excluded faith and the laws of the state from its application. He made it clear that most people should not be trusted with the method.

And then, crucially, he added another section, in which he tried to show that God could not possibly be subject to the level of doubt he was applying elsewhere. Three things, he stated, existed outside the realm of scepticism: his own existence, reason and God.

It didn't work. The section was brief and reluctant. It raised more questions than it answered. And it most certainly did not erect a firewall between his faith in God and his system of doubt.

That put Descartes in a perilous position. The book may have been anonymous, but he was widely known to be its author. Any theologian who was out to get him – and there were now several of them – could claim that his arguments in favour of God were so weak that he was actually trying to spread atheism.

So he made a fateful decision. He resolved to address the problems head on. He would write another book that definitively showed that his system of doubt was not a threat to God.

It would dismantle and defeat sceptical arguments like the evil demon theory, which suggested we didn't really know anything. It would establish God's existence with absolute certainty. And then he could address himself to the problems which really interested him.

In truth, Descartes was reluctant about the whole endeavour. In order to defeat sceptical arguments he would have to describe them, and that was a dangerous thing to do.

'I did not dare to attempt this, because I would have had to explain at length the strongest arguments of the sceptics,' he wrote to an acquaintance in May 1637. 'I was afraid that this introduction, which could have appeared as if it were designed to introduce the views of sceptics, would disturb weak minds.'

As a result, Descartes switched from his native French to Latin. This had the advantage of expanding his learned audience internationally, while excluding uneducated readers – thereby allowing him to say that he had gone out of his way to protect them from febrile ideas.

But it was not enough. Descartes failed beyond his own worst nightmares. Not only would feeble minds come into contact with sceptical ideas, but he was about to write a book which described them so vividly and compellingly that he would be known for centuries as a byword for the very viewpoint he was trying to defeat.

The book was *The Meditations*. Descartes laid it out like a work of fiction. His narrator, who was a kind of composite version of himself, was in a room, by a fire, doubting everything.

He was going to sift through everything he held true and judge whether he could really prove it. If he couldn't, he'd discard it.

He didn't need to take each belief in turn. That would take too long. He only needed to look at the foundations. If those were faulty, the whole construction would come tumbling down.

So he started with his senses. 'How could I deny that I possess these hands and this body?' he asked himself. But he could, because when he was asleep, he was equally certain that his dreams were real, when in fact they turned out to be false.

'There exist no certain marks by which the state of waking can ever be distinguished from sleep,' he said. 'I feel greatly astonished; and in amazement I almost persuade myself that I am now dreaming.'

The threat of dreaming erased all certainty of the physical world. Physics, astronomy, medicine – they were all suspect. But he still had the contents of the mind, the concepts that we give meaning to through our thoughts and which exist independently of physical reality, like maths or geometry. After all, two plus two equals four no matter whether you're awake or dreaming.

But Descartes couldn't be certain of even this. He returned to his fear of an all-powerful evil demon tricking him. It could have inserted false thoughts about mathematics and geometry in our minds. Maybe in reality two plus two equalled five.

This left nothing which could withstand doubt, not even our own thoughts. 'The sky, the air, the earth, colours, figures, sounds, and all external things, are nothing better than the illusions of dreams, by means of which this being has laid snares for my credulity,' Descartes wrote.

He was lost. 'I had fallen all of a sudden into very deep water, I am so greatly disconcerted as to be made unable either to plant my feet firmly on the bottom or sustain myself by swimming on the surface.' Nothing could be relied on. 'What is there, then, that can be esteemed true?' he asked. 'Perhaps this only, that there is nothing absolutely certain.'

This was the moment in the history of ideas – the exact point – when the old world died.

Amid the ruins, Descartes started scrambling around for one thing, just one block of unassailable truth, with which he could start putting the world back together again. 'I shall be entitled to entertain the highest expectations, if I am fortunate enough to discover only one thing that is certain and indubitable,' he said.

And then he found it: a point of truth. He found the self.

He did it with a single thought: If I am being deceived, then there must be a me who is being deceived. Therefore I am.

Everything else can be stripped from you, except that one solitary part. Doubt can challenge all things, but it cannot challenge the fact that you are doubting and therefore definitely exist. 'This proposition – I am, I exist – is necessarily true each time it is expressed by me, or conceived in my mind.'

Or, in Latin: *Cogito, ergo sum.* I think, therefore I am.

It is arguably the most famous sentence in all of western philosophy. And it is also – without hyperbole – the single most beautiful thought in the history of humankind. It is the only thought you can have which is certainly true without any hint of doubt. There is simply no other thought like it. It proves itself, in a circular motion, by virtue of what it contains. It is a closed system of perfect confidence.

Descartes had brought down the entire edifice of knowledge and found just one thing that was certain: the individual.

But that was not all. There was something else contained in the Cogito: a secret partner. The individual was not a blank slate. It had one definable characteristic. It thought. It was only by virtue of thinking that it knew it existed.

'I am a real thing, and really exist, but what thing?' Descartes asked himself. 'A thinking thing.' He had a mind, he had understanding. In other words, he had reason.

This was the moment liberalism was born.

That seems a strange thing to say. Most people don't consider Descartes a liberal. He wasn't even writing about politics. Other major thinkers, like the German moral philosopher Immanuel Kant, are usually considered to be the outriders of liberalism. But it was here, completely by accident, that its basic operating units spluttered into life. The existential truth of the individual replaced the creaky old dogma of church and state.

But it was not a single embryo. The 'I am' could not be proven without the thinking and the thinking could not take place without the 'I am.'

Liberalism and reason were born as twins.

From then on, Descartes frantically tried to build up from this block of truth to where he was trying to reach all along: the existence of God. But suddenly his skills and reasoning betrayed him. From one page to another, he went from some of the most impressive arguments in the history of philosophy to some of the least.

He fired off numerous arguments for God, each seemingly more desperate than the last, each falling apart faster than the previous one. *The Meditations* collapsed as soon as it turned to its original purpose.

All of those pro-God arguments turned to dust. But the preceding thinking, the Cogito, took on a life of its own. Once its truth was revealed, it spread out relentlessly. Within years, students were asking searching questions of their teachers and agitating against the old Aristotelian strictures of their classes. Now, hundreds of years later, it is often the first argument given to philosophy undergraduates.

In truth, the ideas Descartes was outlining were not really that new. Aristotle had a similar thought when he said that 'to perceive that we perceive or think is to perceive that we exist.' St Augustine, the 5th-Century philosopher, did too, when he responded to sceptical arguments by replying that 'if I am mistaken, I exist.' Jean de Silhon, a friend of Descartes, had toyed with similar formulations.

But the history of ideas is not the history of the people who first thought of them. More often than not, it is the history of the person who popularised them. 'As a rule, the man who first thinks of a new idea is so much ahead of his time that everyone thinks him silly,' the 20th-Century liberal philosopher Bertrand Russell said. 'Then gradually, the world becomes ready for the idea, and the man who proclaims it at the fortunate moment gets all the credit.' Descartes was that person, even if he never wanted to be.

Part of the reason the Cogito spread so far and fast was because it was so well written. Despite his stated concerns about uneducated readers, Descartes continued to write 'in the vernacular.' His voice was emotionally rich and appealing. The text was vivid and immediate. It was nothing like the treatises written by other philosophers of the time, or the dialogues which had been popular since Plato. His lack of interest in books left him free of the affectations of the age. His suspicion of learned men pushed him into a much more engaging and democratic form of writing.

The Meditations was eventually banned by the Church, a few years after Descartes' death. It had various theological problems, but the truth was deeper and broader. It was Descartes' whole personality. No matter how much he tried to hide it, he reeked of rebellion. He had prodded and probed until the whole edifice of authority had fallen down.

In its place, he found the individual. He freed humans from being a part of a whole.

We are not a subsection of our family, or class, or tribe, or religion, or race, or nation. We are individuals. We can think for ourselves. We have a capacity for reason. This was the philosophical truth that emerged from the ruins of the old certainties. And from there, it took over the world.

2. AWAKENING

It happened in 1647, six years after *The Meditations* was published. A group of English soldiers and radicals stood in a room in Putney, just outside London. They had taken their king captive. They were at war with their parliament. They had mutinied against their officers. And then they held an advanced debate on political theory.

For centuries, the records of this meeting were lost. But in 1890 a librarian at Worcester College in Oxford made an extraordinary discovery: carefully noted minutes of what took place, written down in an early form of shorthand. It was, as the 20th-Century historian Austin Woolrych said, possibly the most 'exciting archival discovery in any field of British history.' It provided a detailed minute-by-minute account of people hammering out the very early outlines of what would become liberalism, in the frenzy of civil war.

The sophistication of the debate was not by chance. It was the culmination of years of radical arguments, scribbled down in jail cells, smuggled out by sympathisers, published on outlawed presses, spread in the streets and alleyways of London, and whispered through the army ranks. It was the result of a sustained campaign by a group of stubborn, bloody-minded radicals called the Levellers.

They were the first group to process Descartes' existential assessment of the individual into religion and politics. They hadn't read him. They almost certainly had no idea he existed, but at certain moments in history, similar ideas start to emerge in distinct and disparate contexts, like branches of an evolutionary tree. And that was what happened here.

The Levellers' struggle started with King Charles I. England's sovereign had married a Catholic French princess, Henrietta Maria, in 1625, and in doing so created lasting suspicion and resentment against his rule in his Protestant kingdom. During his reign, a form of High Anglicanism was imposed on England that had a grandeur and theatricality to it which looked, to his opponents, a lot like Catholicism. Above all else, Charles believed in the divine right of kings – the notion that monarchs received their authority directly from God and were therefore entitled to exercise absolute power.

Looking back, he seems like a relic of the old world caught in the furnace of the new. But that would not have been how it appeared at the time, even to his opponents. Much of Europe was at that stage moving towards absolutism and would keep doing so for decades to come. Charles saw himself as a moderniser and a reformer, trying to overcome a century of economic inertia and stagnation. He could be a slippery character, prone to lying and misleading people, but he was not avaricious. Despite his many failings, he was a man of principle. He really believed he was God's elect and that to defy him was to challenge the creator.

Similarly, those who fought against him did not see themselves as the harbingers of a new democratic era. They rooted most of their arguments in ancient English liberties, which evoked a bygone – and largely fictitious – age of freedom deep in England's history.

History is not simple or linear. Its characters have a jumble of religious and political convictions that are barely comprehensible to a modern person. But at certain points, shocking new ideas emerge by chance out of economic and social events. And that's exactly what took place.

Charles was being frustrated by parliament. At this point, it was still under his command. He could choose when to call it and when to dissolve it. But it had a hold over him which was far more powerful than God's. It could raise taxes.

For years parliament had been using this lever to keep the king in check. It would only authorise new funds when it had secured something in return. And that meant Charles was stuck. When he recalled parliament, its members challenged his authority. When he didn't, he ran out of money.

For over a decade, he held off from calling them and tried all sorts of other imaginative – and ultimately unsuccessful – ways of raising money. It was known as the Eleven Years' Tyranny. During this period Charles exerted executive control through a kind of mini-parliament called the Star Chamber. This body could pass laws, call witnesses, and torture and execute suspected heretics. It became a byword for arbitrary power among those opposed to the king's rule.

At its head was a deeply reactionary archbishop called William Laud. He was Charles' enforcer.

Laud understood that society was changing at breakneck speed. The shift of people from the countryside into London was forging new kinds of identity. Where people previously thought of themselves as being part of their village and religion, essentially as a part of a mass, they were now being bundled together, cheek-by-jowl, from diverse parts of the country and different social classes, in relatively large numbers. The old ties were fraying. Now there were new identities – of individual churches, Protestant groupings, occupation, and class.

City-living also created the necessary conditions for what we now call news. Information could flow between people much faster in the bustling streets than it could between remote villages. When events took place, outbursts of gossip, rumour and innuendo flew across the city like darting birds, often sparking bouts of mass political activity.

One piece of technology above all others fomented this instability: the printing press.

Laud understood better than anyone the danger this invention posed to the regime. It could super-charge the flow of information so that it no longer required one person to speak to another. Unless it fell under government control, it would challenge religion and the king.

So in 1637, Laud passed a decree through the Star Chamber restricting the number of authorised printers in London to 20. The number of people authorised to cast type was limited to four. Printing domestic news was a criminal offence. Authors and publishers of unlicensed material were interrogated and tortured.

The Stationers' Company – a mixture of a trade union and a professional body with full commercial control of books and printing – was expected to seek out and eradicate any published work that was considered treasonous or heretical or had been published on an unauthorised press. No carpenter, joiner or blacksmith was allowed to make any part of a printer without informing the Company. It became a kind of censorship militia, tracking down banned books and arresting their authors and publishers.

In the summer of 1637, three anti-Catholic writers – William Prynne, Henry Burton and John Bastwick – were hauled before the Star Chamber and convicted of seditious writing. They were fined £5,000 each – an inordinate sum of money – and sentenced to life imprisonment. They were also put in the pillories, had their books burned in front of them, and had their ears cut off. In the case of Prynne, who had already been before the Star Chamber four years earlier, the stumps of his ears left over from his previous mutilation were removed. He was branded with the initials SL, for 'seditious libeller.'

One young man in his twenties was inspired by the plight of three men and the way they stood by their convictions despite their torture. His name was John Lilburne and he would become the closest thing the Levellers had to a leader. He continued to distribute their works until December 1637, when he was caught by Laud's agents and sent before the Star Chamber.

His actions at this point defined his approach to politics for the rest of his life: defiance, legal literacy, a rousing and near-ceaseless insistence on the ancient liberties of the English, and a desire to be as argumentative and stubborn as it was possible for a man to be. As one of his allies once said: 'If there were none living but himself, John would be against Lilburne, and Lilburne against John.'

The Star Chamber secured convictions on the basis of its own witness testimonies, meaning that interrogations doubled up as grounds for prosecution. So Lilburne simply refused to speak except to state his freeborn right against self-incrimination. He also insisted that he could not contribute to the hearing because he had not been subpoenaed. Finally, he told prosecutors, he could not take the oath required of the court until he had been given time to consider its lawfulness. It was like someone had cut him out of the future, which had due process, and pasted him into his own time, which did not. The Star Chamber ruled that he be fined £500, imprisoned, and publicly tortured.

On 18th April 1638, Lilburne was tied to the back of a cart, marched from Fleet Bridge to parliament, and beaten with a knotted three-thronged whip every four paces. Onlookers shouted encouragement to him as he was pulled through the streets.

When he reached Westminster he was put in the stocks. He stared out at the crowd and delivered a calm and eloquent speech on Laud's abuse of authority. Eventually the authorities stuffed a gag in his mouth, so he resorted to staring out at the people around him and regularly stamping his feet as a mark of defiance. From that day on he was known as 'Freeborn John.'

The authorities sent Lilburne back to prison, where they put him in solitary confinement and denied him food, clothing and medical care. He only survived because fellow prisoners smuggled him morsels through holes in the wall.

Lilburne kept on writing from his cell, smuggling out radical anti-Laudian tracts that were published clandestinely. One of them, *Cry for Justice*, sparked huge protests. That was when he came to truly understand the power of the printing press. It was an extremely effective mechanism for mobilising support. You could write a pamphlet, publish, and – within a day – bring out crowds in protest.

Laud had made a mistake. Banning printing did not make it go away, it just drove it underground. By capping the number of legal printers but not apprentices, the Star Chamber probably helped create the economic conditions for an illicit press. Idle trained workers were primed for an approach by radicals and many of the presses that should have been broken up ended up on the black market, where they gave voice to a growing network of anti-Catholic writers in London. These new customers wanted something urgent and quick. Instead of a long book for the nobility, the new product was a A3-sized sheet of paper folded into an eight-page pamphlet.

Hundreds of these could be churned out over the course of an evening using just a single printer. And business was brisk. The area around St Paul's Cathedral became the beating heart of a renegade printing trade. In a maze of decrepit back alleys and dingy buildings, a small army of radicals and criminal publishers smuggled in illegal printers and distributed outlawed pamphlets. They were referred to as 'paper bullets.'

They cost no more than the price of a beer to buy, so even very poor people could read them. At this stage London was surprisingly literate – 60 per cent of people could sign their own name. And those who could not read would often hear the tracts read out in the alehouses and taverns. The pamphlet was the opening salvo in the democratisation of politics.

By 1640, Charles was embroiled in a messy ongoing conflict with the Scots which urgently needed funding. His financial situation was getting desperate, so he finally called a new parliament. It was a catastrophic error. He had bottled up the problem for too long and now it exploded.

As soon as parliament was recalled, its members set to work ensuring they could never be dismissed again. They passed a legal requirement that parliament be summoned at least once every three years and that, if this did not happen, it could assemble on its own, thereby establishing itself as an independent political body separate from the king. Then they accused Laud of treason, threw him in the Tower of London, and abolished the Star Chamber.

Laud's entire system of censorship fell down around him. The liquidation of the Star Chamber created a regulatory vacuum that destroyed the Stationers' Company as an effective political or economic body and triggered a free-for-all in publishing.

The number of titles published jumped from 900 in 1640 to more than 2,000 in 1641, then to 3,500 in 1642. More printed material was produced in that year alone than in the previous century and a half put together. Tellingly, the number of actual pages printed did not increase. These were predominantly pamphlets. The black market and the formal market were now effectively the same thing.

Among the key Leveller figures who rose up in this new anything-goes printing culture was William Walwyn. He was older than most of his Leveller allies and more contemplative. His instincts constantly guided him away from violence and towards calm, reasoned argument. His chief pleasures in life, he said, were 'a good book' or an 'honest and discoursing friend.' Just like all the Levellers, and indeed anyone involved in the politics of the 17th Century, he was deeply religious.

Although modern liberalism is overwhelmingly secular, one of its ironies is that the seeds of its growth were planted by Christians making pious protests against Catholicism.

In 1517, the German pastor Martin Luther had challenged the authority of the Pope by opposing the extravagances of the Catholic Church, starting the Reformation and eventually Protestant Christianity. By the time of the Levellers, this conflict had ballooned to cover the entire continent. It defined the animosity between parliament and the king and was the motivation for the 30 Year War raging in Europe.

Protestantism wasn't homogeneous. After it spun off from Catholicism, it continued to fracture into countless pieces. Some were fairly similar to Catholicism in their political structure. Orthodox Presbyterianism, for instance, which was common in the British Isles, envisaged a state church, a legal requirement that people attend it, and a demand that they worship in a particular way. But some members of other Protestant movements took a different view. For them, the challenge to the Pope's authority extended into a challenge to any religious authority. They saw the relationship with God as personal.

The Puritans were the dominant group in what became the Levellers. They were themselves extremely diverse, with many conservative adherents supporting a national church. But the radical members were more subversive. They believed in a separation of church and civil authority, the autonomy of congregations, and the importance of personal conversion.

Three explosive political thoughts sprang out of that religious outlook. The first was that people should have freedom of religious conscience. They should be able to worship as they pleased, in whichever church they wished. Some radicals even encouraged people to visit numerous churches and listen to different preachers before settling on one.

The second was the notion of the individual. By centring their religious views on a personal relationship with God, radical Puritans undermined the authority structure of society. It wasn't that they wanted individual freedom to find God exactly. In fact, their thinking went in the other direction – they were trying to clear away the man-made clutter to free God's will for the individual. But the end result in the material world was the same.

The third was the notion of doubt. Descartes recognised this when he saw the weakness of human senses in perceiving fire, and again when he stripped away human certainty about truth. Radical Puritans applied the same caution to religion.

They accepted that humankind did not have the spiritual apparatus to know exactly how to worship God. It followed that everyone's personal journey to religious enlightenment should be tolerated, so that people could discover which one was right. Neither the state nor any individual had the right to enforce a style of worship on others. Jesus, as Walwyn noted, used 'no other means but argument and persuasion to alter or control.'

These three ideas – of personal freedom, the individual, and the uncertainty of truth – would become central to liberal thought.

Liberalism did not exist yet and it would have been incomprehensible to any of the people pursuing these views. And yet its starting assumptions were now starting to emerge, half-formed, in a cauldron of dissent.

By this point, the king realised how badly he had misjudged his opponents in parliament. They had wiped out his allies, broken down his mechanisms for exerting authority and begun to assert themselves as an independent political force. So in January 1642, he took decisive action. He charged five members of the House of Commons with treason.

The next day he emerged from his chambers and said simply: 'My most loyal subjects and soldiers, follow me.' Then he strode out and took a coach to parliament, followed by hundreds of armed men. He was going to do with military might what he had failed to do through politics. He was going to humble parliament.

The soldiers lined up at the door of the Commons, drew their swords from their scabbards and cocked their pistols. Charles walked slowly into the Chamber and approached William Lenthall, the Speaker, who chaired debates. 'By your leave Mr Speaker,' the king said, 'I must borrow your chair a little.'

Lenthall got up. Charles sat in the seat and looked around at the MPs in front of him. The five men he was looking for had already fled but the king didn't know that yet. He turned to the Speaker and told him to point them out.

Lenthall's response was a key moment in English history. It would fundamentally alter the constitutional structure of the country.

'May it please your majesty,' he said, 'I have neither eyes to see nor tongue to speak in this place but as this House is pleased to direct me.'

The words hung in the air. They constituted the marking of territory. The king's authority did not extend in that room, among the country's elected representatives. The Speaker was the servant of parliament, not the Crown. It was now explicitly a fully formed and independent source of political power.

Charles marched out the chamber. It was the last time any English monarch entered the House of Commons.

He had been humiliated. Within days he left London for the north of the country, to ensure his safety. A period of shock and dawning realisation followed on both sides. Then, on 22nd August 1642, Charles raised his royal standard in Nottingham. He was going to war with his own parliament and England was about to endure one of the bloodiest conflicts in its history.

Parliament's military fortunes lay with two men. One was Thomas Fairfax, a dashing lieutenant-general whose gallantry and bravery in battle inspired a fierce sense of loyalty from his men. The other was Oliver Cromwell, one of the most mercurial and impenetrable figures in British history.

Countless books have been written about him, but none ever seem to pin him down. He is a body of contradictions and evasions. To some, he is the great defender of parliament. To others, he is Britain's only military dictator. To many he is a monster, because of the crimes he committed later in Ireland.

He is a shadow. At certain crucial moments in the narrative, he simply disappears. At others he speaks at length in favour of one set of ideas only to pursue the exact opposite course of action the following day. His behaviour is often impossible to decipher.

Cromwell came from the lower rungs of the upper class, with a very wealthy grandfather but a struggling father. In his twenties he was diagnosed with melancholia, which was probably some form of nervous breakdown. After that period he became intensely religious.

Cromwell and Fairfax were among the most successful army leaders Westminster possessed. But it wasn't enough. Their forces were subject to a series of military defeats forcing them to retreat ever closer to parliament's stronghold in London. There was a real fear that Charles was going to win the war.

Cromwell used his status as an MP to launch a blistering attack against the existing army leadership in November 1644. He accused it of 'backwardness in all action' and pointedly suggested that many in parliament were unwilling to have the war 'prosecuted unto full victory.'

He was right. Parliament had been split. Some MPs and Lords wanted to end the fighting as soon as possible, sign an agreement with the king imposing their own form of religious government, and then reinstall him so he could enforce it. This was the Presbyterian faction.

On the other side were the Independents. They wanted a much more root-and-branch reform of the system – freedom of conscience and an end to state religion. They believed that churches were voluntary bodies and people could decide whether to commit to them. They did not want to trade one system of coercion for another, but to fundamentally alter the conduct of religion and politics.

This split had a military dimension. The Independents believed that the war had to be won hard. It was only by a swift and firm defeat that the king could be forced to make the radical changes they required.

The Presbyterians were constantly trying to make deals with the king, from the beginning until the bitter end of the war, in order to return to normality, but with their own mild reforms in place. The king flirted with them throughout, always seeming to be open to negotiations but never treating them seriously.

The acrimony in the Commons created a problem. Most MPs agreed that parliament needed its own national army to take the fight to the king, but both sides of the House were wary of it being controlled by the other camp. So they came up with what seemed like a simple solution. They would pass a law banning any member of the Commons or Lords from maintaining military command. It was called the Self-Denying Ordinance.

At the time it seemed pragmatic, even ingenious, but the parliamentarians did not fully grasp what it entailed. They had created a completely new and independent power in the kingdom, as consequential as themselves or the king. And then they were giving it lots of weapons.

This new national fighting force, which was professional and well paid, was called the New Model Army. It proved to be powerfully effective. In a decisive battle on 14th June 1645, the New Model defeated the king at Naseby in Northamptonshire and triggered a complete military collapse of the royalist forces. Leicester surrendered, followed by Bridgwater, Bath, Sherborne Castle, Bristol, Devizes and Winchester.

By autumn, Charles retreated to Oxford, his last bastion, and, realising he was defeated, tried to escape in disguise. He made his way to Scottish forces and surrendered. The war was over.

Or at least that's what people thought. It was actually about to turn into something far messier. Parliament's radical defenders were going to learn a harsh lesson – one which has been experienced by countless other revolutionaries in the years since: those who lead the fight very quickly become as oppressive as those they overthrow.

It started with something called the Ordinance for the Regulating of Printing. After two years of bewilderment in a deregulated printing market, the Stationers' Company petitioned parliament for a return of the licensing system. It dressed up its commercial concerns in political terms. The message to the authorities was that if the state couldn't control books, it couldn't control ideas. And if it couldn't control ideas, it couldn't control anything.

It found a willing audience among the Presbyterians, who were aghast at the boisterous pamphleteers, with their abusive mockery of opponents and the idea, simmering away in the background, that even the poor should engage in political debate.

The Presbyterians accepted the Stationers' Company's request. Blackmarket printers were outlawed, along with any work considered 'false, forged, scandalous, seditious and libellous.'

It was similar to Laud's decree of six years earlier. Extraordinarily, Prynne, the man who had had his ears cut off twice by Laud, was one of the new censorship regime's chief enforcers. 'A turd in your teeth,' Lilburne told his former hero the next time he saw him.

The resistance to this new censorship engendered some of the first works of early liberalism.

The first salvo came from the poet John Milton, a supporter of parliament who shared several friends and printing presses with the Levellers. He wrote a pamphlet called *Areopagitica*, in which he mounted one of the world's first defences of the freedom to publish.

It was 'as good almost kill a man as kill a good book,' he wrote. 'Who kills a man kills a reasonable creature, but he who destroys a good book kills reason itself.'

Milton wasn't the perfect defender of freedom. He was indifferent towards the free speech of non-Puritans and believed in banning seditious works. Nevertheless, he was doing something that would prove crucial in the development of liberal thought. He was acknowledging the concept of doubt, just as the Descartes had in knowledge and the radical Puritans had in religion, and importing it to the world of secular ideas. People did not always know what was true, so free debate was needed to find out.

'Let her and falsehood grapple,' Milton wrote. 'Who ever knew truth put to the worse in a free and open encounter?' Those who refused to engage in free debate were doomed to fossilise and expire. 'I cannot praise a fugitive and cloistered virtue, unexercised and unbreathed, that never sallies out and sees her adversary.'

He was glimpsing something. He didn't quite know what it was yet, but the first moments of understanding were there. It was the fuzzy outline of a liberal hierarchy of virtues – one in which freedom was placed at the foundation, as the precondition of all other goods. 'Give me the liberty to know, to utter, and to argue freely according to conscience, above all liberties,' he concluded.

Despite Milton's efforts, the attacks on the blackmarket printers continued. The Leveller printing operation was in danger of being wiped out. Across London, rebel publishers were playing a cat-and-mouse game with the Stationers' Company.

One of the most celebrated was Richard Overton, who was both a publisher and a writer. He started life as a typical anti-Catholic propagandist, but grew increasingly radical over the years, deploying biting satire and mockery to deflate political opponents. He had his own printing press, people to run it, a distribution network, and the capacity to knock out copy to fast deadlines. This made him a target of the Stationers' Company.

Its enforcers traced his press to an address at Goodman's Fields, where they tried to force their way through the door. The men inside held it shut against them. When it was forced open they escaped down a rope hanging from the upper window, but the press and several books were confiscated.

The Stationers' Company finally found Overton himself sleeping in bed with his wife one morning. He opened his eyes to find one man by his bedroom door, his pistol cocked, and another by the bed, his sword drawn and the blade by his face. 'Tut, tut, tut,' the man said. 'Rise up and put on your clothes.'

They ransacked the house and dragged Overton to Newgate prison by his hair, where they put him in irons. His wife was later arrested and taken to Bridewell prison.

The Levellers were discovering that the new regime felt a lot like the old regime. 'The tyranny over conscience that was exercised by the bishops,' Walwyn wrote, 'is like to be continued by the Presbyterians.'

The radical printing network went back underground. Leveller writing now had to be done in secret – usually from prison cells – and smuggled out to the surviving blackmarket printers.

Those printers churned out about 100 pamphlets an hour, often working all night for one run. Some articles were scattered on the streets at night. Others were sold by street merchants or at bookshops, or chosen by book agents, who would service readers in the countryside.

The air was thick with war and resistance to power. And in that struggle, Leveller ideas started to become more radical.

Most of them were simply committed to freedom of conscience for Protestants and no-one else. But occasionally they would venture into more expansive territory. Jews were included sometimes, along with 'Turks,' who we'd now call Muslims.

At its most radical – and this was very rare – Leveller belief in freedom of conscience even included Catholics. Walwyn's pamphlet *A New Petition of the Papists* allowed for their toleration. Overton's remarkable *The Arraignment of Mr. Persecution* spoke out against persecution for any style of worship or speech. This was extremely far-sighted, given that at the time Protestant England viewed Catholicism less as a religion and more like an enemy military power.

In mid-1646, Lilburne finally pushed his luck too far. The Lords demanded he answer for an anti-Presbyterian pamphlet he had written. At the trial, he simply put his fingers in his ears and refused to hear the charges against him. When prosecutors asked him what he said to the charges, he replied that 'he had heard nothing of it, he had nothing to do with it, he took no notice of it.'

He was fined £2,000, sentenced to seven years imprisonment, and banned from writing or being visited by friends and family. His books were burned in New Palace Yard in Westminster.

When Lilburne was prevented from speaking to his wife Elizabeth in the prison yard, she went into a house 40 yards away and continued their conversation by shouting to him from the window. Eventually, Lilburne's jailer threatened to board up the windows. 'I would pull them down as fast as he nailed them up,' he said, and speak to his wife until they 'sewed up my lips, or cut out my tongue.'

Meanwhile, Overton was in his own cell, writing a pamphlet that would introduce one of the fundamental principles of liberal thought. It was called *An Arrow Against All Tyrants*. Its first line rang with indignation: 'An arrow against all tyrants and tyranny, shot from the prison of Newgate into the prerogative bowels of the arbitrary House of Lords and all other usurpers and tyrants whatsoever.'

Just like Descartes, Overton's writing was free from the presumptions and rigidity of philosophers. He was able to think in a radically different and unaffected way, a process which was given a shot of adrenaline by war and imprisonment.

But unlike Descartes, he was not writing for other intellectuals, or out of a desire for recognition for his intellectual abilities. He was a propagandist and a hack. *An Arrow Against All Tyrants* was a piece of opinion journalism, written for busy people with little to no education, to be read on the street or the alehouse. It was intended to be a call to action, not reflection. The text crackled with urgency. And in that text he first outlined the idea of human rights.

'To every individual in nature is given an individual property by nature not to be invaded or usurped by any,' he wrote.

And there it was. Emerging almost fully formed out of the ancient political culture of the English Civil War: the idea of individual rights. This was a sudden and astonishing elevation in the maturity of political thought. Overton was not demanding the rights of Quakers, or Baptists, or Protestants generally, or even Englishmen. He was reaching out from Puritanism's demand for freedom of conscience to something universal.

The Presbyterians had demanded freedom when they were under threat. But once they were ascendant, they had cast all that aside and behaved like the old regime. So it followed that something more wide-ranging was required, something that applied to everyone, regardless of circumstance, or religion, or political fortune.

And then Overton went one step further. He outlined where

those rights ended: at the exact point at which someone else's rights were infringed. You were free to do whatever you wanted, as long as you did not take away the freedom of others.

'No man has power over my rights and liberties and I over no man's,' he said. 'For by natural birth all men are equally and alike born to like propriety, liberty and freedom. We are delivered of God by the hand of nature into this world, every one with a natural, innate freedom and propriety – as it were writ in the table of every man's heart, never to be obliterated.'

These rights existed outside of religion or the state. They were natural rights, which operated independently of the political world.

In the summer of 1646 the Levellers published something akin to a manifesto: *A Remonstrance of Many Thousand Citizens*. It summarised a clear and practically-minded expression of rudimentary democratic ideas. For centuries people had thought that the king was sovereign and all power could be sourced back through him. But now he was gone. So they had to find the source of legitimate authority elsewhere. The obvious location was the people.

'We possessed you with the same power that was in ourselves,' the pamphlet told MPs, 'for we might justly have done it ourselves without you, if we had thought it convenient.' Insofar as the Commons had legitimacy, this document suggested it was because it represented the people's will.

By the spring of the next year, the Levellers had thrown their weight behind a petition with a 14-point plan for the country. Various attempts were made to deliver the petitions to parliament, but they were brutally suppressed. The petitioners were branded 'rogues,' assaulted, dragged along the ground, and threatened with arrest. When copies were handed to MPs at the door of the Commons they were sent to be burned by the hangman.

The civil war had splintered into a three-way battle between the Levellers, the king and the Presbyterian-dominated parliament. But the radicals were aware of a fourth group: the New Model Army. And this one was more useful than the others, because it had the guns.

In a way, losing the war was the best thing that could have happened to Charles. Until then, he had been the military enemy, with his opponents allied against him. Now, in victory, they were fighting each other.

Formal peace negotiations began with the king. The Presbyterians wanted a quick deal, incorporating his old political and religious structure into their own and then taking control of the country. The Independents in parliament were tentatively making their own advances. If either side could get the monarch on side, they would trump the other.

The king's tactic was simple: flirt and delay. Now he was captured, everyone wanted a piece of him: his cooperation would give either side legitimacy. So he bided his time and welcomed all sorts of advances without having any intention of doing a deal with anyone.

While the king negotiated, the Presbyterians wanted to disband the New Model Army and send its remnants to fight in Ireland. But the soldiers were resentful. They had been used by parliament to win a war and now they were being dismissed. They wanted arrears of pay and indemnity for any crime committed during their service. Men had been put on trial for stealing horses during the war – a charge carrying the death sentence – and they needed legal protection.

Slowly but surely, the Levellers and the army started to realise they had the same enemy.

Lilburne attacked MPs who 'call the army rebels and traitors.' He was joined by Walwyn. Radical printers made sure that Leveller pamphlets were spread around regiments and read around campfires. A printing press was brought into the ranks. Before long, one observer noted that 'Lilburne's books are quoted as statute law' by the soldiers. In the spring of 1647, the phrase 'Lilburne's freedom – soldiers' rights' became a key motto in a growing army rebellion against parliament.

When the Presbyterians in parliament heard of a New Model petition for arrears and indemnity, they branded the soldiers 'enemies of the state.' This enraged the troops, who redoubled their resistance to any further calls for disbandment. If they were cast out of the army, they could be put on trial.

And then they did something remarkable. They started electing representatives.

It started among eight cavalry regiments in East Anglia. Cavalry regiments had higher rates of literacy, so they proved fruitful grounds for Leveller pamphlets. Two men were selected by the others to represent them when discussing their interests with the rest of the army. Then it spread. Several infantry units elected their own delegates. They were known as 'agitators,' although the word at the time meant something more like 'agent.' This was not exactly a mutiny. Many officers were sympathetic and the agitator system had some degree of support from the authority structures of the army.

Colonel Thomas Rainsborough, a celebrated military leader and the best siege-master in the army, was watching with keen interest. He noted the way they selected two out of every troop in an orderly way and 'did nothing that did not become them as soldiers.'

Parliament tried to kill the trend by sending out commissioners to demand the soldiers disband, but it was too late. Fairfax's infantry regiment in Chelmsford simply refused to follow the commissioners' orders and instead began marching towards a general army rendezvous.

Aghast, a Presbyterian lieutenant colonel asked them on whose orders they were marching. 'Orders from the agitators,' the men replied.

The army was operating completely independently of parliament.

The soldiers behaved as soldiers are trained to do. They understood that the first item of business was to secure their artillery. On 1st June 1647, an agitator called George Joyce rode out with his unit to Oxford and made sure the cannons were safely in New Model Army hands.

Then he did something more unusual: he seized the king. He journeyed to Northamptonshire where Charles was being kept and at 10.30 at night, as he lay asleep, entered his room and informed him that he would be moved in the morning, but that under no circumstances would he come to any harm.

The next morning the king walked downstairs to find 500 troopers mounted and ready to take him away. He turned to Joyce. It was a scene which just a year before would have been unthinkable: a king facing a coronet, the lowest commissioned rank in the army. But the conversation which was about to take place was even stranger.

Under whose authority was Joyce acting, the king asked.

'The soldiery of the army,' Joyce replied.

This answer made no sense. If it was an army decision he would have a commission from Fairfax. So the king asked again.

'Here is my commission,' Joyce replied.

'Where?' asked the king.

'Behind me,' Joyce said. And then he pointed back at his men. A democratic army was now making its own decisions.

As baffling as it must have been to the king, it might also have made a kind of deranged sense. Just as parliament had shaken off its royal parent, so its own children were now abandoning it. It was 'as fair a commission,' Charles said, and 'as well written' as he had seen in his life.

From there, Joyce transported him to Newmarket where the army was holding a general rendezvous. Fairfax and Cromwell both made their way there, too. At this stage, they were barely in control of events. Neither really approved of what was happening, although they were sympathetic to the men's demands for pay and indemnity. They were trying to ride the wave, hoping they would still be on top when it crashed.

Fairfax and Cromwell were presented with two documents. One was a list of grievances suffered by the army and the Levellers. The other created a new decision-making body, called the Council of the Army, which would bring together senior command with a pair of commissioned officers and two private soldiers elected by each regiment.

They agreed to it. Perhaps they thought that it would allow the officer class to control this radical new body. But by signing up to it, they created something unprecedented: an army high command that was officially sharing operational power with the rank-and-file.

The army published a document declaring that it was 'no mere mercenary army, hired to serve any arbitrary power of a state, but called forth and conjured by the several declarations of parliament, to the defence of our own and the people's just rights and liberties.' The army then issued a series of demands, including freedom from prison for John Lilburne, Richard Overton, his wife, and other Levellers.

But it also had one other demand: the impeachment of 11 Presbyterian MPs on charges of negotiating with royalists.

This was the one of the first glimmers of the bleak moral irony which would hang over the coming events. Just as the king had done when he first sparked the civil war, the soldiers were demanding the right to remove elected parliamentarians at will. The only difference was that this time it would be done in the name of the people.

The Commons refused to hand over the MPs, but the men themselves withdrew from parliament, probably out of concern for their own safety.

In truth, it was not at all clear that the New Model Army was really representing the people. On the streets of London, there were signs of a royalist counter-insurgency. In June and July 1647, violent demonstrations demanded the return of the king and the abolition of the New Model Army. On 26th July, a crowd broke into parliament, forced its way into the Lords and made the peers repeal a vote castigating a previous demonstration. Then they broke into the Commons and started ordering MPs around.

In the turmoil that followed, Fairfax decided to take matters into his own hands and advance towards the capital. The New Model Army took control of the city instantly. When Fairfax reached the Tower of London he was given a copy of the *Magna Carta*, the centuries-old agreement which had first limited the power of the king. 'This is what we have fought for,' he said, 'and by God's help we must maintain.' The New Model Army alliance with the Levellers was now in control of England.

The newly-democratised army quickly issued its first declaration of executive intent: the Heads of Proposals.

All the previous deals the king had received came directly from parliament. These were the first to be independently generated by a third party. They were concerned not just with limiting his powers, but that of parliament as well. Far from being an occupying power, the army was drawing up the terms for a new constitutional settlement.

It was one of the first instances of what later blossomed into a tenet of liberalism: the separation of powers. The army was trying to prevent too much control being held in one place.

Parliament would no longer be the plaything of the king, but it could only sit for between 120 and 240 days before a new one had to be formed. Seats would be redistributed to make them more representative. The king lost his authority over the military for ten years, but opponents of parliament were barred from office for just five years, meaning he would soon have political representatives. Most importantly, the army did not propose abolishing the bishops, a feature of all previous peace terms. The king even got a legislative veto. Both sides had to accept freedom of religion.

The Heads of Proposals were based on forgiveness for deeds committed during the war and an attempt to lay out a fair and enduring settlement for the future. Charles couldn't have asked for a better deal.

Rainsborough and Henry Ireton, Cromwell's son-in-law, delivered the document to him. If the king would accept it, the army could, in one stroke, restore parliament and the monarchy. The conflict would be over.

The king sat in silence. He read the proposals, then turned to Ireton and said: 'You cannot be without me. You will fall to ruin if I do not sustain you.'

His reply spoke volumes about his failure to understand the historical moment. He was now negotiating directly with an elected, independent army. But his own responses were burdened with the weight of ancient Godly rights, like commandments passed down on stone tablets. He was speaking a different language.

Rainsborough was aghast at the king's response and left enraged. Ireton negotiated for a further three hours, but Charles was pursuing his flirt-and-delay tactic. It would be months before he sent a formal response, by which time the army had lost all patience with him.

From this point on, the army's proposals became much more radical. A document called *The Case of the Army Truly Stated* was drawn up in early October and presented to Fairfax. It contained the usual practical concerns about indemnity for troops, but alongside it there was a clear statement of the moral basis for a new national constitutional settlement.

'All power is originally and essentially in the whole body of the people of this nation,' it read. 'Their free choice or consent by their representatives is the only origin or foundation of all just government.' Parliament was to be dissolved and new elections held. The existing property requirement for voters of a 40-shilling freehold would be abolished. All Englishmen above the age of 21 could vote unless they were an ally of the king.

A date for a debate on the paper was set for 28th October 1647 in St Mary's Church in Putney. It would become one of the most crucial events in the history of ideas.

By the time delegates turned up, agitators and Levellers had already turned the Putney debates on their head. Instead of bringing a copy of the *Case of the Army*, they had suddenly produced a new and even more radical document: the *Agreement of the People*. The basic democratic principles were the same, but *Agreement of the People* was more detailed and far-reaching.

At its root was the idea of inalienable individual rights. The *Agreement* had turned Overton's article into a codified list of legal freedoms. These included freedom from arbitrary imprisonment, freedom of religious worship, freedom from military conscription, indemnity for acts in wartime, the right to refuse any law which was 'destructive to the safety and well-being of the people,' and equality before the law. Discrimination would be prohibited on the basis of 'tenure, estate, charter, degree, birth or place.'

'These things,' it said, pre-empting words which would ring out in America 150 years later, 'we declare to be our native rights.'

It was one of the world's first visions of a liberal society. In many areas, such as indemnity and conscription, the actual rights demanded were clearly a product of their time and circumstance. But what mattered was that the Levellers were outlining an early democratic system in which the public elected people to make laws and then carved out a protected area for the freedom of the individual that those laws could not infringe. There was a demand for democracy, but also a recognition that there were certain things democracy was not entitled to do.

Cromwell chaired the debate. He cut a lonely and thoughtful figure. As chair, he regularly called people to speak only to have them angrily outline his failings. He would then go on to select someone else, only for them to do the same.

Cromwell was ultimately a force for conservatism and many of his comments were plainly self-interested. But he was even-handed enough to chair the debates fairly and the objections he raised to the Leveller plan would highlight problems that liberalism grappled with for years afterwards.

The first day of debate was lost to a largely procedural issue, but something changed on day two.

The men started debating how far the right to vote should be extended. For a few short moments – probably no more than an hour or two – events came completely unmoored from their age. There was no talk of indemnity, or arrears, or the status of the king, any of the other practical concerns which dominated their immediate circumstance. It was pure political philosophy, an era ahead of its time.

Rainsborough and Ireton, who had travelled together a month earlier to hand the Heads of Proposals to the king, now stood opposed to each other. Ireton asked if the agreement would give all men the vote, regardless of whether they had property. In response, Rainsborough delivered one of the most startling and beautiful expressions of early liberalism: 'Really I think that the poorest he that is in England has a life to live as the greatest he, and therefore truly, sir, I think it's clear that every man that is to live under a government ought first by his own consent to put himself under that government; and I do think that the poorest man in England is not at all bound in a strict sense to that government that he has not had a voice to put himself under.'

Rainsborough was going further than just arguing for equality. He was recognising a crucial new element in political thought: consent. He was introducing Descartes' individual 'thinking thing' into politics. The public's approval was the basis for the legitimacy of government.

Ireton was horrified. Abolishing the property requirement meant that people without any investment in the country would exercise political power. One of the first things they would do, presumably, was remove property from its owners. Anarchy would prevail. He insisted: 'No person hath a right to an interest or share in the disposing of the affairs of the kingdom that hath not a permanent fixed interest in this kingdom.'

Rainsborough replied: 'What the soldier has fought for all this while? He has fought to enslave himself, to give power to men of riches, men of estates, to make him a perpetual slave.' No-one could question the interest the soldiers around them had in the country. They had risked their lives for it.

Something profound had been revealed, which would echo through liberal history. What did liberty mean when it came to property? Should it be restricted so that it did not interfere with economic arrangements? Or was it something much more radical? Would it start challenging the existing distribution of wealth?

Neither men could have known it, but they were firing the opening shots in a war that would go on for centuries, between two different approaches to liberalism.

Cromwell then seized the advantage. He pointed out a weakness in the concept of 'the people' with a devastatingly simple question: Which people?

The Agreement claimed to be 'of' the people, but it was not subscribed to by all the people. In fact, hardly anyone outside of that room had even heard of it. And yet here were these men – agitators and Levellers – claiming to speak for the whole country. It might not, Cromwell, pointed out, be any more reasonable than an agreement reached by another set of people.

This was true. Those rioting crowds overrunning parliament had shown that opinion in the country was mixed. Many city-dwellers were sympathetic to the king. Most of the Levellers' supporters were from what was called the 'middling sort' – apprentices, tradesmen, lesser gentry, merchants and craftsmen. The very rich didn't support them – but neither did the very poor.

Indeed, as the debate went on, the men in the hall started trimming the groups who might be counted among 'the people.' Women were the first casualties – in fact, they were never mentioned. It was simply unthinkable they would be given a voice in politics. Foreigners were excluded too. Then servants were removed, then beggars and debtors. This would equate to about a third of the adult male population. 'The people' was whittled down to comfortably-off men.

The franchise under consideration still remained far broader than anything else put forward at this point in history. But something revealing had happened. The self-appointed representatives of the people were excluding whole groups from that category while still maintaining that it gave them democratic legitimacy.

After that, the debate turned back to the more immediate concern about what should be done with the king. But as they discussed his fate, he escaped.

Charles gave his guards the slip and rode south. He got lost in the New Forest, then eventually found his way to the Isle of Wight, where he planned to sail to France, but was instead locked up in Carisbrooke Castle. From there, he tried to coordinate a new bout of warfare, with a Scottish invasion from the north coinciding with royalist uprisings in England.

The confusion and uproar caused by his manoeuvre gave Fairfax and Cromwell an opportunity to suffocate the radical movement in the army.

Fairfax announced a rendezvous where all the soldiers could meet to discuss their position. Soldiers turned up ready to sign off on the *Agreement*. But when they got there, senior officers arrested radical ringleaders.

A new document, called *A Remonstrance from his Excellency Sir Thomas Fairfax*, was put forward containing a classic compromise position – the product of a smart leader who knew how much to concede.

The offer addressed the primary concerns of the army, such as indemnity and arrears. It also promised some vague constitutional reforms, with free and fair elections on 'an equal representation of the people that are to elect,' although quite what that meant in practice was not clear. And that was it. There was to be no formal equality. The franchise was not mentioned. Democracy and individual rights were ignored.

Then Fairfax faced down the soldiers. His natural authority, practical promises, and tactical nous won the day. Nine ringleaders were picked out and three sentenced to death, but only one was executed.

The mutiny was dead. The Leveller dream was broken. But the rhetoric of the people did not go away. Instead, it was taken by the army command and used to justify what it did next.

Fairfax was able to turn his attention to the Scottish invasion and a looming royalist revolt, both of which were suppressed. Charles was defeated once again. And this time there was no more sympathy for him. The demand for him to be tried became a clamour.

A new proposal was written up, which would force the king's trial. It was called *The Remonstrance of the Army*. It was read to the Commons over four hours on 20th November 1648 and heard in deathly silence. MPs knew what it meant. This wasn't just the end for the king. It was the end of their way of doing business.

They delayed its consideration for a week and tried to pursue peace terms with Charles. But the army couldn't be stopped – it moved from St Albans to Windsor, then from Windsor to London.

On the cold, dry morning of 6th December 1648, England experienced its first coup d'état. The army deployed infantry and cavalry units around parliament and inside it, as well as patrols on the streets in the surrounding area. When MPs tried to enter, they found a man named Colonel Thomas Pride standing by the door. In his hand was a list. It contained the names of MPs who had voted to prolong negotiations with the king. Those who were not on the list were allowed to enter. Anyone on the list was immediately detained.

Forty-one MPs were arrested. A total of 110 MPs were formally excluded. Combined with those who voluntarily stayed away, they numbered about 270 of the Commons' 470 members. This was called Pride's Purge.

From now on, it would be known as the Rump Parliament. The Commons was under army control. Parliament declared that 'the people are, under God, the original of all just power.' But it meant nothing.

The king was put on trial in the Great Hall in Westminster. When the impeachment was read out in the name of 'the good people of England,' Fairfax's wife, who was sitting in the public gallery, shouted: 'It is a lie. Not half, nor a quarter of the people of England.'

But protests did not help. The court took a few days to consider the evidence and find Charles guilty. On 30th January, he was escorted under guard from St James's Palace to a scaffold at the Palace of Whitehall. He said a prayer and put his head on the axeman's block. He died at 2pm.

Instead of a democratic revolution, the parliament of the people descended into tyranny. It struggled on for another four years before Cromwell staged another coup and booted out the Rump. Soon enough, he secured the power to nominate his own successor and chose his eldest son. He was king in all but name.

The Levellers faded away. Walwyn retired to write books on medicine. Overton went to the Netherlands with his wife. Lilburne, being Lilburne, was put on trial, acquitted, exiled on pain of death, then returned, was put on trial again, and once again acquitted. He died on bail, in Kent, at the age of 43.

'Though we fail,' he wrote, 'our truths prosper.'

And that was precisely what happened. The Leveller dream had been stripped of meaning and then its language used to justify that which destroyed it. But over the next 150 years, the principles it established would conquer the world.

3. THE THREE REVOLUTIONS

I. The Glorious Revolution

The Levellers' ideals took hold through three revolutions. Each helped lead to the next, in a strange dance of political philosophy, money and geopolitics. It began in England, shifted to North America, then arrived in France.

When the dust settled, the half-formed yearnings for freedom of the English Civil War had transformed the world. But that process was violent. The dream of liberty was still young and ferocious. So when modern freedom did come, it claimed a blood-price, one that was so severe that it threatened to discredit liberalism before it even reached maturity.

It began with two brothers: Charles and James. They were the sons of King Charles I, who had died on the scaffold in Whitehall at the end of the civil war. Their response to that traumatic episode would define the events to come.

Charles, the former king's eldest son, was more canny and astute than his father. He knew just how much to bend, and with whom to form alliances, to ensure his survival. He soon had an opportunity to put those skills to use. England's experiment with Republicanism didn't last long. Just over a decade after the execution of his father, he was invited over from his exile in Holland to become Charles II.

He was ostensibly a Protestant, but suspicion grew about his sympathies towards Catholicism – and it was well founded. His mother was Catholic, his wife was Catholic, his mistress was Catholic, he was in a close alliance with Louis XIV, the Catholic king of France, and his younger brother James was Catholic. That last part was a significant problem, because all of Charles' many children were illegitimate, placing James next in line to the throne. James' Catholicism left a ticking bomb in the febrile politics of 17th-Century England, counting down towards a Papist monarch.

The fuse was lit in 1678, when a conspiracy theory about a French plot to assassinate Charles and replace him with James was fabricated by a fantasist called Titus Oates. For three years, Oates rode a wave of paranoia and incrimination in London, and radicals in the Commons set about trying to remove James from the line of succession. This would solve the problem at a stroke, because James' daughter Mary was a Protestant, who lived in Holland with her husband William of Orange – they could simply sail across the sea to be crowned.

The ensuing battle between parliament and the king was called the Exclusion Crisis.

Charles offered to limit the powers of a future Catholic monarch, but he set himself hard against altering the line of succession. On three occasions between 1679 and 1681, MPs looked on the verge of passing an exclusion bill and he responded by either suspending parliament or putting pressure on the Lords to reject it.

In the furnace of this crisis, two groups emerged who would go on to become the templates for modern political parties: the Whigs and the Tories.

The Whigs led the battle against the king. In a way, they were the successors to the Levellers, although they came from a higher social class and were less radical. They saw monarchy as a man-made institution that was meant to benefit the community and themselves as protectors of the ancient constitution – a hazy repository of Anglo-Saxon law that no-one could properly describe.

The Tories saw monarchy as being governed by divine law, which meant the hereditary succession could not be broken. They believed in the firm authority of the Crown and the Church of England. If James became king, they believed, then so be it. That was the arrangement under English law and English law would defend them from arbitrary government.

Both groups hated Catholicism, but as the Exclusion Crisis wore on, the Tories made a strategic judgement. Out of the twin threats of Catholicism and radical Whigs, they decided it was the Whigs who posed the biggest threat to the British constitution and a reprise of the anarchy of the civil war.

Together, the king and the Tories proved unbeatable. The clamour for exclusion was turned back. Whigs were dismissed from office in local government and pursued in the courts. Some fled into exile. Others were executed. By 1685, the Whigs were a spent political force.

And then something happened which changed everything. Charles died.

It wasn't a Catholic plot which got him in the end – just natural causes. But it made little difference in the overall scheme of things. The Whigs' worst nightmare had come true. A Catholic king now ruled over England.

James II had a brutal authoritarian streak. He had learned it early on, as a teenager, when his father was executed, and then afterwards when he pursued a military career in exile. He was hard, single-minded and inspired by the notion of divine right to believe that he must be obeyed at all times. After one failed rebellion against his rule, he hung up so many body parts of his opponents that the south west of England looked like 'a vast anatomical museum.'

But there was another side to James. He genuinely seemed to believe in religious freedom. His opponents accused him of trying to instigate a Catholic takeover of England, but actually his aim was more moderate than that. It was toleration.

When he ascended to the throne, Catholics were barred from worship, education and publishing by penal laws and from holding office or sitting in parliament by legislation called the Test Acts. He wanted to abolish these restrictions. Once Catholic clergy could compete with Protestants on equal terms, he believed, new believers would follow naturally.

It was a strange battle for liberty, one which can't really be categorised in modern terms. James used arbitrary powers to pursue religious tolerance. His opponents fought against arbitrary power to maintain religious discrimination.

But regardless of its political complications, James' approach had a crucial strategic flaw. He alienated too many people without bringing enough supporters onside to make up for it. The Whigs would always regard him as a Popish king with no respect for parliament. And by breaking his allegiance with the Church of England, he also outraged the Tories.

James increased the size of the army and appointed Catholic officers, tried to stop the Anglican clergy from criticising him in sermons, opened up a Catholic chapel and attempted to break up the Anglican monopoly in university education. In Ireland, which was increasingly viewed as a test case for the kind of regime he wanted to introduce in England, he filled the ranks of the army with Catholics, appointed Catholic judges and put requirements for Catholic membership on institutions.

When parliament asked questions, he simply suspended and dissolved it. He pursued his goal with an abandon that was undiluted by any respect for England's constitutional arrangements. He used his royal powers to suspend the laws against religious nonconformity, exempt individual Catholics from restrictions under the Test Acts, and suspend the penal laws, thereby allowing them to worship freely.

But this only got James half the way. Royal powers could be easily undone by the next monarch. To secure long-lasting change, he needed to formally repeal the penal laws and Test Acts in parliament. So James set about trying to pack the Commons with people who would do his bidding. MPs from the parliament he'd suspended were asked about their willingness to repeal. The local voting system was purged to secure compliant men.

It was a comprehensive assault, but even so, for most of James' reign, Protestants thought they would probably be able to sit it out. After all, his Protestant daughter Mary would be along soon enough and normality would resume. Then, overnight, that presumption fell away.

On 10th June 1688, James' wife bore a healthy son, the first after 15 years of marriage. There was a new Catholic heir to the throne. That meant that anything James did would remain embedded in the English constitution. Protestants were no longer in a waiting game, but a fight for survival.

Seven leading figures in English political life – a bishop and six peers – wrote to William of Orange in Holland pledging their support if he brought a force to England against James. It was an invitation to invade. William had encouraged the offer and, when it came, he accepted it eagerly.

He claimed to act as a defender of English liberties, arriving from overseas to save it from papist tyranny, but in fact his motivation was more cynical. He was locked in a protracted conflict with France. An invasion offered a chance to break the Franco-English alliance and bring the English firmly and definitively into the Protestant block.

It was this geopolitical calculation, more than any of the rhetoric about English liberty, which motivated him. And it would prove decisive in the emergence of liberalism in the years to come.

William set sail with a massive invasion fleet, carrying 15,000 soldiers, 18 infantry battalions and 4,092 cavalry, as well as vast amounts of propaganda to be distributed in England. It arrived on what was later dubbed a 'Protestant wind,' which drove his fleet down the English Channel while keeping James' trapped in the Thames Estuary. They landed at Torbay in Devon on 5th November, the day the last Catholic plot against England was thwarted back in 1605. For many Protestants, it seemed as if God himself were orchestrating events. And that's pretty much how it played out.

Things fell apart for James almost immediately. He left London to take the fight to William, only to find that the capital and other towns and cities were erupting in anti-Catholic rioting. Whig and Tory peers in the north started a rebellion. His commanders fell away and defected to the enemy, followed by the rank-and-file. He developed a severe nosebleed which laid him low for hours at a time, possibly as a result of extreme stress. He may have had a nervous breakdown.

And then, as he gave up fighting and retreated back to the capital, having not even engaged the enemy, he learned that his youngest daughter, Anne, had also deserted him. 'God help me,' he cried. 'My own children have forsaken me.'

All hope was lost. On 11th December James tried to flee the country, boarding a small boat in the Thames and throwing the Great Seal, which authorised legislation, into the water. He was captured by some sailors and taken to an inn, where a crowd abused him. When the Earl of Ailesbury arrived to take him back to London, he found the king sitting in a chair, with a beard, looking exactly as his father had in a painting made at his trial. It felt like history was repeating itself.

But this time there would be no execution. It was simply much easier for all involved if James succeeded in his mission to get out of the country. He was told that he could retire to Rochester, where Dutch troops were given clear orders to allow him to escape. He soon left the house by the garden, which backed onto the Thames, took a rowing boat to the mouth of the Medway and met a ship that would take him to France.

William entered London on the same day James left it. England had been taken with barely a shot fired.

It was called the Glorious Revolution. In the years that followed it would be portrayed as a serene and bloodless event in which parliament finally established itself over the monarchy. In fact it was a mess – a mad scramble of practical necessities under the shadow of foreign military might.

Once the king was gone, the schism between Whigs and Tories, which had been papered over by their mutual loathing of James during the crisis, quickly re-emerged.

The Whigs argued that James had broken the ancient constitution between ruler and people. But they couldn't say where the constitution lay, who signed it, what the mechanism was for enforcing it, or what the consequences were for violating it. In fact, they didn't really want to answer those questions, because to do so would confirm a general right of revolution. Unlike the Levellers, the Whigs were members of the political elite. William's invasion gave them an opportunity to help run the country again. The last thing they wanted was to establish the legitimacy of rebellion.

But they were clear on one thing: the strict line of succession didn't really matter. Now that James had run away, it was parliament's job to select a new monarch.

The Tories felt differently. During the Exclusion Crisis they had elevated the idea of the line of succession to the pinnacle of importance as a sacred principle of English life.

Their remaining convictions were in disarray. They had emphasised royal power and the authority of the Church of England, but James' reign meant choosing between them. So now they were in a state of ideological breakdown, grasping around for convictions they could still hold.

A Convention was launched to reach a constitutional settlement, made up of a Whig-dominated House of Commons and a Tory-dominated House of Lords. The two sides had to find a compromise.

The primary question was who would sit on the throne. If it was Mary, the Tories could claim that the line of succession had been maintained. If it was William, the Whigs could claim the line of succession had been broken and parliament had the right to select monarchs.

In the end, an exasperated William made the decision for them. He issued a threat. If the politicians didn't come to a conclusion quickly, he would simply leave and take his army with him, leaving parliament vulnerable to the French army and the anarchic mob engaging in bouts of anti-Catholic rioting.

That sharpened minds. The Commons and Lords agreed to a resolution that James had broken 'the original contract between king and people' and 'abdicated the government.' The throne was therefore 'vacant.' William and Mary became joint monarchs in principle, with William exercising power in practice.

Both sides would later take advantage of the ambiguity of this statement to interpret the frenzy of what took place in their own narrative. But the real relevance of the Glorious Revolution in the history of ideas did not come from its political settlement. It came from a book, released shortly afterwards, which defined and justified what had happened. The manner in which it did so would interpret events in the most radical way possible and then spread that idea around the world, with profound consequences. It was *The Two Treatises of Government* by John Locke.

Locke had been in the thick of the Exclusion Crisis, serving as a personal assistant to the Earl of Shaftesbury, one of the key players against the king, before fleeing into exile in Holland. Once William and Mary were safely on the throne, he returned to England and started preparing the notes he'd taken during the crisis for publication.

He published *The Two Treatises of Government* anonymously in 1690, a year after the revolution, and only confessed to being the author posthumously, through a codicil to his will. There was a good reason for that caution. Locke was outlining a right of revolution against illegitimate government.

His argument was abstract. It established a logical case for defining legitimate government and the conditions by which it could be judged illegitimate. But it was perfectly obvious which government in particular he was talking about and which actions he was defending.

He described a constitutional settlement exactly like England's, with a hereditary monarch, a House of Commons and a House of Lords, and then outlined the type of actions that would authorise the people to rebel, which happened to be precisely those of Charles and James.

Locke's chief contribution was to take the vague Whig rhetoric around ancient constitutions and a right of resistance to arbitrary government and turn it into something much more specific, with a sound theoretical foundation. All the loose talk of law and history, seen through the mists of a mythical past, fell away. He wasn't interested in that. Instead, he grounded his case in natural rights.

Locke was far more intelligent and far more radical than the Whigs. He was also less cagey: when he talked of resistance, this would be a properly defined right of disobedience. He was making solid the ideas which had drifted around since the Levellers.

Until now, people had grasped for an idea of freedom. Once Locke was done, it was much clearer what that meant. The messy contradictions of the struggle under James, in which monarchy had defended religious freedom and its opponents defended constitutional freedom, would be wiped away. *The Two Treatises* put forward the modern conception of freedom: the right of do-as-you-please.

It was the first comprehensive system of liberalism, the root from which most of the modern strains have grown. And inside it, you could find all the glories, and many of the tragedies, of what would later come to pass.

Locke began by imagining a state of nature, early in human history, before political society, in which people related to one another without being subservient to any political authority. He then used this to evaluate the modern state of his own time.

It was a weird form of reasoning. It's not clear if the state of nature was supposed to present a true account of human origins, or if it was just an imagined framework. But there were actually quite a few arguments like this at the time, possibly inspired by the state-of-nature explanation of humanity in the Bible. Many later readers have found

the whole idea of a state of nature as the basis for a political theory
to be silly and groundless. But this kind of argument had a vital
function in the history of thought. It provided abstraction. It got rid
of the cluttered rhetoric about history and conventions, or even the
notion of divine approval, and instead established the fundamental
characteristics of humanity that could inform modern-day theory.
Its conclusions could then be applied to any society.

Locke's contemporary, the political philosopher Thomas Hobbes,
constructed his influential idea of Leviathan using a similar process.
He deemed humankind to be violent and irrational, resulting in
a state of nature which would be 'nasty, brutish and short.' It was
therefore necessary to have a strong central government that could
prevent a 'war of all against all.'

Locke's view was more positive. He argued that the state of
nature was a place of perfect freedom. Liberty was not a modern
development, the product of rebellious minds. It was the starting
condition of the species. Humans were 'by nature all free, equal
and independent.' They could 'order their actions and dispose of
their possessions and persons as they think fit.' There was law, but
it was not enforced from above. Everyone regulated it themselves,
rationally and equally. 'All the power and jurisdiction is reciprocal,'
Locke said, 'no-one having more than any other.'

He didn't flesh out what was in this law of nature, but you could
see the outline. There was a moral duty towards others. Humankind
ought to be preserved as much as possible. People should protect
themselves and protect others.

The core component of the law of nature was individual rights, a
sphere of personal life which no-one was entitled to interfere with.
'Being all equal and independent,' Locke said, 'no-one ought to
harm another in his life, health, liberty or possessions.'

Possessions played a central role in this world. Property was an
important aspect of individual freedom. But this raised a question:
how exactly did people get property? What made something belong
to someone in a state of nature?

Locke's answer was labour. At the start of human history, God created people's bodies, which they owned, and the land, which was owned in common. But where people used their bodies to work on the land, they converted it into their own private property. 'Whatever he removes out of the state that nature has provided, man has mixed his labour with, and joined to it something that is his own, and thereby makes it his property.'

The type of labour which established property was varied. You could do it by picking an apple from a tree, say, or by hunting, or cultivating land.

There were conditions. You could not waste property, for instance by claiming lots of land and doing nothing with it. You could not take more than you needed either, for instance by collecting lots of apples and letting them rot while others went hungry.

This was Locke's prehistoric assessment of how the right to property first came into existence. But then money came along. This created a permanent store of value, so people would no longer need to hoard apples or other goods. They could sell them, get money in return, and purchase whatever they wanted with it. This initiated the era of exchange, commerce and cities.

Unlike apples, money did not decay. And it was limitless – people could have as much of it as they liked without taking any away from someone else. This meant that the property restrictions Locke had established on waste and excess fell away.

This was a vision of human freedom which had property at its heart. Liberty and property were fundamentally entwined. This was not simply because property was included within a person's individual rights. It was because it improved the condition of humankind in general.

Property turned land that might have had a few apple trees into fields full of crops which could be cultivated to make more food than would have existed otherwise. It thrust humans from subsistence to industry, from scarcity to abundance. 'I think it will be but a very modest computation to say,' Locke wrote, 'that of the products of the earth useful to the life of man, nine-tenths are the effects of labour.'

The money-exchange economy benefited every member of society, because wealth filtered down to those at the bottom, meaning that even those with little or no property would do better than they would if no-one had any.

There was a downside, though. Insofar as people had reason to quarrel, it was often because of property. At first, because things were simple, there wasn't much to fight about. 'The equality of a simple poor way of living,' Locke said, 'made few controversies, and so no need of many laws to decide them.' But as the economy became more advanced, the difficulties became more numerous and complex.

Given that complexity, people were no longer best suited to settling disputes themselves. They were too subjective for that. So they required an impartial body above them to settle conflicts. They needed an adjudicator. And this was the origin of government.

'The great and chief end of men uniting into commonwealths, and putting themselves under government,' Locke said, 'is the preservation of their property.' This moment provided a secure footing for the enjoyment of their 'lives, liberties and estates.'

This was where the ancient constitution existed. It was the point at which people agreed together to create an impartial body to settle their disagreements.

It was telling that, once again, the issue of property had emerged as soon as liberty was mentioned.

It seemed at first that Locke had established a firm line. People's property rights were sacrosanct. Protecting them improved the material condition of society at large. The securing of these rights required the establishment of government. This seemed to chime with Ireton's position in the Putney debates. Liberty was not to interfere with property.

But when you poked away at it, a more complicated picture emerged. It played out in the idea of taxation – a financial payment imposed on an individual or organisation by a government.

Locke rejected the idea that the government could 'take from any man any part of his property without his own consent.' The whole function of political power was to secure individuals 'in the possession and use of their properties,' by which he meant their freedoms but also their belongings.

But Locke recognised that governments had to be funded if they were to function. They could not, he said, 'be supported without great charge.' This would require taxation. The taxation would be legitimate if it was decided with the agreement of the people, either through their own actions or those of their elected representatives. So, to some extent, liberty could interfere with property and indeed it had to in order to function.

Locke also alluded to a more general responsibility than merely funding the government. He was sympathetic to the idea of a general right of subsistence – a basic level of material support that the very poor should receive, which could only be deliverable through taxation.

The law of nature required the sustenance of mankind in general. And that was not just an abstract notion to Locke. He supported it as a matter of government policy. After the Glorious Revolution, he was appointed a member of the Board of Trade, which had a role in economic policy. When the king asked for suggestions to revise the Poor Laws, which supported the destitute, Locke drafted a memorandum insisting that 'every one must have meat, drink, clothing, and firing.' If anyone in a parish died of starvation, he said, the administrative Poor Law officer should be charged with a criminal offence.

Importantly then, Locke had two different assessments of how property played into the debate over freedom. On the one hand, it should be safeguarded as part of individual liberty. On the other, it had to be violated in order to secure the 'life, health, liberty or possessions' of people in general.

Locke didn't resolve the tension between these potentially contradictory views. It's not really clear that he even recognised there was a tension. But it was here, in the shared root of later forms of liberalism, that the two approaches to its economic agenda continued to play out.

No matter which side people took, there was something troubling in Locke's property theory. Even with all the caveats, the centrality of property to his political system created a sense of humanity as small economic units, relating to each other only through negotiation over their mutual non-interference.

His was a slightly lonely and distant kind of society, which didn't seem to reflect any of the vibrancy, identity and community of people's real-life interactions. It kept reducing the great expansive dimensions of human liberty to people's possessions, as if that was ultimately the most important aspect of life.

In time, these questions would explode into era-defining battles for the soul of liberalism, but for now they settled into the background. Because what Locke did next in *The Two Treatises* set the world on fire.

Locke's description of the birth of government provided him with a test for its legitimacy.

The test was quite simple. Where it abided by the purpose for which it had been established – the protection of people's individual liberties – it was legitimate. Where it did not, it was not.

If the king used his power for his own advantage rather than the good of the political community, the government was no longer legitimate. If the king stepped outside of the law, regardless of whether his intentions were decent or not, the government was no longer legitimate.

This had two far-reaching implications.

The first was that political power had to be separated. The king could not judge whether he was breaking the law. That would entail the same subjective personal assessment of disputes that government had been designed to address. So there had to be different functions in the state.

Locke split them in two. There was a legislative power, composed of an assembly of elected representatives. This would pass statute which interpreted the law of nature and specified the punishment if it was broken.

There was then an executive power, which would enforce that statute in specific cases and administer whatever punishment was required for infringement.

Crucially, the legislative power was above the executive power because it could impose limits on it. 'What can give laws to another,' Locke said, 'must needs be superior to him.'

On the face of it, it would seem as if parliament represented legislative power and the monarch represented executive power, but the reality was quite messy. The king could be involved in law making, for instance.

And yet Locke was continuing a core liberal principle established in the Levellers' Heads of Proposals. Power was dangerous. It had the capacity to infringe on individual liberty. So it had to be restrained by being broken up and put in many locations. Legitimacy, Locke said, involved 'balancing the power of government, by placing several parts of it in different hands.'

The second implication was the most striking. It was the exact thing that even the most radical of Whigs had felt suddenly uncertain of during the long battles with Charles and James. It was the right of revolution.

Where the government was no longer fulfilling its function, it was no longer legitimate. The obligations of obedience fell away and the people could replace the government with a new one that abided by the original contract.

'The people are at liberty to provide for themselves by erecting a new legislative,' Locke said, 'differing from the other by the change of persons, or form, or both, as they shall find it most for their safety and good.'

Locke had taken the vague notions of an 'ancient constitution,' simmering away for so long in radical English arguments, and turned them into something viable, with a proper theoretical underpinning, which could apply universally, to any society, at any time, regardless of its legal or political history. He had demanded the separation of powers as a key requirement of legitimate government. And he had established a right of revolution against tyrannical rulers.

But it was arguably even more profound than that. He was articulating a completely different world view from what had gone before, an entirely new set of starting assumptions.

It was liberty, not authority, which was the natural state of humankind. It was government, not rights, which was artificial. And it was individuals, not the state, who decided if the government was legitimate. This was the final philosophical articulation of decades of struggle, from the start of the English Civil War to the close of the Glorious Revolution.

II. The American Revolution

William's plan was an unqualified success. Over the next few years, the rather out-of-the-way kingdom he had invaded grew into a powerful global force. Scotland and England agreed an Act of Union in 1707, creating Great Britain. And this state, with its particularly strong navy, started to focus on overseas settlements, including its 13 colonies in North America.

William's main achievement was the severance of the Anglo-French alliance. After his invasion, England swung into the anti-French camp and grew to lead it. Britain and France entered a protracted conflict, with intermittent bouts of intense warfare for the next 100 years. One of the most significant came in 1756, with the Seven Years' War. It was the world's first truly global conflict, with fighting taking place on multiple continents, involving all the great European powers. By the time it was over, France had been humiliated and Britain had gained undisputed dominance over the eastern half of North America.

That victory came at a price. By 1763, Britain's war debt totalled £137 million.

The obvious way to raise the money was through taxation on trade with the colonies. So Britain made a decision which would turn out to be catastrophic for its North American interests: it raised their taxes.

The Sugar Act of 1764 imposed duties on a range of American imports. The Stamp Act of 1765 applied taxes directly on internal colonial activity. The Townshend duties of 1767 introduced further charges on such goods as glass, paint, paper and tea.

With every tax rise, the rebelliousness of the colonists grew. There was a flurry of radical pamphlets, angry town assemblies, protest associations and outbursts of crowd violence.

Boston, in the colony of Massachusetts, became the epicentre of the resistance. On 16th December 1773, around 50 men smuggled themselves onto a ship and dumped 342 chests of tea, worth around £10,000, into Boston harbour.

Relations between Britain and its American colonies finally broke down altogether. The British passed a series of Coercive Acts to try and hammer down the growing rebellion and in April 1775, redcoats in Massachusetts became embroiled in bloody skirmishes with colonial militias.

If the fighting had been restricted to chaotic militia violence, British officials in America could have quelled it. But the situation was much graver. Under its nose, the colonists had begun to develop a viable governance structure. Committees for the regulation of all sorts of activities had sprung up. A Continental Congress was held in Philadelphia to recognise new local authorities.

When news of the fighting in Massachusetts reached Philadelphia, a second Continental Congress was in session. And then it took the next logical step: it became a de-facto government in order to manage the conflict. George Washington, a Virginia tobacco planter who had led colonial forces in the Seven Years' War, was made commander.

By then, war was inevitable. On 23rd August, Britain declared the colonies in open rebellion.

The colonists saw themselves as part of the constitutional struggle for liberty which had emerged in England. They were steeped in English radical literature and especially Locke's *Two Treatises*.

On 4th July 1776, delegates to the Congress embedded that political heritage into a *Declaration of Independence*. 'We hold these truths to be self-evident,' it read, 'that all men are created equal; that they are endowed by their creator with certain inalienable rights; that among these are life, liberty, and the pursuit of happiness; that to secure these rights, governments are instituted among men, deriving their just powers from the consent of the governed.'

It was an elegant and concise summary of early liberal principles. But the colonists were not just carrying the torch. They were making their own unique contribution. They grounded what had, until now, been lofty sentiment into a practical judgement.

The principle of consent was enacted through a system of democracy. The basic dynamic was presumed to be quite simple: liberty had to be protected from power. In the formulation of the revolutionaries, liberty was the people and power was the government. So it followed that the people had to be made strong and the government weak. 'Society is produced by our wants,' the recently arrived English radical Thomas Paine said, 'and government by our wickedness.'

Central government was rejected in favour of state government. Over the ensuing years, the 13 states legally established the Articles of Confederation to create the 'United States of America,' but most final lawmaking authority remained at the local level.

The second task was to prioritise democratic structures within the states. Electoral districts were structured on equal terms, with annual elections and an enlarged suffrage. Most states introduced elected state governors, who functioned as the executive, but they were weak, with no power to control the meeting of assemblies, veto legislation, establish courts, create electoral districts, or appoint people to office. These rights were handed instead to the legislature.

English radicalism had centred on strengthening parliament's role in tax policy and protecting the subject's rights. But the American Revolution went further. The legislature was not a check on power. It was power. It was handed all the roles that had traditionally been reserved for the king.

The only real restriction on the legislature came from the legislature itself. All the states except for Pennsylvania, Georgia and Vermont mimicked the split in parliament between the Lords and the Commons by creating an upper chamber, or senate, and a lower chamber. This structure – called bicameralism – was intended to check the power of the lower chamber.

But it was a minor concession. Few people believed there was any real need to restrain the democratic will. 'A democratic despotism,' John Adams, one of the patriot leaders, said, 'is a contradiction in terms.'

The revolutionaries had a deep and abiding trust in the voters. Monarchy accorded with Hobbes' idea that people were corrupt and unruly and therefore needed a firm leader to keep them in order. But the states were republics. Like Locke, they presumed that people were fundamentally good and rational. Order would come from below, from the public themselves.

This commitment to the fundamental decency of the people also operated at an international level. The revolutionaries believed that trade would take the place of conflict.

Instead of military alliances, America would have trading partners. 'Our plan is commerce,' Paine said, 'and that, well attended to, will secure us the peace and friendship of all Europe; because it is in the interest of all Europe to have America a free port.'

In 1776, the members of the Continental Congress attempted to encapsulate those ideals in a model treaty, initially for France but envisioned eventually for other nations too, which would operate on the basis of equality and commercial freedom. 'It would put an end forever to all maritime war,' Adams said, 'and render all military navies useless.'

None of the state activity meant anything, however, unless the revolutionaries could win the war against the British. They were fighting against the 18th Century's superpower, with the world's largest navy and a massive well-trained professional fighting force.

But Britain had several difficulties. The first was supply. It was fighting 3,000 miles from home, which made communication and logistics difficult. The second was America itself, which was a vast landscape of wild territories which the revolutionary militias knew better than the redcoats. The third was Washington, who proved a canny military opponent. And the fourth, and arguably most decisive, was France.

In Europe, King Louis XVI had sensed an opportunity in the American Revolution. If the rebels succeeded, he could avenge

France's humiliation in the Seven Years' War and undermine British power.

French conservatives were troubled by the idea of intervention. After all, it would involve supporting republican rebels against a fellow monarch. But it was simply too tempting. Covertly, France began funnelling supplies and intelligence to the revolutionaries. In 1778, it recognised the United States of America as an independent nation. Finally it established a formal military alliance. It was now at war with Britain again, in support of American independence.

France's military contribution was vital. It created a sense of threat in Europe which prevented Britain from sending all the troops it needed across the Atlantic and it proved crucial to the war in America, on land and sea.

By 1781, Britain's campaign was desperate. Charles Cornwallis, the commander of the British forces, marched his army to Yorktown, in Virginia, and found himself isolated. On land he faced a combined American and French army of 17,000 men and at sea his escape was blocked by the French fleet. In October, Cornwallis surrendered to Washington.

The war dragged on for a few more months, but everyone understood what had happened. Britain had lost. The United States of America had won their independence.

The euphoria of the victory, however, didn't last long. There was something terribly wrong with the democratic system the revolutionaries had established. It produced a central state that was too weak to function and chaotic state governments that could be strong-armed by local interest groups. America was discovering one of the central propositions of liberal theory: that democracy is not enough. Without protections, the will of the people can be just as oppressive as arbitrary government.

The problem was that people did not want the same thing. Farmers, who were often in debt, needed low taxes and a halt on court actions over their loans. Merchants and creditors wanted higher taxes on land and the protection of private contracts.

Lawmaking turned into a desperate scramble, fought over by local interest groups. Legislation was 'altered – realtered – made better – made worse,' the Vermont Council of Censors said in 1786, 'and kept in such a fluctuating position, that persons in civil commission scarcely know what is law.'

The idea of 'democratic despotism' now became the threat that most troubled the revolutionaries. It was the state legislatures, not the governors, that were the main threat to liberty. They violated property rights by taking the side of debtors and kept pushing against the boundaries of their role.

Individual states tried to fix the problem, redistributing powers away from the legislature, but by the mid 1780s, most reformers accepted that national action was needed.

In 1787, a convention was called in Philadelphia with the power to revise the Articles of Confederation. The 55 delegates who attended from 12 states – Rhode Island refused to have anything to do with it – expected new powers to be added to the Congress. What in fact took place was the creation of the US Constitution.

It was the moment when America's revolutionaries made their great contribution to liberalism.

It could only have happened at that particular time, in that particular place, with those particular people. In the heat of the moment, it was just another mad scramble, a desperate attempt to save a revolution that was collapsing under its own inconsistencies. But with the advantage of distance, you could see how the unique circumstances translated lofty ideals into an effective democracy. The culture of multiple colonies, the literature of English radicals, and the demands of effective statehood coalesced into a document which finally started answering practical questions about the application of liberal theory.

'Every word of the constitution,' James Madison, its chief architect, said, 'decides a question between power and liberty.'

The constitution was a short, prosaic document. This was not the poetry of the *Declaration of Independence*. It was the section-by-section, article-by-article formulation of its aspirations in legal terms. It was also a product of compromise, between those who wanted greater centralisation of power and those who cherished state independence. It led to positions no-one had originally proposed. But that, too, reflected the democratic practice of its values.

The core achievement of the US Constitution was the separation of power. This idea had been woven into the English radical tradition from the civil war to Locke. But it was given a more sophisticated form by the French judge and philosopher Montesquieu, in his 1748 work *The Spirit of the Laws*.

Montesquieu stressed that good government was incompatible with unified power in the state, no matter where it came from or how it was constituted. Instead there should be three distinct institutions: The executive, the legislature and the judiciary.

The executive, which took the form of the monarch in most European countries, was in charge of external duties, such as defence and foreign relations, and some internal ones, such as the enforcement of the law. The legislature was the body which made law. The judiciary ruled on the law in particular instances.

These institutions had to be independent of one another, but they were also dependent on each other, so that the influence of any one power would not be able to exceed that of the other two, either singly or in combination.

The US was itself an experiment in the separation of power, because of the relationship between states and central government. The authors of the constitution embedded this notion by arguing, in line with the Levellers' *Case of the Army Truly Stated*, that sovereignty lay with the people, and could therefore be expressed at both the local and national level.

But the genius of the constitution was to grapple with that issue while simultaneously establishing a sophisticated and painstaking system of checks and balances at the central level.

The first three articles of the constitution dealt with the legislature, the executive and the judiciary.

The legislature was called Congress. It was bicameral.

The lower chamber, the House of Representatives, reflected the public vote. The representatives of each state were directly elected, in numbers proportionate to each state's population. The franchise was left up to individual states, but it was typically set in a similar way to England's: only men of property could vote. This was less restrictive in the US than it was in England, however, because the vast amount of land in North America meant property ownership was far more common.

The upper chamber was the Senate. Senators were elected, but they were more distant from the public than the representatives. They were not voted for directly, but chosen by popularly-elected state legislatures. They were not representative either. Each state had two, regardless of size. They had a higher age requirement, 30 instead of 25 for representatives, and longer terms, of six as opposed to two years. The intention was to provide a sense of experience and gravitas, a brake on over-excitable public sentiment. Congress was given several categories of specific power, including tax and the regulation of interstate commerce.

Instead of a king, the executive role was taken by a president. The president was to be democratically selected, but again at a couple of removes from the public. States had electors equal to their representation in Congress, who would cast individual votes for the figure they considered best qualified. This was the Electoral College, although the name only became official in 1845.

The president stood alone. He was not elected from the legislature. He picked his own council, had command over the armed forces and control over diplomatic relations.

The judiciary was the least defined of the three branches but it was to operate independently and be made equal to the other two branches. Federal judges were appointed for life to ensure their independence and protect them from popular sentiment.

The branches were balanced against one another with countervailing restraints. The Supreme Court judges, for instance, were chosen by presidential nomination, but with Senate approval. The president could veto a congressional bill, but the veto could be overturned by a two-thirds majority in Congress. The president could be removed by Congress through the process of impeachment.

The constitution could be amended. The first amendment, in 1791, was an important series of individual rights providing protection against state power called the Bill of Rights. The Bill of Rights included freedom of religion, speech, press and peaceable assembly, as well as protections for the accused, like trial by jury. The fifth amendment, on property, had a classic Lockean formulation: 'No person shall be deprived of life, liberty, or property, without due process of law; nor shall private property be taken for public use, without just compensation.'

By entrenching the freedom to write and publish, the constitution in effect safeguarded a fourth institution: the free press. Since the flurry of leaflets during the English Civil War, journalism had proved itself a crucial means of scrutinising power. It was scrappier than the others, without focus or control, but also much freer and wide-ranging, capable of holding all three other power centres to account.

Not all of the decisions taken in the constitution worked. The use of non-proportional representation in the Senate gave excessive power to states with relatively few inhabitants. The inclusion of a presidential nomination to the Supreme Court would eventually create a hopelessly politicised body.

But the real importance of what took place was not its specific form. It was the pursuit of the task itself. Radicals were now reaching an extremely sophisticated understanding of one of the central missions in liberal history: the separation of power – the attempt to carve it up, and balance it, in a web of coordinated tensions, so that it was prevented from ever lying in one place, ripe for misuse.

It was also a crucial moment in the history of liberalism for another reason. It was the first moment that the two forms of tyranny had been fully recognised and addressed. Executive power was only one of the threats which limited freedom. The other threat emerged from the people themselves.

Simply opening up politics to the public would not, on its own, secure freedom. The individual had to be protected from the people as much as from the state. That involved individual rights, embodied in the Bill of Rights, and a restraint in the operation of democratic government, embodied in the US Constitution's checks and balances.

For the first time, a liberal agenda had been established in the genetic code of a nation. And in that genetic code you could already see all the complexities and possibilities to come.

But there was also, at that early point, something much darker. Right there, in a moment of supreme triumph, was one of the great liberal failures. Slavery, the use of humans as property, was protected.

North America had around 500,000 slaves during the revolution – roughly one fifth of the population. Independence had not improved that situation and in many cases it had made it worse. There were more slaves after the revolution than there were at the start.

The possession of slaves was vigorously defended by the southern states. And they succeeded, in negotiations over the constitution, to entrench the arrangement. Fugitive slaves had to be surrendered upon claim. Slaves were counted for three-fifths of a free man in calculations of representation, so they were actually utilised to bolster the political power of slaveholders.

It was impossible to square this arrangement with the *Declaration of Independence*'s insistence that 'all men are created equal.' But then that document, no matter its lofty ideals, was the product of slaveowners. It made explicit what had until then been implicit in early liberal theory: when people spoke of universal rights, they did not really mean it. In fact, they were envisioning a community of the free and whole classes of people were excluded from it.

They included women, whose exclusion was so natural it was not even mentioned, Native Americans, who were treated as foreign nationals, and African Americans, whether they were free or slaves.

This was an injustice that would stain American history, but it was also something much more than that: it was a stain on the foundation of liberalism. The mark it left could not be wiped off, because it demonstrated a fundamental hypocrisy in the application of its ideals.

Universal rights were not registered universally. And the battle to ensure they were would go on throughout the liberal story.

III. The French Revolution

On the face of it, France's decision to participate in the American war of independence had been a success. Britain had been humbled and lost its North American territories. But the cost of victory for the French was extremely high.

The first was prosaic but devastating. Louis XVI had taken on extreme levels of debt to finance the intervention. In August 1788, after a series of tortured reform initiatives, the pack of cards fell down. France was bankrupt.

The second was less immediate but arguably more damaging. The American Revolution had unleashed a powerful thought into the world: that you could start afresh. Anything was possible. Old authorities could be smashed to pieces, not as some kind of utopian dream, but as a practical plan for societal change.

Louis then made a decision which he would later come to regret. In a bid to secure support for a package of financial reforms, he agreed to resurrect an antiquated 500-year-old advisory institution called the Estates General.

This turned out to be a very bad idea. Louis had made the same mistake as Charles I a century earlier. He had revived a political body that he could not control. That set in train a series of events that ended with revolution.

It was not one seismic event. It was a series of small revolutions, each one more radical than the preceding one. And it began in seemingly abstruse arguments about the composition of the Estates General.

This body was supposed to represent the whole nation of France via three hierarchical states: the clergy, the nobility and the third estate – which was ostensibly everyone else, but in reality mostly lawyers and office-holders.

A debate immediately began about what form the Estates General should take. In 1614, it had met in three numerically equal chambers, which voted separately and in order. If this was followed, the clergy and nobility would be able to outvote the third estate. That was intolerable to those who wanted to secure political change. They demanded that the votes of the third estate be doubled and voting take place by head, in one place.

The king gave way on the first but not the second. On 27th December 1788, he announced that the third estate would be doubled and expressed a hope that the other estates would agree to meet and vote in common – but he would not force the issue. It would be up to them to decide.

The Estates General opened on 5th May 1789, following a series of elections for the deputies who would sit in the debates. By the next day it was already clear that it could never be tamed.

The first order of business was verification. This was required before the individual bodies were constituted. The nobles and clergy started getting on with it, but the deputies of the third estate realised that this moment, before proceedings could start, was when they needed to press their case. If they verified separately, they would be drawn into voting separately too. So they simply refused. Instead, they asked the other two estates to agree to talks on joint verification.

Those talks dragged on for weeks. On 10th June, the third estate sent a final appeal to the other two orders asking them to come at once for joint verification. If they failed to do so, it would simply verify itself and proceed as a national assembly, regardless of what the other estates did.

This was the first moment of revolution. As soon as that vote was passed, the deputies had unilaterally given themselves power that they had not been handed by law. The third estate was constituting itself as the legitimate power in the state, regardless of any existing constitutional arrangement.

The resolve of the other two orders started to crumble. At first three parish priests came over, and then eventually most of the clergy and some nobles arrived. On 17th June, the deputies voted to name themselves the National Assembly.

The king offered some fairly imaginative concessions which might have worked if he had tried them a month earlier. But now it was too late. Events had taken on a sense of momentum, of delirious change, which he was unable to stop.

Louis decided upon a royal session to press his case, but the deputies were not informed. So when they arrived for work on 20th June, they found the doors locked and guarded by soldiers. There was outrage. It seemed obvious the king was going to dissolve. In a flurry of activity, the deputies found a nearby indoor tennis court, took it over, and made a vow not to disperse until they had agreed a new constitution for the country.

The king arrived days later and made his offer. There were sweeteners, but the ultimate message was that nothing the Assembly did was valid without his approval. Unprecedented numbers of troops started to gather in the vicinity.

When Louis was done, he told the deputies to disperse and left the room. The Count of Mirabeau told the king's enforcer: 'Tell those who send you that we are here by the will of the people, and will leave only by the force of bayonets.'

The king made one final attempt to try and regain control. In early July, he ordered more troops into the capital, increasing their numbers five-fold in less than a week. Then he fired Jacques Necker, his finance minister, who enjoyed tremendous support in the country. That was the final straw. As soon as he did so, any further plans crumbled in the face of events. The revolution pulsated out, from the assembly to the street, and Paris began to arm itself.

Crowds attacked toll gates around the city and broke into locations where they thought there might be weapons. They found cannon and small arms in the Invalides, a military veterans hospital, and used it to take the Bastille, a fortress in Paris.

The storming of the Bastille would become the defining moment of the revolution. It is celebrated even now in France, on 14th July. But the decisive moment did not take place there. It was in a private conversation between the king and Marshal de Broglie, the minister for war and supreme commander of the forces in Paris.

Weeks earlier, two companies of the French Guards had refused public order duties. Now other regiments looked like they might follow their example. Broglie advised the king that he could no longer rely on the army.

And that was the second revolution. It was the point at which the king could no longer enforce his will. From then on, he had no control over events. The National Assembly was in charge and it would fulfil the task it had set itself. It would write a constitution for France.

The weeks that followed were, without hyperbole or caveat, seismic in human history. They ushered in a new age.

First they destroyed the old world. Until now, France had operated under a feudal regime, where peasants paid dues to their lord and tithes to the church. But in one frenzied, euphoric late-night session, all of that was cast aside.

It started with an amendment, on the evening of 4th August, to abolish feudalism. This was quickly followed by another. Then a bidding war began. Hunting rights, private courts and tolls went next. In the small hours of the morning, the entire infrastructure of financial control fell away. Royal pensions, municipal immunities, tax privileges and exemptions were ended. Tax equality was introduced. Public employment would become equal to all. The central role of privilege in the organisational principles of the French state was destroyed and with it went the existing structure of provincial, local and municipal government.

A week later, when the decisions of that evening were translated into a formal decree, it was quite clear what had happened. 'The National Assembly,' it read, 'entirely destroys the feudal regime.'

Underneath the euphoria and the idealism, though, there was a sense of legal order. The Assembly was still, at its heart, the product of lawyers, of men who respected property rights and desired stability. Feudal duties had to be bought out and were to be paid until that point – even if, in truth, most peasants had little intention of doing so.

With the old order gone, a new one had to be put in its place. And its cornerstone would be a document which was without parallel in human history. It was called the *Declaration of the Rights of Man*.

Unlike similar efforts in England and America, this document was not slotted into a series of historical events to try to safeguard liberty. It was the basis of the entire endeavour. It broke free of the bonds of its era and its place.

It was timeless. It was universal. It was one of those moments in which the ambitions of authors transcend their circumstances. This was the moment Overton had glimpsed in his prison cell, come to fruition: a full codification of the principle of freedom and its maxims. It was the triumph of a century and a half of struggle.

'The representatives of the French people,' it read, 'organised as a National Assembly, believing that the ignorance, neglect, or contempt of the rights of man are the sole cause of public calamities and of the corruption of governments, have determined to set forth in a solemn declaration the natural, inalienable, and sacred rights of man.'

The rights the document protected were 'liberty, property, security, and resistance to oppression.' These were all listed as if they were of equal value, but the document carved out a special place for property in its final article, as an 'inviolable and sacred right,' a status that no other right was given.

'Liberty consists,' it said, 'in the freedom to do everything which injures no-one else; hence the exercise of the natural rights of each man has no limits except those which assure to the other members of the society the enjoyment of the same rights. These limits can only be determined by law.'

This was to be combined with the separation of powers as the cornerstone of legitimate government. 'Any society in which the guarantee of rights is not assured,' Article 16 said, 'nor the separation of powers determined, has no constitution.'

It was a profound moment, not just in the history of France, or even liberalism, but in human development.

Yet there was something else lurking there, under the glory: a germ. It lay in Article six. 'Law,' it said, 'is the expression of the general will.'

And it was this phrase, more than any other, which took the advances of the previous months and drenched them in blood.

The phrase 'general will' dated back to the 17th Century, but in the years before the French Revolution, a Genevan immigrant in France gave it a new meaning. His name was Jean-Jacques Rousseau.

Rousseau was an extremely unusual man. His view of life was bitterly pessimistic, a fount of despair. He yearned to go back to a mythical human past that he wasn't sure existed and dreamed of a utopian future that he did not think could come true. In his later years, he went completely insane.

Humankind, for Rousseau, was naturally good, but it had been corrupted by civilisation. This corruption was very difficult to undo. If it could be achieved at all, it was in such limited conditions, and so easily reversed, that there was little point in trying. This was his general political position and it goes without saying that it made him very lonely.

The Enlightenment philosophers of his day despised him. 'I have received your new book against the human race, and thank you for it,' the theorist Voltaire wrote to him after his second work. 'Never was such cleverness used in the design of making us all stupid.'

The authorities also hated Rousseau, because he was too independent minded and eccentric to stay within the boundaries of political and religious debate. His two most important works – *The Social Contract*, which laid out his political theory, and *Emile*, a treatise on education, both published in 1762 – were banned, confiscated and burned in Paris and Geneva. Having lost both his homes, he became a fugitive.

The persecution shattered his mind. He collapsed into a series of paranoid fantasies in which he was being pursued by a league of malevolent philosophers. The Scottish thinker David Hume took pity on him and brought him to England, but it was too late to salvage his sanity. 'He is like a man who was stripped not only of his clothes, but of his skin,' Hume said.

Rousseau died once he had returned to France, in 1778. But in 1794, with the French Revolution in full swing, his remains were disinterred from an aristocratic estate at Ermenonville, north of Paris, and brought to the Paris Pantheon. He had gone from outcast to national hero. The reason for this change in reputation was his notion of the general will.

'Man is born free, and everywhere he is in chains,' Rousseau wrote, in the opening of *The Social Contract*. 'He who believes himself the master of the others does not escape being more of a slave than they. How did this change take place? I have no idea. What can render it legitimate? I believe I can answer this question.'

Like Locke, Rousseau was concerned with how a state could be deemed legitimate. But for him, the key to legitimacy didn't rest with consent. It relied instead on the state being guided by the general will of its citizens.

This sounded profoundly democratic, but in fact there was nothing about Rousseau's assessment of the general will which was simple. It is arguable whether it was even comprehensible. It did not just refer to the majority view of the population – it was something much stranger.

There were in fact three different kinds of will. People had their own private selfish will as individuals. They also had a corporate will in groups, for instance as a church or a political party. And then they had the general will. This was a kind of collective consciousness, where people identified with the entirety of the citizenship: they set aside their own personal concerns and acted as part of a greater whole. The general will was an almost mystical thing – a kind of transcendent manifestation of people's abstract common interest.

In specific circumstances, with sufficient development of consciousness, under unique voting conditions, the general will would emerge. And at that point, like atoms being drawn together, divergent views would be cancelled out and corresponding ones strengthened. 'Take away from these same wills the more and the less which destroy each other,' Rousseau said, 'and the general will remains as the sum of the differences.'

The general will was real and was always right, by definition. It represented the correct answer to the common good. If society was properly organised, the majority view would equate with the general will. If it was not, it would not.

To that extent, Rousseau's theory was a rejection of the liberal tradition of doubt. He believed that definite right and wrong existed. People voting in the right conditions would find it by virtue of their collective consciousness.

Rousseau called this freedom. But he did not mean personal freedom. He meant political freedom – the freedom to have a voice in politics. In the real world, the implications of what he was proposing for individual liberty were catastrophic.

Unlike Overton and Locke, Rousseau did not carve out a space for individual rights outside of democratic decision-making. Instead, he put absolute faith in people's collective consciousness to find the common good. When they came together to express the general will, they became something called 'the sovereign.' Their individual rights were subsumed into the whole. This meant 'the total alienation of each associate, together with all his rights, to the whole community.'

There were no protections. 'Whoever refuses to obey the general will will be forced to do so by the entire body,' Rousseau wrote. 'This means merely that he will be forced to be free.'

He then created space for an unusual figure in the constitutional landscape. They were called the legislator. The legislator's job was to establish the conditions for the legitimate state through the nurturing of 'virtue.' In this context, 'virtue' meant the enlightenment of collective consciousness in pursuit of the common good. The legislator would not achieve this through argument or reason. Instead, they would mostly opt for non-verbal symbolism, like festivals and ceremonies, to cultivate the 'inner force which penetrates the soul.' They would have a magnetic character, a charisma strong enough to shape a type of personality from the varied multitude of the citizenship. They would be a man-god. They would be of the 'gods on earth.'

Strictly speaking, Rousseau cannot be blamed for what came next. He never advocated revolution. He was against violence. 'The liberty of the whole of humanity,' he said, 'did not justify shedding the blood of a single man.' The legislator he envisioned was not a master, but merely a guide. He wasn't even really proposing a system for political life, but rather engaging in a strange and depressing experiment to demonstrate the failures of civilisation. Most of the people who spoke in his name had barely read him and did not seem to understand him.

But books are dangerous things. Ideas change the world. And every aspect of what came next was right there in the text. Not just in the French Revolution, but in the horrors that would follow.

It was in the dismissal of individual freedom in the name of the group, the rejection of rights, the insistence that there existed absolute truth about right and wrong, the assertion of a single collective will, and the idea, above all, that one man could claim to represent it, using their charisma, through a form of mystical identification.

In the centuries to come, these ideas would claim millions of lives. The bloodshed began in the French Revolution, as the triumph of the *Rights of Man* descended into barbarism and murder.

The Assembly started breaking its own commitments in the *Rights of Man* almost as soon as it turned to its original purpose.

It was hard to remember, given everything it had been through, but the original reason for the Estates General to meet had been the disastrous state of the French national finances. And that problem had not gone away.

The deputies came up with an idea for addressing it. They would nationalise the church lands. The clergy strenuously objected, arguing that this would be a blatant assault on property rights, but they were unable to halt the appropriation. By itself seizing church land would not solve the issue however. Selling off that much property would take time and the short-term debt was pressing. So the Assembly decided to create I-owe-yous based on the value of the land, which could be used to pay creditors. These IOUs were called assignats. On 17th April 1790, they became legal tender for use within the French economy.

In the summer of 1790, an ecclesiastical committee in the Assembly composed a Civil Constitution of the Clergy, which unilaterally reformed centuries of practice without consulting the Pope. On 27th November, the deputies voted to dismiss any cleric who refused the new arrangements. The test would be an oath, sworn after mass the next available Sunday. Only around half the clergy felt they were able to subscribe. Those who did not became known as refractory priests and were subjected to intimidation and abuse. In Paris, hostile crowds stopped them and their congregation from exercising their freedom of worship.

In the years that followed, this would be considered a decisive moment. Two things seemed to have happened at once: property rights were violated and then, immediately, individual rights were violated. That suggested there really was some kind of fundamental relationship between the two.

As soon as property rights had been broken, the economic consequences also appeared to spiral out of control. Most people didn't trust the assignats. They often refused them and, worse, started to hoard the traditional coinage, driving it out of circulation. A mythical currency began to kill real money. The assignats quickly started to trade well below their face value and the price of goods started to rise.

The debate over the clerical oath sparked a bitterly polarised split between conservative Catholics and radical supporters of the revolution, who congregated around the new political clubs springing up around Paris. The most influential was the Society of the Friends of the Constitution, commonly called the Jacobin club, after the monastery in which its meetings took place. It was a mixture of a campaign movement, political party and debating society. Before long it became the intellectual epicentre of the revolution, with 200 deputies and 1,000 others as members.

It started pumping out newspapers and organising festivals and marches. And in its nightly meetings, in front of large crowds, many of the most influential figures of the revolution got their first political experience and developed their power base.

Among its members was a little-known deputy called Maximilien Robespierre.

'He is a stern man,' a British observer said in March 1791, 'rigid in his principles, plain, unaffected in his manners, no foppery in his dress, certainly above corruption, despising wealth. I watch him very closely every night. He really is a character to be contemplated; he is growing every hour into consequence.' That prediction was prophetic. Before long, Robespierre would become one of the key figures in French politics.

He was able to exert such influence because of the mangled contortions of France's evolving constitution. Most Assembly deputies accepted Locke and Montesquieu's insistence on the importance of the separation of powers and tried to lock it into the new arrangements. But there was an aversion to a bicameral legislature. Having just spent gruelling months fighting for the assembly to sit and vote together, the deputies did not want to split it in two again.

The king, who remained as the executive, was an additional problem. No-one took his proclamations of support for events at face value. It was quite clear that, if he was given the opportunity, he would turn back the revolution and punish those involved.

Soon how he might do that became clear. Countless nobles were escaping France and heading out to neighbouring countries, which were governed by monarchs making belligerent threats against the revolutionary regime. If they succeeded in an invasion, the king would be reinstalled with all the despotic powers he had before the Bastille fell.

Then on 20th June 1791, Louis tried to slip out of Paris. He left behind a long manifesto denouncing the revolution.

The escape attempt didn't get far and he was quickly returned to the capital, but the event put the Assembly in a difficult position. Their constitution placed executive power with the king. That no longer worked, because he quite plainly couldn't be trusted. But nor could they get rid of it without having to start all over again.

So the Assembly simply lied. It pretended that he had been kidnapped and then, behind closed doors, stripped the king of his functions. There was now, in practice, no separation of power. The liberal principle that power be split up and divided fell away. The Assembly had total authority.

Shortly after the king's attempted escape, war with Austria arrived.

It was greeted with jubilation. Most revolutionaries believed the conflict would restore discipline in the army and bring some level of domestic stability. Foreign peoples, inspired by the sight of free citizens, would follow the French example towards liberty.

In fact, the opening stages of the war were a disaster. French forces dissolved upon contact with the enemy. And suddenly the jubilant aspirations of national glory were replaced by a search for scapegoats. 'Everywhere you hear the cry that the king is betraying us,' one Jacobin said, 'the generals are betraying us, that nobody is to be trusted.'

One of the king's ministers, Jean-Marie Roland, wrote a public letter that criticised the monarch and warned that the French people were starting to see him as 'the friend and accomplice of conspirators.' It was the kind of challenge which couldn't be tolerated. The king dismissed him, along with three other radicals.

That decision would change the course of events. Until this point, popular resentment of the king could be contained by the authorities. Now it erupted in a way that no-one could control. The revolution ceased being the project of well-to-do lawyers in the Assembly and came under the authorship of crowds in the street.

They were called the sans-culottes, meaning 'without breeches.' It was once a derogatory phrase referring to the clothing of the lower classes, translating approximately as 'scum.' But now it was embraced by activists to demonstrate authenticity and revolutionary commitment. They organised themselves through the Sections – small local assemblies under the Paris Commune, which ran the city.

On 10th August, the central committee of the Sections proclaimed itself an Insurrectionary Commune. A group roughly 20,000 strong marched on the king. His Swiss guards opened fire, but they were hacked to pieces with knives and pikes.

Louis was transferred to a medieval fortress, whatever little power he had left now completely gone. But the decisive constitutional precedent which had been set was not really about him. It was about the Assembly. It had not sanctioned the attack. Like the king, it was no longer in control. The power it held had transferred to the sans-culottes. And there was no restraining force against them, because all the power had been held in one place.

The majority of deputies went to ground. In a desperate bid to placate the crowds, the Assembly made George Danton, an aggressive radical whose political career had taken place exclusively in the Sections, minister for justice. But that simply handed over more influence.

The Assembly was dissolved, elections held, and a new legislature, called the National Convention, established. But the underlying reality had not changed. The deputies were not in control. 'Never forget,' one warned his colleagues, 'that you were sent here by the sans-culottes.' The armed crowds were the watchdogs of the revolution.

On 21st September, the Convention abolished the monarchy. The king was put on trial, but there was no doubt as to the verdict. For him to be acquitted would have meant the revolution was guilty. On Monday 21st January 1793, Louis went to the scaffold, trying to protest his innocence, his voice drowned out by drums.

His death did not end the turmoil. Far from any kind of general will, French politics was breaking down into different tribes. In the Convention, the 'extreme left' Montagnards – whose lead figures included Robespierre, Danton and the radical journalist Jean-Paul Marat, a proponent of massacres as political solutions – faced off against the more moderate Girondins.

On the streets, Jacques Hébert led the Hébertists, with his angry, expletive-ridden newspaper *Le Père Duchesne*. The radical Catholic priest Jacques Roux led his left-wing followers, the Enragés or Enraged Ones.

Regions outside of Paris were also in unrest, this time in opposition to the sans-culottes. In the department of the Vendee, there was violent resistance, with crowds chanting 'long live the king and our good priests.' In Marseilles, a committee was formed demanding an end to 'the anarchy of a few men of blood.' In Lyon, the local Jacobin commune was overthrown. In some cases these regional rebellions were royalist, in others they supported the revolution but opposed the recent turn of events.

Many of the debates centred on France's economic problems. Most deputies in the Convention still clung, despite the expropriation of church lands and the issuing of the assignats, to the traditional defence of property rights.

By 1793 this was becoming a difficult position to sustain. The worth of the assignats continued to fall throughout the chaos of the preceding year. They were now at just over half their face value. Coinage was still being hoarded. Food supply was being damaged by the war. The price of basic goods was volatile and often rose suddenly.

On 12th February, a group from the Sections called for a new idea, called the 'maximum.' They wanted price controls on basic commodities.

It was overwhelmingly rejected by the deputies. 'The people,' Robespierre said, should not be concerned 'with miserable shopping lists.' Even Marat, who believed hoarders should be guillotined, opposed the idea.

But they were increasingly unable to hold the line. Later that month, the sans-culottes lost patience and started to attack grocery shops. By April, Robespierre, noting the instinct of the crowd, started to shift position. He made a speech to the Jacobins and the Convention questioning the sacred principle of property rights and arguing that they were subordinate to the general interest.

On 1st May, 8,000 demonstrators descended on the Convention and demanded the introduction of a maximum price for bread. This time the Montagnards gave in. The next day a law was passed setting a maximum price for bread and grain and broader powers for local authorities to search and requisition property. By the autumn it had expanded to set prices on all sorts of goods, including tobacco, clothing, and food and drink.

It was a turning point in the revolution. The new order turned decisively against property rights. Within a year of the price control on bread, France was on its way to becoming a fully controlled economy. And once again, the dismemberment of property rights seemed as if it walked hand-in-hand with a broader collapse in individual freedom.

Faced with a growing regional revolt and under constant fear of military invasion, demands grew from the Jacobin club and the Sections for tougher action to root out and punish traitors. Committees of Surveillance were established throughout the country to track suspects and foreigners.

On 26th May, Robespierre swung the spotlight decisively on the Girondins, with a speech at the Jacobin club in which he 'invited the people' to rise up against the Convention's 'corrupt deputies.'

Days later, thousands of armed men were posted around the Convention and forced back with swords anyone who tried to leave. They handed in a petition calling for the arrest of 29 Girondin deputies. Most deputies abstained, but the move was supported by the Montagnards, who were eager to eliminate their rival faction and now used to submitting to the demands of the crowd. The Girondins were given up.

With them gone, the Convention agreed a plan which had been long discussed by the Sections: a Revolutionary army, composed of battle-hardened sans-culottes, who would go to the countryside and punish traitors.

On 26th July, Robespierre joined a recently established organisation: the Committee of Public Safety. It was intended to work alongside the pre-existing Committee of General Security as, in Danton's words, 'a hand to grasp the weapon of the Revolutionary Tribunal.'

A new constitution was written up, but its content did not really matter. As soon as it was passed it was suspended, quite literally, in a box above the Convention hall.

'In the circumstances in which the Republic finds itself,' the radical deputy Saint-Just said, 'the constitution cannot be set up; it would be destroyed by means of itself, it would become the guarantee of attacks on liberty, because it would lack the force necessary to suppress them.'

In other words, liberty was a threat to liberty. Or, as Robespierre put it a little later: 'We must organise the despotism of liberty to crush the despotism of kings.'

Technically, the Convention should have dissolved itself at that point, as the National Assembly had done after passing the constitution in 1791. But it was decided that it wasn't the right time for that either.

This was the death of any meaningful notion of freedom in the French Revolution. Individual rights had been sliced away in the attacks on refractory priests, prisoners, hoarders, moderates, and ultimately anyone who would not support the new order. Now the freedom of political participation had been robbed of any mechanism of expression.

The only real political value left was that of the general will, as expressed by the sporadic violent demands of the sans-culottes. This, as the demonstrators kept insisting, was the self-mandated will of the people. The fact that many others across the country were now in active opposition to it did not challenge it. It simply meant they had to be silenced.

On 5th September, thousands of sans-culottes, with Hébert at their head, stormed into the Convention. They forced it to pass a series of laws, including the expansion of the Revolutionary Tribunal and the immediate establishment of the Revolutionary Army.

This was the spark which created the Law of Suspects. Under its terms, anyone could be arrested if, 'either by their conduct, their contacts, their words or their writings,' they had 'showed themselves to be supporters of tyranny, of federalism, or to be the enemies of liberty.'

These were blanket terms, so broad as to defy meaning. It was, in effect, a universal arrest warrant. Robespierre made it clear that any normal court procedure was old fashioned. Proving guilt was surplus to requirements. Instead the collective consciousness of the virtuous would provide the mechanism for justice.

'Public notoriety accuses a citizen of crimes of which no written proof exists,' Robespierre said, 'but whose proof is in the hearts of all indignant citizens.'

The general will had replaced democracy, the separation of powers, the rule of law and individual rights. There was nothing to restrain it. All that was left was for various figures to try and take authorship of it and aim it against their enemies.

This was the Terror.

The first targets were the radicals themselves, who threatened Jacobin dominance. Robespierre branded Roux a foreign spy. He was arrested, then released, then arrested again. When he eventually found out his case would be tried by the Revolutionary Tribunal, he pulled out a knife and stabbed himself several times, but failed to kill himself. Less than a month later, he tried again and succeeded.

Marie Antoinette, the queen, was charged with manipulating the king, orchestrating orgies, incest, funding the Austrian emperor and organising massacres. She was found guilty within an hour. The next day her hair was cut off and her hands bound behind her back. She was put in an open cart to be slowly carried through jeering crowds to the Place de la Révolution, where she was guillotined.

The Girondins followed her. No documents were produced, no lawyers for the defence were permitted, and they had no right to speak except in response to the prosecutors' questions. They were executed the day after their verdict. It took 36 minutes to cut off 22 heads.

In the first nine months of the Terror, 16,000 people died under the guillotine's blades.

The first stage of the Terror was primarily a decentralised and anarchic affair. Local Revolutionary Armies sprang up around the country, probably comprising about 40,000 men at their height. They were recruited regionally, using their knowledge of the area to find suspects. Together with the local Committees of Surveillance, they rounded people up and passed them on to the Revolutionary Tribunal.

The range of people targeted therefore had a local flavour. Offences noted down in the administration of the Terror included 'plots,' 'attitudes' or 'writings.'

Identity cards, which had originally been introduced for foreigners, now became mandatory for all citizens. Those found without them were arrested and imprisoned. Around half a million people were arrested at some point in the Terror.

Most victims were not rich. Just nine per cent of death sentences were imposed on nobles and less than seven per cent on clergy. Two thirds of those officially condemned were just ordinary people.

Many would have been indifferent to politics, or just caught in one of those areas where different armies demanded different allegiances and they didn't keep up with the shifting requirements of loyalty.

Foreigners often found themselves targeted by suspicious locals, as did eccentrics and loners. Many of the victims were simply strangers who entered a community and became subject to rumours. The fevered climate of paranoia entrapped precisely the people it always targets: those who are slightly different.

Outside of Paris, the main task of the Terror was to annihilate the resistance movements. It was accomplished with murderous abandon.

'Lyon will lose its name,' the Convention decreed. 'It will be destroyed.' At first they tried killing people by firing squad. When this proved too time-consuming, they switched to a guillotine. But even that was too slow, so they started firing cannon filled with shot directly into crowds of people. By the time they were done, nearly 2,000 were dead.

In the port of Nantes, the Convention's envoy, Jean-Baptiste Carrier, also found the guillotine was too inefficient for the rate of death he required. So he tried a different method, in which 90 priests were hogtied in a holed boat in the Loire and sunk. This technique, called a 'vertical deportation,' became one of his primary methods. Around 1,800 people were killed in this way.

The great swells of anger and violence against the church took on a new form too, with sporadic attacks on refractory priests turning into a policy of formal dechristianisation. It began with a local initiative in Nièvre and then spread out across the country, with churches destroyed and priests pressured into marrying.

The Paris Commune soon made it an official policy and Notre Dame cathedral was reclaimed as a 'Temple of Reason.' In several areas festivals were held in which priests were forced to renounce their faith and declare themselves ready to marry, ideally to a nun. About 20,000 priests were bullied into renouncing their faith.

It was in this chaos that the Committee of Public Safety took full executive control. All power had been laid in one place at the Assembly, then claimed by the sans-culottes, then surged out chaotically around the country. There were no institutions or formal restraints to stand in the way. In December 1793, representatives from the Convention were called back to Paris and the local Revolutionary Armies were abolished.

The will of the people became the will of the Committee of Public Safety. And more often than not, that meant the will of its most influential member: Robespierre.

'What is the end towards which we are striving?' he asked the Convention. 'The peaceful enjoyment of liberty and equality. What then is the fundamental principle of democratic or popular government, that is to say the essential underpinning which sustains it and makes it work? It is virtue, which is nothing other than the love of the land of your birth and its laws. This sublime sentiment supposes a preference for the public interests above particular interests.'

He was becoming the man-god. The legislator. The charismatic figure who could mystically connect with the true soul of the people without the inconvenience of democratic mechanisms to establish what they wanted.

Throughout the spring and early summer of 1794, Robespierre cleansed the Republic, eradicating those who fell short of virtue.

The Hébertists went next. Twenty of them were arrested and sent before the Revolutionary Tribunal, accused of fomenting insurrection.

They were executed on 24th March. The crowds were no kinder to them than they had been to anyone else. Hébert, who had mocked his enemies for their fear when they faced 'the national razor,' fainted several times on the way to the guillotine and screamed when he was put under the blade. His executioners entertained the crowd by stopping the blade just over his neck three times before they finally beheaded him.

Danton fell days later. 'The word virtue made Danton laugh,' Robespierre said. 'How could a man, to whom all idea of morality was foreign, be the defender of liberty?' He went to the guillotine on 5th April, along with his allies. 'Within three months,' he shouted at the shuttered windows of Robespierre's house, as he was carried to his execution, 'you will follow me.'

It was the end of the sans-culottes as the dominant power in the Republic. Many had been co-opted into the formal political system with places in the surveillance committees, which were now answerable to the Committee of Public Safety. The Paris Commune, with few ringleaders left to defend it, was purged and turned into a pliable organ of the central power structure. The debating clubs of the capital were closed down, or replaced by offshoots of the Jacobins. The central revolutionary army was dissolved.

The special terror courts in the regions were closed and all cases handled by the Revolutionary Tribunal in Paris. And then, under new centralised control, the killings continued.

During June and July 1794, 1,515 people were executed in Paris. The social composition of the victims changed. Some 38 per cent of noble victims and 26 per cent of clerical victims died in this period. It was now a form of social cleansing.

Robespierre reversed the dechristianisation process and established a Cult of the Supreme Being, launched on 7th May with a speech in the Convention on virtue and Rousseau's political theory.

A celebration of this strange new secularised religious worship was tabled for 8th June. It was a festival suitable for the mysterious mechanisms of the legislator, with an artificial mountain built in Champ de Mars, marked by trees of liberty, and a procession, led by the members of the Convention, with their president Robespierre at its head. He delivered two more speeches, on virtue and republican religion.

'It's not enough for him to be master,' one of Danton's old allies muttered as he watched him. 'He has to be God.'

In the end, Robespierre's downfall came because of a strategic mistake. His waves of paranoid conspiracies became ever greater until it became clear that they might crash over anyone.

'Let us say that there is a conspiracy against public liberty,' he told his colleagues in the Convention on 26th July, 'that it owes its strength to a criminal coalition which is conspiring right in the heart of the Convention.'

The deputies watched him. This meant some of their number would be targeted next. But then he went further, to one of the two committees which formed the government. 'This coalition has its accomplices in the Committee of General Security, and in the offices of this committee, which they dominate.'

And then he took another step further still. 'The enemies of the Republic have set this committee against the Committee of Public Safety, and thus created two governments. Members of the Committee of Public Safety have joined this conspiracy.'

Those were the words which ended him.

His mistake was twofold: the breadth of the accusations and the lack of specificity.

In the jittery paranoia of the Terror, deputies were concerned to make sure their own positions were safe. But Robespierre's speech meant anyone could be branded an enemy of the people.

All members of the Convention and the two committees were now at risk. And he had not named who he was speaking about, so no-one felt protected.

At first, the Convention obediently, in cowed sullenness, started to debate whether to publish his speech. But then one deputy rose up. 'Before being dishonoured,' he said, 'I shall speak to France.' The resilience he showed encouraged others to come forward. One challenged Robespierre to name the members of the Convention he was accusing. He refused. There was uproar.

By the next day Robespierre's attempts to speak in the Convention were drowned out by protests and cries of 'down with the tyrant.' His authority was collapsing in front of his eyes. In the midst of the chaos, a little-known ally of Danton shouted above the noise: 'It's time to conclude. Vote now on the arrest of Robespierre.'

The vote was held immediately. His arrest was adopted unanimously.

He was executed on 28th July 1794, alongside several allies. In the days that followed there was one final bloodbath, of the Jacobins and members of the Insurrectionary Commune. And that was how the Terror was brought to an end. Within a month of Robespierre's death, its central institutions had been dismantled.

But the consequences of these events went far further. In the years which followed, they would define how people saw individual freedom.

For conservatives, it was proof of the dangers of liberty. A revolution had come with freedom at its heart and it had ended in a terrible wave of blood.

The phrase 'individualism' emerged, for the first time. But it was not celebratory. It was an expression of disgust at what had triggered the Terror.

'Individuals pass like shadows,' the influential Irish conservative Edmund Burke concluded. 'The commonwealth is fixed and stable.' The focus on the individual had created an 'unsocial, uncivil, unconnected chaos of elementary principles.'

Louis Veuillot, a militant Catholic propagandist, agreed. 'The evil which plagues France is not unknown,' he said. 'Everyone agrees in giving it the same name: individualism.'

For a while it seemed that the concept of the individual was tarnished beyond repair. Liberalism had snuffed itself out before it had attained adulthood.

But there was one man, above all, who understood the true lesson of what had happened and could rebuild liberalism in its shadow. He recognised that the Terror was not the result of too much individualism, but too little.

His name was Benjamin Constant.

4. CONSTANT

Benjamin Constant was a maniac. He seldom met a woman he didn't try to sleep with, regardless of her marital status. He gambled himself into oblivion, time and time again, despite enormous inherited wealth. He let down every friend he ever made. He had to escape from almost every major European city to avoid his creditors, or angry husbands, or heartbroken lovers. He condemned political enemies in the strongest possible terms and then allied himself with them when he thought it might be of benefit. He was an hysteric, an egomaniac, a liar, and a cheat.

He was also the world's first truly modern liberal. His achievements were legion. He sketched out a blueprint for modern liberalism from the ruins of the Terror. He was one of the world's first cosmopolitans, with a genuinely global lifestyle and sense of identity. He outlined a form of political theory which orbited around personal freedom. He articulated the idea that society was as much of a threat as the state. And, most importantly of all, he introduced the notion of the individual as a fully established political unit.

'For 40 years,' he said, 'I have fought for the same principle: liberty in all things, in religion, in philosophy, in literature, in industry, in politics. By liberty, I mean the triumph of the individual, as much over a government which seeks to rule by despotic methods, as over the masses who seek to render the minority a slave of the majority.'

Constant was the advent of something approximating the modern age. He is us, for the first time, appearing suddenly almost fully formed in the past, free from the bonds of place, truly liberated, but also terribly lonely, yearning for something and never able to articulate quite what.

But Constant's influence is today barely even mentioned, except by a handful of academics as a punchline to the Napoleonic era. He was derided in his own time, labelled a moral delinquent in the age that followed, and largely forgotten in ours.

And yet, when you get past the shambolic lifestyle – the catastrophic strategic misjudgements, the failed relationships, the shattered alliances, the hopeless self-harming love affairs – you find something truly remarkable: one of the greatest thinkers of the modern period.

Constant was an experiment, created from birth to prove a theory. His father, Juste Constant was a wealthy and eccentric Swiss colonel who was obsessed with the idea that you could take a child and fashion them into an ideal version of your values if you had complete control of their upbringing.

So Constant was intended to be his father's prodigy. He would be instructed in lofty academic subjects from an early age and sent to the best tutors in Europe to create a true Renaissance man for modernity.

Not all of Juste's experimental subjects were so lucky. In 1761, he stumbled across an intelligent young girl called Marianne Magnin in a village and proceeded to kidnap her, pay off the parents, and have her tutored in isolation so that she could be turned into the perfect mistress.

By 1772 – when Constant was four, Marianne 20 and Juste 46 – she was made the child's carer. Later on, after Constant's mother died, she became Juste's wife. It wasn't until Constant was in his thirties that he learned her true identity. By that stage she had been his older sibling, his tutor, his guardian, and then his step-mother.

Constant was sent away from Switzerland to a series of tutors, but here the experiment stalled. The young boy ended up being instructed by a series of chancers and drunks. He was a science experiment conducted by an inept researcher.

Nevertheless, Constant developed at incredible speed. By five he was learning Greek, Latin and mathematics. By seven, he was spending eight to ten hours reading novels and philosophical treatises. Before puberty he was writing like a novelist.

'Dear author of my days,' he wrote to Juste Constant at the age of 12. 'I have been told that fathers always regard the productions of their children as works of surpassing merit, even though they are often no more than a bundle of reminiscences strung together without literary art. In order to demonstrate the falsity of this rumour I have the honour herewith to offer you this work, being quite certain that, although I wrote it, you will not find it good; and that in fact you will not have the patience to read it.'

The basic elements of Constant's adult personality were already there in this note: the pinpoint intelligence, the lucidity, the snarky irony, the sense of emotional distance, and the perpetual attempts to please an emotionally incompetent father.

By the time Constant was a teenager it was obvious that he only really had two social interests: gambling and women. Over and over again, he would be sent to a foreign city to study, quickly disgrace himself, flee, be rescued by his father and sent somewhere else, only for the cycle to begin again.

He was sent to Erlangen, in Germany, at 13, where he fought two duels, learned to gamble, fell in love, and was then recalled by Juste and sent to Edinburgh. The only record of him reading anything there was a copy of Descartes' *Meditations*, which he donated to the Speculative Society library. After 18 months he had accumulated so many gambling debts that he had to escape to London. From there he went to Brussels, where he met Marie-Charlotte Johannot, the wife of a French politician, slept with her, and ran away again back to Switzerland, where he met the wife of the British ambassador to the Court of Sardinia, fell passionately in love with her, was rejected, tried to fight a duel on her behalf, and was ordered away.

In Paris, he met a wealthy 17-year-old heiress and proposed to her as a way of clearing his debts. He was rebuffed, so he made advances towards her mother, who also rejected him. He then tried to swallow a phial of opium in an inept suicide attempt. The ensuing embarrassment was so severe he left for England, where he travelled around the country on a white horse.

From there he was sent to work in the Court of the Duke of Brunswick, in what is now north Germany. Not long after he arrived, he saw a woman weeping on a sofa. He approached her and asked her what was wrong. She told him she was unloved, so he proposed to her on the spot. They were married the next year and bitterly unhappy a year after that.

Very quickly he started seeing other women. She responded by having an affair and setting up a menagerie, which eventually grew to include 120 birds, 36 cats, eight dogs, and two squirrels. 'I live surrounded by hordes of cats, birds, dogs and casual acquaintances,' he wrote to a friend. 'There is also her lover. Such is the company in which I pass my days.'

And then, in September 1794 – having squandered his talent and racked up a series of failed affairs and gambling debts – he ran headfirst into Germaine de Staël. For the first time, he had met someone whose volatility, intelligence and sexual appetite outweighed his own.

For the next 18 years, they would form the power couple standing up to the might of Napoleon Bonaparte's police state. But it wasn't a happy relationship. It was deranged. And yet out of its rubble, Constant built a psychological picture of himself which he would convert into a new unit of political analysis.

Staël was the daughter of Jacques Necker, the French finance minister whose dismissal by Louis XVI triggered the storming of the

Bastille. Her education had mostly been in the bustling world of the Paris literary salons, where her mother would place her by her feet as a young child and encourage her to take part in debates about Shakespeare and Rousseau.

She married a baron but his interest in her only extended to her dowry, so she pursued a string of intense love affairs. She was inexhaustible in reading, socialising and politics. 'When she is present,' one observer noted, 'other people just become the audience.'

Staël had been present at every major historical moment of her period, from the opening of the Estates General to the execution of Louis XVI. She was initially sympathetic to the revolution, but the treatment of her father – who was mocked by the sans-culottes in Paris for his opposition to the assignats – warned her that something was wrong. When the revolution entered its most violent period, she knew she had to escape or be killed. She fled to Switzerland.

From there, she created an underground European network to smuggle aristocrats out of France. Many had been her family's political enemies a few years previously, but now she was paying vast sums of money to secret agents to spirit them to safety. She believed anyone who was being threatened deserved her assistance, whatever their social or political background. Many of them would then gravitate towards her, until she maintained a travelling circus of lovers, former lovers, would-be lovers, radicals, aristocrats, exiles and bohemians, which moved across Europe in search of large houses in areas where the locals would not raise too many eyebrows at the unconventional living arrangements.

'Tell me,' Staël asked a friend when she realised it was time for the group to move on again, 'whether you could find some house not far from your own where I could bring M. de Narbonne and another younger man whose name I mentioned to you. Would it be possible for us all to live together, supposing we were three or four? What would be the moral and political reaction out there to such a scheme?'

Their lifestyle was opulent in the extreme. At the mansion Staël occupied in Coppet, Switzerland, there were 15 servants in the kitchen alone, weekly dinner parties featuring dozens of people, and regular theatrical performances in the library. Staël hated punctuality or orderliness, so she encouraged chaos. Breakfast was at 10am, dinner at 5pm and then a further meal at 11pm, but no-one was expected to keep set hours and were laughed at if they did. Staël entered whichever room she liked, whenever she liked, day or night.

'There was no order at all,' one guest said, 'nobody knew where to go, where to meet, where to wait. Everybody's door was open. Once a conversation started, one set up one's tent in the place it had begun and remained there for hours.'

She met Constant at a party. He fell in love instantly, but she was not convinced. 'This evening, I came across a man of great wit,' she told one of her lovers, 'not very handsome but extraordinarily amusing.'

At first, Staël resisted Constant's infatuation and his multiple daily love letters, but after a few months he seized his chance. One of her lovers, a Swedish count called Adolph Ribbing, was away, and another, Mathieu de Montmorency, was fading in her affections. So he pursued her in the only way he knew how: by acting out a mock suicide attempt.

Anyone else would have looked at this spectacle and concluded that Constant was, at best, emotionally illiterate, but Staël was susceptible to precisely this kind of dramatic gesture. Her response to at least one marriage proposal was to throttle herself. So, in a troubling indication of what was to come, she drew closer to him after this demonstration of his affections. Two monstrous and self-obsessed egos were circling each other, ready to embrace.

After 18 months of daily pleas and elaborate demonstrations of heartbreak, Staël finally relented and their friendship blossomed into a romance. By now, Constant was divorced, but she was still married, so they contented themselves with a written declaration of love.

'We promise to dedicate our lives to each other,' it read. 'We declare that we regard ourselves as indissolubly bound together, that our future destiny shall be in every sense a common destination.' By October she was pregnant, with what was probably Constant's child, although it was impossible to be sure.

In the years after the Terror, a fragile sense of stability returned to France and the couple moved to Paris, where they established a salon at the Swedish Embassy on Rue du Bac. They didn't know it, but it was only a brief respite in between tyrannies, a heart beat of calm between Robespierre and France's new ruler, Napoleon Bonaparte. The Sardinian general would soon arrive in the French capital and begin a new era of control.

Staël had followed Napoleon's exploits from afar. Once he arrived in Paris, fresh from an arduous campaign in Egypt, she tried to bring him into her orbit.

Their first meetings, however, were catastrophic. He seemed completely indifferent to her, making a few obligatory remarks about her father at the party they were both attending, issuing a misogynistic comment, and then moving on to talk to other guests. She was outraged.

Staël decided that she needed to make more of an impression, so she went to another party he was attending, accosted him in public, and then, when he retreated into the house, followed him all the way to the bedroom door. Napoleon closed and locked it but she started knocking and demanded to be let in. He said that he was undressing. 'What matters that?' she replied. 'Genius is always clothed.'

It did not go down well. Napoleon decided he couldn't stand Staël, but the truth was that Necker's daughter could still make a useful political ally. His brother was dispatched to ask if she wanted to work with him. 'It is not a question of what I want,' she replied. 'It is a question of what I think.' It was a typical Staël statement – principled, courageous and egomaniacal. For Napoleon, it was interpreted as a declaration of war. Staël was now mortal enemies with the man about to take over France.

The coup came in 1799. Constant watched it from the streets. 'I saw the collapse of representative institutions in France for the next

14 years,' he wrote later. 'In everything Bonaparte does, he looks only to his own elevation.'

As first consul, Napoleon set up four bodies to run the country: the Senate, the legislative body, the Council of State, and the Tribunate. They looked to outward appearance like liberal institutions, but it was a trick. Every pillar was designed so that it could only provide minimal resistance to Napoleon's will.

In the background, Napoleon installed the apparatus of a police state, under the justification of France's continued and seemingly endless state of war. Newspapers were closed down. The remaining press became utterly sycophantic. War was glorified. Opposition groups were put under surveillance, private letters opened by authorities and informers deployed to report on conversations in the street. A climate of suspicion fell over Paris.

Constant and Staël were under no illusions about the type of regime that was being created, but instead of opposing it from the outside, they tried to influence it from within. Constant was appointed a tribune, via a nomination from a friendly senator, on 24th December.

Within just two weeks he was already marked out as a troublemaker. On 4th January 1800, Napoleon had warned the new tribunes in a fiercely worded newspaper article not to disturb the calm waters of the dictatorship.

The intention was clear. There was a proposal before the Tribunate the next day that would put an arbitrary time limit on its debates. It was part of a broader effort to fetter the institution's ability to scrutinise and restrain the government.

Staël and Constant wrote a speech denouncing the measure. That evening they held a grand reception at their home. As their guests drank and gossiped, the pair discussed their plan. 'Your rooms tonight,' Constant warned her, 'are crowded with people who interest and amuse you. If I make that speech tomorrow, they will be empty.'

Staël shrugged. 'One must abide by one's convictions,' she replied.

The next morning Constant fired off his salvo in the Tribunate, rejecting the time limit, warning of the dangers of tyrannical leadership and asserting the right of even an advisory body to hold the government to account. The response was instantaneous. He and Staël were now on the black list. 'I was due to have many, many people to dinner at my house,' he wrote. 'Only two turned up.'

The loyalist press launched a savage counter-attack on the couple and Staël in particular. 'This woman discourses about metaphysics which she does not understand,' one newspaper wrote, 'about morals, which she does not practise; about the virtues of her sex, which she does not possess.'

Napoleon's response was simpler. 'These intellectuals are like vermin in my clothes,' he said. 'I shall shake them off.' His chief of police summoned Staël and told her in no uncertain terms to spend some time in the countryside. After a short period safely back in Paris, she was once again being forced into exile.

Constant stayed behind in the Tribunate, fighting a daily battle against increasingly authoritarian laws. He used high rhetoric, but most of what he did was legislative trench warfare, battling line-by-line over bills and challenging the kind of broadly written statute which would give the government sweeping powers.

'Whatever life may have in store for us,' he wrote to his uncle, 'we must serve the cause of freedom to the very end. To follow one's conscience and be answerable to it alone is the only way not to be eaten up by uncertainty.'

It was a valiant battle, but doomed. In January 1802, Napoleon expelled him and other troublesome colleagues from the Tribunate.

Constant watched the Napoleonic regime grow ever more authoritarian, and took notes. Years later, when it was safe, he would finally publish them, in a pamphlet titled *The Spirit of Conquest and Usurpation and Their Relation to European Civilisation.*

It was a horribly prophetic piece of work, which correctly diagnosed the nature of military leadership and showed how it necessarily descended into what would later be called totalitarianism. Constant was identifying, classifying and explaining liberalism's future enemy before it even existed.

At the heart of the problem was war itself. Where the military existed to defend the nation against threats, it was benign. But as soon as it was used to conquer foreign lands, as it had been in Napoleonic France, it became toxic. It corrupted the institutions and freedoms it was supposed to protect.

The problem for leaders like Napoleon was that the public weren't actually that interested in military glory, especially when it came at the expense of their wealth and their children's lives. So a series of lies had to be fabricated to secure their support and pretend that an initiative which was essentially hostile was fundamentally defensive. Wars of aggression became issues of 'national security.'

The public relations requirements of military expansion required that the truth be turned on its head. 'Authority would have to work upon the intellectual faculties of the mass of its subjects,' Constant concluded. 'It would have to banish all logic.'

At first language would be twisted to accommodate the propaganda, but eventually it would be reversed altogether so that terms meant their polar opposite. 'All words would lose their meaning,' he said. '"Moderation" would presage violence; "justice" would announce iniquity.'

Nearly a century and a half later, amid the rise of more oppressive police states, the English journalist George Orwell would stress this mutation. But it was Constant who first noticed how military systems perverted language.

Those who refused to believe the lies of the generals, or at least pretend they did, would be battered into submission. The totalitarian regime would inject itself into the minutia of people's day-to-day lives. 'Coercion will have to fill the gap left by sophistry,' Constant said. 'We shall see spies and informers, those eternal resources of force, encouraged and rewarded. We shall see fathers punished for the faults of their children, the interests of children separated from those of their fathers.'

And rising on top of it all would be a monstrous threat to the character of humankind: the demand for conformity. A uniform view of politics, religion, patriotism and lifestyle would be demanded of all citizens. The singular image of the great dictator would wallpaper over the endless diversity of human life.

'Above all, uniformity is the great word nowadays,' Constant warned. 'It is a pity that no-one cannot pull down the towns to rebuild them all on an identical plan, level the mountains, so that the ground may be the same everywhere, and I am surprised that the inhabitants have not all been ordered to wear the same costume, so that the master may no longer encounter any irregular mixture or any shocking variety.'

Constant was evoking, over a century before it happened, the horrors of the 20th Century, where the individual would be subsumed entirely into the group. 'Variety is an organism,' he wrote, 'uniformity a mechanism. Variety is life, uniformity is death.'

But there was an alternative to war. It was trade.

Constant picked up the commitment to international commerce which inspired the American revolutionaries. This, he believed, would inevitably replace an age of conquest. It was a peaceful way of securing the same objective: access to resources. 'Commerce is an attempt to obtain by mutual agreement what one can no longer hope to obtain through violence,' he concluded.

Constant and Staël may have been united in their struggle against Napoleon, but their own relationship was fraying at the edges. Constant had been inferior to her since the start, both socially and romantically. Now that the early euphoria of his infatuation was fading, that started to grate.

Staël began pursuing multiple love affairs again and often brought back the men with her to live in the strange social menagerie she'd created.

Constant was tired. He was nearly 40 and the flames of passion were starting to flicker out. He wanted comfort, and emotional security, and an end to the intense drama of the bohemian circuit.

'I am isolated without being independent,' he wrote. 'I am completely subordinate to her without being at one with her. I see the last years of my youth slipping away with neither the peace of solitude or that sweet affection which comes from a legal union.'

The relationship was the source of amusement and condescension in Paris' political circles. The press mocked Constant for being the puppet of Staël, polite society thought their living arrangements were immoral, and his family was ashamed of the whole arrangement – especially the fact that she seemed to be funding his lifestyle.

Their relationship deteriorated badly. 'Terrible scene, terrifying, insane,' he wrote in his diary in 1807, after some undescribed argument. 'Appalling things said. She is mad, I am mad. How will it end?'

Then, not long afterwards: 'A frightful scene which lasted till 3am. I do not enjoy being asked to make love, after ten years of a love affair, when each of us is approaching 40 years of age.'

Finally, he came to his decision. He had to escape. He would break away from Staël, find someone suitable and get married. 'I shall marry this winter,' he resolved. 'Obviously I must marry, if only to get to bed at a reasonable hour.'

But there was a problem with his strategy. Constant could simply never maintain his feelings. Over and over again, his relationships followed the same despairingly predictable pattern: he would fall madly in love with someone, pursue them at the expense of everything else, and then, once he had secured their affections, lose all interest. His love for Staël was especially intense, but it had only really delayed the process by a few years.

'I have noticed,' his friend Isabelle de Charrière once told him, 'that when you express a feeling, it is on the point of disappearing.'

After a string of affairs, Constant finally settled on someone he considered wife material: Charlotte von Hardenberg. She was an old girlfriend who had never stopped loving him, despite her marriage. In October 1806, while staying in Paris, she offered an ultimatum in the form of a letter: 'I cannot believe you are indifferent, and I will prove it to you by speaking to you with confidence. I am alone here: Monsieur Du Tertre thinks I am still in Germany. He is not due to return before the end of the month.' Constant went immediately.

The affair with Hardenberg lasted for two years until, in June 1808, they married, in secret, in a Protestant ceremony in Basel. Constant told his new wife he would go off immediately to tell Staël the news and finally end it with her.

He did the first, not the second. In fact, he did not come back at all. Hardenberg would not see him again for six months. He had once again become embroiled in his life with Staël.

This pitiful state of affairs continued for the next three years. 'Their story,' Constant's biographer William Holdheim later wrote, 'is perhaps without parallel in the annals of human weakness.' Constant would live with Staël and then, when he could make an escape, go and see Hardenberg. He had turned his wife into his mistress and his mistress into his wife.

When it eventually ended, in spring 1811, it was not because of anything Constant did – he was cowardly and indecisive to the last – but because Staël had finally found a lover who was not willing to accommodate his rivals. His name was John Rocca, a handsome 23-year-old Genevan soldier recovering from wounds he'd received on the battlefield in Spain. He had no interest at all in Staël's intellectual debates. 'Speech does not happen to be his language,' Staël said. He immediately took a dislike to Constant and challenged him to a duel. Constant calmly accepted, went upstairs and started preparing his will. He was quite experienced at duelling but he had no chance against a military man half his age. It was only Stael's intervention, and her demand that Rocca promise to never kill Constant, that stopped it taking place.

And then, finally, with all pride and goodwill gone, Constant said goodbye to Staël and went off with Hardenberg to Germany. Their brutal romance was at an end. Within a year, he had already tired of his wife. But despite it all – and further affairs, as well as countless visits to prostitutes – they stayed together until he died.

It's strange that any romantic relationship would form part of the story of political ideas, especially one which was as toxic and immature as Constant's with Staël. But something happened when he tried to process it. By a weird kind of alchemy, he took the geographical dislocation of exile, the sneering condescension of society and the contradictory impulses of his emotions and turned them into something else: a new type of political unit, which he called the individual.

Constant's first attempt to articulate what this unit looked like came in a novel called *Adolphe*. It was the only fictional work he finished, although in truth it was barely fictional at all. It was heavily autobiographical.

Adolphe, the protagonist, was Constant. He made no real attempt to hide himself. 'No confession that I have ever read,' one of his acquaintances wrote, 'provide one with so exact a self portrait.'

The plot was simple. Adolphe was a young, isolated man who found it impossible to behave in the way expected by a dull, conformist society. That society was a deadening weight, always attempting to shape people into identical units through social penalties and rewards. The world was full of people who judged others for living lives which were not identical to their own.

Adolphe kicked back against these expectations, but he also knew that society's disapproval would hurt his family, suffocate his social life and limit his career. Eventually, he met Ellenore, the long-term mistress of a married man.

As soon as she accepted his advances, the relationship soured. 'We lavished caresses upon each other and talked of love,' Adolphe recounted, 'but we talked of love for fear of talking about something else.' He became suffocated by her affections. At the end of the novel, she recognised that he no longer loved her, and simply shrivelled up and died.

The moment she passed away, Adolphe realised what he had lost. 'How my heart now cried out for that dependence which I had often hated,' he exclaimed. 'I was a stranger to the whole world.'

The novel reflected Constant's life. Just like him, the protagonists were completely free from national identity. He had been educated all over Europe and continued to flit between countries throughout his adult life, either because of political exile or romantic adventure, as he alternately chased and hid away with Staël or Hardenberg. National boundaries meant as much to him as the separation between towns. He was, quite literally, a rootless cosmopolitan.

'I have always made it a point of vanity,' Constant wrote, 'to detest my own country.' That view was shared by many of his closest associates.'You and I,' one of his best friends once told him, 'when we are together, belong to no country.'

The characters in *Adolphe* lived the same way. They constantly travelled between countries, but there was almost no description of the countryside or the cultures in the places they stayed. They had no loyalty or even much affection for any particular location or culture.

Constant's strange relationship with Staël, with their bizarre living arrangements and the social stigma of being a kept man, led countless friends and family to judge him. He grew used to treating society as a threat, a universal force which was trying to turn everyone into one uniform type, with uniform habits and uniform desires.

And then, finally, there was the sense of uncertainty in his own mind. Reading *Adolphe* is like drowning. It is a claustrophobic experience in which you're trapped with Constant's endless doubts about what he wants and why.

Constant shuttled between desire and aversion, love and resentment, a yearning for belonging and then independence. He simply did not know what he wanted. And then he had the crucial thought, the one which took his self-obsessed ramblings and turned them into something political. If he did not know what was good for him, then society didn't either. And if so, it had no right to tell him how to live.

People had already toyed with these ideas. There was a tradition in French literature of treating humans as elusive and changeable. The Romantic movement in England and Germany was talking about individualism in a way that was starting to feed into political discourse. But Constant was doing something different. He was carrying the torch of doubt – lit by Descartes, carried into the religious realm by the Puritans and the secular arena by Milton – and bringing it to the next stage, one which was arguably more radical than all the others: the individual's personal life.

In 1812, Napoleon was broken by Russia. He had taken Moscow only to see the enemy melt away, his own army humbled by the harsher adversaries of hunger and cold. A long westward retreat, through the endless snow and mud, finally shattered the French military machine.

Constant could see that France was about to return to monarchy, but he felt that, with his influence, it could be a constitutional one, along British lines, which respected individual freedom. He started looking around for viable contenders, but he was no better at picking political winners than he was at gambling.

Eventually he threw in his lot with Jean Bernadotte, the Crown Prince of Sweden. By the time he'd done so, it was already obvious that he had bet on the wrong horse. Louis XVIII, brother of the executed Louis XVI, was proclaimed king in April 1814 and Constant was out in the cold.

A year later, Napoleon escaped his island jail of Elba, slipped past the British and landed in Fréjus, in southeastern France. This time Constant did a 180-degree turn and backed the French king. It was another unwise decision.

The former emperor's victory was perfectly predictable, but Constant pressed ahead with a series of damning attacks on him anyway. By the time a waspish article written by Constant was published on 11th March 1815, Bonaparte was about to retake the country. When he eventually arrived, Constant had to go into hiding.

He considered fleeing, but then, in a winning moment of chutzpah, he reversed course, returned to the capital and set up a meeting with Napoleon's brother Joseph, to convince him that, even though they'd been enemies for years, he might make a useful ally. Incredibly, given the vitriol Constant had thrown at him, he was not just forgiven by Napoleon, but invited to write the new constitution of France.

It is almost impossible to imagine what was said during this meeting that it could have so quickly and efficiently turned Constant's errors of judgement to his benefit. 'If we regard Constant as an ordinary opportunist,' his biographer Harold Nicolson concluded, 'we miss the whole interest of his story. The originality of Constant lies in the fact that he was one of the most extraordinary opportunists that has ever lived.'

For the press of the time, the reaction was less generous. Constant was treated as a pathetic and laughable hypocrite, whose public utterances meant nothing because they would be reversed the next day. That view was completely justified: Constant swapped political loyalties with the wind. But it was ultimately a superficial assessment of his behaviour.

Certainly he didn't care about political organisations, or leaders, or systems of government. At various times he was a monarchist, a Bonapartist and a republican. These were all just vehicles to further his political philosophy. But that philosophy was completely unchanged throughout his adult life. He never once, under any circumstance, deviated from his commitment to liberal principles. And in whatever system he found himself, he fought for checks on power and a strengthening of individual freedom, often to his personal detriment.

Remarkably, after years in the political wilderness, he seemed to have suddenly found a willing audience with his former enemy. Napoleon wanted to rebrand himself as a liberal ruler. 'One is not the same man at 45 that one was at 30,' the former emperor said. 'The repose of a constitutional monarch might suit me quite well.'

Constant's draft constitution – nicknamed 'le benjamin' – put liberal theory into practice. It guaranteed freedom of the press and religion, individual rights, an elected parliament, an independent judiciary and limits on conscription. Napoleon hated every word of it.

'It's not exactly freedom he wants,' Constant realised. And indeed it wasn't. The two continued to battle over the document until it became clear that, once again, Constant had backed the wrong horse. After months back in charge, Napoleon was defeated at Waterloo and his regime was toppled.

'The wretches,' Constant said of the political enemies circling the leader. 'They served him with enthusiasm when he crushed liberty, they are abandoning him when he is establishing it.' After a reign of just 100 days, Napoleon abdicated.

Constant was now in trouble. He was on the list of Napoleon's allies, so Louis XVIII's impending return was likely to lead to exile. But once again, he somehow pulled victory from the jaws of ineptitude.

Instead of running, Constant sat down and wrote a memoir of his time with the emperor, justifying his actions as a pragmatic way of trying to protect France from the inevitable establishment of autocracy. After reading it, the king smiled and personally crossed out Constant's name from the list of exiles.

'You seem to have convinced the king,' a friend informed him.

'That does not surprise me,' Constant replied. 'I almost convinced myself.'

'Le benjamin' was discarded, but the period had not been wasted. It gave Constant vital experience of trying to formulate a governing structure for a country. He was now in a position to synthesise his artistic work on the uncertainty of the individual with the practical implementation of a political constitution.

The resulting project was called *Principles of Politics Applicable to All Governments*. It was one of the first efforts to formalise modern liberal thought into a coherent political programme.

Constant embedded the idea of the individual at the heart of his political philosophy. This individual bore an uncanny resemblance to the tortured psychological profile he had outlined in *Adolphe*. In other words, it was basically him.

They were unmoored from society. They were a bundle of semi-realised desires and needs. They were to be protected from the interference of the majority, whose judgemental ideas about family life and morality threatened to curtail their freedom. They were not to be forced to do what others thought was best for them. No-one really knew what was best for anyone.

The individual was like a light. Constant could shine it anywhere and the true moral form of what he was looking at would reveal itself. The first thing he illuminated was exactly what had happened during the early period of liberalism.

He was able to write with extraordinary clarity about the truth of what took place in the English Civil War. 'We see the English legions,' he said, 'who, with their own hands, had broken the throne of kings and shed their blood for twenty years to establish a republic, spring into action with Cromwell against that nascent republic and impose on the people a tyranny more shameful than the chains from which their valour had delivered it.'

He could see the reason for the bloodbath of the Terror. And he could see clearly what was responsible for these events.

The problem was not that the destruction of old authority structures had unleashed anarchy. The blame resided in a different direction entirely. It lay with Rousseau and his theory of the general will.

'The mistake of Rousseau and of writers who are the greatest friends of freedom,' Constant realised, 'comes from the way their ideas on politics were formed. They have seen in history a small number of men, or even one alone, in possession of immense power, which did a lot of harm. But their wrath has been directed against the wielders of power and not the power itself.'

He went on: 'Instead of destroying it, they have dreamed only of relocating it. It was a plague; but they took it as something to be conquered; and they endowed the whole society with it. Inevitably it moved from there to the majority and from the majority into a few hands.'

It followed that the whole idea of 'the people' was suspect. There was no will of the people. There never had been. There was only the varied will of individuals, which even they themselves would struggle to articulate in a consistent way. Any political movement that proclaimed the will of the people would eventually be taken up and misused by one leader – whether it was Cromwell or Robespierre or whoever came next. They'd claim to represent this mythical entity, summon up tremendous power, and use it in their own interests.

It was true that the people were sovereign, as the Levellers and the American revolutionaries had claimed. But as soon as that power was recognised, it had to be limited. Each individual had to be protected by a set of inalienable rights – first envisioned by Overton and codified by the *Rights of Man* – against interference by the state, church and society.

'There is a part of human existence,' Constant wrote, 'which necessarily remains individual and independent and by right beyond all political jurisdiction.'

The right to privacy, to get on with your life without other people interfering, was now at the heart of the political project. Constant was seeking not just to protect individual rights. He was making them the starting point for all political discussion. Any interference with them whatsoever had to be carefully justified.

'Sovereignty exists only in a limited and relative way,' he wrote. 'The jurisdiction of this sovereignty stops where independent, individual existence begins. If society crosses this boundary, it becomes as guilty of tyranny as the despot whose only claim to office is the murderous sword.'

He went on: 'When a government of any sort puts a threatening hand on that part of individual life beyond its proper scope, it matters little on what such authority claims to be based. Even if it were the whole nation, except for the man it is harassing, it would be no more legitimate for that.'

It was not just the state that was to be limited from interference. It was anyone and everyone who might start peeking through other people's windows to see what they were getting up to. The secret police, the busybody preacher and the nosey neighbour were all manifestations of the same problem.

This was the tyranny of the majority. And unless there were restraints on it, it would target those who lived differently. Sometimes these individuals would be religious minorities, sometimes political factions. More often than not they would be free thinkers, dreamers and eccentrics: the people who could not, or would not, fit a universal social mould.

'To defend the rights of minorities is to defend the rights of all,' Constant said. 'Everyone in turn finds himself in the minority. The whole society is divided into a host of minorities which are oppressed in succession. Each one, isolated to be made a victim, becomes again, by a strange metamorphosis, a part of what is called the exalted whole, which serves as a pretext for the sacrifice of some other minority. To grant the majority unlimited power is to offer to the people en masse the slaughter of the people piecemeal.'

By anchoring his political ideas in the individual, Constant had found a universal political programme which would protect everyone. To secure the rights of one was to secure the rights of all. This was the beauty of individualism: it was the only true path to universalism.

'If anyone thinks these maxims dangerous,' he concluded, 'let him think about the other, contrary dispensation which authorised the horrors of Robespierre and the oppressions of Caligula alike.'

It was an extraordinary piece of writing – a sudden and powerful upgrade in the power and maturity of liberal thought. And then Constant brought in a new element, which would prove crucial in the internal struggle within liberalism to come. He went back to the property question.

He did so in a way that was vastly more sophisticated than previous thinkers, because he had access to significant improvements in the field of economics. The chief figure in that improvement was a Scotsman called Adam Smith. Using his contributions, Constant was able to develop new lines of argument for how freedom existed in the material world.

Smith was born in Kirkcaldy in 1723. He lived a fairly uneventful life, teaching in universities in Edinburgh and Glasgow. But his contribution to intellectual thought would make him a pioneer in the history of ideas. His 1776 book, *An Inquiry into the Nature and Causes of the Wealth of Nations*, was the foundation of modern economics.

It has since been misrepresented into a far cruder and more pessimistic assessment of the human personality than Smith himself intended. His other major work, *The Theory of Moral Sentiments*, offered a much more generous view, in which people were capable of all sorts of selfless and charitable acts. But people's economic behaviour, which forms the basis of *Wealth of Nations*, was different. Their relationship to each other in the market was not based on fellow-feeling or altruism. It was based on self-interest.

'Man has almost constant occasion for the help of his brethren,' Smith wrote, 'and it is in vain for him to expect it from their benevolence only. He will be more likely to prevail if he can interest their self-love in his favour, and show them that it is for their own advantage to do for him what he requires of them. Whoever offers to another a bargain of any kind, proposes to do this. Give me that which I want, and you shall have this which you want, is the meaning of every such offer.'

He went on: 'It is not from the benevolence of the butcher, the brewer, or the baker that we expect our dinner, but from their regard to their own interest. We address ourselves, not to their humanity, but to their self-love.'

This self-interest inspired a unique dynamic. It was called supply and demand.

It wasn't a new idea. There was a reference to similar notions in the sacred Tamil text *Tirukkural*, composed over 1,000 years earlier. Locke had described a mechanism of this sort as well and countless traders over the centuries had presumably discovered its truth without bothering to write it down as economic theory. But Smith articulated it in a more advanced and accessible way.

He argued that there were two kinds of price: a natural price and a market price. The natural price was the sum total of all the costs that went into a product, such as the rent of the land and the payment of labour. The market price was the amount it eventually sold for. This could be less than, the same as, or more than the natural price. It was the result of how many people wanted the product, which was called demand, and how much of it there was, which was called supply.

If lots of people wanted something that was being produced in small quantities, they would be willing to pay more for it and the price would rise. Other producers would see that there was a lot of profit to be made and start making it themselves. Eventually there would be more supply and the price would fall. But if few customers wanted a product, the price would fall. People would stop producing it, because it didn't make much profit, until there was a reduction in supply and the price would eventually rise.

This price mechanism gave people all sorts of vital data about scarcity and desire. And it meant that production suddenly became efficient. The profit motive encouraged cheaper production, driving down costs and maximising national output.

Importantly, this was not achieved by planning. It flowed naturally from people's self-interest. Each individual, Smith said, in the single most famous metaphor in all of economics, was 'led by an invisible hand to promote an end which was no part of his intention.'

This system operated at peak efficiency when it was the natural product of people's instinctive economic behaviour. Whenever officials tried to interfere with it, they simply ended up jamming unnecessary material into its cogs. The best thing for everyone was that it was left well alone. And that meant the government had to get out the way.

Indeed, Smith said, the state should have only three duties. The first was defence. It had to safeguard its people from 'the violence and invasion of other independent societies.' The second was justice. It had to protect, 'as far as possible, every member of the society from the injustice or oppression of every other member of it.'

The third was the most interesting. It involved the creation and maintenance of 'public works, and certain public institutions, which it can never be for the interest of any individual, or small number of individuals to erect and maintain.' In other words: the taxpayer should step in to fund projects where the market mechanism would fail, such as the building of roads and schools.

'The public can facilitate this acquisition,' he said, 'by establishing in every parish or district a little school, where children may be taught for a reward so moderate, that even a common labourer may afford it; the master being partly, but not wholly, paid by the public.'

Like Locke, Smith was one of the great foundational thinkers of modern society. Nearly every economic school which followed cleaved to his assessment. But those who clung to him most closely tended to forget this final, public works element of his thinking. Instead, the notion of a minimal state, concerned only with defence and arbitration, took hold among those who celebrated his name.

However, Smith was extremely concerned about the wasteful spending of government. Even though state borrowing was at very low levels compared to the present day, he believed that the debts the government ran up would 'oppress, and will in the long-run probably ruin, all the great nations of Europe.'

The debts would get larger and larger, demanding more and more tax to pay it off. 'When national debts have once been accumulated to a certain degree, there is scarce, I believe, a single instance of their having been fairly and completely paid.'

States therefore had to balance their budgets. The basic demands of personal finance were the same as national finance. 'What is prudence in the conduct of every private family can scarce be folly in that of a great kingdom,' Smith said.

This notion took a firm hold on those who came after him. It became something close to a sacred economic commandment, to be followed at all times, by people across the political spectrum.

The Wealth of Nations was an explanation and defence of capitalism – a system of production organised for profit. And it fitted liberalism like a glove.

It seemed to tick all the boxes. It began with the individual. It based its function on the assumption that no-one had the right to tell the individual what to do – no king, no lord, no planning committee had the right to interfere. Each person was working for their own betterment, in freedom, in the marketplace, buying and selling whatever they liked. This activity created competition, which resulted in efficiency, which in turn increased the material wealth of society.

And that created a powerful new idea in liberalism: market equilibrium. This was the notion that the economy worked best when it was left alone by the state. This idea was present in Locke's celebration of the increased abundance that came from labour. But with Smith's elaboration, it became vastly more practical and intuitive.

Until now, the liberal defence of property had rested mostly on the notion that people's property rights were rooted in their individual rights. In the wake of the French Revolution, this notion seemed more powerful than ever before. After all, the attacks on the individual rights of refractory priests had begun after the confiscation of church lands. The lunacy of the Terror had coincided with the introduction of the maximum. But Smith's notion of the invisible hand introduced a second argument. By interfering with property rights, the state was undermining the efficiency of the market and reducing the wealth of everyone in society.

Writing decades after *The Wealth of Nations* was published, Constant accepted that the state did have a right to interfere with property. 'Society,' he said, 'has rights over property it definitely does not have over the freedom, lives, and opinions of its members.' But regardless, he concluded that it would be best if society left it completely alone.

Governments that tried to interfere with property always did more harm than good, he believed. Some had pursued 'progressive taxation, compulsory borrowings, and taxes directed solely against the wealthy,' he noted. 'These measures have been so fully rebuked by experience, however, that it is almost superfluous to demonstrate their futility and danger.'

Left alone, property would solve all the injustices which people wanted to alleviate through their interference. Property moved. It churned through human ownership without anyone needing to get involved.

'If property were immobile and always stayed in the same hands,' Constant said, 'it would be a most improper institution. It would split the human race in two. Such is not the essence of property, however. In defiance of those who possess it, it tends to a continual changing of hands.'

The job of government, therefore, was to stay out of the way. 'The simplest and surest means of encouraging the widening ownership of property would be to abolish all the laws which oppose it,' Constant concluded.

Taxation was to be kept at an absolute minimum, and not to go much further than guaranteeing the internal and external security of a country. 'The natural interest of any nation,' he said, 'is that taxation be lowered to the least possible.' He also broadly accepted Smith's argument on national borrowing, which he considered 'morally and politically unfortunate.'

In making this argument, Constant was one of the first to set out the laissez-faire approach to liberalism. The phrase roughly translates as 'let things be.'

Superficially, it seemed powerfully convincing. As Constant was writing, the industrial revolution was driving Britain forward, largely free of the government regulation that Constant and others disliked. As Smith had insisted, production was booming.

But if you looked a little deeper, there was a terrible human cost. Working conditions were atrocious. Some machines were designed specifically to be small enough for children to use. Cotton textile workers died of lung disease from the dust. The poor would sleep 15 to 20 to a room, with only one toilet. Life expectancy in poor areas of Manchester was just 17 years.

If the increase in production was increasing the churn of property through many people's hands, then it was happening very slowly. In fact, society in Britain and France remained deeply unequal. And despite his warning of anything which might 'split the human race in two,' Constant did in fact view society as split in two – between those who owned property and the property-less.

Those with property had the opportunity of leisure and were consequently often called the leisured class. This is what gave them the time to think about politics, appreciate art and explore different lifestyles. Those who did not have property were too hard at work to have any opportunity for that.

In Constant and Staël's kitchen, 15 servants embodied this divide. They worked away below stairs while the leisured class held political discussions upstairs. These servants too may have wished to dismiss all social convention, criss-cross Europe in search of love, and follow their true desires. But they could not afford to. They too may have wished for privacy, but could not secure it while sleeping whole families to a bed. Their individuality was difficult to discover or protect while working 80 to 100 hours a week.

'Only property secures this leisure,' Constant concluded. 'Only property can render men capable of exercising political rights. Only owners can be citizens. To counter this with natural equality is to be reasoning within a hypothesis inapplicable to the present state of societies.' That situation, he believed, would pertain indefinitely. 'The vast majority,' he said, 'will always be deprived of leisure.' So Constant's desire to 'let things be' went further than just economics. It was a more general assessment of the world, a resistance to challenging or peering too deeply into its social structures.

This was, in essence if not in form, a further elaboration of the community of the free, which had excluded people on the basis of their race and gender in America. Under Constant's formulation, it excluded those without property.

For the time being, it was quite easy to ignore these issues. People with property had power and voting rights, while those without did not. That meant that laissez-faire liberalism was fairly untroubled by any opposition.

But that situation would not last much longer. As the franchise expanded, these questions would become impossible to ignore. And the answers would emerge from a strange location: one of the most famous advocates of Adam Smith's economics.

5. HARRIET AND JOHN

They met at a dinner party in London, sometime in 1830, with nothing in their favour. She was a mother of two, with another soon on the way, trapped in a stultifying marriage. He was the half-broken product of a child experiment, turned into a faulty human logic machine by a distant and obsessive father. Theirs would be the greatest love story in the history of ideas.

Her name was Harriet Taylor. His was John Stuart Mill. By the time their romance was over, they had turned liberalism into the fully formed system of political thought we know today.

We know hardly anything about Taylor before she met Mill. She has barely been written about, except in relation to the man she loved. Even today, there are no biographies of her and only one attempt to collect her writings.

She was born in 1807 and then, in typically Victorian fashion, married off by 18. Two of her older brothers died of tuberculosis when young men. Two others left for Australia. Her father was a bitter penny-pincher. Her mother was a narcissist. Her sister Caroline was married to a wife-beater.

We can't get to know Taylor through her life story. Very little of her writing has survived, outside of the books she wrote with Mill and the letters the two penned each other. But there are left-over bits of communication which bring her to life. Scraps of paper survive containing half a conversation, usually with her daughter, presumably scribbled down when at a concert or a show, or perhaps at a social event when they didn't want others to hear. This is how we find her. These snippets of writing reveal a warm, witty, mournful, incisive personality, bursting with feeling and opinions.

'How long have you given up the beautiful way you used to put up your hair? I miss it so,' she wrote in one. Her daughter then wrote some remark, lost to us, on another piece of paper. Taylor replied: 'NO – you are JUST what you were – only now you neglect your beauty. So do I when I am quite alone.'

Another response, then: 'How frightful is anything worn which suggests money.' And finally: 'I never had that satisfaction, of feeling harmoniously dressed. It requires thought and trouble and I don't give enough of either.'

She was the kind of woman Victorian society had no idea what to do with: confident, intelligent, funny, with a devastating turn of phrase and a refusal to accept her status.

About Mill, we know infinitely more. His life story isn't told in scraps of paper, but in scholarly journals and weighty biographies. He was born in 1806. His father, James Mill, had the precise same idea as Juste Constant: children were a blank slate. With the right educational conditions, you could mould them into a kind of superman, a perfect intellectual ideal. Unlike Juste Constant, however, James Mill was highly intelligent and deeply committed. There would be no tutors for his son. He would take full control of every aspect of his development and account for every aspect of his learning and personality for every minute of the day.

Not long after John Stuart Mill was born, his father met the philosopher Jeremy Bentham. Together they formed an intellectual partnership in pursuit of a philosophical theory called Utilitarianism – the belief that the purpose of life is to secure the greatest happiness for the greatest number of people.

Benthamite Utilitarianism is a closed system of moral thought, which answers any question that might be asked. And it seems to make a simple, almost childlike kind of sense. But as soon as you start following this rule to its natural conclusion it has a strange habit of turning people into monsters.

Imagine that you are in a boat carrying your mother and a scientist you do not know, who is potentially capable of developing a cure for cancer. The boat starts to sink and you can only save one person. The strict Benthamite ethics would demand that you leave your mother to drown and save the scientist, because that's the outcome likely to spread the greatest happiness to the greatest number. It makes perfect moral sense, but it is also devoid of human emotion. No-one could be expected to live their life like that. As the philosopher Bernard Williams remarked many years later, if you considered saving the scientist rather than your mother, you just had 'one thought too many.'

Bentham and James Mill set about trying to turn his child into the Utilitarian ideal: a man constructed entirely of reason and able to operate at the highest possible levels of rational thought. The kind of man who would save the scientist. It was, as the 20th-Century liberal philosopher Isaiah Berlin put it, 'an appalling success.'

John Stuart Mill was initiated into what one of his biographers, Alice Rossi, described as 'perhaps the most intensive study regimen any child has ever been subjected to.' By three he was learning Greek. By six he had written a history of Rome. By seven he was reading Plato. By eight he was learning Latin. By nine he had already read the Iliad dozens of times. By 11 he was on Aristotle. By 12 he had consumed whole libraries of Ancient Greek and Roman texts, studied logic and oratory, and developed a comprehensive understanding of Athenian institutions, legislation and governance. By 13 he had completed a full course in political economy.

At 15 he was finally given the last part of the puzzle: a copy of Bentham's philosophy. He had been created for this moment. His entire life had been reverse-engineered so that his mind would be most receptive to this work when it was handed to him.

Mill experienced it as a moment of spiritual transcendence. 'I felt taken up to an eminence from which I could survey a vast mental domain, and see stretching out into the distance intellectual results beyond all computation,' he wrote. 'I now had an opinion; a creed, a doctrine, a philosophy; in one among the best senses of the word, a religion.'

James Mill had succeeded. He had created the ultimate Utilitarian man. He had turned his son into a 'dry, hard logic machine.'

And that was all the outside world really saw. John Stuart Mill's autobiography, which was published posthumously, seemed the product of this creation, as if he had remained that pulverised young boy even decades later. It was almost unreadably dense, with a normal sentence running for 12 lines and some paragraphs running for pages. There was barely any mention of his feelings.

For years, this was considered the defining evidence of a man who had been robbed of the capacity to feel anything and turned into a sterile computation device. As the right-wing liberal Friedrich Hayek observed: 'Of what in the ordinary sense of the word we should call his life, of his human interests and personal relations, we learn practically nothing.'

But then something interesting happened. An earlier draft of the autobiography surfaced. It had been bought in London in 1922 by Jacob Harry Hollander, a professor of political economy at Johns Hopkins University in Baltimore, and taken to the US. When Hollander died, in 1940, it was stored in a warehouse with the rest of his library until it was bought as a job lot by the University of Illinois. And then, finally, in 1961, it was published.

The earlier manuscript completely changed the meaning of the published text. It showed that under the dry, rigid sentences, there was a yearning and a sadness that Mill contemplated making public and then decided against. It revealed an aching desperation underneath the writing.

Suddenly a whole new side to his childhood emerged. The early manuscript detailed how the relentless study and his father's refusal to let him play with other children had left Mill so physically incapable that he would struggle to do up a tie, even as an adult. He attempted several passages in which he described these defects in detail, then decided against them and simply wrote: 'I consequently remained long, and in a less degree have always remained, inexpert in anything requiring manual dexterity.'

Mill described how he had been left friendless for the entirety of his childhood. His father was the only person he spent meaningful time with, and he was a cold, distant, punishing figure. 'I thus grew up,' he wrote, 'in the absence of love and in the presence of fear.'

When John was old enough to start making his way in the world, he found friends in the debating societies of London. He was clearly a genius, but he came across as a half-finished human. 'Of the world, he knew nothing; and above all of woman he was as a child,' his friend John Roebuck said. 'He had never played with boys; in his life he had never known any, and we, in fact, who were now his associates, were the first companions he had ever mixed with.'

And then, at the age of 20, he had a nervous breakdown.

It started with a single terrible thought. He had been grown, almost as if from a petri dish, to foster a rational Utilitarian world, in which the greatest happiness would be the basis of all political calculations. But what if it all came true? What if every change he desired in society actually happened? Would he be happy? The answer, he realised with horror, was: 'no.'

'At this my heart sunk within me,' he wrote. 'The whole foundation on which my life was constructed fell down. I seemed to have nothing left to live for.'

Mill fell into depression. His collapse was simultaneously political and personal. The Utilitarian system he had been raised to promote was based on happiness, but he himself would not be made happy by its achievement. His own life and the validity of the political system fell as one. Eventually he contemplated suicide. Why should he be 'bound to go on living,' he asked himself, 'when life must be passed in this manner?' In a typically systematic way, he set a deadline. 'I did not think I could possibly bear it beyond a year.'

After six months, something happened to stop the countdown. Mill was reading a memoir by the French historian Jean-François

Marmontel and came across a passage which, tellingly enough, described the death of his father. Suddenly the kindling took flame. He felt something.

'A vivid conception of the scene and all its feelings came over me,' he wrote, 'and I was moved to tears. From this moment my burden grew lighter. The oppression of the thought that all feeling was dead within me was gone.' For the first time perhaps in his life, he realised he was capable of emotions.

He started to put himself back together, to remake himself from his own priorities, rather than his father's. His saving grace was poetry. Bentham had breezily written off this entire form of literature by insisting it was all 'misrepresentation,' but Mill found that it gave him a will to live.

He thought the verse of the Romantic poet William Wordsworth contained 'thought coloured by feeling, under the excitement of beauty.' His newfound friends were aghast. Wordsworth was considered a sentimentalist and a reactionary in Utilitarian circles. But Mill didn't care. Being unfashionable with the Benthamite set was better than being suicidal. He went from Wordsworth to Percy Shelley, Alfred Tennyson and Samuel Coleridge.

Poetry didn't just give him a taste for art. It gave him a taste for rebellion. If verse offered a reason to live, perhaps there was something useful in other things he had been told to ignore. He began exploring conservative thinkers who were frowned upon by his political allies.

Chief among these was the Scottish philosopher Thomas Carlyle. Carlyle was a great wit, with a merciless turn of phrase, whose history of the French Revolution is considered one of the greatest ever written. He was also a racist – which was common at the time, although even in Victorian society he was considered extreme – and arguably a forerunner of fascist thought. He envisioned a class of strong individuals shaping society through history.

Mill rejected the racism and the idea of a leadership class, but he noticed something useful in the overall approach: this notion of the individual, which could be easily extracted and applied – in an egalitarian way – to the whole of mankind.

'Even if there were errors,' Mill concluded, 'there might be a substratum of truth underneath them.' He started to become obsessed with the idea of 'half-truth' – that there were little slivers of validity in everyone's philosophy, which he could discover and reassemble, through a kind of empathetic intellectual archaeology.

He had been raised to have complete faith in one system of thought, but now he grew wary of the idea that any ideology could provide all the answers. The whole idea of a 'universal synthesis' was flawed.

'If I am asked what system of political philosophy I substituted for that which I had abandoned, I answer: no system,' he wrote. 'Only a conviction that the true system was something much more complex and many-sided than I had previously had any idea of.'

Mill never quite gave up on Utilitarianism, although the work he did on it in later life mangled it out of the shape fashioned by his father and Bentham. What he did give up on was the idea that it could provide a total scientific system for understanding the world. Instead, he saw it more as a framing device, a way of arming people with the right questions.

He had been broken into smithereens, emotionally and intellectually, and reassembled himself again, using parts shunned by his father and Bentham: emotions, poetry, and an openness to new ideas. Then he met Taylor.

We don't have much written evidence for the close relationship that blossomed between Taylor and Mill in the first year or so after they met. Instead, we have to piece it together from scraps in the historical record, like a kind of Victorian romance detective investigation. Most of the evidence about it has been destroyed, either by them or by their friends acting on their instructions.

Accusations of adultery could ruin reputations forever, especially those of women. It would have destroyed their ability to promote their political ideas. And anyway, Taylor's husband was, in Carlyle's words, an 'innocent dull good man.' She was out of love with him, but she didn't want to hurt him.

The only scrap, very short and extremely telling, is from Taylor's close friend Eliza Flower. She'd just read an article she enjoyed. This was a period before the name of the journalist was printed in magazines, but she knew them both well enough to see that it was clearly by one of them. She wrote to Taylor: 'Did you or Mill do it?' So we know that within a year of meeting they were considered to be intellectually indistinguishable by those closest to them.

About the same time, there was an argument. Almost certainly, Taylor's husband demanded she stop seeing Mill. She accepted it and wrote to him cutting off contact. He reluctantly agreed, but made one last desperate plea. 'At whatever time, in whatever place that may be so, she will find me always the same as I have been, as I am still.'

It worked. Within months contact resumed, but now it was conducted in hushed conspiratorial tones. 'Yes dear,' Taylor wrote to him, 'I will meet you, in the chair, somewhere between this and Southend – the hour will depend on what your note says tomorrow.' And then, a little later: 'No-one has ever loved as you love me nor made their love one half quarter so happy.'

The rumour mill of London society went into overdrive. Carlyle's wife reported that Taylor had 'ogled Mill successfully so that he was desperately in love.' He passed on the gossip to another friend. 'It is the fairest Mrs Taylor you have heard of, with whom, under her husband's very eyes, he is (platonically) over head and ears in love.'

Mill was horrified by the whispering going on around him. He began, in Carlyle's phrase, 'suffering the clack of tongues.' In the summer of 1832, he made some kind of declaration to Harriet. The letter has been lost. Given the reply, it was probably an expression of love, together with anguish about the gossip spread about them, and a frustration with the fact that she remained married to another man.

'I am glad that you have said it,' she replied. 'I am happy that you have. There has never yet been entire confidence between us.'

A year later, Taylor left her husband. She decided on a trial separation from both men, in which she would spend six months in Paris and decide what to do next. Before she went, she spent one last evening with Mill. 'Far from being unhappy or even low this morning,' she wrote the next day, 'I feel as though you had never loved me half so well as last night.'

Soon enough, he travelled out to see her. For six blissful weeks, they were away from the prying eyes of London society. 'To be with him wholly is my ideal of the noblest fate for all states of mind and feeling which are lofty and large and fine,' Taylor wrote to a friend.

But it wasn't to be. The consequences of a divorce were too severe. For a start, it was legally extremely difficult and would require an act of parliament. Secondly, it would deprive Taylor of any contact with her three children, who under Victorian law would remain the property of the husband. Finally, it would break John Taylor's heart and turn him into a laughing stock.

Instead, she returned to London and created an arrangement that would be unusual even now. She would stay married to her husband, maintaining the external presentation of the marriage and his reputation, but she would pursue her relationship with Mill, making sure that they only ever went out socially together with very close friends.

The gossip machine again spluttered into life. One night, when Taylor and Mill went to an evening event together, his friend Roebuck reported that 'a suppressed titter went around the room.' The next day Roebuck travelled to Mill's house to advise him that he was in danger of making a fool of himself. But he'd misjudged the strength of Mill's feelings. Anyone who ever spoke ill of Taylor, or passed any critical comment on their relationship whatsoever, up to and including his own family, was instantly cut off. When Roebuck returned to see Mill the next day, he found that his friendship with him was at an end.

It was just the start. Mill began to cut himself off from a society he had only just entered. Eventually the judgements and social isolation got the better of him. In a fit of frustration, he lashed out at Taylor, criticising her for failing to leave her husband and insisting that he was in danger of falling into an 'obscure, insignificant and useless life.'

Taylor wrote back immediately. 'Good heavens have you at last arrived at fearing to be "obscure and insignificant?"' she wrote. 'What can I say to that but: "By all means pursue your brilliant and important career."'

Even if Mill was prepared to bend to the swirling gossip and innuendo, she refused to do the same. 'I know what the world is,' she wrote. 'I have not the least desire either to brave it or to court it – in no possible circumstances should I ever do either.'

She explained why she could not get a divorce. Bentham himself might have approved of its Utilitarianism. 'I should spoil four lives and injure others,' she wrote, referring to her husband and their three children. 'This is the only hesitation.' But also she refused to accept the idea that she should be separated from Mill.

And that was it. Mill made no more attempts to drag her out of her marriage. It sounds terrible, but they seemed to be perfectly content. Their letters burst with love and admiration for one another, even after years of being together. Nothing changed as they grew older. The notes they sent to each other in middle and old age read like they were written by lovestruck teenagers. Taylor's dual marriage provided a space for her and Mill to develop their romance and their working relationship.

It's hard to fully capture the scale of the contribution made by Taylor and Mill. They consolidated liberalism into a coherent system of political thought. They developed the left-wing answer to liberalism's property question. They finally challenged the notion of a community of the free. They outlined a liberal way of life. Perhaps most importantly of all, they established the notion of autonomy as a motor within liberal thought.

Today, all of this is associated with Mill. He is the father of liberalism. Whole libraries could be built on the literature dedicated to him. But there are no books about her. History wiped her away.

Insofar as she is mentioned, it is as an air-head flirt, who happened to attract the attention of a great philosopher, or alternately as some sort of scheming seductress, a kind of liberal femme fatale. These interpretations are mutually contradictory – she was either useless or she was powerfully manipulative, but she could not be both. And yet you often see them expressed by the same writer in the same piece.

'I believe he was literally the only person who was the least impressed by her,' wrote Harold Laski, the British economist and Labour party chairman. 'She had a knack of repeating prettily what Mill said.' Another writer concluded: 'Harriet of the incomparable intellect was largely a product of his imagination, an idealisation, according to his peculiar needs, of a clever, domineering, in some ways perverse and selfish, invalid woman.'

A Mill scholar in the late 19th Century waspishly remarked: 'Men have been blinded by affection, bewitched by womankind, but John Stuart Mill out-Herods them all.'

Scholars of Mill frequently made Taylor into a kind of intellectual laundering service. Any thoughts of his they found objectionable, or which didn't fit with their assessment of him, could be attributed to her malign influence. Any thoughts they approved of had nothing to do with her. Even Hayek, who did so much of the early research into their relationship and without whom her communication might well have been lost to us entirely, fell victim to this tendency when trying to explain away Mill's left-wing tendencies.

But the truth was actually quite simple. There is extensive evidence for it, both through documents and their own consistent explanations. It is that they operated, in certain key works, as a joint intellectual partnership.

Mill himself was extremely clear about how their working relationship operated. 'When two persons have their thoughts and speculations completely in common, when all subjects of intellectual or moral interest are discussed between them in daily life, when they set out from the same principles and arrive at their conclusions by processes pursued jointly, it is of little consequence in respect to the question of originality which of them holds the pen,' he wrote.

Mill was fastidious about stating which bits of his work were done independently of Taylor, which were the product of their general conversations, and which were formal joint productions in which both should be considered authors.

As Mill noted, 'the most valuable ideas and features in these joint productions – those which have been most fruitful of important results, and have contributed most to the success and reputation of the works themselves – originated with her.'

Their working relationship seems to have been almost completely seamless. Early manuscripts show Taylor making edits in pencil which Mill then wrote over in ink. Among her documents, researchers found small slips of paper in which a sentence would occasionally begin in one handwriting and finish in the other's.

The most important works of the philosopher known as John Stuart Mill were in fact jointly produced by him and Harriet Taylor. Liberalism had a mother. And she was erased.

The treatment of Taylor was part of a pattern. Until this point, women were not even an afterthought in liberal history. Descartes barely seemed aware of their existence. The Levellers didn't refer to them in their speeches or pamphlets. The *Rights of Man* were just that. Constant showed little interest in restrictions on women's freedom.

That ended with Taylor and Mill. They reinvented the whole system.

Like Locke, they began by putting forward a vision of life before society. But this was not an attempt at contract theory based on a state of nature. 'Society is not founded on a contract,' they said, and 'no good purpose is answered by inventing a contract in order to deduce social obligations from it.' Instead, the pair were seeking to tell real history, as it might have been.

Before the state, there was simply force. Some possessed lots of it, either through their own strength – a hard man taking what he wanted – or by working with others. Others had less. Perhaps they were physically weaker, or there were fewer of them.

Then authority emerged, and with it the law. But it did not challenge the power relations that had been created by force, it simply legitimised them. It took what was anarchic and unpredictable and transformed it into something which abided by rules. 'They convert what was a mere physical fact into a legal right,' Taylor and Mill said. People kept as slaves with sticks and stones were now kept as slaves by law. Land appropriated by fists was now secured through statute.

Over the course of human history – and especially since the revolutions in England, America and France – the grip of brute force had started to weaken. Absolute kings had become constitutional monarchs. Feudal lords had been discarded. But one part of society had seen almost no change at all. The slavery of women had lasted from the dawn of civilisation until the Victorian period almost completely intact. The liberal revolution had taken place without even noticing that it was ignoring half the population.

'From the very earliest twilight of human society, every woman (owing to the value attached to her by men, combined with her inferiority in muscular strength) was found in a state of bondage to some man,' Taylor and Mill wrote. 'Originally women were taken by force, or regularly sold by their father to the husband. After marriage, the man had anciently the power of life and death over his wife. She could invoke no law against him; he was her sole tribunal.'

Marriage in Victorian times had not 'lost the taint of its brutal origin.' Wives were 'bondservants' of their husbands. His permission was required for anything. 'From this state she has no means of withdrawing herself. If she leaves her husband, she can take nothing with her, neither her children nor anything which is rightfully her own. If he so chooses, he can compel her to return, by law, or by physical force.'

Women were property, nothing more. 'Marriage is the only actual bondage known to our law,' they concluded. 'There remain no legal slaves, except the mistress of every house.' This was the feudal relationship of serf and lord embedded in the living room and the marital bed, an era after it had been eradicated in wider society.

Countless male radicals had fought against this injustice when it came to economic or political relationships, but not when it came to women. After all, they were the winners. 'When we ask why the existence of one-half the species should be merely ancillary to that of the other,' Taylor and Mill wrote, 'the only reason that can be given is that men like it. It is agreeable to them that men should live for their own sake, women for the sake of men.'

Some men were good husbands – caring, kind and thoughtful. But that did not make the legality of the situation any less real. Many men were not good husbands at all. And those who wanted to be abusive could pretty much do whatever they liked. 'Practically the evil varies,' they wrote, 'from being slowly murdered by continued bodily torture, to being only subdued in spirit.'

In Victorian homes, behind locked doors, countless women and children were suffering the cruelties of unrestrained tyrannical husbands. Sometimes it was beatings. Sometimes it was verbal and emotional abuse. Sometimes it was rape. And sometimes it was murder.

A full 122 years before marital rape was criminalised in England, the pair railed against the husband's right to 'enforce the lowest degradation of a human being, that of being made the instrument of an animal function contrary to her inclinations.'

They campaigned in cases where wives, children or domestic servants had been beaten or murdered by a domestic despot. Working together, Harriet and John wrote countless pieces of campaigning journalism on live court cases. Where the accused was set free and they thought the evidence warranted it, they pursued them regardless, urging readers to consider them 'acquitted murderers.'

'I should like to have a return laid annually before the House of Commons of the number of women who are annually beaten to death, kicked to death, or trampled to death by their male protectors,' they wrote, with cold fury. 'And in an opposite column, the amount of sentences passed, in those cases in which the dastardly criminals did not get off altogether. We should then have an arithmetical estimate of the value set by a male legislature and male tribunals on the murder of a woman, often by torture continued through the years, which, if there is any shame in us, would make us hang our heads.'

Even for women who were lucky enough to never be beaten, raped or murdered, the system of male dominance was a mental prison. It created a society which dedicated itself to diminishing their character and turning them into the playthings of the other half of the population. The idea of being free in any meaningful sense was gone. Instead, they were turned into passive objects, whose entire lives were predicated on the importance of satisfying men.

The process began as soon as a female child entered education. 'Women are educated for one single object, to gain their living by marrying,' they wrote. 'To be married is the object of their existence and that object being gained they do really cease to exist as anything worth calling life or any useful purpose.'

Women were denied any real control over who they married. Only very liberal families offered them much choice in the matter. And even then they couldn't make an informed choice, because such a high value was placed on virginity. 'Girls enter into what is called a contract perfectly ignorant of the conditions of it,' Taylor and Mill wrote, 'and that they should be so is considered absolutely essential to their fitness for it.'

Once the girl was married, there was only one further purpose to her: creating a child, ideally a male one. Women were either 'mothers or nothing' and once they had become a mother 'they shall be nothing else.'

The entirety of a woman's lifetime was therefore defined by sex. Before marriage, her worth was measured by the absence of it, and after marriage it was measured by its product. Women had been reduced to their biology.

Instead of learning about the world, women had been instructed to define themselves by the desires of men. This meant, to all intents and purposes, that they were to become good slaves. 'Meekness, submissiveness, and resignation of all individual will into the hands of a man represent an essential part of sexual attractiveness.'

Women were moulded into un-liberals, human beings without the capacity to make free choices about their lives. 'Not self-will, and government by self-control, but submission and yielding to the control of others.'

Taylor and Mill acknowledged that a middle-class Victorian wife obviously had a more comfortable life than the feudal serf toiling in the field. But the impact on her development as a person had, if anything, been more severe. 'What is now called the nature of women is an eminently artificial thing – the result of forced repression in some directions, unnatural stimulation in others,' they wrote. 'It may be asserted without scruple that no other class of dependants have had their character so entirely distorted from its natural proportions by their relation with their masters.'

Taylor and Mill were addressing a whole half of the population and suggesting that their brains have been wired wrong by an oppressor class, who happened to be their husbands and fathers. But in fact the argument was much more radical than that. It had implications for liberalism that went beyond the treatment of women.

It was not enough to simply seek as much freedom as possible within existing society, as Constant had done. You had to ask yourself how much freedom could be achieved if society was redesigned.

This thought was the precise opposite of the sentiment behind laissez-faire. It would not 'let things be.' It urged the opposite: shake things up. Turn the world over. Do not just accept the way things are.

They were concluding that liberal principles, consistently applied, made the world more equal.

This came partly from Utilitarianism. For all of its weaknesses, 'the greatest good for the greatest number' was inescapably egalitarian. And with that theoretical upbringing still humming away inside him, Mill instinctively noticed the proper radicalism within liberalism.

Earlier liberals had talked of the freedom of the individual. But from the Putney debates to Constant they had then quickly acted to limit those who could benefit – women were excluded, and those without property, and other races, and slaves. Now Taylor and Mill finally recognised the weakness of that proposition. Freedom was for everyone.

'The only school of genuine moral sentiment is society between equals,' they said. 'We deny the right of any portion of the species to decide for another portion, or any individual for another individual, what is and what is not their "proper sphere."'

Towards the end of his life, Mill became the member of parliament for Westminster. He was the only philosopher in this book to become an elected politician and, predictably enough, he was terrible at it. He simply couldn't lower himself to the level of debate demanded of him. As the Victorian journalist Walter Bagehot put it: 'What did the Westminster electors know of Mr Mill? What fraction of his mind could be imagined by any percentage of their minds?'

But Mill did achieve one rather remarkable thing. In 1867, as an electoral reform bill was going through parliament, he put forward an amendment making one small but incendiary change: It took out the word 'man' and replaced it with the word 'person.' For the first time in British history, female suffrage – the right of women to vote – was put before parliament.

It was defeated, although it secured a respectable 73 votes. No-one had thought it would pass. That wasn't its function. It was intended to serve as a springboard for the campaign for women's votes in Britain, which Mill helped lead alongside his young friend Millicent Fawcett.

When the Commons finally passed a law granting women the same voting rights as men in 1928, 55 years after Mill's death, an elderly Fawcett watched from the public gallery. Afterwards, she led a delegation of women to his statue in Embankment, and laid a wreath in his memory.

The battle over gender also had to be fought on economics. Taylor and Mill looked at liberalism's effort to address the property question and found it to be insufficient.

The fact it came from them was surprising. Mill's father had supported Adam Smith's theories. David Ricardo, an early classical economist, had been a regular visitor at the family home.

For most of his life, John Stuart Mill had accepted the basic maxims of this school of thought: the sanctity of private property, the drive of human self-interest, and the idea that competition was the most efficient way of increasing the wealth of a country.

He set out his own economic thinking in the *Principles of Political Economy* in 1848, a tremendously successful book which positioned him as one of the intellectuals of Victorian Britain. It was a fairly typical piece of hands-off-the-market laissez-faire analysis. Prices were defined as a result of the interaction between supply and demand. Along with profits and wages, they always found their natural level as a result of market forces.

It also made the liberal case, previously outlined by the American revolutionaries and Constant, for the role of international trade as a means of spreading ideas, increasing the output of the world and, most importantly, stopping war.

'It is hardly possible to overrate the value, in the present low state of human improvement, of placing human beings in contact with persons dissimilar to themselves, and with modes of thought and action unlike those with which they are familiar,' Mill said. 'Commerce is now what war once was, the principle source of this contact. It is commerce which is rapidly rendering war obsolete, by strengthening and multiplying the personal interests which are in common opposition to it.'

But despite his laissez-faire upbringing, there was another side to Mill. Even as a young man, he had been indignant at the inequality he saw all around him. By the age of 20, he was demanding that resources be distributed 'the nearest to equality.'

For many liberal thinkers, property rights were an intrinsic good. They were within the protective shield of individual life that no-one should interfere with. The state had limited powers to tax people or restrict their economic activity.

Constant had taken this further and defended property rights on an instrumental level. In other words, they were valuable on the basis of what they accomplished. The invisible hand mechanism, which led from self-interest to competition in a free market, increased productivity and gave people more advantages than they would have were the state to intervene.

Mill took this instrumental view of property and started asking searching questions of it. Was uncontrolled competition providing the goods? Was it increasing material wealth for everyone? Was it expanding freedom?

The answer, very often, was yes. In the majority of cases, competition improved the condition of the poorest workers. 'With the exception of competition among labourers, all other competition is for the benefit of the labourers, by cheapening the articles they consume,' he found. 'Competition even in the labour market is a source not of low but of high wages.'

Non-interference in the market should remain the default position, he concluded. State efforts often limited individual free agency, and even where they didn't they tended to increase government power, overburden the state, and deprive people of their capacity for spontaneous action. 'Laissez-faire, in short, should be the general practice,' he said. 'Every departure from it, unless required by some great good, is a certain evil.'

But then he departed from the standard formulation, to striking effect. 'I confess I am not charmed,' he said, 'with the ideal of life held out by those who think that the normal state of human beings is that of struggling to get on; that the trampling, crushing, elbowing, and treading on each other's heels, which form the existing type of social life, are the most desirable lot of human kind.'

It was not enough to simply say that production and accumulation were increasing. The key test, as it had been with gender, was egalitarian. It was whether 'the mass of the people' were benefitting.

And on this point, the free market was a failure. Most of the technological achievements of the industrial period had not yet proved their worth to the majority of people experiencing them. 'It is questionable if all the mechanical inventions yet made have lightened the day's toil of any human being,' he found.

This was a fundamental distinction between Mill and Constant. Constant had been prepared to accept the permanence of a leisured upper class. Mill wanted to destroy it. 'I do not recognise as either just or salutary,' he said, 'a state of society in which there is any "class" which is not labouring.'

The landed classes were using rent to get rich without doing any work on the land. Their money, Mill decided, 'falls into their mouths as they sleep.' This warranted a degree of state action which seems radical even now. Inheritance, he said, should be limited to an 'amount sufficient to constitute a moderate independence.' The whole notion of land ownership had to be rethought. It was fine to own a house and a small garden, but the accumulation of large tracts of property was morally unjustifiable. The earth was a 'gift of nature to the whole human race.'

Mill envisaged a much more fundamentally equal society, involving a 'well-paid and affluent body of labourers; no enormous fortunes, except what were earned and accumulated during a single lifetime; but a much larger body of persons than at present, not only exempt from the coarser toils, but with sufficient leisure, both physical and mental, to cultivate freely the graces of life.'

He was rejecting the easy laissez-faire dismissal of economic arguments, the wave of the hand that discarded the real lived experiences of human beings in favour of an assertion that in all times, at all places, society would be worsened by state interference.

Instead, he was bedding his analysis in the third role of the state Smith outlined in the *Wealth of Nations*: the maintenance of 'public works and certain public institutions.' These were areas where the market failed and state action was needed.

This duty was often ignored by the laissez-faire liberals who followed Smith, with the state reduced to just external defence and internal justice. But Mill fixed pointedly on it and expanded it.

Like Smith he recognised the need for public provision of schooling for everyone. And like Smith he thought that public necessities like roads and canals might also require government assistance, but he updated this principle for the industrial age. Numerous public works were best done by local government, or under its oversight. This included natural monopolies such as gas and water, where, 'though perfect freedom is allowed to competition, none really takes place.'

The state was also required to protect collective decision making, for instance where workers grouped together to demand a limitation of the working day to nine hours. This should be established in law to give force to the decision. Scientific research would also often require government funding.

And there was one final area, which would go on to become more important than any of the others: welfare. In his treatment of this issue, Mill showed how far he had deviated from classical economists' insistence on self-interest.

'Human beings should help one another, and the more so in proportion to the urgency of the need,' he said. 'None needs help so urgently as one who is starving.'

This required a kind of embryonic welfare state – the provision of government help to those in genuine need. It was not to be too generous, or else people would lose their initiative to work. Recipients should not get as much as they would by having a job. But they had to receive enough to cover essential costs.

Even though Mill had started from the basis of classical economics, his conclusions were far reaching. In fact, they were unlimited. 'In the particular circumstances of a given age or nation, there is scarcely anything really important to the general interest which it may not be desirable, or even necessary, that the government should take upon itself,' he said. This included 'roads, docks, harbours, canals, works of irrigation, hospitals, schools, colleges, printing-presses.'

Mill's updating of liberal economic thought was subtle and gradual. Unlike the criticism of gender relations, it was not all-out assault on the old order. It evolved out of his previous work, through new editions of the *Principles*, growing from classical economics, challenging a point here, a principle there. But it was the start of a school of liberalism which stood opposed to laissez-faire. It was egalitarian liberalism. It would not let things be, but instead prod away at them, ask questions, demand change, and test the success of freedom by the extent to which it resulted in equality.

At the heart of it was a profound idea. The binary 'state versus market' debate was infantile. It was dangerous to suggest, as some socialists were starting to, that the state should provide everything. But it was also absurd to pretend that the market could do the same. The question of how far the government should interfere in the market, Mill said, in a comment that would echo into the future of liberalism, 'does not admit of any universal solution.'

Both had to be kept in check. Both had to be embraced for what they could do and prevented from doing what they could not. They were suitable for different things at different times. And the way to establish that was not to adopt uniform rules. It was to assess these issues instrumentally, case by case.

Despite their indescribably weird romantic situation, Taylor and Mill had settled into a blissful long-term love affair. 'When I think that I shall not hold your hand until Tuesday,' Taylor wrote, years into the relationship, 'the time is so long and my hand so useless.'

This lasted for over a decade. The 1830s passed. They spent most of the 1840s going on long European trips and gradually withdrawing from social life. Partly it was the gossip. But it was also that each needed only the other.

John Taylor died from bowel cancer in 1849 and, after a respectable interlude, the pair finally married, two decades after they first met. Ahead of the ceremony Mill wrote a statement rejecting the powers the marriage contract gave him: 'I, having no means of legally divesting myself of these odious powers, feel it my duty to put on record a formal protest against the existing law of marriage, in so far as conferring such powers, and a solemn promise never in any case or under any circumstances to use them.'

Finally, after years of waiting, they settled into married life without any gossip or complications to distract them. Mill reduced his journalistic output considerably. They moved out the centre of London to Blackheath, where they hardly saw anyone and barely even wrote to friends. Mill made tea and played the piano for Harriet, making up the music as he went along.

We don't know much about their relationship during these years. They were finally together all the time, so the letters stopped. Then, after a couple of years, they started up again. Health reasons had forced them to start spending more time apart, usually by having to seek relief in southern or coastal climates. 'This is the first time since we were married my darling wife that we have been separated and I do not like it at all,' Mill said after departing. 'How I long for the first sight of that dear handwriting.'

In Rome, he had an idea. They should write a book on the idea of freedom itself. 'The more I think of the plan of a volume on liberty, the more likely it seems to me that it will be read and will make a sensation,' he wrote. 'We must cram into it as much as possible of what we wish not to leave unsaid.'

The couple got to work, but it would be their last project together. In November 1858, not long after it was finished, Taylor died. They had been heading off to France to find a retirement home when she developed a severe cough. In a panic, Mill fired off a letter to the doctor, but it was too late. She passed away in a hotel room in Avignon.

For one day, Mill sat alone with the body. His loss was incalculable. She had not just been his wife, or his intellectual partner. She had been his salvation. The logic machine had found someone who could free his feelings. To the outside world, there was just the relentless machine-gun fire of his reasoning. But with her, he was tender. Now that part of his life was gone.

'For seven and a half years that blessing was mine,' he said of his marriage. 'For seven and a half years only.'

The attacks on her character, from female and male writers alike, started almost as soon as she was gone and lasted until the present day. She was 'in all probabilities a frigid woman,' according to the academic Max Lerner. Her concern about domestic violence was due to 'morbid inclinations,' Mill's biographer Ruth Borchard concluded, and she suffered from 'a deep-seated masochism unfitting her for normal physical love.'

The Cambridge professor Stefan Collini called her an 'imperious, paranoid, unpleasant woman.' Diana Trilling, the American literary critic, branded her 'one of the meanest and dullest ladies in literary history, a monument of nasty self-regard, as lacking in charm as in grandeur,' with 'no touch of true femininity, no taint of the decent female concerns.'

In the month she died, Mill sent the manuscript for their final project to his publisher. Unlike his other works, there would be no updated editions or revisions. It was a memorial to their relationship and their principles. It was, for Mill, a sacred text. 'The conjunction of her mind with mine,' he wrote, 'has rendered it a kind of philosophical text-book of a single truth.'

On its first page, Mill gave a proper account of Taylor's qualities, which the following decades of abuse would not be able to touch. He wrote: 'To the beloved and deplored memory of her who was the inspirer, and in part the author, of all that is best in my writings – the friend and wife whose exalted sense of truth and right was my strongest incitement, and whose approbation was my chief reward – I dedicate this volume. Like all that I have written for many years, it belongs as much to her as to me; but the work as it stands has had, in a very insufficient degree, the inestimable advantage of her revision. Were I but capable of interpreting to the world one half the great thoughts and noble feelings which are buried in her grave, I should be the medium of greater benefit to it than is ever likely to arise from anything that I can write.'

The book would go on to become the single most important work in the history of liberalism. It is *On Liberty*.

The achievements of *On Liberty* were threefold. First, it turned the notion of individual freedom into a principle which could understand and reach conclusions about almost any political issue. Second, it developed a much more complex understanding of the role of doubt in liberal history and used it to produce one of the strongest arguments for free speech ever made. And finally, it used these ideas to outline a liberal personality and lifestyle. Liberalism became a vastly more advanced and sophisticated system of thought. In many respects, it is the liberalism we know today.

'The subject of this essay,' Mill and Taylor began, 'is the nature and limits of the power which can be legitimately exercised by society over the individual.'

Mill greatly admired Constant. He believed he was a true liberal among 'intriguers' and described his death as a 'misfortune for the world.' Now he and Taylor would take his central philosophical idea of individual freedom and make it more sophisticated.

The French Revolution helped to free people from the tyranny of the state, but it had raised a new threat, typified by Rousseau, of the will of the people. 'The will of the people practically means the will of the most numerous or the most active part of the people,' they argued. 'The people, consequently, may desire to oppress a part of their number; and precautions are much needed against this, as against any other abuse of power.' They branded this the 'tyranny of the majority.'

This meant there were actually two threats to the individual: the state and society. Society's threat to the individual was if anything more alarming than that of the state, because it could reach deeper into people's lives.

'When society itself is the tyrant,' Mill and Taylor wrote, 'its means of tyrannising are not restricted to the acts which it may do by the hands of its political functionaries. Society can and does issue its own mandates: and if it issues wrong mandates instead of right, or any mandates at all in things with which it ought not to meddle, it practices a social tyranny more formidable than many kinds of political oppression.'

The solution they invented was called the harm principle. It was extremely simple. 'The only purpose for which power can be rightfully exercised over any member of a civilised community, against his will, is to prevent harm to others,' they wrote. 'His own good, either physical or moral, is not a sufficient warrant. In the part that merely concerns himself, his independence is, of right, absolute. Over himself, over his own body and mind, the individual is sovereign.'

The harm principle is like a marker in history. The second it is articulated, liberalism vaults from the past into a practicable system of thought for our own time. Even Constant, who in any number of ways was years ahead of his time, often reads like a product of a far-off age. But the moment the harm principle comes into play, the examples we think of suddenly become strikingly modern.

Taylor and Mill's liberalism applies to the world around us: smoking bans, the hijab, the teaching of creationism in schools, gay marriage, immigration, cannabis legalisation, sugar tax, euthanasia. The harm principle is like a switch. You hit it, and you're in the modern world.

It is one of the most elegant ideas ever expressed in political philosophy. It is at once uniquely simple but also endlessly complicated.

The basic premise can be understood by even young children: When something concerns only the individual, no-one has a right to interfere. But when it can harm others, they can.

And yet from that distinction countless fiendishly complex moral questions arise. Political and economic debate springs from it, curling and twisting in innumerable unpredictable directions.

The initial question was obvious. What is 'harm' exactly?

Many acts affected others but should not be centrally controlled. 'An individual may be hurtful to others, or wanting in due consideration of their welfare' without actually violating their constituted rights, Taylor and Mill accepted. Acts such as spitting on the pavement for instance, or swearing in front of an elderly man could be 'justly punished by opinion though not by law.'

This was not, the couple were at pains to point out, a world devoid of moral judgement. 'It would be a great misunderstanding of this doctrine to suppose that it is one of selfish indifference, which pretends that human beings have no business with each other's conduct.'

You could disapprove all you wanted. And if someone did something which you found unpalatable, you could avoid or chastise them. Perhaps they were a serial liar, or cheated on their partner, or wasted all their money on gambling. All these things could rightfully earn someone the contempt of their peers. And this was potentially positive. It meant that people could pressure others to be more considerate. Moral judgement could advance humankind.

What you could not justifiably do was force them to stop. If they wanted to commit errors and become a 'subject of distaste,' that was ultimately up to them.

But where exactly was that gap, between 'harm' and 'wanting in due consideration of their welfare'? After all, there really is no action on earth which only affects yourself. Not even the fiercest defender of public health would suggest that someone should be jailed for eating too many sweets, but that action will affect their family, if they develop a heart condition, and it will affect society, if the condition requires the care of a publicly funded health service.

Taylor and Mill knew the line was blurred. 'No person is an entirely isolated being,' they conceded. 'It is impossible for a person to do anything seriously or permanently hurtful to himself without mischief reaching at least to his near connections and often far beyond them.'

But to have defined the difference, or exhaustively listed which acts fell into each category, would have gone against the spirit of the proposal. People had to make their own decisions, based on the unique situation. The harm principle was designed to assist in debate, not to decide it.

There were, however, basic individual liberties that could not be touched: freedom of thought and conscience, the freedom of 'expressing and publishing opinions,' freedom of lifestyle – 'of doing as we like' – and freedom of association.

It all sounded completely harmless and uncontroversial, even in the Victorian era. But that was only in the abstract. When these values were actually turned into a practical reality, they were nearly always met with angry resistance. That much has not changed between the Victorian era and our own. 'There is no doctrine,' they warned, 'which stands more directly opposed to the general tendency of existing opinion and practice.'

To demonstrate the principle, the book branched out into multiple examples. But these were not intended to be hard-and-fast rulings. They were 'specimens of application.'

Nevertheless, the examples accomplished three things. First, they showed that from seemingly uncontroversial principles extremely radical propositions followed. Second, they highlighted the way that liberal thought quickly burrowed down into detailed policy-making. And finally, they revealed the highest possible achievement of liberal behaviour: the reluctant acceptance of things which you personally found to be distasteful.

The first point seemed to rise up, cloaked in shadow, from otherwise innocuous examples. Taylor and Mill cited Cromwell's attack on music and parties after the English Civil War. The Puritans, they pointed out, had banned 'all public, and nearly all private, amusements: especially music, dancing, public games, or other assemblages for purposes of diversion.'

This was obviously wrong and no-one in Victorian times would have thought it reasonable. It was unfair for people of a particular religious or moral persuasion to prevent others from doing what they like, as long as they weren't hurting anyone. But as soon as this premise has been accepted, it becomes impossible to resist much more challenging examples.

What about the use of recreational drugs, for instance? In our own times, these are banned in almost every country in the world. Arguments can be made about their effect on others, but these are no different to the arguments that could be made about the impact of alcohol on others – from ill-health to violence, addiction and family breakdown. According to the harm principle, it is very difficult to defend banning recreational drugs on liberal lines. And yet hardly any country on earth has decriminalised them.

Another example in *On Liberty* addressed the sale of poison – items with a conventional legal use but which could also be deployed to kill someone. The question here was 'how far liberty may be legitimately be invaded for the prevention of crime.' And here the second finding burst forth: the harm principle quickly translated into detailed policy-making. If the poison – say, a cleaning product – was banned, countless people would lose their freedom to purchase something that was useful for harmless activities. But if there were no restrictions on its sale, some unlucky people could end up losing all their freedoms if they died from being poisoned. Murder, after all, is the ultimate anti-liberal act – it eradicates the freedom to make any future choices.

The solution was to create an impediment to improper use of the poison without detection. This required the seller being compelled by the state to fill out a register with the time of sale, the name and address of the buyer, the precise quality and quantity sold, and the purpose of the purchase. Such restrictions would be tedious for normal consumers to comply with. They would all lose a little bit of freedom, in the time and effort expended. But their freedom to purchase the item would be secured, while the freedoms protected by the prevention of murder would be enhanced.

Very quickly, liberalism descended into day-to-day, granular policy-making. The harm principle hovered over everything, requiring carefully-judged regulation, form-filling, and case-by-case judgement. It was a world of balanced interests.

These two cases showed the strange counter-intuitive character of liberalism. It was at once daringly radical – authorising countless actions which would be considered intolerable by the majority of people – and also practical and even-handed.

The next cases, however, took Taylor and Mill into awkward territory. They involved the treatment of women, and showed how far they were prepared to go against their own instincts.

The first involved Mormonism, or more specifically its commitment to polygamy – an arrangement where a man can marry multiple women. The couple hated the idea. 'Far from being in anyway countenanced by the principle of liberty, it is a direct infraction of that principle,' they decided, 'being a mere riveting of the chains of one half of the community, and an emancipation of the other from reciprocity of obligation towards them.'

Nevertheless, and despite the demands of many in Victorian society for a 'civilising' disbanding of Mormon colonies, polygamy had to be tolerated. Those women may have been subject to an unequal culture, but it was their free choice to enter into it. 'This relation is as much voluntary on the part of the women concerned in it, and who may be deemed the sufferers by it, as is the case with any other form of marriage institution,' they concluded.

There was, however, one caveat. There had to be 'perfect freedom of departure.' This was a crucial point. People were able to enter into unequal contracts, but they had to be able to walk away from them.

A basic principle was being articulated, which would become a source of controversy in liberalism in the 20th Century. You could decide to live life with less freedom, but there had to be entry and exit rights. You had to enter of your own free will and have the ability to leave when you wanted.

A similar issue arose with prostitution. Taylor and Mill hated the practice. Mill thought it was 'disgraceful and immoral.' But none of that mattered. It had to be allowed, if a person was freely choosing to engage in it.

These were not easy answers. They were not satisfying. They were emotionally challenging. Taylor and Mill did not pretend that they felt at ease about polygamy and liberalism did not designate indifference. But it did require that someone could get past their own feelings about something and ask themselves whether it was freely chosen or harmed others. It was a two-stage form of political thought: one in which you felt a certain way about a thing, and another where you asked yourself whether your feelings should have any role in its restriction.

Objecting to something and then allowing it was not a defect in the system. It was the peak of liberal action: the point when a liberal lived up to their convictions.

Taylor and Mill then introduced a new layer of complexity to the oldest element of liberalism: the concept of doubt.

For Mill, this was personal. When he was at his worst, in the abyss of depression, it was poetry that had turned his life around. His father and Bentham scorned it. His fellow Utilitarians sneered at it. But when he sat there, utterly alone, contemplating suicide, being open to other ideas had saved his life.

From there he had begun exploring the views of people who were opposed to his own. To his friends' dismay he had sympathetically engaged in dialogue with reactionaries like Carlyle. He never accepted their world view, but he found in their writing aspects which he agreed with – a sentimental view of nature, the role of the individual in history, and the importance of strong institutions for managing social change – and incorporated them into his own.

Mill became fixated with how to condition the brain to accept new ideas and reject tribalism. Internationalism helped. A trip to France when he was young left him with a lifelong fascination for the country and he came to believe that a deep understanding of another place could inoculate people against national parochialism.

Learning another language embedded this lesson even deeper. It taught people that there were whole concepts that their own language could not even articulate, and by doing so opened up the mind to the limitation of its own thoughts. Knowing another language dampened ignorance and intellectual overconfidence.

'Without knowing the language of a people, we never really know their thoughts,' Mill said. 'Unless we do possess this knowledge, of some other people than ourselves, we remain, to the hour of our death, with our intellects only half expanded.'

Mill had a lifelong commitment to dissent and the clash of ideas. It is a term that has taken on a tedious, angry resonance nowadays. In the first decades of the 21st Century, we associate it with warring political tribes, talking over each other on current affairs programmes, neither showing the least interest in ever changing their position, their own behaviour more readily explained by their sense of identity than by any appreciation for argument.

But for Mill it was not just about conflict. He despised the 'blind rage' with which different schools of philosophical thought went into battle with one another.

Opposition was only the opening stage of the battle of ideas. It was also about synthesis. Intellectual progress came from finding that which was true or meaningful in your opponent's argument and incorporating it into your own.

At the heart of that thought was an astonishingly humble realisation: that there could be truth in the words of someone you disagreed with. Sometimes it was just a trace element. Sometimes it was a sizable chunk.

Truth existed. It was real. But most schools of thought held just a morsel. 'Conflicting doctrines, instead of the one being true and the other false, share the truth between them.'

In *On Liberty*, Taylor and Mill fashioned this layered and multifaceted view of truth into a powerful new argument for free speech. It was the most accomplished take on the subject since Milton's *Areopagitica* more than 200 years earlier.

The starting premise was the fundamental intellectual acceptance of doubt. No-one was infallible: not the state, nor any religion, nor any individual, and even less public opinion. 'If all mankind minus one were of one opinion,' they said, almost quoting Constant word for word, 'and only one person were of the contrary opinion, mankind would be no more justified in silencing that one person, than he, if he had the power, would be justified in silencing mankind.'

They then reiterated Milton's argument on the necessity of truth and falsity clashing to establish valid ideas. If an opinion was true, banning it robbed us of the opportunity to realise its truth. If it was false, a ban prevented us from recognising the validity of the opposing idea.

But then they took another crucial step. The idea of a clash of false and true arguments was simplistic. In reality, truth was shared among arguments. False ideas could have truth in them, and true ones falsity. Many opinions were broadly true, but 'seldom or never the whole truth.' The search for truth was like a detective story. You found scraps here, scraps there, and had to pull together a unified whole.

'They are a part of the truth,' they said, 'sometimes a greater, sometimes a smaller part, but exaggerated, distorted, and disjoined from the truths by which they ought to be accompanied and limited.'

It followed that there should be almost no limits to freedom of speech. Certainly, causing offence was not enough. Most political ideas, and especially radical world-changing ideas, such as Galileo's views on astronomy or Taylor and Mill's views on women's rights, would upset people, sometimes deeply. Mankind, in whatever time and in whatever society, was powerfully susceptible to convention. Any idea that challenged the assumptions of that period was liable to be deemed offensive. To silence offence was to end progress.

But there was one limit: the incitement to violence. This marked the specific point at which free speech encroached too far on people's other freedom – namely their freedom not to be assaulted or killed. 'An opinion that corn-dealers are starvers of the poor,' they said, 'ought to be unmolested when simply circulated through the press, but may justly incur punishment when delivered orally to an excited mob assembled before the house of a corn-dealer.'

Notice how high the bar was set. It was not enough for the inciting opinion to be expressed generally in a newspaper during peaceful times. The incitement had to occur in a time and place at which it was directly and immediately likely to cause harm. It was also important that the example was specific. The assessment of incitement was not based solely on the words themselves, but on the likelihood that they would be acted on in the context in which they were said.

As before, Harriet and John were less concerned about state censorship than the suffocating impact of society. In truth, the days of Lilburne being put in the stocks in Westminster were long gone. The danger was now less dramatic but perhaps more dangerous: social stigma.

'Our merely social intolerance kills no-one, roots out no opinions, but induces men to disguise them, or to abstain from any active effort for their diffusion,' they warned. 'The price paid for this sort of intellectual pacification is the sacrifice of the entire moral courage of the human mind.'

The person themself was not the only victim. In the end, all of humankind suffered. 'Who can compute what the world loses in the multitude of promising intellects, combined with timid characters, who dare not follow out any bold, vigorous, independent train of thought, lest it should land them in something which would admit of being considered irreligious and immoral?'

They did not know as they were writing, but in the same year that *On Liberty* was published, Charles Darwin would finally release his book outlining the theory of evolution, *On the Origin of Species*, after 20 years of nervous delay. It would be the most explosive assault on the religious account of existence since Galileo and a perfect demonstration of their argument. Had Darwin – or Alfred Russel Wallace, who came to the theory at the same time – been more afraid of ridicule, the world might have been denied the truth they'd discovered.

Running against popular opinion could be lonely and dangerous. Anyone who truly thought independently risked losing friends, social respect and even career advancement, but this was the duty of being a truly free individual. Anyone who did not have this confidence, no matter how truthful their opinions might happen to be, was not truly thinking.

'Truth gains more even by the errors of one who thinks for himself,' Taylor and Mill said, 'than by the true opinions of those who only hold them because they do not suffer themselves to think.'

This bravery of speech was only part of the story, though. True liberals had to do something else too, which was arguably even more difficult: listen to those who disagreed with them. They had to open themselves out completely to the most compelling, informed, effective and eloquent attacks from the opposing position. 'He must feel the full force of the difficulty,' they stressed.

This required something even greater than confidence and independence. It required empathy. It needed the imaginative capacity to experience ideas from the perspective of someone else. And that quality was hard to find anywhere. Out of 100 so-called 'educated men,' Taylor and Mill estimated, barely even one truly behaved in this way. 'Their conclusion may be true, but it might be false for anything they know: they have never thrown themselves into the mental position of those who think differently from them.'

The demand – emotionally and intellectually – required an extraordinary mixture of confidence and humility. All of a sudden, it became clear that *On Liberty* was not really a manifesto at all, or even a work of political philosophy. It was a self-help book. It was an instruction manual to living a life of truth.

Society had little interest in people living this way. 'The majority,' Taylor and Mill said, 'being satisfied with the ways of mankind as they now are, for it is they who make them what they are, cannot comprehend why those ways should not be good enough for everybody.'

Like Constant, Taylor and Mill recognised the contradictory tugs of the human need for freedom and the human demand for conformity. And also like Constant, they visualised conformity as a machine and diversity as biology. 'Human nature is not a machine to be built after a model and set to do exactly the work prescribed for it,' they said, 'but a tree, which requires to grow and develop itself on all sides, according to the tendency of the inward forces which make it a living thing.'

The machine, however, was winning. It was relentlessly crushing individuality. This wasn't just political. It went far beyond the expression of opinion. It was a deep-seated phenomenon about the way people lived their lives.

'Every one lives as under the eye of a hostile and dreaded censorship,' they warned. They'd stopped asking themselves what they wanted and instead asked what people typically did, or what people of their type did, or, worse still, what people of a higher class did.

It was not that people 'choose what is customary, in preference to what suits their inclination,' Taylor and Mill continued, damningly. 'It does not occur to them to have any inclination, except for what is customary. Thus the mind itself is bowed to the yoke.'

Individual nature was relentlessly crushed in this engine of conformity, of people second-guessing themselves, of basing their actions by the behaviour of others, of behaving as a bird in a flock, of fitting themselves into smaller and smaller spaces to win the acceptance of family, friends and co-workers, 'until, by dint of not following their own nature, they have no nature to follow: their human capacities are withered and starved.'

This culture was a form of tyranny, just as real – and arguably even more dangerous – as the reign of Charles I. 'Whatever crushes individuality is despotism, by whatever name it may be called.'

But why was this happening? It seemed to go against the whole tide of human history from which liberalism had sprung. The industrial revolution had driven an even faster surge of workers from the countryside to the cities. People were being unchained from the tight-knit communities and religious identities of old and freed to form new ones in the metropolis.

But in a dark twist of irony, it was precisely the forces that had helped give liberalism life which Taylor and Mill believed were encouraging social conformity. Specifically two types: information exchange and democracy.

Having propelled the Leveller movement, the pamphlet had evolved into the newspaper. Free speech provisions, such as in the US Constitution, had turned this into an informal fourth institution in the separation of powers. But there was a darker, illiberal side to the free press. It had taken a firm hold over the political and social assumptions of readers and was now operating as a stigma-affirmation programme, responding to people's instincts about right and wrong ways to behave.

'The mass do not now take their opinions from dignitaries in church or state, from ostensible leaders, or from books,' Taylor and Mill explained. 'Their thinking is done for them by men much like themselves, addressing them or speaking in their name, on the spur of the moment, through the newspapers.'

These views won greater traction in the political class because of the expansion of the franchise. 'At present individuals are lost in the crowd,' they said. 'In politics it is almost a triviality to say that public opinion now rules the world.'

From a vantage point of two centuries later, Taylor and Mill's foresight is startling. They had spotted the beginnings of a feedback loop in which mass media – starting with newspapers and then radio, television and finally social media – would receive public opinion, affirm it, amplify it, then beam it back into the public, in a constant self-perpetuating cycle.

As full representative democracy was first established and then mythologised, public opinion became an extra moral force, which then pushed legislators into responding to its wishes.

Sometimes the public opinion was tolerant and desirable. Sometimes it was mean-spirited and prejudiced. Almost always it was sudden and transitory, leaving behind legislative effects which would fester for years. Public scares – over gay sex in Victorian times, Communist infiltration in 1950s America, hippies in the 60s, or dance music in 90s Britain – would translate, through feverish media reports, into social prejudice and repressive legislation.

Taylor and Mill's solution to this problem was simple. It was a key moment in the development of a liberal culture: You had to have agency over your life. You had to ensure that every decision you took and every action you made was on the basis of what you truly wanted, rather than because you were seeking the approval of others.

'He who does anything because it is the customs, makes no choice,' they said. 'He who lets the world choose his plan of life for him, has no need of any other faculty than the ape-like one of imitation.'

On Liberty is often criticised, both in its own time and ours, as being a somehow cold vision of the world, as an attempt to promote an atomised society of isolated individuals, with no responsibilities to each other, whose only relationship to humanity is through the mediation of the harm principle. But that is not so.

The harm principle was merely there to protect each individual against unwanted interference by others. The central argument of the book was not for any particular form of society. It was simply that people truly chose their lives, rather than have it chosen for them.

But here, unusually for them, Taylor and Mill blinked. They gazed down at the full extent of the permissiveness and freedom that they were promoting, seemed to gasp, and then took a step back. No matter how modern and far-sighted their morals were, they were still Victorians. And there was an idea they could not let go of: of higher and lower pleasures. These had been with them their whole life. They were a vestigial element of Mill's Utilitarianism.

'Lower pleasures ' covered things like sex, food and drink. Mill considered them the 'animal appetites' which consisted of 'mere sensation.' The 'higher pleasures' covered more profound activities. They were 'of the intellect, of the feelings and imagination, and of the moral sentiments.'

There was no prohibition on trying all these things. But Taylor and Mill believed that people free to have sex and also read philosophy would come to the conclusion that philosophy was more enjoyable.

That is a controversial proposition, but it's also quite a revealing one. There was an unspoken assumption operating under all the permissiveness. Mill and Taylor were promoting freedom in lifestyle in the same way that the Puritans promoted freedom in worship: not because there was no right way, but because there was and we were yet to discover it.

They valued diversity, but they assumed that once people tried everything, they would want to become rational, philosophy-reading liberals. They would, in other words, want to become exactly like them. It was subtle, but there was a hint of uniformity lurking in the text.

This is how it always goes with liberalism. Its proponents make the case, they outline the argument. And then, in nearly every case, they step back from the radical logical implications.

But even when they do so, they have secured a new level of progress.

Mill and Taylor did so with a beautiful and earth-shattering idea, one which had been fermenting since Descartes but never expressed with such confidence or theoretical sophistication. You had to have autonomy. You had to think for yourself.

'In this age,' they said, 'the mere example of non-conformity, the mere refusal to bend the knee to custom, is itself a service. Precisely because the tyranny of opinion is such as to make eccentricity a reproach, it is desirable, in order to break through that tyranny, that people should be eccentric.'

This was the final testament to their love affair.

6. DEATH

Two new systems of government emerged in the 20th Century: communism and fascism.

They were, on the face of it, polar opposites, and indeed they considered themselves implacable enemies. But underneath the opposition, there was a common strain of thought. They were both dedicated to the destruction of the individual.

For a long time, it felt like nothing of this sort could ever happen. The half century after Mill's death in 1873 seemed like a period of liberal triumph.

It was the creation of the world we know today. Universal male suffrage was spreading. Technological developments were bringing people closer together. The railway, car and bicycle were reducing the restrictions of physical distance, while the telephone, cinema and radio reduced mental distance. Industrialisation was hastening urbanisation. Large cities of over 100,000 people became quite common and a handful of metropolises – places like Berlin, London, Paris and Vienna – had over a million.

There was a slow but noticeable improvement in the lives of the working poor. Average pay was now enough to buy more than just the bare necessities. States were tentatively interfering with the market, for instance by introducing restrictions on child labour. There was even an embryonic welfare state developing, notably in Germany in 1871 with the introduction of an industrial accident insurance scheme. Other countries followed, with initiatives like health insurance, unemployment insurance and an old age pension.

Europe was peaceful. From 1871 to 1914, no European power ordered its troops to fire on those of another European power.

For most liberals at the time, there was a sense that history was on their side. People were becoming wealthier and less prone to superstition. As times progressed, they were expected to become more rational and free.

One of the core assumptions of liberalism – put best by the Anglican bishop Mandell Creighton – was that 'we are bound to assume, as the scientific hypothesis upon which history has been written, a progress in human affairs.' Peace, democracy and freedom were in the ascendant.

It was a comforting story. But if you started probing, it did not hold true.

The peace was real enough, but it was localised. Instead of fighting each other, European forces were colonising the world.

Imperialism, the practice of taking control of another territory and exploiting it economically, had entered its most frenzied period. Between 1880 and 1914, most of the world outside Europe and the Americas was partitioned into territory under the formal or informal control of a handful of western states, including Britain, France, Germany, Italy, the Netherlands, Belgium and the US. They divided up around a quarter of the earth's surface between them and distributed it.

This didn't involve much fighting. Western powers were too strong economically and militarily for their colonial targets. But there were wars, and when they happened they were conducted with a savagery which was entirely in line with the past. During the Boer War, between 1899 and 1902, the British first experimented with the use of concentration camps, killing thousands of women and children through malnutrition and starvation.

The trade which took place between colonised and colonising countries was not free. Colonised countries were required to sign unequal trade agreements which deprived them of the ability to set their own trading rules.

And even putting aside colonialism, the peace in Europe was unstable. It was not the product of good relations, but of fear.

Two great military power blocs had arisen. Germany had a rock-hard alliance with Austria-Hungary. Austria had taken over Bosnia-Herzegovina, leading to conflict with Russia, which formed an alliance with France. Britain attached itself to the latter camp to limit German power. The great powers of Europe were frozen into opposing coalitions.

For a while, this acted as a form of deterrence. A dispute between any of them could trigger total war with all of them, so they always tended to back down. But each time a disagreement arose, the process became more fraught. There was a storm brewing, which would discount forever the liberal assumption of inevitable human progress.

At the end of the 19th Century, something moved. There was a shudder which was felt around the world. It was as if something old and terrible had been lying dormant and it woke suddenly from a slumber.

It started with a wastepaper basket, in the Germany embassy in Paris, in 1894. It belonged to a German military attache called Maximilian von Schwartzkoppen. Every day he would read letters or reports coming in and throw them in the basket.

What he didn't know was that his cleaner was a spy. Every week she would go into his office, clear out the rubbish, and hand it to her bosses in the Statistical Section of the French army's General Staff. Schwartzkoppen's communications travelled in a direct line from his bin to French intelligence.

On 26th September, a French army commander called Major Henry found something unusual in the most recent haul. A flimsy piece of paper contained details of French artillery and changes in military mobilisation plans. This information had no business being in the hands of a German military attaché. There was a spy in the army.

Within days, suspicion settled on one man: Alfred Dreyfus. There was no evidence that it was him. But Dreyfus had one gigantic disadvantage. He was the only Jew on the General Staff.

The army manufactured a case against him, supplementing a file of previous communications sent to Schwartzkoppen with forgeries. On 31st October, the story broke in the press. It was incendiary. One newspaper in particular led the way: *La Libre Parole*. It was a violently anti-semitic publication edited by a man named Édouard Drumont.

Anti-semitism – prejudice against Jews – had a long and bloody history in Europe, involving sporadic massacres, expulsions and forced conversions. But Drumont's writing started to outline a modern variant of this age-old hatred. He moulded together several types of anti-semitism. The first was an ancient Catholic suspicion of the 'Christ-killers,' bolstered by a still-present reactionary hatred of the French Revolution. The second was a pseudo-scientific racism based on the physical characteristics of individuals. The third was a left-wing hostility towards capitalism, and especially banking, which Jewish people were seen to embody. The fourth was the notion of a plot by Jewish outsiders to undermine the integrity of the nation.

Dreyfus was found guilty. He was brought to the courtyard of the École Militaire, a military academy, as a public crowd massed outside. He was stripped of everything, piece by piece: his badges, his gold braid, his insignia, every button, every mark of rank and finally his sword, which was smashed in two. Then he was paraded in front of each side of the square, as he desperately repeated: 'Innocent. Innocent. Long live France.' Hardly anyone could hear him. Outside, the crowd roared: 'Death to the Jew. Death to Judas.'

Dreyfus was deported to Devil's Island, a penal colony in French Guiana infamous for its harsh conditions, with a survival rate, in its worst periods, of just 25 per cent. He was the only inhabitant apart from his guards, who were forbidden to talk to him. He lived in a tiny hut, four metres by four metres. Eventually he was shackled to the bed. That was be his home for the next four and a half years.

He should by any right have died there, but then an unlikely saviour emerged. His name was Georges Picquart. Outwardly he was little different to those around him – an anti-semite, an army officer, a member of the General Staff, convinced, as the whole country was, of Dreyfus' guilt. But Picquart turned out to be a man of principle nonetheless.

In June 1895, six months after the conviction, he took over as head of military intelligence. It soon became clear to him that French military secrets were still finding their way to the German embassy. He concluded that another spy must be operating in the General Staff. As he worked his way through more rubbish from the German embassy, he found a letter, ripped into tiny pieces, addressed to a French army official named Charles Esterhazy. Picquart placed Esterhazy under surveillance and had his staff collect up pieces of paper with Esterhazy's writing on them. Then he discovered something that blew the case wide open: his writing matched the original letter perfectly. Dreyfus was innocent. Esterhazy was the spy.

Picquart took his findings to his superiors, expecting them to take action. Instead, they were horrified. His investigation threatened to reveal the army conspiracy against Dreyfus.

Picquart was ordered to Tunis, in north Africa, where they expected him to die in the brutal military campaign there. When that failed, they had him arrested, court marshalled for leaking secret information, and dismissed. The army drew up a new forgery, which attempted to demonstrate beyond all doubt that Dreyfus was guilty.

By this point the Dreyfus Affair had very little to do with spying. It had become a culture war over national identity. The army and the church represented old authority and the purity of France. They were opposed by intellectuals and liberals – Jew-lovers – who lacked sufficient patriotism. To be against Dreyfus was to be for France. To be for him was to be against it.

Émile Zola, an influential novelist and journalist, was one of the few figures in the latter camp. He knew that if he spoke out, people would listen. But he also understood that this would not save him from the consequences. If he proclaimed Dreyfus' innocence, all the pent-up hatred of the debate would be directed at him.

On 13th January 1898, *L'Aurore* newspaper carried a front-page article by Zola headlined *J'Accuse*. It was one of the most impactful pieces of journalism ever written. In point after point, it amassed the evidence of Dreyfus' innocence and the army cover-up. It was not so much published as detonated.

Something in France snapped when *J'Accuse* came out. The next day, the police received a note. 'What is about to happen in Paris is a much more dangerous riot,' an informant wrote. 'It will have a definite goal, the looting of Jewish shops.' Hundreds of students appeared in the streets in the Place de la Sorbonne and the Latin Quarter shouting 'Down with the Jews.'

The next day the protests grew. 'Their numbers are constantly swelling,' a policeman reported. When they reached the Place de la République, customers in neighbouring cafes heard the chants and many got up and joined the protests. On the Champs-Élysées, the crowd began to pick out certain passers-by and shout: 'Dirty Jew.' The *Libre Parole* newspaper gleefully told readers: 'Like scalded rats, the Jews no longer know which way to turn.'

A political meeting was called bringing together the anti-semitic groups. Drumont brought in Jules Guérin, the leader of the Anti-Semitic League. He was a charismatic thug, surrounded by butcher boys from the local slaughterhouses who operated as his shock troopers. 'Physically, he's a tall and strong man,' a police report said. 'He never goes out without an enormous bludgeon on him.'

The League itself was organised according to strict obedience to his command. 'The leaguists obey Guérin as soldiers obey their colonel,' a police spy told his superiors. 'Discipline is absolute.' He invented a cane, made of oak with a head of thick steel or lead, which he called the Anti-Jew and distributed to followers, to attack suspected Jews in the streets.

The cults around Drumont and Guérin were unusual, not just in their discipline, but in their hero worship. The men seemed to almost bathe in the violence around them. They revelled in it, even worshipped it. It was an expression of potency, of national virility, of politics as action rather than thought.

The rhetoric throbbed with hatred. Chants, newspaper headlines and mass-produced posters attacked 'vile Hebrews,' 'dangerous parasites,' and 'cosmopolitan Jewry.' One newspaper ran a guide to spotting Jews: 'A hooked nose, enormous, hairy ears, an accent there's no mistaking.'

Leading 'anti-Dreyfusards' talked of an international Jewish plot against France. Jews were portrayed as immensely wealthy and able to bribe even the richest government. But they were also grotesque, dirty degenerates, almost subhuman beings who would spread disease. These two ideas were mutually incompatible. If Jews were so primitive, how had they managed to perpetrate such a complex global conspiracy? But this did nothing to stop the conspiracy theories spreading and in fact made them more powerful. There was no scenario they couldn't warp into anti-semitism, from low crime to international politics.

The use of conspiracy theory provided a political narrative anyone could understand: the country was being undermined by a secret group of traitors. France's various misfortunes, from the economic to the military, could now be explained with a simple story which, most usefully of all, had a villain. If only the villain was expelled or killed, the problems would go away.

The conspiracy theory was attractive precisely because it was false. The real, complex reasons for national decline could be dismissed. Anything bad that happened could be blamed on the conspirators and anything good credited to the nationalists. The nationalists could never be proved wrong, or held to account for their actions, because this form of political rhetoric was completely divorced from objective reality. It operated in a parallel never-never land of fantasy.

The Jews made an ideal scapegoat. They were the 'wandering race' in an age of nation states. They were in every country, but had none of their own. They were the perpetual immigrant.

Enormous posters started to appear all over Paris calling for a national demonstration. All troop leave was cancelled and soldiers forbidden from fraternising with crowds.

Wherever Zola went, he faced the mob. They mocked and screamed at him. He was called a traitor. Finally, less than a month after *J'Accuse* was published, he was put on trial for libel.

In late February, Zola was found guilty. 'For five minutes, people enthusiastically stamped their feet,' the newspaper *Le Matin* reported. 'All hats waved on the end of canes, lawyers tossed their caps in the air. Many wept, others embraced one another as if they had just escaped a cataclysm. Then a rhythmic chant, muffled at first, but becoming more pronounced in a tremendous crescendo, rose toward the vaults of the Palais. "Death to the Jews. Death to the Jews."'

The anti-semitism juddered outward, from Paris to Bordeaux, Angers, Marseilles, Caen, Nancy, Dijon, Nantes, Bar-le-Duc, Avignon, Normandy, Lorraine, Provence, Lyons, Rennes, Tours, Clermont-Ferrand. From big cities to small towns, like a political virus.

Most Jews tried to hide away, hoping it would pass. But it did no good. Many found that those they considered friends had joined the mobs outside their homes, throwing rocks at their windows in the night and threatening to set them on fire.

Where Jews did fight back, they were blamed for the violence. In the northeastern town of Bar-le-Duc, a local rabbi approached two men selling a song entitled *We'll Kill Dreyfus* and asked them to stop. The crowd turned on him at once. In a town with just 18,000 residents, a mob of 1,000 marched around chanting his name and shouting: 'Down with the Jews.'

Not long after Zola's conviction, the legal tide turned. Major Henry's crude forgery was discovered. He confessed, was arrested, and then slit his own throat. Esterhazy fled to England. The verdict against Dreyfus was annulled and he was returned home – frail, broken, barely able to speak after years of social isolation. After a long series of legal and political clashes which lasted for six years, his and Picquart's convictions were overturned.

But the anti-semitism that the Dreyfus affair revealed would not be so easily put back in a box. It was an old hatred, ever present in Europe. But now it was being given a spectacular new force, through the mass media of posters and newspapers, the militarised hero-worship of nationalist organisations, and a highly effective conspiracy theory that could appeal to left and right.

A new kind of political thought was emerging, which worshipped the group and attacked perceived outsiders. Liberalism's modern enemy was revealing itself.

In 1914, the powerbloc deterrence system finally broke down. In the end it took very little. Archduke Franz Ferdinand of Austria and his wife Sophie were assassinated by a Bosnian Serb nationalist. It should have been a minor local incident, but the system of national allegiances acted like trip-wires that ended in a continent-wide conflict.

Austria-Hungary declared war on Serbia. Russia mobilised for war against Austria and Germany. Germany declared war on Russia and France. Britain declared war on Germany. Austria-Hungary declared war on Russia.

It took just a few weeks, from 28th June to 6th August, for half a century of peace in Europe to collapse.

The world war which followed was the most destructive conflict Europe had ever known. Within weeks, thousands of miles of trenches had been dug into the mud, within metres of enemy lines. The great technological advances of the era were now directed towards slaughter: machine guns, chemical warfare, tanks and aerial bombardment.

Four years later, when the guns stopped, tens of millions of people were dead, or injured, or missing. An entire generation had been lost.

In the years that followed, people would yearn for the return of the pre-war days. But that world was gone. Wartime command economies had wrecked the normal function of the state. War debts and currency fluctuations plunged international trade into chaos. When demobilisation took place, many countries collapsed into mass unemployment. Emotions were driven to fever pitch by a sense of loss and grievance. And something new had emerged from the chaos: the world's first communist state.

Russia fell to communist revolution in October 1917, under the leadership of Vladimir Lenin. It based its new programme of government on the work of Karl Marx.

Marx was a dishevelled German thinker writing in the 19th Century. His early years were spent writing philosophy in Germany, France and Belgium and getting chased out of wherever he was by the police. His later years were spent predominantly writing economics in London, where he tried to produce a scientific analysis of capitalist development.

Marx's main philosophical and economic concern was labour – the way in which humankind worked to adapt its environment. Throughout history, Marx argued, human labour had operated under different types of political control. First there had been primitive communism, where everything was held in common. Then there was slave society, where labourers were owned by a master. Then feudalism, where they were technically free but worked on their lord's land. And finally capitalism, where they worked for a wage using machinery owned by their employer.

'The history of all hitherto existing society,' Marx wrote in the opening pages of the *Communist Manifesto*, 'is the history of class struggles.' Class was defined by a group's relationship to the means of production, which were the tools and raw materials used to make products. The bourgeoisie – such as factory-owners – controlled the means of production and the proletariat sold their labour to them.

In Marx's time, the means of production were developing at an extraordinary rate in the form of factories, coal mines, railways and utilities. But Marx believed that by creating the huge workforce necessary to run them, capitalism was giving birth to its own grave-diggers. The vast ranks of the disenfranchised, propertyless industrial working class would bring down the system.

In the first post-revolutionary stage, called socialism, they would seize the means of production and establish the 'dictatorship of the proletariat.' In the second stage, called communism, private property would be abolished and everything held in common. As the material condition of society changed, people's social personality would evolve, and the era of exploitation and injustice would pass away.

Unlike most socialist ideas of the time, which were typically quite dream-like, Marx framed his theory in scientific language. His argument, certainly in his later years, was not really moral. He did not want capitalism brought to an end because it was wrong or cruel. It would simply pass away as a consequence of historical development, as naturally as the motion of large bodies under Newtonian physics or the mutation of organisms under Darwinian evolution.

Marx's theory was an impressive intellectual achievement. It is difficult to even begin to describe the extent of its influence, not just to communist thought, but to social democracy and anarchism. By the latter part of the 20th Century, one third of the world's population lived under governments which claimed to follow its ideas.

At his best, Marx showed genuine concern for the individual, particularly in the world of work – a sphere of life which consumed the majority of people's time but which many liberals had ignored.

His vision of communism was not one of crushing uniformity, but a rich landscape of individual freedom. 'In communist society,' he wrote, 'where nobody has one exclusive sphere of activity but each can become accomplished in any branch he wishes, society regulates the general production and thus makes it possible for me to do one thing today and another tomorrow, to hunt in the morning, fish in the afternoon, rear cattle in the evening, criticise after dinner, just as I have a mind, without ever becoming a hunter, fisherman, shepherd, or critic.'

But as attractive as that vision was, Marx's theory followed a pattern that western philosophy had seen before. It replicated Rousseau.

Instead of focusing on the individual, Marxism suggested that the authentic self was at the social level in the form of class. The true emancipation of humankind did not come from personal liberty, it came from the freedom of the group. Those who could perceive this, and its scientific basis, had authentic consciousness. Those who could not were experiencing false consciousness.

Like Rousseau, Marx concluded that individual rights were therefore surplus to requirements. There was no need to protect the individual against the state. In the *Critique of the Gotha Programme*, the closest Marx came to spelling out the practicalities of how a communist revolution should play out, he branded individual rights 'dogmas' and 'obsolete verbal rubbish.' He lashed out against 'ideological nonsense about right and other trash.'

Such thinking had proven disastrous under capitalism, but under communism it was even more fraught with danger. What was being proposed was the polar opposite of laissez-faire liberalism: the provision by the state of all material life. Its power over the individual would be limitless.

Vladimir Lenin was the leader of a minor Russian communist party, the Bolsheviks. This left him with a theoretical problem: why was the working class failing to achieve authentic consciousness?

His solution was called vanguardism. A politically enlightened group was needed to raise the consciousness of the rest of the class.

This would be done by the leadership of the Bolshevik party, which later became the Russian Communist Party. And like that, with one step, Marx's dictatorship of the proletariat became the dictatorship of the Communist Party.

Almost immediately upon taking power, the Bolsheviks proceeded to try and eradicate the individual.

From the very earliest days of the revolutionary government, the party was at war with the concept of a personal life. The private sphere provided a potential source of opposition to communist control. A private life emphasised the individual and the family, rather than the correct historical grouping of the proletariat, and was therefore to be replaced by a socialised consciousness necessary for the creation of true communism.

'The so-called sphere of private life cannot slip away from us,' commissar for education Anatoly Lunacharsky said in 1927, 'because it is precisely here that the final goal of the revolution is to be reached.'

This involved an attempt to eradicate the family unit and replace parents with the state. 'By loving a child,' the Soviet educational thinker Zlata Lilina said, 'the family turns him into an egotistical being, encouraging him to see himself as the centre of the universe.'

The primary purpose of the school system was no longer strictly education. It was, in the words of one Soviet education theorist, to 'nationalise' the child – to erase the notion of individualism from their psychology.

'The young person should be taught to think in terms of "we,"' Lunacharsky said in 1918, 'and all private interests should be left behind.'

Most of that learning took place on an instinctive level, through the creation of socialist ritual and practice. Children were encouraged to form their own school police, to write denunciations of fellow pupils and hold trials of transgressors in the classroom. Marches, songs and oaths became a fixture of pupils' day-to-day life.

A communist league for children was set up, called the Pioneers, and another for young people aged 15 and up, called the Komsomol. Once in the latter group, members were treated as grown-up commmunist activists. They were charged with exposing 'class enemies' among their parents and teachers and took part in mock trials of 'counter-revolutionaries' in school.

The process of destroying the family also focused on living arrangements. A policy known as 'condensation' relocated the urban poor into rooms in the family homes of the wealthy. This wasn't simply an economic move. It was part of a broader attempt to replace the family unit with communal habitation.

By the mid-1920s, new homes were built on this principle. At the most radical end, Soviet architects drew up plans for 'commune houses' that obliterated almost all privacy. Even underwear was to be owned and used in common. Cooking and childcare would be assigned on a rotating basis and everyone would sleep in a large dorm room, with private rooms maintained only for sexual purposes.

Few of these buildings were ever built, but the broader plan of forcing people to live together, with shared rooms for cooking, dining and bathing and a small private space for sleeping, became the standard for the urban population.

The battle for authentic consciousness was particularly acute for those within the party, predominantly because of concerns that non-working-class Russians would join in order to thrive under the new regime.

Members were asked to write regular short autobiographies giving details of their social background, education, career, and the evolution of their political thought. Party members were told to denounce anyone they suspected was ideologically impure.

No aspect of a party member's life was private. Anything they did reflected on the party. The phrase 'party unity,' which was common at the time, did not just mean the solidarity of members. In the words of Soviet expert Orlando Figes, it required 'the complete fusion of the individual with the public life of the party.'

Once the party accused a member of something, it was seen as a further crime to proclaim one's innocence. This was an act of dissent against the will of the party. In fact, any expression of personal conviction, or private conscience, was considered an act of rebellion.

The Russian word for conscience, 'sovest,' which carried the implication of a private dialogue with the self, almost disappeared from official usage from 1917. It was replaced by the word 'soznatel'nost,' which implied an elevated revolutionary logic.

This mission was a failure. The collective personality was not created. Instead, something else happened. The private self retreated into the mind. People put on a public mask, of an ideal Bolshevik-approved proletarian completely disconnected from the reality of their internal life.

This was called 'internal emigration.' As time went on, it would consume the entire country. But for now it was relegated to party members and their families, large sections of the working population in the cities, and those whose background made them vulnerable to repression.

Germany, like Russia, emerged from the war a shattered, defeated nation.

The government had borrowed huge amounts of money to pay for the war. Once the fighting was over it had to pay it back, alongside harsh reparations to the victorious powers and the expenditure required to transition its economy to peacetime. But its ability to do so was severely restricted, not least because it had lost key industrial areas to the peace treaty.

The government tried to print more money, but this crashed the value of the currency. Before the war, a dollar had been worth four German marks. By the end of the war it was worth twice that. Then it spiralled out of control. In April 1919, it was 12 marks. In

December 1922, it was 7,000 marks. By the same time next year, a dollar was worth 4,200,000,000,000 marks.

Money simply lost all meaning. The mint's printing presses could not keep up with the new denominations. Workers collected wages in wheelbarrows and rushed to buy products before the prices could rise again. This was called hyperinflation.

Other countries were similarly affected – in Austria, for example, prices reached 14,000 times their pre-war level. But the effect in Germany was unprecedented in world history. They reached a billion times their previous level.

There was a brief period of economic improvement between 1924 and 1928, with a rise in exports, industrial production and wages. Then the Wall Street Crash hit.

On 24th October 1929, there was a sudden outburst of panic selling on the New York stock exchange, with a further breakdown on 29th October. As values plummeted, desperate traders tried to sell them off quickly, driving prices further into the ground. Ten billion dollars were wiped off the face of major American companies – twice the amount of money in circulation in the US at the time.

The chaos and misery went on for years. Tariffs – taxes on goods crossing national borders – were raised to protect domestic producers, resulting in tit-for-tat responses by other states. Countries keen to maintain a balanced budget cut spending. Banks collapsed, leading to a disintegration of private sector demand. As the public lost faith in financial institutions, they kept more money in cash. The banks that survived preferred to keep their money on hand rather than lend it, which further reduced spending.

Germany's recovery since inflation had been partly financed by investment from the US. When American banks started calling in the loans, German industrial production collapsed. Small banks started to fail in 1929 and 1930. By 1931, the big banks were under pressure. The country sank into a deep depression. By 1932, one in three German workers was unemployed.

The situation was ripe for communist exploitation. The German Communist Party's national membership soared from 117,000 in 1929 to 360,000 in 1932. Many Germans suspected that their country was about to follow Russia into revolution.

But the communists faced a powerful enemy: fascism.

These two systems of thought seemed to be polar opposites. They fought each other in the streets and defined themselves in opposition to one another. But in fact there was an underlying similarity. Fascism did for race what communism did for class. The individual was disregarded. Instead, the authentic social self was to be found in an organic racial community.

In Italy, which had fallen to the fascist dictator Benito Mussolini, this was called 'la raza.' In Germany, it was the 'volk,' which translated as the people with a racial connotation. The will of this racial grouping was encapsulated by the leader.

The race was singular, pure and good, but it had been undermined by an international Jewish conspiracy. With only minor changes, this conspiracy followed the anti-semitic formulation of the Dreyfus Affair – pseudo-scientific racism, left-wing hostility towards capitalism and right-wing anxiety around the integrity and security of the nation.

As in 1890s France, the conspiracy theory could be moulded to fit any historical circumstance. Jews were responsible for undermining the war effort in 1918 and therefore for Germany's military defeat. Jewish merchants were responsible for the economic chaos of hyperinflation and the Great Depression. A Jewish-Bolshevik conspiracy was responsible for the growth of the Communist Party. These explanations were contradictory, but that simply served to make them more powerful and adaptable.

Adolf Hitler first emerged on Germany's far-right political scene in 1919, as an unremarkable, 30-year-old rank and file soldier. But those who saw him make speeches at meetings of the tiny German Workers' Party noticed something else. He was an extremely powerful public speaker.

He would usually start very quietly, so that the audience would have to lean in to hear what he was saying. Then, gradually, he worked himself up into a climax of frenzied energy. 'After this, there was only one thing for me,' a young nationalist said after witnessing one of his speeches in the 1920s, 'either to win with Adolf Hitler or to die for him.'

Hitler rose through the renamed National Socialist German Workers' party, or Nazi party, turning it into his personal fiefdom. By 1927, he had moved from addressing small beer-hall meetings to massive displays of demagoguery, speaking at rallies attended by up to 40,000 devotees.

Unlike the great political philosophies of communism, conservatism and liberalism, fascism had no intellectual heft. There was no Karl Marx, or Edmund Burke, or John Stuart Mill, no learned Victorian debate to fall back on. Fascism did not communicate through the mind. It was pumped into the heart and pursued with the fist.

Fascist communication operated on the level of emotion, via vitriolic rhetoric, mass-ceremonies and organised violence. A powerful visual architecture was developed, including a rigid fascist salute – of an outstretched arm, met by the leader in a crooked backward acceptance gesture – elaborate standards to carry flags, the Nazi swastika symbol, ritual fascist ceremonies, an emphasis on marches and parades, and poster campaigns representing Germany as a physically perfect Aryan man smashing his minuscule political enemies.

Glorified violence was one of the chief methods of communication and political advancement. It was a reflection of the underlying ideology. Thinking, reading and debating were weak and effeminate. Strength demonstrated the vitality of the party and thereby the nation.

In 1920, the party first developed its paramilitary wing. It was initially called the 'hall protection' group, then the Gymnastics and Sports Section, then the Storm Division, or SA. They were colloquially known as the brownshirts. It was a thug enforcement unit, who swaggered through the streets with knuckle dusters and rubber truncheons.

A separate unit was developed called the Protection Formation, or SS. This was initially conceived as a personal bodyguard for the leader but it soon became an internal party police and then the core elite of the new racial order. The SS embodied all that the Nazis admired in humankind – racial purity, discipline, unquestioning obedience, and lawless violence.

The Great Depression hugely improved Hitler's fortunes. The Nazis went from the ninth largest party in Germany in 1928 to the largest in 1932. And then, in the opening days of 1933, Hitler became Reich chancellor.

On 30th January, a torch-lit procession of brownshirts and the SS was organised to celebrate the appointment. Melita Maschmann, a young girl, was taken to watch it by her parents and saw a man being attacked and left on the ground with blood streaming down his face.

'The horror it inspired in me,' Maschmann recalled later, 'was almost imperceptibly spiced with an intoxicating joy. "We want to die for the flag," the torch-bearers had sung. I was overcome with a burning desire to belong to these people for whom it was a matter of life and death. I wanted to escape from my childish, narrow life and I wanted to attach myself to something which was great and fundamental.'

In Russia, a new group was being created as the enemy of the proletariat. They were the kulaks.

The word had once designated a peasant who was doing well and could hire labourers. After the revolution, it changed into something more dangerous.

Peasants themselves were difficult to incorporate into Marxist theory. Marx believed they did not count as a class and therefore had no class consciousness. Lenin suggested they had the potential for revolutionary activity, but that those with smallholdings, as property owners, tended to think like capitalists. His successor, Joseph Stalin, made that distinction a matter of life and death.

Over the 1920s, the word kulak changed to designate a wealthy peasant and then eventually any peasant who opposed or resisted the state. 'Anyone who expressed discontent was a kulak,' Ekaterina Olitskaia, who wrote a memoir of the time, said. 'Peasant families that had never used hired labour were put down as kulaks. A household that had two cows, a cow and a calf or a pair of horses was considered kulak.'

Part of the reason for that changed definition lay in the food supply. In 1928, Stalin established the Five Year Plan – a programme that envisioned a massive 20 per cent increase in national industrial production. This would require a large and consistent provision of grain, provided by the peasantry in the countryside for the proletariat in the cities, as well as a further supply for export. The hard currency earned by the export market would then be used to buy the machines and tools for industrialisation.

In order to secure so much grain, Stalin established large collective farms. Peasants were told to give up their land and nearly all of their possessions – certainly their animals and their equipment – and join the collective. Some would be able to stay in their home, but others would live in communal houses and barracks, eating in common dining rooms. They would no longer earn their own money, but instead be paid in day rates – not with cash, but with goods in kind. In other words, they would be fed in exchange for their labour.

At first it was optional, but when party cadres were sent out into the countryside on a recruitment drive, they found few takers. The Bolshevik hatred for the kulaks grew. For a decade, Bolshevism had promised material plenty, but provided grinding poverty. The narrative of the kulak traitor offered an explanation for the misery.

'The kulaks stood between us and the good life,' party loyalist Pasha Angelina wrote, 'and no amount of persuasion, constraint or ordinary taxation was sufficient to move them out the way.'

This was the point at which Stalin ordered the liquidation of the kulaks as a class. Set quotas were introduced dictating how many kulaks were to be removed, how many exiled, how many resettled in other villages, and how many were to be put into a new system of concentration camps known as gulags. At this point who was considered to be a kulak ceased to matter. If too few kulaks were rounded up to satisfy the numerical requirement from Moscow, they had to be created.

Ukrainian authorities were told to arrest 15,000 kulaks, exile between 30,000 and 35,000 kulak families, and remove 50,000 to a region on the White Sea. Belarus, for comparison, was to arrest 4,000–5,000. The Central Black Earth province was to arrest 3,000–5,000.

Kulaks were branded 'enemies of the people,' which suggested they were national as well as class enemies. 'We were trained to see the kulaks not as human beings but as vermin, lice, which had to be destroyed,' one activist said. The people, or proletariat, were pure and good. So something was required to explain the hardship of the Soviet system. The kulaks were given that role.

Between 1930 and 1933 over two million peasants were exiled to Siberia, Northern Russia, Central Asia, or other usually uninhabited areas. They were forced into villages which they were forbidden to leave. When the families arrived, they found nothing: no food or shelter, no preparations. Many died on the way or on arrival.

Around 100,000 were put into concentration camps, where they became a slave labour force.

During the late 1920s and early 1930s, the chief architect of the gulag system, Naftaly Aronovich Frenkel, had created a model Soviet camp on an archipelago on the White Sea called Solovetsky. Food was used as a tool of control. Prisoners were divided into three groups according to physical activity: those capable of hard work, those capable of light work, and invalids. Each group received a different set of tasks with quotas to fill, called norms. If they achieved the norm, they were fed accordingly. The strong lived. The weak died.

Soviet officials began forcing peasants to join the collective farms. Targets set in July 1930 demanded that 70 per cent of households in the main grain-growing region were to have joined by September 1931. The target was soon raised to 80 per cent.

'You must assume your duties with a feeling of the strictest party responsibility, without whimpering, without any rotten liberalism,' one Communist party leader told local organisers in the Volga region. 'Throw your bourgeois humanitarianism out of the window and act like a Bolshevik worthy of comrade Stalin. Beat down the kulak agent wherever he raises his head.'

Many peasants resisted the only way they could: by slaughtering their own cows, pigs, sheep and horses and then eating the meat, or salting and storing it, or selling it – anything to make sure it did not fall into the hands of the authorities. Between 1928 and 1933 the number of cattle and horses in the Soviet Union almost halved. Others burned barns full of animals rather than see them go to the Soviet state.

Hundreds of thousands of peasants were forced onto the collectives. They were worse off than they had been under feudalism. They lost the freedom to make their own money, or to go where they wanted. They lost the choice over how to work and instead had to follow central command. They were not given money, but paid in kind with grain and potatoes.

Production fell. People tried to work as little as possible. The most productive workers had been exiled, deported or killed. Techniques developed over generations were ignored in favour of centralised mandates. Theft became endemic. The property of the collective was seen as belonging to no-one, so any social stigma about stealing quickly dissipated. This prompted a harsh response from the state. 'Kulaks, the de-kulakised and anti-Soviet elements all steal,' Stalin said. 'Crime must be punished with ten years or capital punishment.'

On 7th August 1932, the Soviet Union passed an edict which seemed to explicitly invert the property provisions in the *Rights of*

Man. 'Public property,' it read, 'is the basis of the Soviet system; it is sacred and inviolable, and those attempting to steal public property must be considered enemies of the people.' This rule unleashed another sudden inflow of inmates to the camp system.

Bad weather, combined with the chaos of collectivisation, provided a poor autumn and spring sowing season. It was soon clear that the 1931 totals would fall well below target.

Hundreds – perhaps thousands – of farms which failed to reach grain acquisition targets were put on blacklists. They were banned from purchasing any manufacturing goods, or receiving kerosene or matches, so that even if they were able to find food they would not be able to cook it. All trade in grain, seeds, flour or bread between blacklisted districts was restricted, as was any form of credit. They were stopped from growing, or preparing, or purchasing anything at all.

People tried to flee the region in search of food. But in January 1933, Stalin closed the border of Ukraine. An internal passport system was introduced for cities and peasants prohibited from obtaining them. Any peasant found in a city was to be sent back to their place of origin.

Soviet teams operated across Ukraine, entering people's homes with long metal rods, designed to prod any surface in search of grain. They searched attics, chimneys, roofs, cellars, ovens, beds, underneath rubbish, in wells – anywhere it might have been hidden. They took any other food they found. They killed family dogs. They took the bread from people's tables.

Anyone who wasn't starving was under suspicion. Not long after that, anyone left alive was treated as a potential kulak. If they had food, they should have given it up. If they did not, they were kulaks.

Starvation was endemic. 'People didn't look like people,' a peasant from Kiev province said. 'They were more like starving ghosts.'

Old people, adults and children all deteriorated in the same way. 'All alike,' a Soviet agent said. 'Their heads like heavy kernels, their necks skinny as a stork's, every bone movement visible beneath the skin on the arms and legs, the skin itself like yellow gauze stretched over their skeletons. And the faces of those children were old, exhausted, as if they had already lived on the earth for 70 years.'

In total, at least five million people died of hunger between 1931 and 1934 across the Soviet Union, including 3.9 million Ukranians. Ukrainians referred to it as Holodomor, a combination of the word 'holod,' for hunger, and 'mor,' for extermination.

Within six months of coming to power, Hitler had destroyed any remnants of opposition in Germany.

In February 1933, sections of the constitution protecting freedom of expression, freedom of the press, freedom of assembly and freedom of association were suspended. People could be detained indefinitely, without a court order. The state was given the power to spy on letters and telephone communications, launch house searches and confiscate property. The next month, Hitler passed an Enabling Act which rendered the Reichstag parliament powerless and allowed his Cabinet to make law on its own.

The communists were the first victims. The party was completely banned from 6th March. By the end of the year, communists estimated that 130,000 of their members had been imprisoned and 2,500 murdered.

The Marxist Social Democrat party went next. First its support base in the trade union movement was eradicated. On 2nd May, brownshirts and SS squads burst into every Social Democratic trade union office in the country. All trade union newspapers were taken over and all branches of trade union banks occupied. Leading union officials were taken into custody, where they were beaten, humiliated and sometimes killed.

Without the trade unions, the Social Democratic party had no power. On 10th May, its assets and property were seized, leaving it unable to operate. On 21st June, it was banned.

The Catholic Church, and its political party, the Centre Party, was handled more delicately, but nevertheless silenced. Its newspapers were closed down and some leading Catholic politicians, writers, lawyers and journalists arrested. The party was dissolved following a Concordat with Rome on 5th July, which contained an empty promise not to close Catholic lay organisations.

By the summer of 1933, Germany was a one-party state.

The mass arrests required by this initiative led to the development of the Nazi's concentration camp network. Heinrich Himmler, the leader of the SS, was appointed Provisional Police President in Bavaria, where he announced the opening of a 'concentration camp for political prisoners' in Dachau, just outside Munich.

On 22nd March, two hundred prisoners were transferred in four police trucks from state jails. On 11th April, four Jewish prisoners were taken out the gate and shot dead. By the end of May, 12 inmates had been murdered or tortured to death.

Theodor Eicke, a senior colonel in the SS, was made commandant. He introduced a sense of order and consistency to the sadism that went on inside. Set punishments were introduced for various infractions, from execution by hanging or firing squad to solitary confinement and hard labour. The Dachau camp became a closed system, with its own subculture of symbols, codes and structures. It was, in the words of survivor Eugen Kogon, 'the theory and practice of hell.'

From there the concentration camps grew across the country. Within the first few months of 1933, at least 70 camps had been established, alongside the various torture cellars and makeshift prisons still in operation.

The Nazi party simultaneously suffocated any potential for resistance within society. The formal institutions that separated power, like the civil service and local government, were taken over. Radio stations, newspapers, magazines and cinemas were 'coordinated.' But the process went much further than the traditional centres of resistance to executive rule. The Nazis took control of universities, employment centres, health insurance offices, hospitals, professional associations, veterans organisations, theatres, opera houses, boy scouts groups, local choirs, and sports associations. Outside of the home and ale house, every area of social interaction was brought under the party's control.

Jews were purged from the professions and civil society. The Law for the Restoration of the Professional Civil Service in April 1933 banned Jews from state employment. Similar provisions banned Jewish lawyers, Jewish teachers and Jewish academics.

In 1935, the Nazis began purging Jews from social life. Anti-semitic roadsigns were erected on the entrance to many towns and villages, with slogans such as 'Jews enter this locality at their own peril.' In many areas they were banned from going to cinemas, libraries, or restaurants.

The Law for the Protection of German Blood and German Honour outlawed marriage between Jews and non-Jews and banned sexual relationships outside of marriage. This was called 'race defilement.' The definition of sexual activity was soon expanded to include any kind of physical contact, including an embrace or a kiss on the cheek. Soon people were singled out for being friendly to Jews, or maintaining non-sexual friendships with them, or allowing them in their shops.

Life for Russia's urban working class in the 1930s was better than it was for the peasants in the countryside, but not much better. Most had just a single pair of clothes and hardly ever enough food.

The greatest competition was for the most prized asset of all: living space. What people really wanted, above all, was a sliver of privacy. 'Future generations will never understand what "living space" means to us,' Nadezhda Mandelshtam, a Russian writer, wrote. 'Innumerable crimes have been committed for its sake. Who could ever leave this wonderful, precious 12 and a half square metres of living space? No-one could be so mad.'

Communal apartments dominated. They were constructed to establish a system of mutual surveillance. In each establishment there would be an elder, who ran households like a dictatorship, including telling people when to wash, and yardsmen, who patrolled the territory.

People knew everything about everyone: What their daily timetable was like, what they ate, when they drank, who they socialised with or spoke to on the phone, and what about. The paper-thin walls meant there was no real privacy, even in the private sleeping areas.

'It was a different feeling of repression from arrest, imprisonment and exile, which I've also experienced, but in some ways it was worse,' one resident said. 'In exile one preserved a sense of one's self, but the repression I felt in the communal apartment was the repression of my inner freedom and individuality.'

Outside of the home, a vast network of spies created a culture of mutual surveillance. Anyone could be a spy or police agent. Even one's children, drilled by youth leagues to report class enemies, could not always be fully trusted. According to one senior police official, one in every five office workers was a spy. Spies were in every school, factory, and apartment block.

New enemies of the people joined the kulaks – priests, merchants, criminals, sex workers, gypsies and other ethnic groups. Ethnic minorities, including Armenians, Chinese, Finns, Germans, Greeks, Koreans, Latvians and Poles, were deported or executed. Foreigners were always suspect, especially if they stood out. 'Every single black I knew in the early 1930s,' Robert Robinson, a black Communist who moved to Moscow said, 'disappeared from Moscow within seven years.'

Those with foreign connections were also vulnerable. Diaspora nationalities, like Poles or Germans, with families across the border, were often rounded up, as were Greeks, Iranians, Chinese, Romanians, Koreans and others.

Those who maintained any kind of international dimension to their lives came under suspicion, even if it was only a pen friend, or the capacity to speak another language.

Stalin branded the enemies of the people 'vermin,' 'pollution,' 'poisonous weeds,' or 'filth.' Waves of terror washed over the civilian populace. By the middle of the 1930s the gulag system had a slave labour force of 300,000 people.

German society was turned into an undifferentiated mass, whose only communication with itself was through the leader.

In the violent first few months of 1933, as the thugs of the SS and the brownshirts took over, the attacks were broad in scope, hoovering up anyone who criticised the Nazi party or might do so, including perceived deviants, independent thinkers, intellectuals, eccentrics, vagrants and general non-conformists. This process was widely reported, because part of its aim was to instil a sense of fear and obedience in the public.

The Gestapo, Hitler's secret police force, was established as an all-seeing eye of state surveillance over the populace. In reality, it was not particularly large and had comparatively few agents, most of whom were office workers rather than field operatives. But the Gestapo did not need a big staff, because it could rely on paid informers, information tortured out of political enemies and, crucially, denunciations sent in by the general public.

In the city of Saarbrücken, for example, 87.5 per cent of cases of 'malicious slander against the regime' were sent in by the public – innkeepers, people in bars, work colleagues, those who overheard conversations in the street, even family members. Often the crimes of those tracked down were simple jokes, or mild statements of resentment. But this did not matter. Even a speck of discontent was treated harshly, because it was a refutation of the Nazi party's central proposition: that the people were singular and represented in their entirety by Hitler.

The lowest level of social control was the block warden, who was assigned over a group of houses. By 1938, there were two million block wardens. They were replicated at work by officials from the Nazi Labour Front, employers, foremen and members of the Nazi Security Service. 'Nobody dares to say anything anymore,' one German wrote in his diary in 1933, 'everyone's afraid.'

Robert Ley, head of the Nazi Labour Front, said that 'the only person in Germany who still has a private life is a person who's sleeping.' But in fact this was not true. Even in their sleep, the German people were subject to the regime. When the journalist Charlotte Beradt composed a file of people's dreams in Nazi Germany between 1933 and 1939, she found the notion of surveillance and obedience had penetrated deep into their internal life.

The Nazi term for the process of complete social and institutional control was 'gleichschaltung.' This was the party's view of society under its rule: uniform, conformist, undifferentiated, exposed, and dictated in all characteristics and action by the will of the centre.

Hitler's power over the party had enveloped the German people. He was the man-god, the legislator made manifest – not as a tutor toward the general will, but as the embodiment of the people through the notion of race leadership, mediated through his charisma.

'The authority of the leader is total and all-embracing,' concluded the constitutional lawyer Ernst Rudolf Huber, 'within it all resources available to the body politic merge; it covers every facet of the life of the people; it embraces all members of the German community pledged to loyalty and obedience to the leader. The leader's authority is subject to no checks or controls; it is circumscribed by no private preserves of jealously guarded individual rights; it is free and independent, overriding and unfettered.'

Constitutional authorities developed a consensus that legislation itself, even thought it was still passed, was ultimately unnecessary. Hitler's verbal utterances were considered legally binding.

Once Hitler's rule was established over other political forces, he began to eradicate the social pollution that had infected the master race. From 1935, the camp system was reorientated away from socialists and communists towards habitual criminals, the long-term unemployed, so called 'deviants' and 'racial degenerates,' and 'asocials' – a broad category which eventually came to include prostitutes, gypsies, tramps and beggars.

By 1938, there were around 21,000 inmates. An inverted triangle was put on the left breast of their striped uniform: black for asocial, red for political, violet for Jehovah's Witnesses, pink for gay men. Jews were designated as one of these categories, usually political, but with a yellow triangle stitched underneath, the right way up, so it formed a star of David.

The Jews were in a different category to other victimised groups. They were more than just an obstacle to Nazi rule, or a pollution of the race. They were the enemy, the representatives of an international conspiracy which intended to destroy the people. By this stage, they had been purged not just from civil society but from the social life of the country.

On the evening of 9th November 1938, Hitler issued instructions for a massive bloody coordinated reprisal against Germany's Jews in retaliation for the shooting of a junior official in the Nazi embassy in Paris. That night, virtually every synagogue in Germany was set on fire. At least 520 were destroyed, alongside 7,500 shops. Jews were woken in bed by knocks at the door. The Gestapo and brownshirts ransacked their homes, smashing the furniture and windows, throwing out books and valuables and beating the inhabitants.

Between 9th and 16th November, 30,000 Jewish men were arrested and taken to the concentration camps at Dachau, Buchenwald and Sachsenhausen. The total number of people killed was between 1,000 and 2,000.

Between 1937 and 1938, Stalin's paranoia turned inwards. It was called the Great Terror. By the time it was over, 1.3 million people had been arrested for crimes against the state. At least half of them were executed.

The camps shifted from being places where people often died of neglect to places where people were deliberately worked to death and sometimes murdered. Starting in 1937, Stalin signed orders sent to local NKVD bosses with quotas of people to be arrested in given regions. Some were to be sentenced to the first category punishment of death. Others were to be sentenced to the second category punishment of camp imprisonment for between eight to 10 years. Azerbaijan, for instance, was to provide 1,500 first category arrests and 3,750 second category. Georgia was to provide 2,000 first category arrests and 3,000 second category.

Those arrested under Article 58 of the prison code, which included 'counter-revolutionary' crimes, were designated 'enemies of the people.' This category applied to anyone who voiced criticism of the regime or might even think it. 'An enemy of the people,' secret police boss Lavrentiy Beria said later, 'is not only one who commits sabotage, but one who doubts the rightness of the party line.'

A decree in 1937 made it possible to arrest women as 'wives of enemies of the people.' The same applied to children. Officially this was termed 'Member of the Family of an Enemy of the Revolution.'

Once someone was arrested, their entire social and professional network usually went with them. 'Arrests rolled through the streets and apartment houses like an epidemic,' the author Aleksandr Solzhenitsyn wrote. 'They passed on the infection of inevitable arrest by a handshake, a breath, by a chance meeting on the street.'

The fear of arrest became so all-encompassing that the basic ability to talk came under threat. 'One cannot speak of anything or with anyone,' the Russian writer Mikhail Prishvin wrote in his diary, in a scrawl so tiny he believed it could not be read with a magnifying glass. 'The whole secret of behaviour is to sense what something means, and who means it, without saying anything. You have to eliminate completely in yourself any remnant of the need to "speak from the heart."'

Anyone under the age of 30 was particularly susceptible to the system's crushing uniformity, because they were the children of the revolution. They had been programmed since birth to place all faith in the party and to relinquish their own individual judgement.

Older people had a better chance of maintaining a capacity to distinguish objective reality from the regime's propaganda. But for many of them, the mask they had put on had become their true face. 'I began to feel,' one citizen said, 'that I was the man I had pretended to be.'

It was a common sentiment. One woman wrote in her diary: 'My inner self has not gone away – whatever is inside a personality can never disappear – but it is deeply hidden, and I no longer feel its presence within me.'

Those arrested were taken to the local prison, where they were registered, photographed and fingerprinted. This was the first stage of what inmates called the gulag 'meat-grinder,' which involved arrest, interrogation, torture, transportation, forced labour, starvation and death.

'You are already not a person,' Inna Shikheeva-Gaister, who was arrested for being the daughter of an enemy of the people, said. 'And around you there are no people. They lead you down the corridor, photograph you, undress you, search you mechanically. Everything is done completely impersonally. You look for a human glance – I don't speak of a human voice, just a human glance – but you don't find it. You have become an object.'

Prisoners were tortured into making confessions. They were beaten, their faces smashed in, their organs ruptured. Some were put in solitary confinement, or their family were threatened. Women were raped, or threatened with rape. One of the most common forms of torture was sleep deprivation, which could last for days or weeks, until sanity snapped.

In January 1938 the population of the camps was 1.8 million. Inmates did every kind of work imaginable – mining gold, nickel and coal, logging, building roads, canals, airports, and housing, making weapons, military aircraft, chemicals and children's toys.

An entire vocabulary developed for the 'living dead' – the class of people in the camps who were closest to death. They died of starvation, or diseases of starvation, or vitamin deficiency: scurvy, pellagra, diarrhoea. Others died at work from the unsafe conditions. Some committed suicide. Some were murdered in mass killings.

The dead bodies were stacked until there were enough to warrant a mass burial, when they were loaded naked onto sledges. Before they left the camp gate, an officer would smash the skull with a pickaxe to ensure they were dead. They were then dumped into large ditches.

No death certificates were written. No-one knew where the bodies were buried. Their families were not told they had died. No-one in the camp would be informed of their death.

Between 1929 and 1953, when Stalin died, 18 million Soviet citizens passed through the gulag system. A further six million were internal exiles. A minimum of 2.7 million people died in the gulag system and exile villages.

On 1st September 1939, Germany invaded Poland. Two days later, France and Britain declared war. Stalin and Hitler had deferred their own conflict in a secret pact that carved up eastern Europe between them, but it didn't hold long. At first light on 22nd June 1941, Germany invaded Russia. The Second World War would become the largest and most deadly conflict in human history.

It radicalised the Nazi regime. 'The war made possible for us the solution of a whole series of problems that could never have been solved in normal times,' Hitler said.

A project code-named Aktion T-4 was developed for the eradication of the mentally unwell or the disabled, which included schizophrenics, epileptics, the senile, the deaf, the blind, those suffering from Huntington's disease and those experiencing 'feeble-mindedness,' a broad category into which any kind of social deviant might be included.

Albert Widmann, an SS officer in the Criminal-Technical Institute of the Reich Criminal Police Office, was tasked with developing a mechanism of gassing victims with carbon monoxide. He built an experimental model in the old city prison at Brandenburg. It was an airtight chamber, three metres by five, lined with tiles to make it look like a shower room, so that those entering it would not panic. A gas pipe was fitted to the wall to introduce the fumes into the chamber. A viewing window was installed in the door.

The first experiment was conducted in late 1939. Senior officials took turns to watch through the window as eight patients were murdered. The experiment was a success. The gas chamber went into regular service, alongside several others built in asylums or former hospitals repurposed as killing stations during 1940.

Patients were collected in large grey coaches. On entering the institution they were told to undress and an identifying number was stamped on their body. They were photographed, then taken to the chamber in groups of 15 to 20. Any who were anxious were injected with tranquillisers. Once inside, the doors were locked and doctors released the gas. Around 80,000 people were killed in this operation.

The killing of Jews in the war initially took place in a chaotic manner, as a result of local initiatives spurred on by demands from the leadership in Berlin.

At the start, the deaths were of Jewish men. At least 5,000 and probably as many as 10,000 were killed in Vilnius, Lithuania, in the summer of 1941, for instance. Three SS Security Service units in Riga, Latvia, killed 2,000 Jews in a wood outside the town in July. Ostensibly these units claimed to be killing the 'Jewish-Bolshevist leadership cadre,' although in reality they often murdered the entire male population.

Two significant policy changes then took place. The first was the formal inclusion of people who were clearly not engaged with any form of military resistance. The second was the expansion of the killing to women and children. By August, SS brigades were systematically shooting the entire Jewish population.

The parameters of this change were set by Hitler and articulated, through repeated verbal orders, by Himmler. By the end of 1941, across the whole of eastern Europe, the overall number of murders committed by the SS Security Service Task Forces and their associated military and paramilitary groups had reached probably around half a million Jews.

It was clear at this stage that the Nazi plan was for the extermination of the Jewish race, but mass shootings were not efficient enough to achieve that and they were having a debilitating effect on the men ordered to carry them out. 'Despite the fact that up to now a total of some 75,000 Jews have been liquidated in this way,' one Task Force report stated, 'it has nevertheless become apparent that this method will not provide a solution to the Jewish problem.'

A solution was provided by the T-4 programme and initiated in Poland. A camp was established at Belzec in November 1941, to serve as a base for gassing vans. A similar centre was established at Chelmno.

Jews were transported to the centre from the Nazi controlled ghetto, then taken to the vans. The vans at Chelmno would take 50 people at a time, driving from the camp to some woods 16 kilometres away, gassing them as they went. They would then unload the bodies in ditches dug by Jewish prisoners. Sometimes a mother would succeed in saving her baby by wrapping it tightly enough to block out the fumes. In these cases, the babies' heads were bashed against a tree. The total number of people killed at Chelmno was 360,000.

Establishing the gassing operations in fixed camps improved efficiency. The first finished construction at Belzec in February 1942. The chamber was fitted with an airtight seal and pipes which supplied the fumes from nearby cars. On 27th March, the first batch of prisoners was delivered and immediately gassed.

A second camp was built in Sobibor, with construction starting in March 1942, and a third at Treblinka, in the summer. These three camps murdered 1.7 million people.

A further killing station was established at a pre-existing concentration camp called Auschwitz, selected because of its good communications and remoteness from major population centres. Where the other camps had been intended to kill the Jews of Poland, Auschwitz was intended to kill Jews from surrounding countries, including those transported from Germany itself.

Instead of exhaust fumes, a chemical pesticide called Zyklon B was used. It was tested on Soviet prisoners of war in 1941 by forcing the men into an airtight room and then shaking the powder down on them from holes in the roof. The warmth generated by the bodies turned it into a deadly gas. Two chambers were built at Auschwitz, Bunker I and Bunker II. The first deaths using this method took place on 20th March 1942.

When prisoners arrived at Auschwitz they were forced out the transport with dogs and whips and made to line up. They underwent selection by SS doctors, who asked them a brief series of questions and gave them a cursory medical examination. They were then separated between those who were fit to work and those who were not. Those under 16, mothers with children, the sick, the old and the weak were moved to the left, loaded into trucks, and murdered. Those who were fit for work were taken to the labour camp, where they were tattooed with a serial number and registered. Periodic selections would then be imposed on this group, with any found no longer fit to work taken to the gas chambers.

The first victims of the gas chambers were Jews from Slovakia and France. They were followed by Jews from Poland, Belgium and the Netherlands. From July 1942, transports began to arrive from Vienna, then in the winter from Berlin, Romania, Croatia, Finland, Norway, Bulgaria, Italy, Hungary, Serbia, Denmark and Greece.

Over its lifespan, between 1.1 million and 1.5 million people were killed in Auschwitz, approximately 90 per cent of them Jews. Around 400,000 were considered fit for work. Of these, at least half died from malnutrition, exhaustion, disease or hypothermia.

In total during the war, around three million Jews were killed in the extermination camps, 700,000 in the mobile gas vans, 1.3 million by being shot, and up to a million from hunger, disease or murder. Around six million Jews were killed by the Nazi regime and its allies.

This was the consequence of liberal failure. This was what happened when the individual was destroyed.

7. NEW WORLD ORDER

Everything that followed the war was based on one overriding moral objective: to never let it happen again. Nazi Germany was defeated. The Soviet Union retreated behind the Iron Curtain, dividing Europe between capitalism and communism. Western liberalism now had to demonstrate that it could be reinvented to avoid the horrors of the past.

That project began with economics.

The property question had divided liberalism from the beginning, when Ireton faced Rainsborough across the floor of the Putney debates. It had developed into a split between the laissez-faire wing, exemplified by Constant, and the egalitarian wing, exemplified by Taylor and Mill.

This debate now had a new urgency. The economic chaos after the First World War had ravaged Europe. The Great Depression which followed led directly to the triumph of the Nazi party. If liberalism was going to survive, if it was going to prevent totalitarianism, these types of events could never be allowed to reoccur.

There had to be a new way of looking at economic questions. It would be found through an intense life-long struggle between two liberals: Friedrich Hayek, representing liberalism's right wing, and John Maynard Keynes, representing its left.

It translated itself, in practical terms, into two overriding concerns. For Hayek, the primary aim of economic policy was to lower inflation – the rate at which things become more expensive. For Keynes, it was to lower unemployment – the number of people out of work. These two elements became the battleground for a new internal liberal battle over what freedom entailed.

Hayek was born to a patriotic Austrian family just months before the 19th Century turned into the 20th. Austria had been badly hit by hyperinflation after the First World War. It had bankrupted itself to pay for the war-effort, and then it had to deal with the consequences of that decision, alongside brutal punishments by the victors and an all-pervading sense of national humiliation. People began to starve. A beer cost a billion marks. Stoves were lit with million mark notes. The Hayek family life savings became worthless.

Hayek realised that a society where money had lost all value teetered on the edge of chaos. It could not offer true freedom, only the freedom of the jungle. He never forgot that. For the rest of his life, the moral imperative of preventing the ravages of inflation would dominate his work.

He began his academic career at the University of Vienna, then worked in a government body administering war debt, before landing a post at the London School of Economics (LSE) in 1931. Here, he was a man out of place. His thick Austrian accent meant he struggled to make himself understood in English. Most of his opinions stemmed from the Austrian school of economics, which almost no-one in Britain had read.

Nowadays, Hayek is treated as a conservative, but that's not right. He was a liberal. He believed in the freedom of the individual and his views, whether economic or political, flowed from that concern. When he failed to abide by his convictions, for instance when in his old age he voiced support for dictatorships, he betrayed himself as a liberal, not as a conservative.

Hayek had a towering intellect. But he had the very grave disadvantage of being pitted in a fight with one of the most charismatic, eloquent and successful men in the history of ideas.

John Maynard Keynes lived like a true liberal. He was impossible to define. In fact, his life seemed a near-constant effort to defy the very concept of definition. He was a promiscuous and outspoken gay man, well before it was socially accepted or even legal. Then in 1925, he married the ballerina Lydia Lopokova, in a move that startled his friends. But it was not some attempt to garner a more respectable reputation. His letters to her – written most days – were brimming with passion and sexuality.

He was utterly practical and yet known for his theoretical works. He lived a life of passion and feeling, but spent his career at the highest reaches of British political life and left behind a body of ruthlessly academic economic doctrine. He loved art, but also played the stock, property, commodity and currency markets. He worked with British prime ministers and held talks with American presidents, but he surrounded himself with a group of gay and straight friends, connected by interlocking love lives, who spent their time agitating for social change. Socialists called him a conservative and conservatives called him a socialist.

Keynes was gifted with an extraordinary ability to communicate. He knew exactly the right level to pitch his theories, whether it was in a radio broadcast to the general public, a parliamentary committee, or an economics textbook. His writing was clear, colourful, witty and lit up with vivid examples.

Those who met him were taken aback by his intelligence. Bertrand Russell, the philosopher who utilised several hundred pages of symbolic logic to prove that one plus one equals two, said: 'Keynes' intellect was the sharpest and clearest that I have ever known. When I argued with him, I felt that I took my life in my hands, and I seldom emerged without feeling something of a fool.'

The clash between Hayek and Keynes defined the future of economics and pitted two tribes against one another in an acrimonious dispute that dominated their lifetime and our own. But at the heart of it lay an uneasy friendship.

They first met at a joint LSE-Cambridge University event in 1928. Keynes was in his mid-forties and Hayek in his mid-twenties. Within seconds, they started arguing.

'We at once had our first theoretical clash – on some issue of the effectiveness of changes in the rate of interest,' Hayek later recalled. 'Though in such debates, Keynes would at first try ruthlessly to steamroller an objection in a manner somewhat intimidating to a younger man, if one stood up to him on such occasions he would develop a most friendly interest even if he strongly disagreed with one's views.'

Neither men held back when criticising the other's work. Their written jousts, conducted mostly through letters and articles in academic magazines, were aggressive and bad-tempered, as were their private assessments of the other side's failings.

'The wildest farrago of nonsense yet,' Keynes scrawled over his copy of Hayek's essay *Capital Consumption* in 1932. Reviewing another of Hayek's works, he concluded: 'It is an extraordinary example of how, starting with a mistake, a remorseless logician can end up in Bedlam.' But slowly, despite these public and private salvos, their personal relations blossomed into a genuine, if testy, friendship.

When the LSE was evacuated from London to escape the Blitz in 1940, Keynes intervened to make sure his rival could have a room near his own at King's College. 'We shared so many other interests, historical and outside economics,' Hayek recalled. 'On the whole when we met we stopped talking economics. So we became personally very good friends.'

The Nazi bombing eventually reached Cambridge and the staff at King's were tasked with sitting on the roof all night with shovels, so they could tip incendiaries off the roof before they started a fire. On one evening in 1942, Keynes and Hayek shared rooftop watch duties, and sat together until the early morning, watching in the sky for signs of German planes.

Both men knew what those planes represented: the fascist enemy. They were united in opposition to tyranny and, once the war was over, agreed on the moral imperative of never letting it take over again. But they did not share the same assessment of why those pilots had come to sit in those Nazi planes, flying over England and dropping bombs on them.

Hayek recognised a central truth: that fascism and communism were variants of the same evil. They might appear as polar opposites, but they reflected a similar effort to destroy individual freedom. The individual liberty he cared about, however, was not diversity or freedom of thought. It was the freedom to operate in the market.

His central principle was the price point, when two individuals agree to a sale. This, he thought, was the real will of the people. It represented the amount someone was willing to pay for something and the price someone was willing to sell it for. In a world of infinite complexity the price point was something real, firm, and full of meaning. It told you, through the consensual agreement between two individuals, all sorts of information about scarcity and demand. It was a sacred moment of liberty that must be protected from interference.

If you put your faith in this price point, in this meeting of minds, it would reveal extraordinary truths. But if you eradicated it or even tampered with it, you would cause terrible harm. Hayek believed that even modest state manipulation would likely cause economic collapse, such as the 1930s slump. Such crashes may have looked like the market had gone crazy, but in fact they were the result of the state getting involved in the economy.

The problem lay in the lowering of interest rates – the amount of money a borrower has to pay back to a lender. Interest rates were set by central banks, which were connected to the state. They had a powerful effect on a country's economic performance.

When interest rates were low, people could borrow more cheaply, which led them to buy more goods and services and therefore increased spending. There was so much money in circulation, however, that businesses selling products realised that they could start charging more, which would trigger inflation.

When interest rates were high, it was harder to borrow and more attractive to put money in a bank account, so people spent less and demand for products fell. Eventually, businesses would lay off workers and you could end up in a recession. The balance between these two scenarios was crucial to a country's economic performance.

Building on the work of his mentor, Ludwig von Mises, Hayek believed that low central interest rates had prompted banks to lend more money than was justified by the real state of the economy. But because the loans had been cheap, businesses had borrowed the money to buy machinery to make more goods.

Such machines were called capital goods. Capital goods are the product the consumer doesn't see. If someone buys bread from the bakery, that bakery will have had to buy products to produce the bread, like a dough mixer, a large oven and a bread slicer. Those are capital goods.

According to Hayek, the purchases of capital goods hadn't reflected future demand for the products they would make. They had only been purchased because there was a lot of credit available. It was a malinvestment, triggered by the central bank's bad decisions.

Once the machines were ready, they didn't have enough customers to serve. The economy slowed down. And then central banks were left with a problem. If they kept interest rates low, inflation would grow. But if they raised them, investment would slump and there would be a downturn.

The fault lay not with the market but with the central banks setting interest rates. This had interfered with the true functioning of the economy and in particular the relationship between savings and investment. The capital goods theory explained how interference in the economy made things worse, but it was grounded in a philosophical assumption. Hayek believed that the economy was too complex to be understood and manipulated. He rejected the idea that economists could look down on it from above, like a town planner looking at a scale model, and work out what to do. And because people couldn't understand the economy, their attempts to interfere in it would make things worse. Hayek's was the latest formulation of Constant's argument that the market was best left alone.

The only thing economists could rely on was the price point. The individuals deciding on a price weren't perfect. They didn't have absolute knowledge of the present or the future. But their decisions told you something real. If you left them alone, the price point would return to an equilibrium that truly represented supply and demand.

For Hayek, this argument was never just about economics. It was political. Any central interference in the economy breached the age-old liberal principle that the government should be restrained.

If unfettered, the state would rip into property rights, and then, like a hungry animal, interfere more and more, until it eventually became the all-controlling monster of Stalin's Russia. This was a complete rejection of Mill's argument that there could be no 'universal solution' to the state/market question. For Hayek, any state intervention created a slippery slope to tyranny.

'Once the free working of the market is impeded beyond a certain degree,' he said, 'the planner will be forced to extend his controls until they become all-comprehensive.'

Most of Hayek's writing was obtuse, technical and dry. But on one occasion, he let himself go and expressed his profound fears over a slide to totalitarianism. It was called *The Road to Serfdom*.

He thought the book would be read by a few hundred people, but an abridged version was included as a *Reader's Digest* edition in the US. It exploded. A million copies were ordered. *The Road to Serfdom* became a gospel for right-wingers in America and Britain and Hayek developed a cult following.

Keynes read it while crossing the Atlantic in summer 1944. 'The voyage has given me the chance to read your book properly,' he wrote to Hayek when he reached America. 'In my opinion it is a grand book.

You will not expect me to accept quite all the economic dicta in it. But morally and philosophically I find myself in agreement with virtually the whole of it; and not only in agreement with it, but in a deeply moved agreement.' They were, once again, as they had been on the roof of King's College, united in their opposition to fascism.

But there was a problem. Smuggled away in the text, Hayek admitted that he was in fact willing to accept some state interference in the economy. He believed there should be control of weights and measures, for instance, and that the state could step in 'where competition cannot possibly do the job.' He even believed that the state could provide 'a comprehensive system of social insurance.'

Keynes focused on the concession. 'You admit here and there that it is a question of knowing where to draw the line. You agree that the line has to be drawn somewhere; and that the logical extreme is not possible. But you give us no guidance whatever as to where to draw it.'

Then he delivered the blow. 'As soon as you admit that the extreme is not possible, and that a line has to be drawn, you are, on your own argument, done for.'

Hayek's theories also had an empirical defect. Since the Great Depression, countries had begun to interfere with their economies more and more, in no small part due to aggressive lobbying by Keynes. In America, President Franklin Roosevelt had started a project called the New Deal involving state-organised public works. That was a decade old and yet America had not yet descended into a fascist dystopia. 'Your greatest danger ahead,' Keynes told Hayek lightly, 'is the probable practical failure of the application of your philosophy in the US in a fairly extreme form.'

Keynes' followers treated the capital goods theory of economic slumps with scorn. During Hayek's first attempt to demonstrate it in England one member of the audience looked up at the scrawl of triangles and mathematical formulations on the blackboard and concluded that Hayek was in 'a pitiful state of confusion.' Hardly any economist now subscribes to the capital goods theory.

Despite the complexity of his reasoning, Hayek's view of the market was also ultimately quite simplistic. He envisaged it as a natural force, but in reality it was ordered by humans. The limited liability company, the central bank, and intellectual property were all human inventions that enshrined certain value judgements. Activities such as child labour and slavery were banned. All of this amounted to interference in the market.

But Hayek's biggest problem wasn't the lack of evidence or even the fragility of his theories. It was political. Ultimately, he provided very few solutions. His was a manifesto for inaction. In the event of a slump, and even with people out of work and begging in the streets for food, as they had been during the Great Depression, Hayek had little to offer.

'The most we may hope for,' he said, 'is that the growing information of the public may make it easier for central banks both to follow a cautious policy during the upward swing of the cycle, and so to mitigate the following depression.'

This approach was politically possible before universal suffrage. When the victims of economic downturns could not vote, it had been easy for right-wing liberals to dismiss calls for action with the excuse that it would only make things worse. But those days were over. The West was now almost fully democratic. The victims had a vote. And at the ballot box they demanded that something be done.

Liberals had seen what happened when you didn't intervene. Communism and fascism had appealed to voters out of the chaos of the old laissez-faire economics. That couldn't happen again.

When Keynes had looked in the sky for those Nazi planes, he was thinking something else entirely.

The Nazi regime had come to power on a wave of discontent following the Great Depression. And depressions, he believed, were the result of a failure of aggregate demand in the economy.

People weren't buying or investing enough. So businesses made less money, economic activity declined, profits tumbled and workers were made unemployed. Those who were put out of work then had even less money, bought less, and the economy spiralled downwards.

'We get into a vicious cycle,' Keynes said. 'We do nothing because we have not the money. But it is precisely because we do not do anything that we have not the money.'

The Great Depression was finally brought to an end when governments needed to spend huge amounts of money to pay for the war effort. But if countries were able to stimulate demand to pay for war, why could they not do it in times of peace?

'Hitherto war has been the only object of governmental loan-expenditure on a large scale which governments have considered respectable,' Keynes said. 'In all the issues of peace they are timid, over-cautious, half-hearted, without perseverance or determination.'

There were a few different methods of stimulating demand in peacetime. Keynes' favoured method was through fiscal policy – the use of tax and spend by government to affect economic conditions.

The state could stimulate demand through fiscal policy in two ways. The first was through tax cuts. If the state cut taxes, people would have more money to spend. But Keynes' chief method of encouraging demand was through a second option: public works. Instead of letting people wallow in joblessness, they could be employed on big projects needed by society – building roads, homes, even cinemas.

There was a danger to all this. It was Hayek's old enemy: inflation. Increased investment would lead to increased demand, which would lead to increased prices. If the public works programme failed to turn into sustainable long-term employment, those who fell out of work would be worse off than they had been in the first place, because goods and products would now be more expensive. For Hayek, this was extremely likely, because any state action was likely to be counter-productive.

Inflation was indeed expected. Whenever demand increased there was likely to be an increase in prices. But Keynes did not accept that inflation was the main economic danger or that the employment would be unsustainable. The stimulus, he said, would not just provide the jobs in the public works programme. It would create even more jobs.

This was because of something called the multiplier. The people given jobs on public works programmes would be paid wages which they would use to buy things. The workers employed by the state to dig a road, for instance, needed a cafe to buy their lunch and transport to take them to the site. The businesses they patronised would then have more money and spend more themselves. Demand therefore rose and business confidence along with it. Private sector growth came from public sector stimulus.

The consequence of public works was that, in the short term, the national debt would grow. Increased spending would lead to more employment even if taxes were raised to pay for it, but funding it through national borrowing would have a bigger effect. Keynes was therefore taking aim at one of the central faiths of classical economics since the time of Smith: balanced budgets.

It was wrong to treat this as irresponsible, or to make a comparison between national and household finances, as Smith had. In fact, more revenue would flow to the exchequer and less would be spent on unemployment benefits, making it easier to pay back the debt in the long run. 'It is a complete mistake,' Keynes said, 'to believe that there is a dilemma between schemes for increasing employment and schemes for balancing the budget – that we must go slowly and cautiously with the former for fear of injuring the latter. Quite the contrary. There is no possibility of balancing the budget except by increasing the national income, which is much the same thing as increasing employment.'

This was just the tip of the iceberg when it came to Keynes' rejection of right-wing liberalism. In truth, his entire system went against the consensus on non-interference in the market.

'We are brought to my heresy,' he said gleefully. 'I bring in the state; I abandon laissez-faire.'

Non-interference had left millions destitute and hopeless, driving them into the welcoming arms of totalitarians and precipitating a level of slaughter previously unknown to humankind. Left alone during a downturn, the market had not found equilibrium, particularly not with employment.

'It is obvious that an individualist society left to itself does not work well or even tolerably,' Keynes said. 'The more troublesome the times, the worse does a laissez-faire system work.'

He was aiming to destroy not just the economic arguments of the time, but the underlying assumption behind them: that the self-interest of each individual necessarily improved the lot of all.

'It is not true that individuals possess a prescriptive "natural liberty" in their economic activities,' Keynes said. 'There is no "compact" conferring perpetual rights on those who have or on those who acquire. The world is not so governed from above that private and social interest always coincide. It is not a correct deduction from the principles of economics that enlightened self-interest always operates in the public interest.'

This was a war on laissez-faire, but not from fascism or communism. It came from within liberalism. Keynes was trying to address the defects of balanced budgets, supreme property rights and the invisible hand in a way that would strengthen the rest of the system. 'Individualism, if it can be purged of its defects and its abuses, is the best safeguard of personal liberty,' he said.

Keynes was tracing the line of egalitarian liberalism forward from Mill's *Principles of Political Economy*, in which he had held open the possibility that state intervention in the economy could increase, rather than limit, freedom. It was the next stage in the historic compromise between the state and the market.

Despite the odd caveat, Hayek's vision of the world was fundamentally puritanical. Its whole notion of the slippery slope, from well-meaning interference to totalitarianism, forced advocates to treat any instance of state intervention as tantamount to tyranny.

Keynes' vision was intent on finding a middle ground. The free market would do what it did best and the state would do what it could not. In liberal terms, it meant that the market and the state were to be treated with the same degree of scepticism. Both were necessary. Both, in the right way, at the right time, were advantageous. But both were also a potential threat to freedom. They had to be held in check.

It also had philosophical implications. The individual in the Keynesian world was not just an isolated atom bouncing around a rampantly competitive world. They were grounded in society.

In Keynes' system, the whole could still benefit from the self-interest of the individual. But he introduced a vital addition. The individual also succeeded because of the good of the whole.

The multiplier demonstrated that people's fortunes were bound up with one another. They were not alone. They were not defined exclusively by their self-interest. They relied on one another.

Keynes outlined his ideas in a book called *The General Theory of Employment, Interest and Money*. It was published on 4th February 1936.

'It is a badly written book, poorly organised,' Paul Samuelson, an economist at the Massachusetts Institute of Technology, concluded. 'It is arrogant, bad-tempered, polemical, and not overly generous in its acknowledgements. Flashes of insight and intuition intersperse tedious algebra. An awkward definition suddenly gives way to an unforgettable cadenza. When it is finally mastered, we find its analysis to be obvious and at the same time new. In short, it is a work of genius.'

The General Theory began as a kind of rebel text, studied and debated by young economists away from class. 'The old economics was still taught by day,' John Galbraith, a leading Keynesian recalled. 'But in the evening, almost everyone discussed Keynes.' It then spread quickly outward and converted more followers. By the time the Second World War was over, the age of laissez-faire had passed with it.

One of the oddities of Keynesianism was just how influential it proved to be. In the strict sense, it was no more than a programme for ensuring demand during a downturn, through a commitment to full employment. Once that period of instability was over, things would go back to normal and, in Keynes' words, 'the classical theory comes into its own again from this point onwards.'

But the political effects of Keynesianism went much further. It established the principle that the market did not always reach equilibrium. The self-interest of the individual did not always provide the answers. The state could interfere. And once that was acknowledged, everything changed.

Suddenly all the caveats to classical economics in Smith and Mill, on market failure and the need for welfare provision, took on full life. There was a push towards the nationalisation of industries, from coal mining to railways and aviation. A much more generous and comprehensive welfare state was introduced, which would help people through the struggles of life. New mothers would receive financial assistance to help care for their children. The disabled would receive social security benefits. Education and health were provided for free in many countries.

Governments started regulating business. The market was no longer deemed to be wholly rational and self-righting, so it followed there was a need to make sure that firms behaved in a way that respected the public's economic and social welfare. New laws controlled how factories treated the environment or endangered species, and protected workers and consumers. The rights of the individual took precedence over the freedoms of business.

Government was no longer viewed as simply a threat, or just as a nightwatchman overseeing national security. It now had a more general and active role to help and protect people.

Keynes' insistence that the government had a duty to maintain full employment was accepted around the world. The Australian premier, John Curtin, introduced a 'full employment in Australia' programme in 1945. In Britain, the wartime coalition established full employment and a full welfare state as national goals. A National Health Service was established after the war, which would help anyone, for free, at any time, to treat any condition. It was one of the most daring, radical inventions in British political history and became the UK's most cherished institution.

The new welfare system actually improved social mobility. It achieved precisely the transfer of property envisaged by Constant – not by leaving the market alone, but by interfering with it. High taxes were imposed to fund better services, so that the poor, the disabled and the needy were able to improve their situation.

By 1959, Keynesian economics had worked well enough that one of its followers, the British prime minister Harold Macmillan, could win an election under the slogan: 'You've never had it so good.'

The US was motoring ahead. It had experimented with an embryonic form of Keynesianism in the 1930s, when Roosevelt had tried to address the bank closures and job losses with the New Deal. This had provided direct relief to the jobless, old age pensions, employment insurance and a public works programme, building everything from dams to aircraft carriers, schools to bridges. Millions entered the government's payroll.

Banks were brought under control. Many had gone bust after the Wall Street Crash. But in 1933, Congress had passed the historic Glass-Steagall Act. Banks were able to borrow from the Federal Reserve, an organisation created as a lender of last resort, which would prevent them collapsing if they ran out of ready cash. But there was a stick as well as a carrot. They were barred from engaging in risky activity. Commercial banks for ordinary citizens were separated from investment banks, which typically dealt with businesses.

Most advanced capitalist countries introduced similar restrictions on banks. Bank crises largely became a thing of the past, a horrible memory of the days before they were tamed. Banking became respectable and a bit dull.

'Thirty-plus years ago, when I was a graduate student in economics,' the economist Paul Krugman said in 2009, 'only the least ambitious of my classmates sought careers in the financial world. Even then, investment banks paid more than teaching or public service – but not that much more, and anyway, everyone knew that banking was, well, boring.'

In 1946, the year Keynes died, President Harry Truman signed the Employment Act into law, establishing the 'responsibility' of federal government to 'promote maximum employment.'

Unemployment and welfare payments incorporated Keynesian mechanisms without requiring government action. When the economy slumped, they would rise in line with people being made redundant. This achieved precisely what Keynes wanted: an increase in spending, typically through national debt, which would stimulate demand. These were called automatic fiscal stabilisers. In the 1950s, they helped minimise three short US recessions under President Dwight Eisenhower.

A wave of prosperity followed, with average families for the first time owning a house, a car, and modern appliances like a refrigerator and a washing machine.

In 1957, the Russian launch into space of Sputnik, the world's first human-made satellite, triggered half a century of space-race projects between the US and the Soviet Union. And that created a kind of sci-fi Keynesian fiscal stimulus. NASA, the US space agency, got a suitably astronomical $18.7 billion annual budget, with another $20 billion spent on rockets and satellites.

In the 1960s, John F Kennedy became the first explicitly and self-consciously Keynesian president. 'I gave them straight Keynes and they loved it,' he told his economic adviser after his first speech to Congress.

Crucially, however, Kennedy's Keynesianism did not rely on public works. It focused instead on the other fiscal mechanism to stimulate demand: tax cuts. Keynes himself had been open to this approach, but it caused controversy among his disciples in the

1960s. Galbraith, who had written Kennedy's stump speech on economics, branded it a 'reactionary' form of Keynesianism.

Kennedy was assassinated in 1963, but his successor, Lyndon Johnson, pushed through the programme, cutting general income tax rates and slashing the top level from 91 per cent to 65 per cent.

The effect was striking. Federal tax revenue increased by $40 billion, economic growth shot up from 5.8 per cent in 1964 to 6.6 per cent in 1966, and unemployment fell from 5.2 per cent in 1964 to 2.9 per cent in 1966. Inflation stayed low.

In December 1965, *Time* magazine made Keynes Man of the Year. 'Today, some 20 years after his death, his theories are a prime influence on the world's free economies,' it said. 'The modern capitalist economy does not automatically work at top efficiency, but can be raised to that level by the intervention and influence of the government.'

Johnson combined the tax cuts mechanism with a full-throated commitment to public spending. Federal entitlements drove down poverty, everyone over the age of 65 received health care in the form of Medicare, and those who could not afford insurance were offered Medicaid.

This period saw an explosion of wealth and material plenty the likes of which were unknown in the history of humankind: colour TVs, international airline travel, multiple cars.

Between the 1950s and 70s, the highly regulated, highly taxed advanced capitalist economies experienced massive growth. Per capita income in western Europe grew at a remarkable 4.1 per cent a year. Economies were stable. Unemployment was all but eliminated.

This had cultural effects which went far beyond economics. There was, for the first time, a notion of leisure – not for a set class, as it had been in Constant's day, but for everyone. People were not constantly scrambling to avoid destitution. They had the time and the money to dedicate to whatever gave them enjoyment: sports, hobbies, families, pop culture.

Material plenty created something new: the teenager. Until the post-war period, you were a child and then you were an adult. There was nothing in between. But increased wealth, improved higher education provision, and the possibility of escaping parental observation provided by cars and public transport changed all that. It created an ornate ante-room between childhood and adulthood.

The invention of the teenager allowed a space for self-creation, for people to discover who they were and what they liked outside of their family, at exactly the point where they were intellectually and emotionally capable of it, but not yet so stuck in their ways that they found it difficult to do. It became a stage of life that was profoundly amenable to the creation of the individual.

The next bit of repair work on liberalism applied to international relations. Free trade between countries, which had been celebrated by Constant and Mill as a barrier to war and was supported by liberalism's left and right wing, would be encouraged. But the dog-eat-dog nature of the international system would be replaced by a rules-based order.

The governments of the interwar years had been driven into bitter tit-for-tat trade wars, in which they'd pulled up the tariff drawbridge to protect domestic producers.

The job now was to create a global trading system, one based on fairness and cooperation. The first step took place years before the end of the war, in 1941, with a remarkable document called the *Atlantic Charter*. It was the product of a diplomatic mission with impossibly high stakes. On 4th August, British prime minister Winston Churchill and the chiefs of staff boarded a battleship for a journey across the Atlantic Ocean, in conditions of total secrecy. If they had been found by German U-boats, it would have meant the destruction of Britain's political and military high command.

The destination was Placentia Bay, just off Newfoundland in Canada, where Roosevelt had travelled on the heavy cruiser USS Augusta. 'I have an idea that something really big may be happening,' Churchill said as he left his ship. 'Something really big.'

After days of negotiations, the two men emerged with a one-page document comprised of eight clauses describing their vision of a 'better future for the world.'

The *Atlantic Charter* was extraordinarily far-sighted. The first few clauses dealt with the immediate issues of the war. But in clause four, something changed. In a remarkable act of foresight, the document started to outline the first glimmers of what a post-war international trading system would look like. It reflected an understanding between the two men that the financial and trade chaos of the interwar years had been a dress rehearsal for military conflict.

It pledged that the UK and US would endeavour 'to further the enjoyment by all states, great or small, victor or vanquished, of access, on equal terms, to the trade and to the raw materials of the world which are needed for their economic prosperity.'

The next clause promised to 'bring about the fullest collaboration between all nations in the economic field with the object of securing, for all, improved labour standards, economic advancement and social security.' It was a statement of intent. Once the war was over, they were promising to bring order to the international trading system.

The first major international treaty that came from this was the General Agreement on Tariffs and Trade (GATT) in 1947. Its central proposal was that countries work together, in partnership, to agree on a maximum tariff for each good. They would then reduce them, bit by bit, in rounds of negotiation, until that tariff was as low as possible.

At the heart of the system was a rule called Most Favoured Nation. This prevented countries from discriminating in their trade regime. It meant that if Britain put a tariff on whisky from Japan at 10 per cent, for instance, it had to also maintain that rate for everyone else.

It was a block against trade warfare. In the past, if Japan had upset the UK for some reason – either economic or political – the UK would have been able to punish it by increasing tariffs on important Japanese exports for a few weeks. Under GATT, such targeted protection would no longer be legal.

Countries were allowed to unilaterally change tariffs with a single country only in two scenarios: if they provided a much poorer country privileged access as a gift, or if they signed a free trade agreement. This was a specific deal in which two partners lowered their tariffs with each other in order to have a closer economic relationship. The thinking was that these sorts of examples would encourage other states to do their own deals and get equally advantageous access to each other's markets, lowering tariffs further.

None of this was easy. Negotiations between the US and UK were particularly fraught, with the US pushing for immediate Most Favoured Nation provision and Britain hoping for much slower movement. Keynes himself believed that Britain's post-war economic situation required the use of tariffs to protect domestic industry.

'It is an absolutely beautiful day,' US negotiator Winthrop Brown reported home on 30th September 1947. 'The lake is very blue, the hills look like a picture postcard, and the only blots on the landscape are British preferences about which I spend most of the night dreaming.'

The British succeeded initially, but it didn't last long. The signatories to GATT started a series of multilateral trade rounds, from the 1940s to the 1990s, which saw countries reduce their protection levels. By the end, tariffs on industrial goods had been cut right down – although agricultural goods, which are always more sensitive, remained high.

On 15th April 1994, GATT modernised and expanded. One hundred and twenty-three nations signed an agreement turning it into a new international body: the World Trade Organisation (WTO). Today, there are 164 members, including all major trading countries.

A key component of this evolution was the transformation of the existing dispute system into something more closely resembling an international court. Previously, the role of trade law in resolving disputes between the GATT signatories had been somewhat optional. When two GATT members disagreed about something, they could convene a panel of legal experts to advise them who was right. But both parties had to agree a ruling, or it just sat there unenforced.

Under the WTO, the dispute settlement system was locked into place. If a WTO member felt another member wasn't following the rules, they were obliged to hear them out, accept the convening of a panel and accept its ruling as final. The only way out was to appeal to a new appellate court.

Unlike the panels, which would only be called when a dispute arose, this appellate court would sit permanently, with a fixed team of appointed members. Whatever it ruled was binding. On the basis of its decisions, members could raise tariffs against another country within specified limits in response to unfair treatment.

It was a difficult, sensitive, painstaking, generational process, full of late night meetings and claims of unfairness. But the trade rounds boosted global prosperity. During the 25 years after the war, the world economy grew by an average of five per cent a year. World trade rose by about eight per cent per year. And wealth didn't just grow. It was more widely shared. In the liberal democratic world, per capita income sky-rocketed.

By putting in place firm equal rules for trade, the liberal system was increasing the wealth, and consequently the freedom, of the world. But it was about much more than just trade. It was a demonstration that countries could work together to settle their differences, according to a set of rules that applied to the powerful and the weak alike.

In Europe, the scale of national cooperation reached levels never before known in the history of humankind. It started with trade. But at its heart was something much deeper. It was a rejection of nationalism at the deepest possible level.

Europe had now collapsed into war twice, dragging the rest of the world with it on both occasions. If it happened a third time, there was a good chance there would be nothing left. The moral response was therefore to bind nations together, more tightly than they had ever been bound before, so that the entire economic justification for warfare would become logically incoherent.

It started with a speech by Churchill in 1946, in Switzerland, in which he called for a United States of Europe. 'I wish to speak to you today about the tragedy of Europe,' he told his audience. 'This noble continent, comprising on the whole the fairest and the most cultivated regions of the earth, enjoying a temperate and equable climate, is the home of all the great parent races of the western world. If Europe were united in the sharing of its common inheritance, there would be no limit to the happiness, to the prosperity and the glory which its people would enjoy.'

That project began with coal and steel. This was not an accident. These two products were essential to conducting war. If countries could bind those industries together, military conflicts between them would become incomprehensible.

In 1951, under the Treaty of Paris, six countries took that decisive step. Belgium, France, Italy, Luxembourg, the Netherlands, and West Germany formed the European Coal and Steel Community. It was the polar opposite of the response to the First World War. Back then, France had stripped Germany of its coal industry. This time, France and Germany's coal industries joined together.

In 1957, the six countries took one step further, with the European Economic Community.

It developed a customs union. Customs unions do two important things. They harmonise tariffs at the same level on the outside and eradicate them entirely on the inside. If the US sent a banana to Italy, it would face exactly the same tariff as if it sent it to Holland. But if Italy sent a banana to Holland, there would be no tariffs at all. Not on anything. Goods could move freely, without customs checks or payments, across the whole of the customs union.

Those two elements really added up to one thing: the creation of an embryonic single trading entity. Customs checks are a laborious and time-consuming process. They slow down trade between countries and create barriers to companies sending goods overseas. The customs union made them vanish.

Over the next few decades, the European Economic Community grew in size and complexity. Denmark, Ireland and the UK joined in 1973. A little later, the remaining dictatorships of Europe in Greece, Spain and Portugal restored democracy and joined too. Toward the end of the 20th Century, eastern European countries became member states.

Eventually, the renamed European Union (EU) comprised 28 member states, representing half a billion people and a quarter of world's GDP. Its constitutional structure was based on the separation of powers. A Council, comprised of the leader of each member state, operated like a government. A Commission took a role like that of the civil service. A parliament of elected representatives from regions of each member state, called MEPs, acted as the legislature. And a European Court of Justice functioned as the judiciary.

It had become something much vaster than simply coal and steel. It was an entirely new kind of creation, a democratic international organisation which melded whole economies together.

At its heart was the single market.

This initiative solved a universal problem in international trade: domestic regulation. Countries often passed laws affecting goods within their territory. They legislated for welfare standards in the food industry, for instance, or the kinds of chemicals allowed in construction. Once that regulation was in place, it created a barrier to trade. It meant that the goods coming into the country had to be checked to ensure that they complied with that nation's rules.

The European solution was to make all the rules the same, wherever possible.

The single market removed the last obstacle to cross-border trade. There was now no need for any checks on goods within its internal borders. A product could be sent from one end of Europe to another, passing through several countries, without ever being stopped.

The same applied for many services and for capital. And it applied in one other way too, which would constitute one of the remarkable liberal accomplishments in the post-war period. It applied to people.

Anyone, from any European member state, could now go to live and work in any other member state.

Nothing like this had ever existed before. Until the 20th Century, people had been restrained from free movement by money and technology. Long-distance travel simply wasn't viable and when finally it was, it wasn't affordable. Once international travel did become possible, with the possibility of large-scale flows of people, wealthy states quickly put restrictions on who could live there.

The European free movement policy eliminated those rules within the continent. It stripped the state of its power to refuse entry or residence status to EU citizens. For the first time, the individual was being given the freedom to move freely in space. This freedom was restricted to Europe, but as soon as it was established, some people began to dream of something even more ambitious.

No-one thought it would be easy. But for those with the right eyes, with the right temperament, it was at least now conceivable. Perhaps, in the not so distant future, other continents would unite their economies along the European model. Eventually, they would sign trade deals with one another, in which free movement could be included. And suddenly it was not so hard to imagine a world in which each individual could travel freely and without hindrance, for any purpose, and as long as they wished, to anywhere on earth.

It was a dream of a world without borders. A world where the state's ability to block and bar and interfere with the individual as they travelled had finally been brought to an end. Where people's rights to live and move were valued above the state's right to stop them. For now it was just an aspiration for the distant future. But for the first time, the path was visible.

The project to end nationalism through trade had begun with a commitment to eradicate war. And now it was slowly morphing into something else: a vision of truly global freedom.

The final part of the post-war edifice was arguably the most important: human rights. The fascists and communists had destroyed all protections for the individual and then tortured, abused and exterminated minorities.

The liberal solution to this behaviour was individual rights – first articulated by Overton in his prison cell, then codified in the French Revolution's *Rights of Man* and fleshed out by Constant, Taylor and Mill. A force field of protection would be thrown around everyone that would block interference by society or the state.

But these rights had always had a fundamental problem. They might have referred to all people, but in truth they only applied to the citizens of the country declaring them. And they had to be upheld by the state – the very entity that posed the greatest threat to them.

The post-war rights project would be different. It would operate globally. In 1946, the newly formed United Nations, an organisation dedicated to international cooperation to solve world problems, appointed a commission to establish a set of universal human rights.

It collected an extraordinary and eclectic group of individuals, including a Lebanese philosopher, a French public law specialist, a Chinese scholar, and a Chilean judge. The chair was Eleanor Roosevelt, a progressive campaigner and wife of the former American president. They met in a disused gyroscope factory in upstate New York and over the course of 81 meetings thrashed out the *UN Declaration of Human Rights*.

'All human beings are born free and equal in dignity and rights,' article one read. 'They are endowed with reason and conscience and should act towards one another in a spirit of brotherhood.'

The second article established the universality of the rights. They applied to everyone, regardless of 'race, colour, sex, language, religion, political or other opinion, national or social origin, property, birth or other status.' Article three guaranteed 'the right to life, liberty and security of person.'

This was the beating heart of the document.

Articles four to 20 then amassed the liberties that had been assembled over centuries of liberal thought: protection from slavery, or torture, or unlawful detention, the right to equal legal status, to be presumed innocent until proved guilty, to privacy, to free movement within a state and the right to leave it, to asylum, to get married and start a family, to own property, to worship according to whatever religion you choose, to freedom of thought and speech, and to freedom of assembly.

Article 20 and 21 enshrined core democratic values, like the right to peaceful assembly, election and participation in government. Then things became more radical. The next set of rights reflected the new liberalism of the post-war era. They included basic economic demands.

Article 22 guaranteed each individual 'social security' and 'the economic, social and cultural rights indispensable for his dignity and the free development of his personality.' Article 23 guaranteed the right to work in 'just and favourable conditions' and, crucially, protections against unemployment. Work was to be non-discriminatory and provide 'just and favourable remuneration ensuring for himself and his family an existence worthy of human dignity.'

Article 24 guaranteed 'rest and leisure,' including paid holidays. Article 25 created a right to a set standard of living, including 'food, clothing, housing and medical care' and financial security in the case of unemployment. Article 26 protected the right to education.

The General Assembly adopted the declaration by a vote of 48 to zero, with eight abstentions and two non-votes, on 10th December 1948. Finally, for the first time in centuries of liberal struggle, the idea of universal rights for all people had taken on a concrete shape free of national borders.

The first type of rights – the old liberal ones – were branded first generation rights. The second type – the new Keynesian-tinged ones – were branded second generation rights.

The asylum right branched out into its own separate structure. It was the result of a haunting memory from the war. In 1939, a ship named the St Louis, carrying 900 Jewish passengers, had set sail across the Atlantic to escape the Nazi regime. It stopped first in Cuba, but no-one was allowed to disembark. Then it went to Miami in the US. The passengers could see the lights of the city, but immigration authorities prevented them from getting off. Then they appealed to Canada and they too turned them down. So they retreated, back across the water to Germany, where a third of them were subsequently murdered in the Holocaust.

That memory hung grimly over the post-war allies. Their response to it was the Refugee Convention, signed in 1951 and then beefed up with a Protocol in 1967. Anyone with a well-founded fear of persecution on the basis of nationality, politics, religion, or membership of a particular race or ethnic group, now had a right to seek and be granted protection by another country.

In this, as in all parts of the post-war settlement, the message was simple: never again.

†

For all its fresh global energy, the UN Declaration of Human Rights had a significant weakness: it was not directly enforceable. After all, nation states still passed laws and the UN did not.

But that was not as much of an obstacle as people imagined. These rights were enforced in all of the liberal democratic states and those states were the ones with the most economic and political power. Very quickly, they became a set of required standards a country had to meet before it could be treated as modern and civilised, with all the international benefits that would bring. They became the moral foundation for the new global system of liberalism.

They also slowly drifted into international law. In the years that followed, a set of international treaties was drawn up under the auspices of international bodies such as the UN which set out the human rights obligations binding states. Once national governments signed up to them, the treaties gradually exerted influence over how key domestic actors, such as legislators and judges, developed national law. And slowly they became a legal reality.

The domestic enforcement of international human rights law became much more immediate and direct with the creation of the European Convention on Human Rights (ECHR). This comprehensive set of first generation rights entered into force on 3rd September 1953 under the auspices of a new body, called the Council of Europe. It was distinct from the European Union, but as the years went on it acted as a sort of ante-room for membership. Any country trying to get into the EU first had to sign up to the Convention.

The Convention had one very significant difference to the UN Declaration: it had a court, which was established in Strasbourg. Anyone whose country had signed up to it could take their case to this court and have it heard by a judge. It was a seminal moment in the relationship between individual liberty and the separation of power. For the first time, the state was no longer wholly in control. The individual now had rights over the state which could be secured by going over the head of their government to an independent court.

No longer was the state responsible for upholding rights. It was no longer being trusted with acting in a way that limited its own power. Now, there was a place outside of its reach that could guarantee the freedom of the individual.

The actual operation of the court was quite complicated. It could not force the state to change its law. If it found in the individual's favour, it would come to a ruling and state an incompatibility between national law and international human rights law. This ruling triggered a dialogue.

But in practical terms, this rarely made any difference. National governments were under political pressure to abide by the rulings, so countries regularly amended their laws to conform with Strasbourg. European human rights lawyers quickly began to treat it as the key forum for pursuing their claims.

Things became even more efficient in the year 2000, with the creation of the Charter of Fundamental Rights of the European Union. Human rights cases which went against EU law now had instant effect. A ruling in favour of the individual would not just result in a statement of incompatibility. It would automatically change the law itself. And changed EU law would apply not just to the nation of the individual who brought the case, but the entire continent.

Top: Galileo faces the Inquisition in 1633, where he was found 'vehemently suspect of heresy' for heliocentrism. On hearing what happened to him, Descartes held back on publishing *The World*.
René Descartes: 'I am a real thing, and really exist, but what thing? A thinking thing.'

The Putney debates in October and November 1647 proved a decisive moment in the history of political thought. 'And therefore truly, sir, I think it's clear that every man that is to live under a government ought first by his own consent to put himself under that government.'

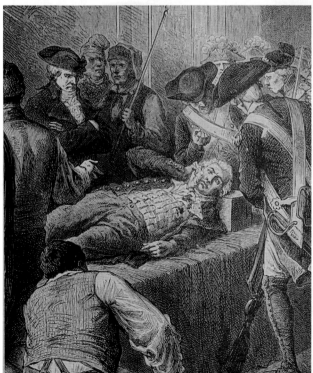

Top: Louis XVI is put under the guillotine blade on 21st January 1793. He tried to protest his innocence, but his voice was drowned out by drums.

Left: Robespierre shot himself in the jaw, shortly before his own encounter with the guillotine, on 28th July 1794. The ensuing bloodbath of the Jacobins and members of the Insurrectionary Commune finally ended the Terror.

John Maynard Keynes: His extraordinary life brimmed with achievement and surprises. He fell deeply in love with his wife, Lydia Lopokova, after previously living as a gay man.

Eleanor Roosevelt: Holding the UN Declaration of Human Rights. For the first time, the idea of universal rights for all people was enshrined in a global document, free of national borders.

Top and Right: Equal rights campaigners in the second half of the 20th Century. The fight for equality rooted itself in liberal ideas and aspired to universal values, unlike some of the social justice movements which came later.

Below: George Orwell and Isaiah Berlin (not pictured) recognised the importance of a sense of belonging.

Top: Activists protest against the US family separation policy in New York City on 18th July 2018. Each new act against immigrants led to demonstrations, as liberals stood firm against nationalism.

Right: The United Kingdom's flag is lowered and removed from the European Parliament building in Brussels on Brexit Day, 31st January 2020.

All these changes limited national sovereignty.

The Most Favoured Nation provision made it difficult for a state to tinker with its tariff rates. The harmonisation of regulations in the EU meant its member states could no longer make all the rules on goods and services for themselves. The creation of human rights law put strict limits on what countries could democratically decide about the treatment of people in their territory.

These decisions flowed from democratic principles. They had been made by elected governments and at any time the public could elect a government to undo them. Nevertheless, they were a limitation on national democracy. They restricted the types of policies which elected governments could pursue.

In some cases that compromise reflected centuries of liberal theory. Liberalism, from its very earliest moments, had tried to balance the rights of the individual with democracy. International human rights law was just the latest stage in that process. It limited what government could do to individuals, even if those measures were supported by a majority of voters.

But other aspects were entirely new. Since the English Civil War, liberalism had been experimenting with how to distribute power to avoid tyranny. Until now, power had been separated at the domestic level, through institutions like the courts. Now something fundamental was happening. Power was being split and allocated internationally.

Countries in the WTO, EU and Council of Europe were pooling their sovereignty. They were accepting that there were some decisions they could no longer make for themselves. Instead they would make them together.

That would, in many cases, give them greater influence, because the impact of their activity was no longer limited to their territory. But in many cases they would also have to abide by decisions that went against them.

That was the price they paid. In return, they received material and political security, immense trade advantages, the right of their citizens to move wherever they pleased, protections against tyrannical government, and the absence of war.

It was a trade off. And in those years after the war, with the memory of bloodshed still fresh, people felt it was worth making.

8. BELONGING

The New World Order represented the next stage of liberal development. It was an advanced experiment in international cooperation, individual rights and the control of the market.

But economics only partly explained the rise of communism and fascism. To really understand why totalitarianism had taken root, you had to go much deeper, right into the human heart, and deal with the difficult things you found lying there. You had to address something liberals had always found it hard to talk about: identity.

Many liberals of the 19th Century, not yet chastened by the horrors of the 20th, had envisaged a straight line of societal progress. They assumed that as people became more free, they would shed their attachments to the group. Communal identity would fall away in favour of liberty, reason and autonomy.

But that hadn't happened – quite the opposite. As people lost their connection to the church and their local area, they seemed to yearn for a new sense of community, which they ultimately found in class and the nation. The reasons that communism and fascism triumphed weren't just about joblessness and bank closures. They were about culture. They were about belonging.

Liberals had almost nothing to say about this. Their model of the individual – from Locke's atomised economic units, to Constant's cosmopolitan traveller, to Taylor and Mill's emphasis on autonomy – seemed inimical to patriotism.

The liberal project was built like an adjudication system between individuals who related to each other through the negotiation of their political rights and their exchange in the market. They just didn't know how to speak this kind of language, to recognise people's need to be part of something larger than themselves, their need for a sense of place.

As difficult as the property issue was, liberals had a tradition to draw on to address it. Cultural issues, on the other hand, made them uncomfortable.

And then two men in England tried to address the problem. One of them was English and never fitted in. The other wasn't and always did. They were both, at heart, outsiders. Their names were George Orwell and Isaiah Berlin.

Orwell was a stubborn socialist journalist, made for dirty typewriters and trench warfare. Berlin was a philosopher nestled into the institutional splendour of Oxford, made for fine restaurants and glamorous dinner parties.

But as distinct as they seemed, they shared crucial qualities. They despised the Third Reich and the Soviet Union in equal measure. They were committed to the notion of the individual. They believed in basing political ideas on what could be practically demonstrated. And they were fascinated by the question of belonging.

It was through their work, conducted at the same time and in the same country, but culturally a million miles apart, that liberalism's relationship with identity started to be articulated.

Once Orwell was dead, he turned into a British myth – a heroic, plain-speaking visionary, with a piercing glare and an unflinching commitment to the truth. It was true, in its way. But life is made of many parts which myths cannot encompass. He was also, in many of his personal relationships, shy, awkward and dejected. He was always on the edge of things.

That characteristic seemed to have already been established by 1911, when he headed off to boarding school at the age of eight, on reduced fees. 'I had no money,' he said later. 'I was weak. I was unpopular. I had a chronic cough. I was cowardly. I smelt.' By the time he left, the institutional snobbery had broken him down. 'Failure, failure, failure – failure behind me, failure ahead of me – that was by far the deepest conviction that I carried away.'

He succeeded in getting the scholarship that took him to Eton, but by this point he was already extremely distant. 'Standing aside from things,' a contemporary said when asked to describe him, 'observing, always observing.' Upon graduation, most of his fellow pupils went to university, but Orwell set off for Burma, a recent annexation to the British Empire, as part of the Indian Imperial Police.

Here, too, his colleagues found him strange and removed. He spent much of the time alone, usually reading. Unlike most recruits, he took time to learn about Burma culture, including its cinema and folklore. He attended the church of the Karen ethnic group, learned the language fluently, and acquired some small tattoos on each knuckle which were favoured by rural Burmese to protect against bullets and snakebites.

Politically, he didn't quite fit in either. There was a left-winger in there somewhere, but also a standard-issue Burma police authoritarian. He subscribed to the progressive magazine *Adelphi*, for instance, but would also get so frustrated by it that he occasionally nailed it to a tree and used it for target practice.

And then something happened, which would help define the kind of man he became. A working elephant went on a rampage with an attack of 'must' – a hormonal surge which leads them to behave aggressively. Orwell set off to deal with the problem, but when he found the animal, rifle slung behind his back, he suddenly had second thoughts.

'As soon as I saw the elephant I knew with perfect certainty that I ought not to shoot him,' he wrote. 'It is a serious matter to shoot a working elephant – it is comparable to destroying a huge and costly piece of machinery. His attack of "must" was already passing off. Moreover I did not in the least want to shoot him.'

But this personal judgement quickly collided with social expectations. 'At that moment I glanced round at the crowd that had followed me. It was an immense crowd, two thousand at the least and growing every minute. And suddenly I realised that I would have to shoot the elephant after all. The people expected it of me and I had got to do it; I could feel their two thousand wills pressing me forward, irresistibly.'

That crowd never really dissipated. It was always there, behind the words he wrote, throughout his life – a reminder of the group's demand to stop thinking for yourself.

In 1927, after nearly five years service, he came back to England on leave and had a realisation, with 'the first sniff of English air.' He would quit the police and become a writer.

Much of that writing was spent formalising his role as the perpetual outsider, operating amid the underclasses of the early 20th Century. He spent some time homeless and wrote it up as *Down and Out in Paris and London*. He investigated life among England's deprived mining communities for *The Road to Wigan Pier*.

It was the 1930s. The great horrors of what was about to happen to the world were starting to make themselves felt. And Orwell had noticed that something was terribly wrong. He was trying to articulate something, a hole at the centre of people's lives, an absence, and the dangerous political movements which it might be filled with.

For a time, he believed it was religion. People had once felt intense comfort during religious observance, but now religion's decline was leaving that sentiment with nowhere to go. Humans had lost their soul, he thought, and not yet found anything to put in its place. 'Very few people,' he said, 'apart from the Catholics themselves, seem to have grasped that the church is to be taken seriously.'

During this period he started attending church. His spiritual involvement was limited – he never seemed to have any faith in God and in fact treated anyone's belief in an afterlife as proof of their dishonesty. But he enjoyed participating in ceremonies.

They seemed to offer him a kind of safety. He befriended a local clergyman at an Anglican church in Hayes, sat through the services and even offered to paint one of the church idols.

In his novel, *A Clergyman's Daughter*, published in 1935, the protagonist, Dorothy, meditated on her own loss of faith. And there Orwell sought to grasp the thing that was missing.

'In another and deeper sense,' he said, 'the atmosphere of the church was soothing and necessary to her, for she perceived that in all that happens in church, however absurd and cowardly its supposed purpose may be, there is something – it is hard to define, but something of decency, of spiritual comeliness – that is not easily found in the world outside. It seemed to her that even if you no longer believe, it is better to go to church than not; better to follow in the ancient ways than to drift in rootless freedom.'

The turning point in Orwell's life came during the Spanish Civil War. It was, in a way, the turning point of the whole pre-war era. From that moment on, the alarming developments in Europe and Russia – the growth of fascism and communism – suddenly took on a specific military dimension and it became clear to almost everyone that another world war was likely.

The civil war started in July 1936, with a military revolt by General Francisco Franco that aimed to destroy the left-wing Popular Front government. It had been intended as a coup d'état, but Franco hesitated and the government armed the trade union militias, leading to a protracted conflict between pro-government forces, called Republicans, and pro-Franco forces, called Nationalists. Soon enough, Stalin intervened on the side of the former and Hitler on the side of the latter. It turned Spain into a dress rehearsal for the Second World War.

The war galvanised opinion across the world. Thousands of foreign sympathisers joined the Republican side via the Communist-dominated International Brigades. Orwell set off to help them. 'I had promised myself to kill one fascist,' he said, 'after all, if each of us killed one they would soon be extinct.'

But it wasn't the fascists who ended up defining what happened to him. They were shadows, over the hills in the distance, who he barely came in contact with. It was what happened on his own side.

What Orwell found in Barcelona was a patchwork of militias, including the anarchist CNT and the Marxist but anti-Stalinist POUM. It was this latter group that he fell in with, largely by accident.

Those early days in Barcelona were euphoric. A social revolution was taking place, in which old forms of hierarchy were being torn down. Deference was being replaced by egalitarianism, authority by anarchist organisation. But when he returned to the city to see his wife after four months fighting on the front line, something had changed.

All armed forces were being incorporated into the government-mandated Popular Army. The CNT and POUM were holding out, but found themselves forced into street battles with the orthodox left as it slipped under Soviet influence. The diverse, grassroots anti-Franco resistance movement was starting to suffocate under Stalin's control.

During one clash, fought between gunmen over the rooftops of Barcelona, Orwell watched a man nicknamed Charlie Chan, who appeared to be a Russian secret service agent, corner those fleeing and tell them it was all the result of an anarchist plot. 'It was the first time,' he said, 'I had seen a person whose profession was telling lies.'

Orwell left this depressing state of affairs to return to battle, but it was to be short lived. At dawn on 20th May 1937, as he came to relieve a guard, a sniper shot him through the throat.

'There seemed to be a loud bang and a blinding flash of light all round me,' he said, 'and I felt a tremendous shock – no pain, only a violent shock, such as you get from an electric terminal; with it a sense of utter weakness, a feeling of being stricken and shrivelled up to nothing.'

The bullet had narrowly missed the main artery. His war was over. He decided to secure a discharge, return to England and get back to writing.

But that decision came too late. He was now associated with the POUM. While he was securing his release papers, the Stalinist liquidation of the party began. It was declared illegal, its buildings seized and everyone connected with it imprisoned.

Orwell returned to the Hotel Continental in Barcelona clutching his release papers and found his wife in the lounge. She walked up to him in a relaxed manner, smiled, put her arm around his neck and whispered: 'Get out.' A warrant had been issued for his arrest.

For a few frenzied days, their lives were in danger. But with good luck, and a side serving of bravery and perseverance, they managed to get back home.

As the train rolled back to London, he watched 'the barges on the miry river, the familiar streets, the posters telling of cricket matches and Royal weddings, the men in bowler hats, the pigeons in Trafalgar Square, the red buses, the blue policemen – all sleeping the deep, deep sleep of England.'

Spain made Orwell realise that Stalinism and fascism were equivalent evils. 'The Spanish war and other events of 1936–7 turned the scale and thereafter I knew where I stood,' he said. 'Every line of serious work that I have written since 1936 has been written, directly or indirectly, against totalitarianism and for democratic socialism.'

In the years to come, conservatives would seek to downplay Orwell's socialism, so he could be turned into a typical anti-Soviet figure of the Cold War, but that was to misunderstand him. He was a socialist, albeit one with an unshakeable commitment to personal freedom. 'I have been convinced that the destruction of the Soviet myth was essential,' he said, 'if we wanted a revival of the socialist movement.'

But he wasn't simply a socialist with liberal sensibilities. He was something else, something really quite unusual. He had split himself in two. There was the civilian, who fought for socialism.

And then there was the writer, who was a liberal, by professional duty.

'Almost certainly we are moving into an age of totalitarian dictatorships,' he wrote in 1940, 'an age in which freedom of thought will be at first a deadly sin and later on a meaningless abstraction. The autonomous individual is going to be stamped out of existence. From now onwards the all-important fact for creative writers is going to be that this is not a writers' world. For as a writer he is a liberal, and what is happening is the destruction of liberalism.'

This did not mean that loyalties – for instance to socialism – did not exist or could be wished away. It simply meant that they could not overrule the personal imperative for honest writing. 'Group loyalties are necessary,' he said, 'yet they are poisonous to literature, so long as literature is the product of individuals.'

By 1941, the bombs had reached England. While they fell, the socialist side of Orwell saw an opportunity for revolution. As it happened, he turned out to be mistaken, but his consideration of the possibility revealed a glimpse of how liberalism could find an accommodation with patriotism. It was an essay called *The Lion and the Unicorn*.

For a while Orwell had presumed that what people were missing was the church. But now it seemed clear that it was something more powerful. Patriotism, he wrote, had 'overwhelming strength' – Hitler and Mussolini had grasped its importance and exploited it in their rise to power. Those who opposed them had not and had paid the price.

People's need for belonging would never go away, Orwell warned. There would never be a world of Constants, adrift from their nation, cosmopolitan, floating between countries as if they were towns. You could either accept this fact and incorporate it into your political agenda, or leave it to the fascists and let them have a monopoly on people's sense of identity.

Orwell chose the former path. He was not being merely strategic, though. He really felt patriotic. His writings were full of long, loving descriptions of the English countryside. He was constantly concerned with a proper sense of place, with a full appreciation for where he was, whether it was Burma, Spain, Wigan, or Southwold.

Orwell's English patriotism did not demand conformity. It did not suggest homogeneity. It was an individual expression of admiration that could only have come from someone who had never quite fitted in, with the kind of eyes and attention to detail which that status gave him. He found the love of his country in tiny details – 'solid breakfasts and gloomy Sundays, smoky towns and winding roads, green fields and red pillar-boxes.' But out of these details he began to paint a picture of a country with general characteristics that were mildly and yet instinctively rebellious.

'All the culture that is most truly native centres round things which even when they are communal are not official – the pub, the football match, the back garden, the fireside and the "nice cup of tea,"' he wrote. 'The liberty of the individual is still believed in, almost as in the 19th Century. But this has nothing to do with economic liberty, the right to exploit others for profit. It is the liberty to have a home of your own, to do what you like in your spare time, to choose your own amusements instead of having them chosen for you from above.'

You could question all of this. Assessments of national character are never entirely free of myth. They are generalisations. But Orwell's conclusions mattered less than how he arrived at them. He envisioned the individual choosing what they wished to associate with in the national culture, not a homogeneous sense of exclusive identity imposed on them from above.

His aim was to incorporate love of country into the socialist political agenda, so that the working class would be inspired to revolt. That project was a failure. But in that failure there was a deep insight, which could be adopted by liberals. It was possible for those who admired freedom to still feel a deep affinity with the nation, without in any way reducing their commitment to the individual.

In 1945, with the war over, Orwell started to refine this idea in a way that incorporated his abiding concern with objective truth. He did it in an extraordinary essay called *Notes on Nationalism*.

Nationalism was the dark side of patriotism. It was what happened when you allowed those without a love of the individual to establish a monopoly on the love of country. Orwell defined it in two ways: uniformity and the absence of independent moral judgement.

'By "nationalism" I mean first of all the habit of assuming that human beings can be classified like insects and that whole blocks of millions or tens of millions of people can be confidently labelled "good" or "bad,"' he explained. 'But secondly – and this is much more important – I mean the habit of identifying oneself with a single nation or other unit, placing it beyond good and evil and recognising no other duty than that of advancing its interests.'

He then made an interesting intellectual leap. He extended the nationalist instinct he was describing to many other kinds of group loyalties: religious, cultural and political. Its form could be a church, or a class, a party, even pacifism. In England at the time, he thought the dominant form was 'old-fashioned British jingoism.'

As soon as this group identity took hold, people's capacity to form independent thoughts started to disintegrate. Eventually, the objective world of evidence and universal moral standards simply disappeared. A British Tory would defend self-determination in Europe but oppose it in India. Outrages like hostage-taking or forced labour would be treated as either acceptable or unacceptable depending on who did them.

Such group loyalists were simply uninterested in facts that did not fit their world view. Newspapers then emerged to cater to their lopsided perceptions. Those papers reported in a way that would only ever pander to the prejudices of their readers. And suddenly the impression of the world that people experienced had no connection to what was really happening. Politics drifted from reality.

This was a pathway that anyone could end up taking if they were not vigilant about their own independent judgement. It meant individuals had a duty to analyse their opinions, to repeatedly challenge whether they corresponded to reason and evidence, to maintain a perpetual vigilance against the temptations of their allegiances. 'I do believe that it is possible to struggle against them, and that this is essentially a moral effort,' Orwell said. 'The emotional urges which are inescapable, and are perhaps even necessary to political action, should be able to exist side by side with an acceptance of reality.'

Orwell was grasping for something profound. There was a fundamental struggle between the individual and the group. But unlike many previous liberals, he had not simply given up on the group and aspired solely towards individual identity. He was acknowledging the struggle as a basic fact of political life – one which would never go away, could not be dispelled by theory. It tugged at the heart. The yearning for belonging had to be simultaneously accepted and restrained.

He had not settled this vexed issue. But he had done something important. He had identified it. And he had set out the broad parameters as to how it might be resolved. The goal was the accommodation of belonging. And the means to achieve it were freedom and truth.

Having pushed it in striking new directions, Orwell then took liberalism back to its roots. He didn't do that in a piece of philosophical theory, or even a newspaper article. He did it through science fiction. It was called *Nineteen Eighty-Four*.

He set off to write it in 1947, on the Scottish island of Jura. The very act of creating it was a struggle. In the previous three years he had lost his wife, his mother and his sister in quick succession. He was plagued by the advanced stages of tuberculosis and his writing retreat was a taxi, two boats, a bus and a train away from the nearest hospital.

And yet, over the next two years, he got it down on the page – first as a written scrawl, then again in a total rewrite, and finally as a typed manuscript, which he churned out, propped up in bed with a typewriter, a cigarette hanging out his mouth, in between bouts of fever and bloody coughing fits, at a pace of 4,000 words a day, every day. By December 1948, it was done. A year later, he was dead.

What he left behind was one of the most evocative and influential works of liberal theory ever published.

By 1973, sales had passed one million in the UK and at least 10 million in the US. Copies were smuggled into Czechoslovakia, Hungary, Poland and Russia. *The Washington Post* called it 'the most famous, the most frequently alluded-to book written in the last 25 years.' Its terms – Newspeak, Big Brother, Thought Police, Room 101, doublethink – have entered the public lexicon. Barely a day goes by without them coming up in political discussion, even now.

Orwell had done something that no other liberal had managed: he had stitched liberal thought into popular culture. He created a world that was so vivid and morally impactful that it buried itself deep in people's political assumptions.

In *Nineteen Eighty-Four*'s futuristic world, one of the regional super-states, Oceania, was ruled over by a nominally socialist party called Ingsoc. Its figurehead was a man called Big Brother, a Stalin archetype whose face beamed down on everyone at all times.

Winston Smith, the book's protagonist, despised Oceania's regime and found a kindred spirit in Julia, a party member who worked in the same building. They embarked on an illicit sexual relationship before meeting O'Brien, a senior official who claimed to be part of a conspiracy to destroy the party. But it was a trap. Smith and Julia were arrested and sent for re-education.

The oppression, conformity and re-education in Oceania almost perfectly mirrored the demolition of liberalism by totalitarianism. Orwell introduced the idea of a telescreen – a two-way video connection which allowed the party to monitor what was happening in people's homes. It worked to create precisely the kind of always-on behaviour control which the mutual surveillance of the Soviet system produced in its own citizens. Winston made a constant effort to maintain a facial expression that would protect him from scrutiny, in the same way that many Russians during Stalin's regime had worn a public mask to conceal their true feelings.

Orwell understood that fascist and communist regimes wanted to exercise absolute control over the individual. Of course, this meant physical control, but more importantly it involved mental control. By writing a diary, Winston 'had committed the essential crime that contained all others in itself. Thoughtcrime.'

The Ingsoc regime was dedicated to the end of all thoughtcrime. A new kind of language was introduced, Newspeak, which aimed to reduce and reformat vocabulary to the extent that critical or individual thoughts were no longer even possible.

The central struggle of *Nineteen Eighty-Four* was not really Winston against the system. It was the ability of the brain to remain individual under the crushing oppression of the party. 'Nothing was your own,' Winston thought, 'except the few cubic centimetres inside your skull.'

Once he was captured, this proposition was tested to destruction. The party set about trying to identify and destroy that autonomy through relentless beatings, torture and degradation. In his torture chamber, after what may have been weeks or months of physical and psychological abuse, Winston was left with only one thing to cling to: objective reality. He understood a central principle. 'Freedom is the freedom to say that two plus two makes four. If that is granted, all else follows.'

Objective reality existed outside the control of the party. The authorities could do anything to you – kidnap you, destroy the evidence of the past, bludgeon you into submission with propaganda, fake all the information you received, make you betray your friends – but as long as objective reality existed, you could still hold on to something. You could still come to independent judgements. Without it, there was no hope. The party would have full control.

In asserting this, Orwell's liberalism reached further back than any of the other modern thinkers – past Taylor and Mill, Locke, Overton and Rainsborough – to Descartes. The defence that Orwell found to totalitarianism was as old as liberalism itself: the individual rational self, capable of constructing hypotheses about the world around it.

That possibility was unacceptable to Ingsoc. It wanted to break Winston completely. After endless rounds of torture, he was finally interrogated by O'Brien himself. Reality did not exist in the individual mind, he told him. 'Whatever the party holds to be truth, is truth.'

At the crucial moment, as Winston was ready to be broken, O'Brien told him: 'You do not exist.' Winston's mind cascaded downwards under obscene psychological pressure and tried desperately to reach out and grab the Cogito.

'Once again the sense of helplessness assailed him,' Orwell wrote. 'He knew, or he could imagine, the arguments which proved his own non-existence; but they were nonsense, they were only a play on words. Did not the statement, "You do not exist," contain a logical absurdity?'

But his position was hopeless and soon enough his grip slipped. He submitted completely to the party. The Cogito had been undone. Liberalism had been strangled at birth.

Winston was considered harmless enough to be released. As the novel came to an end, he sat in a cafe and, totally defeated, traced a slogan in the dust on the table: '2+2=5.'

There was no light, no sense of hope in the story. Orwell had presented a vision of a hellish future without objectivity or individuality. For many critics, that was too much. The darkness was just too severe, the sense of human fragility too bleak. But they had misunderstood.

Orwell wasn't trying to portray a world without hope. He was writing a call to arms. He wanted to demonstrate the extent of the threat from totalitarian thought. And he wanted to show how it could be defeated. The defence lay in a vigorous defence of objective reality. That was the only route to freedom, as it had been since the dawn of the Cogito.

Back in real-world England, there was another man who would take that commitment and pursue it. Like Orwell, he was taking the empirical reality of the 20th Century, the fact that people demonstrated a clamour for belonging, and trying to enmesh it in liberal theory. The manner in which he did so would drive liberalism to the brink of the abyss and then leave it with a startling new formulation. He was Isaiah Berlin.

Berlin's sense of identity was composed of three parts: his Russian birth, his Jewish heritage and his English ideas.

'I am a Russian Jew from Riga,' he said, 'and all my years in England cannot change this. I love England, I have been well treated here, and I cherish many things about English life, but I am a Russian Jew; that is how I was born and that is who I will be to the end of my life.'

He carried this outsider status with him wherever he went. But unlike Orwell, he was never on the edge of things. He was right in the heart of them. Even as a young child he was immensely popular. By adulthood, he was enjoying some of the most prestigious positions in British academia. He was awarded the Most Excellent Order of the British Empire in 1946, knighted in 1957, and appointed to the Order of Merit in 1971. He dined and gossiped with the most powerful and influential people on earth.

Unlike perhaps any other thinker in this book, he was profoundly contented. When asked about life, he said: 'I wish it would continue indefinitely. Why not?'

His intellect operated at an astonishingly high level. He was fluent in English, French, German, Italian, Hebrew, Latin, Russian and Ancient Greek. He showed, in the words of Henry Hardy, his principal editor, 'the unexpectedly large possibilities open to us at the top end of the range of human potential.'

He did not write. None of his important political works were intended to be books – they were just packaged into print afterwards. He did not sit alone and study either. What he did, arguably better than anyone alive, was talk. When he came to formulate his thoughts, he dictated them, so that in the end there was no actual writing, there was merely the transcription of what he had said.

His speech was like a machine-gun fire of ideas and associations, delivered at impenetrable speed. The poet TS Eliot described it as 'torrential eloquence.' When he was in Washington, Berlin was told that he would need to speak more slowly if he wanted Americans to understand him. 'Yes I know, I know, I know,' he replied. 'But if I did, I should be quite a different person, quite a different person.'

Those who knew him well were eventually able to understand what he was saying. When his biographer Michael Ignatieff first spoke to him, all he could hear was the relentless stream of words, seemingly with no break. But after 10 years of interviewing him, he began to get used to the 'arcane precision' of his speech.

'Even if the subordinate clauses open up a parenthesis that seems to last forever, they do close, eventually, in a completed thought,' he concluded. 'Each sentence carries clarity along its spine with qualification entwined around it. This darting, leaping style of speaking is a style of thinking: He outlines a proposition and anticipates objections and qualifications as he speaks, so that both proposition and qualification are spun out in one and the same sentence simultaneously.'

Towards the end of his life, a Russian accent started to creep back into his speech. And that made something clear. His upper-class Oxford intellectual voice was not natural. It was an impersonation by a Russian Jew from Riga, who had poured himself into a British mould, but spent the years in Britain thinking very deeply about what it meant to truly belong.

Berlin was born in Riga, the capital of Latvia, in 1909, then part of the Russian empire. At the time Russia restricted the entry of Jews into certain trades and professions, but Riga lay outside those regulations.

Then the First World War arrived. Russia and Germany faced off against one another, leaving his community – German-speaking with Russian citizenship – in a difficult place. The Russian high command, blaming Jews for helping the enemy, started to deport them beyond enemy lines. Berlin's father moved the family to Andreapol, a small town an hour or so away.

An old rabbi became his first teacher, teaching him and other pupils the Hebrew alphabet. 'Dear children,' he told them, 'when you get older, you will realise how in every one of these letters there is Jewish blood and Jewish tears.' And Berlin did realise it. Decades later, when he recounted this story, he stared out the window, visibly moved, and said: 'That is the history of the Jews.'

The family were shifted to St Petersburg just in time to see the regime disintegrate during the Russian revolution. He was seven and a half when he saw a group of men bundle past with a municipal policeman who had stayed loyal to the tsar, probably on the way to his death. Soon the Bolsheviks were censoring newspapers and armed men appeared at the doors of their apartments ordering them to form a house committee.

In 1919 the family tried to move back to Riga, but the experience was distressing. They were forced off the train and told they would have to spend a week in a Russian bath for delousing. Only a bribe avoided it. The ensuing train journey saw fellow Latvians sit in their carriage and deliver a constant stream of anti-semitism. When his mother spoke out, they accused her of being a Russian spy and police came on board to arrest her. Another bribe was required to release her.

That was the breaking point. There was clearly nowhere left to call home. So in February 1921, the family moved to England. Berlin arrived a young child with no English, but within months he'd assimilated into his new environment. When a boy in school called him 'a dirty German' the other boys beat him up. This habit would continue throughout his life. He was able to be accepted almost instantly, almost everywhere.

After school he went to Corpus Christi College in Oxford, gaining a first class degree in classics and the John Locke Prize in philosophy, and then, in 1932, he won the prize fellowship at All Souls. He was the first Jew ever to receive the honour. The story of his appointment ran in the *Jewish Chronicle*. The chief Rabbi wrote him a letter of congratulations. At the age of just 23, he was already well known and part of one of the most elite institutions in the country.

When John Plamenatz, a Serbian political philosopher, was elected to All Souls years later, he confided in Berlin that he always felt alone when in a room with a pair of Englishmen, because he felt a silent conspiracy between them. Berlin couldn't understand what he was on about. He loved England and attributed to it a fundamental liberal civility which accorded with Orwell's view.

And perhaps that was why he found it so easy to fit in. Because he projected back to the English all the stories they liked to tell themselves about themselves. Or perhaps he was just doing as Orwell had done, and selecting those parts of national identity that he liked himself. Regardless, that was how he viewed belonging – as a choice. When he was asked about his father's pride in his Hassidic ancestors, Berlin was dismissive. Origins did not matter. They were a full stop. Taking pride in them was a form of surrender to a determinism of the bloodline. Instead, he valued his mother's outburst at the anti-semites on the train to Riga, the moments you learned from and used to piece together your own identity.

Like Orwell, he was fascinated by the religious embrace that could be placed around that sense of belonging, despite rejecting the belief itself. 'I have never known the meaning of the word God,' he said. 'I cannot even claim to be an atheist or an agnostic – I am somewhat like a tone-deaf person in relation to music.'

But regardless, Berlin kept to the Jewish festivals all his life. They were an expression of allegiance and provided a sense of meaning. 'Stone-dry atheists,' he said, 'don't understand what men live by.'

In the summer of 1934, he made his first trip to Palestine, which was then in a tense stand-off between Arabs, Jews and the British Colonial Office, that governed the area. When the train through the Sinai desert crossed into Palestine a Jewish conductor in uniform asked for his ticket. Berlin was surprised to find that he had burst into tears. It was the first time he had ever seen a Jewish person in a position of authority.

But once inside he found something odd. He did not feel comfortable. 'As for the Jews,' he wrote, 'they are most odd and fascinating, and I felt equally uneasy with them and away from them, like relations one hasn't seen for 30 years or something.'

Berlin was a Zionist. The creation of the state of Israel, he believed, would restore to Jews 'not merely their personal dignity and status as human beings, but what is vastly more important, their right to choose as individuals how they shall live.' But his joint loyalties – to Britain on the one hand and Jewishness on the other – were about to be sorely tested.

It began with the Second World War. The fighting provided a stark reminder that there was a level of British life to which he would never be admitted.

Berlin volunteered for war work immediately, but was told that he could not take up a position because he was born in Latvia. He was left in Oxford with nothing to do while others went off to make themselves useful.

And then an opportunity presented itself. An associate said he could secure him a position as a press officer at the British embassy in Moscow. Berlin jumped at the chance. He'd been keen to return to Russia throughout his adult life and was desperate to help.

The plan fell apart as soon as he arrived in America, en route to Russia. But with typical good luck, he was instead offered a job with the British embassy's press service in New York. He started small, going through press clippings to compile a weekly report for the Ministry of Information on American public opinion. His reports became so influential that he was soon asked to provide a weekly summary of US opinion for the Foreign Office, working out of the British embassy in Washington.

His talent for lunching, dining and gossiping was set free, in service of his country. He amassed a vast web of American contacts – journalists, editors, congressmen, lobbyists, everyone who mattered – and used it to tease out information from the deepest recesses of the American government.

His dictated weekly summaries had the most indiscreet revelations edited out and were then sent to the Foreign Office and from there to other departments, including the Cabinet Office. Soon Churchill himself was reading them. He was intrigued enough to ask who wrote them. The Foreign Office reply read: 'Mr Berlin, of Baltic Jewish extraction, by profession a philosopher.' The prime minister found them impressive but perhaps a bit too colourful. 'The summaries are certainly well written,' he told his confidant, Anthony Eden. 'I have a feeling that they make the most of everything.' Eden replied: 'I agree. There is perhaps a too generous Oriental flavour.'

So even there, playing a crucial role for the country and publishing material which was read across the political establishment, there was an unavoidable sense that Berlin was still not quite British – just a bit too exotic, a tad too Jewish.

That Jewish identity started to put him in delicate situations. He developed a two-sided role in which he advised British officials on how to manage the Jewish lobby in the US while simultaneously advising the Jewish lobby on how to handle the British.

In June 1943, that balance tipped in one direction. London was concerned that Arab support for the war effort might be lost if they came to believe that a victory would result in a Jewish state in Palestine. The American ambassador shared that concern and urged Churchill and Roosevelt to issue a joint statement insisting the issue be deferred until after an Allied victory.

Berlin found this intolerable. So he took a decisive step. He secretly informed leading figures in the Jewish lobby of the plans. They exploded in anger and demanded the president cancel the declaration. Then he told the British that the news of the declaration had somehow leaked out, while covering up his role as the leaker. It worked. On 8th August, the US State Department informed the British it was withdrawing the declaration.

The Foreign Office was outraged. It demanded Berlin discover how the Jewish lobby had discovered the information. He made up a purposefully amusing story, whose tone served to conceal his culpability. That worked too and the issue was forgotten. But it had revealed something profound about his mixed identity. When it came to it, he placed his Jewish loyalties over his British ones.

In 1945, as the war wound down, he was given a new assignment that would put him in touch with the third part of his identity. He was sent to Moscow to provide a dispatch on American-Soviet-British relations in a post-war world. His experience there brought his childhood back to him immediately. He had not heard his native language spoken on the street since he was a boy. 'I had forgotten,' he said, 'that such emotions and expressions existed.'

They were, he told his parents, the fullest weeks of his life. 'Need I describe to you the crunching snow, the cupolas of the churches, the crisp air, the peasants, the fur caps, the Russian timbre of speech in the streets, the distant sound of the Red Army men singing as they march?'

But it was in St Petersburg, now renamed Leningrad, that he would have the meeting which changed his life. Her name was Anna Akhmatova. She was one of the most important Russian poets of the 20th Century. The Communist Party had taken everything from her. Her first husband had been executed by the Soviet secret police in 1921. The authorities killed or imprisoned countless of her friends in an attack on the intelligentsia. She was deemed a proponent of the introspective 'bourgeois aesthetic,' and vilified by the state and her former supporters. Her work had been banned in 1925 and she hadn't published anything for two decades. Most people outside of Russia presumed she was dead. But she was very much alive.

One evening she and Berlin sat on opposite sides of a room in her apartment and talked for hours, covering every topic that came into their heads, from the personal to the abstract. When he rose, kissed her hand and left, he discovered that it was 11 in the morning.

The connection they established that night stayed with them forever. He was the first visitor for decades from a Europe she had lost all contact with. She was the living embodiment of the pride of Russian culture, somehow still breathing, still unbeaten, after years of persecution. An encapsulation of moral and artistic integrity, of the ability of the soul of a country to withstand decades of intellectual assault.

'He will not be a beloved husband to me,' she wrote afterwards, 'but what we accomplish, he and I, will disturb the 20th Century.'

Berlin returned home in April 1946, at the age of 37, and renewed his academic career. For the rest of his life, he channelled his internal struggles into one of the most startling, challenging and contentious explorations of liberal theory of the 20th Century.

What he did is not easily defined. He was not a systematic thinker. He was deeply suspicious of those who constructed complete systems of thought. Nor was he really clear when he was speaking in his own voice. Much of his work involved imagining himself as a thinker in history in order to realise previously hidden elements and connections. You have to disentangle him from the parts he played.

His work covered different areas of philosophy – from epistemology to ethics and politics. Sometimes it demanded and other times resisted being amalgamated into a clear summary. He was a proper liberal in this respect. He resisted definition. He did not fit into any kind of normal intellectual, moral or political category. He was also inconsistent and often unclear. His work was a beautiful mess, a kind of playdough, out of which you could mould any number of political ideas.

What united his thoughts, however, was his unending and consistent belief in the freedom of the individual. He fought for this principle all his life. This is the value you have to keep uppermost in your mind when you follow Berlin down some twisting and treacherous paths.

It began with belonging. This wasn't some kind of irrelevance, as many liberals had treated it, or something for people to discard as they grew more sophisticated. It was a central feature of the human condition. Like Orwell, Berlin was intent on looking at how people really behaved in their day-to-day lives, and prioritising that empirical self over abstract theories.

'This rejection of natural ties,' he said, 'seems to me noble but misguided. When men complain of loneliness, what they mean is that nobody understands what they are saying: to be understood is to share a common past, common feelings and language, common assumptions, possibility of intimate communications – in short, to share common forms of life.'

Language played a particularly important role in this. Belonging was bound up with the experience of being understood and thereby achieving recognition. My own people, he said 'understand me, as I understand them; and this understanding creates within me the sense of being somebody in the world.' This understanding predominantly operated at the national level and was often expressed through patriotism.

But belonging was not the only good in the world. It was unusually powerful, a fundamental aspect of human need, but there were others. Some were universal, others operated only at particular times, in particular cultures. Liberty. Equality. Justice. Mercy. Courage. Studiousness. Hedonism. Romantic love. Friendship.

Art. Charity. Berlin was going beyond the celebration of freedom, to the things it made possible, and basing his philosophy on them. They all mattered. Everything started with them.

This idea was called pluralism.

These goods did not always happily coexist. They often came into conflict with each other. 'Some of the great goods cannot live together,' he said. 'That is a conceptual truth. We are doomed to choose, and every choice may entail an irreparable loss.' His world was one of constant unavoidable moral tragedy. It existed not just in society but 'within the breast of a single individual.'

People were all, in their lives, impacted by the tragedy of competing goods. Those who stayed single, for instance, lost the sense of contentment and reassurance that could come from starting a family. Those who started a family lost the excitement and vitality that could come from being single. Those who embraced the heroic virtues of the ancient Greeks – of it being 'honourable and glorious for a man to fight for his country' – had to give up the Christian value of turning the other cheek.

Berlin illustrated this idea with an actual case from wartime. A government official had discovered that leaks were coming from his office. If they continued, the lives of the people fighting Nazi Germany would be put at risk. But he had no idea who was leaking, so he sacked everyone. They would never be able to get another government job. And worse, they would go the rest of their lives with the suspicion of treachery hanging over them. But the leak had been stopped. Lives were saved.

Berlin happened to believe that he had done the right thing, but that didn't really matter. His point was that there was no right answer. It was a moral tragedy.

At their most severe, these tragedies were the result of something called incommensurable goods. These were values that were 'equally ultimate,' for which there was no common measure to establish a fixed way of deciding between them. They were often fundamental: liberty and equality, justice and mercy, freedom and belonging.

'If, as I believe,' he said, 'the ends of men are many, and not all of them are in principle compatible with each other, then the possibility of conflict – and of tragedy – can never wholly be eliminated from human life, either personal or social.'

Think back to the thought experiment that was used to dismantle Bentham's rigid Utilitarianism: you are in a boat with your mother and a scientist who might one day cure cancer. The boat sinks and you save your mother.

Berlin wouldn't question that decision. But he asked people to realise that it was still a tragedy. Values clashed – personal affinity with social obligation – and you picked one of them. No-one, apart from a few hardened Utilitarians, would condemn you for it. But a tragedy took place nonetheless.

There was a very stark consequence to all this, one which the human mind, and especially the minds of those who are interested in politics, finds intolerable: there would be no happy endings. There would never be a day in which the problems of humanity would go away. Conflict was a fundamental attribute of the human condition. It would never stop.

This, for Berlin, was a description of humanity as it really was. It was an empirical assessment of how humans actually behaved, rather than how philosophers pretended they did.

Berlin looked back through the history of thought. It was, in most cases, a history of denying the reality of human life. Philosophers kept insisting that there was a mythical authentic self that lay separate to the way people truly behaved.

This was what Rousseau and Marx had done. They had imagined a collective higher self – either in the general will or class consciousness – which was disconnected from how people acted in real life. And then their disciples, in the years after their death, had tried to bludgeon humans into the desired shape, at terrible cost.

But Berlin did not restrain himself just to the standard enemies of liberalism. He turned his guns on liberals themselves.

It wasn't just the idea of a collective higher self that was the problem. It was any notion of dividing humans into different selves. It was anything we introduced beyond their actual demonstrable behaviour.

Taylor and Mill, for instance, had promoted the idea of higher and lower pleasures, which suggested that there was a higher self there – one which was rational and autonomous – that sat above the self that was animalistic or frivolous.

Once that distinction was drawn, it was easy for rulers to start suppressing people's actual activity in order to liberate their supposedly true self. The very idea of an authentic self, even at an individual level, opened the door to tyranny. 'This is one of the most powerful and dangerous arguments in the entire history of human thought,' Berlin insisted.

There was a sense in Berlin's work that this was where liberalism was heading all this time. This was what happened when it really committed to empiricism, to the individual, to freedom. But there was also a sense that he had done something terribly dangerous.

He had let the genie out the bottle. Liberals had spent generations not opening the box marked 'belonging' for a reason, because as soon as one of them did so, all sorts of troubling conclusions started spilling out.

Berlin's logic seemed to eradicate any hope of a unified system of political thought. It challenged any claim to liberal superiority.

His theory of pluralism appeared to make freedom, reason and autonomy – the totems of liberalism – equal to everything else. They were just values, like all the others, no greater than honour, or strength, or beauty.

If that conclusion was accepted, then very bad things happened. It opened the door to moral relativism – the view that there are no universal principles and no dominant philosophy. Freedom would have no greater purchase than any other value, it would offer no basis upon which to judge people's actions or government policies. Anything would be tolerable. Nazism and Stalinism would be just as valid as anything else.

Berlin's process of thought seemed to open up a terrible abyss. It was as if freedom and empiricism had committed suicide.

For some people, that's how it stayed. There have been many anti-liberal figures who embraced Berlin. For them, he opened up a set of truths that were far more dangerous than he understood. Pluralism made liberalism extinct.

But that was not Berlin's intention, nor was it entailed by what he said. Out of the rubble of what he did to liberalism, you could piece together a response to his questions which repaired its structure.

It started with the goods which Berlin had described – all the various values, desires and ideals of human life.

They were important. They mattered. They reflected the full range of human life as it was really lived. So it followed that decent societies should encourage as many of them as possible and ensure people could embrace them if they wanted.

Human lives were defined by the choices they made out of these values: to go to war or stay home and look after your father, to dedicate yourself to scholarship or campaign for political change, to earn lots of money or help the vulnerable in charitable work. If society was to reflect actual human behaviour, it had to allow for those choices to be made. And that entailed a rejection of any act that limited them. 'If pluralism is a valid view,' Berlin said, 'then toleration and liberal consequences follow.'

Choice was therefore the central focus of the human experience. It was essential to the self.

This thought freed liberty from the suffocating pressure of Berlin's pluralism. To choose you must be free. It therefore stood above all other values as the precondition upon which they could be explored. If pluralism was true, Berlin said, 'the necessity of choosing between absolute claims is then an inescapable characteristic of the human condition. This gives its value to freedom.'

But how were these choices to be made? Sometimes Berlin seemed to suggest that it was just by jumping one way or another – as if justice and mercy, for instance, would be selected almost at random. But at other times he stressed that reason could be used to make choices between incommensurable goods.

The key to this lay in the context of the decision. Take the Utilitarian boat example. In this case, the person would rationally save their mother, because the role of personal affiliation was stronger than the requirements of social obligation. But in a different type of example – if they were a judge presiding over a case that involved their mother, for instance, or if they were an official awarding a public contract – they might rationally not allow personal affiliation to overrule social obligations.

In most legal situations, justice took precedence over mercy. But there were situations where that might not apply. When South Africa emerged from a system of apartheid – a form of institutionalised racial segregation – in the mid-90s, the government instituted a Truth and Reconciliation process. It offered an amnesty for the crimes of the past. Mercy was prioritised over justice, in the name of national unity.

What was crucial in these instances was a capacity to assess the context in which they took place. Even if values could not be weighed in the abstract, they often could be in particular cases. 'The concrete situation,' Berlin said, 'is almost everything.'

This assessment of values in context involved reason. And liberals had a story about how that kind of reason was accomplished, told best by Taylor and Mill. It was the story of autonomy – of an individual being educated enough to assess what they wanted in life, of being able to stand back from a situation and take a critical look at their desires, free from the crushing influence of their society or the culture around them. This was therefore a requirement of the choices at the heart of human life.

Berlin's earthquake had flattened liberal thought. But liberty, reason and autonomy could be retrieved from the wreckage and placed back on top as the chief principles of political society. They were meta-values, which could be used to appraise everything else meaningful in human life. However, they required a further meta-value, another guiding principle over the others. It was moderation.

If it was true that there would always be conflict and moral tragedy, the system governing human life had to involve a generous assessment of human imperfection and disagreement. It was based on accepting conflict, not pretending it could be eliminated. And that entailed a kindness in disagreement, a gentleness in the management of division.

'The collisions, even if they cannot be avoided, can be softened,' Berlin said. 'Claims can be balanced, compromises can be reached.'

These, then, were the tests. Berlin's liberalism encouraged people to embrace the full varieties of life in whatever manner they wanted – whether it was patriotism, hedonism, duty, romance, charity or anything else. But the embrace of those values stopped the moment they challenged freedom, reason, autonomy or moderation. Because to undermine those values was to undermine the capacity to embrace values in the first place.

After all that destruction, what was left? It seemed like a liberalism that didn't look all that different from what came before. Freedom, reason and autonomy were back on top, as the guiding principles of political society, joined by moderation.

But if you looked a little closer, this new liberalism was meaningfully different, in the sophistication with which it answered questions that had dogged it for centuries.

Berlin had committed liberalism more deeply to its founding ideas: of doubt, complexity and empirical reality. It fixed its gaze on what humans actually did, instead of what philosophers thought they should. It was more truthful, permissive and humane.

But there was something else, something properly vital, which stood above all that. By placing values at the foundation of his thoughts, Berlin had given liberalism a human warmth.

Until Berlin, there had often been the sense of liberalism perhaps being slightly cold. Locke's theory was developed with the aim of settling property disputes. Even Taylor and Mill, who understood and celebrated the diversity of human life, were fundamentally concerned with managing the rules of non-interference between individuals.

But Berlin's theory was built out of the confusing joys and agonies of the human experience. His liberalism was not just a way of managing the disputes which emerged, but also encouraging as many of the goods as possible. Liberalism was required as the guardian of human life in all its diversity and complexity.

It was liberalism that safeguarded love, honour, disinterest, obsession, discipline, joy, stoicism and everything else. It protected people's ability to choose what they wanted, did not lie to them about what that would entail, and ensured that each value was underpinned with a consideration for individual freedom.

That included, most importantly of all, the value upon which Berlin had himself laboured: belonging.

Both Orwell and Berlin had started with acceptance. They accepted that patriotism mattered to people. Not all of them perhaps, and not all the time, but enough to make it a powerful source of identity and self-definition.

Orwell's response to that acceptance was political and personal. Politically, he urged liberals to recognise the force of patriotism so that fascists could not monopolise it. Personally, he recognised that the tug of belonging and group membership must be mediated by a commitment to truth and objectivity.

Berlin's response was philosophical. If liberalism was grounded in the individual, he argued, then whatever the individual cared about was important. Liberalism was bound, by its own principles, to recognise and appreciate an individual's aspirations. Patriotism mattered because it mattered to the individual. And it stopped mattering the moment it restricted the individual.

What emerged was a liberal patriotism, one which was regulated by freedom. It was the individual love story which sprang from within, not the slab of uniformity imposed from without. It was open. It was diverse. It was plural.

9. CRASH

Hayek's counter-revolution began in April 1947, at the top of a mountain in Switzerland.

Laissez-faire liberals were in a state of disarray after Keynes' victory, but Hayek did not give up. 'Everywhere I went I met someone who told me that he fully agreed with me, but that at the same time he felt totally isolated in his views and had nobody with whom he could even talk about them,' he said. 'This gave me the idea of bringing these people, each of whom was living in great solitude, together in one place.'

He invited about 60 people to Hotel du Parc, on Mont Pèlerin. Thirty-seven turned up. Among them was a young Chicago economist in his mid-thirties named Milton Friedman. 'Here I was, a young, naive provincial American, meeting people from all over the world,' Friedman later recalled, 'all dedicated to the same liberal principles as we were; all beleaguered in their own countries, yet among them scholars, some already internationally famous, others destined to be.'

The meeting was barely noticed at the time, even in economic circles. But the people who attended its annual summits, in particular Friedman, would eventually turn back the Keynesian tide.

Hayek and Friedman presented it as a liberal fight against authoritarianism, but there was nothing authoritarian about Keynesianism and they did not have a monopoly on liberalism. In fact, they were engaged in a liberal civil war: the right wing of liberalism versus the left.

Friedman entered Hayek's movement when it was at its weakest. The man himself was completely defeated. Suffering from recurring bouts of clinical depression, Hayek eventually retreated back to Austria. 'His ideas were not fashionable,' his son Laurence said. 'Nobody seemed to listen to him. Nobody seemed to agree with him. He was alone.'

A new leader emerged in Friedman. His economics were actually very different to Hayek's. He believed the economy could be understood and that limited state interference – through strict monetarism, the setting of rules to maintain a slow and steady growth in the money supply – was acceptable.

But they were as one on the fundamental need to defeat inflation wherever it raised its head and in the belief that unemployment was not the crucial target of economic policy. And they were united more broadly than that, on their politics. Any interference in the market outside of monetarism was counter-productive and risked tyranny. For Friedman, even licensing procedures for doctors and regulations of pharmaceuticals should be scrapped. It was a complete rejection of Mill's insistence that economic issues did not admit of a universal solution between state and market. There was a solution: it was the market.

In the 1970s, events conspired to swing the political needle decisively in their favour: inflation started rising out of control. There were several reasons for it. A pointless and protracted US war in Vietnam encouraged military spending. Militant trade unionism pushed up wages. And most importantly, coordinated action by oil-producing states drove up the price of fuel.

Then something happened which should not have been possible: inflation rose alongside unemployment. It was called stagflation. It was the worst of all worlds.

In 1974, Hayek was awarded the Nobel Prize for economics. It was as if he had suddenly been brought back from the dead. The Nobel committee tried to sidestep any accusation of political bias by having that year's award shared between him and a Keynesian economist, but it didn't matter. The act of recognition handed Hayek and his followers an intellectual status he had been denied for 30 years.

He made the most of it. At the award ceremony, he walked up onto the stage and declared the end of Keynesianism. 'I regard it as fundamentally false,' he said, 'and to act upon it, as we now experience, as very harmful.'

In the UK, stagflation gave Hayek a new disciple: Margaret Thatcher. She would sunder, once and for all, the Conservative party's acceptance of the post-war economic settlement. Once she secured the leadership in 1975, she marched into a party policy meeting, took out a copy of Hayek's book *Constitution of Liberty*, slammed it on the table, and said: 'This is what we believe.'

From opposition she watched and waited as inflation and a seemingly endless series of strikes decimated the Labour government in the second half of the 1970s. In the Winter of Discontent in 1978/79 the country all-but came to a standstill during industrial action.

Thatcher initiated a no-confidence vote in the Labour government, won the ensuing election and was elected prime minister. The victory came just ahead of Hayek's birthday. 'Thank you for the best present to my 80th birthday that anyone could have given me,' he wrote to her. She replied with typical missionary zeal. 'I am very proud to have learned so much from you over the past few years,' she said. 'I am determined that we should succeed. If we do so, your contribution to our ultimate victory will have been immense.'

The free market project, started in lonely isolation at Mont Pèlerin in 1947, was now at the heart of British government.

Shortly after Thatcher was elected, the Hayekians took America. In November 1980, the former Hollywood actor Ronald Reagan was elected US President with the slogan: 'We can get government off our backs, out of our pockets.' The mantra perfectly encapsulated what Reagan brought to the movement: an ability to translate laissez-faire economics into simple language with a down-at-home charm and easy manner.

'Reagan knew Hayek personally,' the right-wing American politician Newt Gingrich explained. 'He knew Milton Friedman personally. I don't think you'd ever get Hayek on the Today show, but you could get Reagan explaining the core of Hayek with better examples and in more understandable language.'

In a little over a decade, Hayek had gone from the wilderness to having his disciples running two of the world's major economies. He sensed a historic opportunity, a sudden change in the global economic and political landscape.

'When I was a young man, only the very old men still believed in the free market system,' he said. 'When I was in my middle ages I myself and nobody else believed in it. And now I have the pleasure of having lived long enough to see that the young people again believe in it.'

The tide had turned. Politically, the Keynesians were firmly out of power. The free market economists were in.

The process adopted to kill off inflation was brutal. It began under the presidency of Democrat Jimmy Carter, but went much deeper under Reagan. Paul Volcker, chairman of the Federal Reserve, decided to deepen the recession in a bid to kill off inflation, by raising the interest rate. In 1981, the year Reagan was inaugurated, it touched 21 per cent. These were levels, in the words of German chancellor Helmut Schmidt, that had not been seen 'since the birth of Christ.'

Inflation was strangling western economies and the need to kill it off was paramount. But the manner in which it was pursued demonstrated no respect at all to the Keynesian principle of trying to avoid unemployment. Hiking rates while simultaneously slashing welfare and lowering taxes for the wealthy seemed designed to punish the poor and reward the rich.

The increase in interest rates coincided with a surge in competition for western manufacturing jobs, particularly from East Asia, as multinational companies trawled the Earth for the lowest labour costs and highest productivity. This was possible because of the global free trade policy supported by liberalism's left and right wing, but its consequences were allowed to play out with pitifully little help for those left behind.

In what would come to be called the Rust Belt, many plants closed for good. The great steel centres of the US, stretching from Buffalo, New York, to Gary, Indiana, were replaced by Mexico, South Korea, Brazil and China. In the north of the US, the centre of cities like Detroit – which had made so many cars its best-known record label was Motown – fell into decay and dereliction. Unemployment in the US rose from around seven per cent in July 1981 to nearly 11 per cent by December 1982. Between 1979 and 1983, 2.4 million American manufacturing jobs were lost.

In the UK, traditional British industrial centres like Manchester, Liverpool and Sheffield, and mining areas in England and Wales, were devastated. Nationally, unemployment rose to over three million – nearly 12 per cent of the workforce – and didn't fall below that level until 1987. Factories, shipyards and coal pits closed. Many areas never fully recovered.

High-paying factory jobs that had boosted millions of families into the middle class disappeared, reversing advances in social mobility. There were no Keynesian programmes to employ people in public works. They stayed out of work. And the longer unemployment went on, the worse its effects became. Skills became outdated. Individuals lost confidence. People become less likely ever to find employment.

Unemployment was passed down from generation to generation. When work was found, it was in low paying retail or hospitality jobs, whose meagre wages were a drop in the ocean next to the riches made in capitalism's headquarters in Wall Street, the City of London and Silicon Valley, the heart of the new tech industry.

The state retreated from the market. Government spending was cut, particularly in education, housing and transport. Trade unions were legally restrained. Taxes were cut, especially for the wealthy. Nationalised industries were privatised, particularly in areas like gas, water, steel, airlines and rail. Sectors were deregulated.

In some areas, such as aviation and trucking, these changes were positive, leading to greater competition and reduced prices. In others, such as electricity, private companies ended up with vast monopoly powers, which they sometimes went on to abuse. But in truth, there was no case-by-case assessment of state or market anymore. Laissez-faire had become something close to a religion.

The financial markets were freed from the shackles placed on them after the Great Depression. Thatcher carried out a 'big bang' deregulation of the City, Britain's financial heart, bringing international capital flooding into London in a gigantic wave. American and European investment banks set up shop. The walls between investment banks and retail banks fell down.

In America, New Deal bank regulations imposed to prevent a recurrence of the 1930s slump were chipped away through the 1980s. The Depository Institutions Deregulation and Monetary Control Act of 1980 shot holes in the wall dividing investment and retail banks. Further relaxations came from the Garn-St Germain Act of 1982 and new rules allowed by the Federal Reserve in 1987.

And then, like an eclipse, an event took place which suggested some grand historical direction to all this change. The Soviet Union collapsed.

'I told you so,' Hayek said, when communism ended in 1991. It was the last major political event he would ever see. He died a year later, at the age of 92.

The end of the USSR was considered the complete historical triumph of the laissez-faire model. Two opposing economic extremes had faced each other: communism and unfettered capitalism. And now one of them was victorious. The American political economist Francis Fukuyama suggested it could effectively be 'the end of history.'

For years, politicians and academics all over the western world acted as if that was the end of the story, as if all matters of economic consideration in human affairs were now closed. By the time centre-left parties had fought their way back into power in the 1990s – under Democratic President Bill Clinton in the US and New Labour prime minister Tony Blair in the UK – they had largely accepted the deregulation agenda.

These leaders were not, as some subsequently claimed, identical to conservatives. They invested in social programmes in a way the preceding governments never had. Health and social services, which had dwindled into chronic dysfunction through lack of funding, were revitalised. But there was an acceptance of the core proposition that the market performed best when left to its own devices.

Clinton summarised the approach neatly in his 1996 State of the Union address. 'We know big government does not have all the answers,' he said. 'The era of big government is over. But we cannot go back to the time when our citizens were left to fend for themselves.'

The aggressive deregulation of the financial sector continued. In the US, the 1994 Riegle-Neal Interstate Banking and Branching Efficiency Act removed regional limitations on bank growth, allowing banks to merge and expand. Between 1998 and 2007, the assets of the five largest retail banks – Bank of America, Citigroup, JP Morgan, Wachovia, and Wells Fargo – more than tripled. The assets of the five largest investment banks – Goldman Sachs, Morgan Stanley, Merrill Lynch, Lehman Brothers, and Bear Stearns – quadrupled.

In 1996, the Economic Growth and Regulatory Paperwork Reduction Act required federal regulators to review their rules every decade and solicit comments on 'outdated, unnecessary, or unduly burdensome' requirements. It created an obsessive zeal for slashing regulation, even among regulators themselves. The Federal Deposit Insurance Corporation's 2003 annual report featured a photograph of officials with banking industry representatives using a chainsaw and pruning shears to cut 'red tape.' Any regulator which tried to stick to its job of controlling the financial sector was met by an avalanche of industry lobbying and legal action. It was, in the words of Securities and Exchange Commission chairman Arthur Levitt, a 'kind of a blood sport.'

Then finally, in November 1999, Clinton eradicated the last remaining vestiges of Glass-Steagall-era restrictions. The Gramm–Leach–Bliley Act allowed banks, no matter their origins, to bounce between retail and investment operations.

Under Blair, British bank regulation was streamlined into a single light-touch entity, the Financial Services Authority (FSA). 'The philosophy of the FSA from when I set it up,' its first chair said, 'has been to say "consenting adults in private? That's their problem."'

A deregulating causal cycle developed between the City of London and Wall Street, in which both lobbied, usually successfully, for their own government to lower and limit regulation of financial services so they could stay competitive with each other.

These measures were supported by the new chairman of the Fed, Alan Greenspan. He repeatedly put forward the argument that there was no need to regulate financial services, because they would do it themselves by virtue of market logic. Contracting parties would only enter into beneficial deals. There would be no demand for unduly risky manoeuvres.

This type of private regulation was considered far more powerful than any kind of state regulation. 'The market-stabilising private regulatory forces,' Greenspan insisted, 'should gradually displace many cumbersome, increasingly ineffective government structures.'

Pay shot up. Adjusted for inflation, executive pay in the financial sector grew annually by only 0.8 per cent in the 30 years after the Second World War. But the rate picked up in the 1970s and hit 10 per cent a year from 1995 to 1999. By 2005, the average bank executive was taking home $3.4 million a year.

Banking was no longer boring. It was as exciting a career as you could go into and certainly the best paid. Some of the brightest minds in physics, maths and computing were drawn away from their work towards finance. In the early years of the 21st Century, at least 40 per cent of Ivy League graduates became bankers.

But underneath it all, something was going badly wrong.

The key development in what was about to happen lay in the transformation of consumer borrowing into investment products. And at the heart of that was a financial trick called securitisation.

It began with mortgages. These were the biggest loans most people took out in their lifetime. They allowed people on average salaries to split up the payments for a home over a number of years, so that they were manageable.

During the Keynesian era in the US, this was a fairly simple process. In the 1960s, a homebuyer would typically get a 30-year loan, on a fixed interest rate, with a five per cent down payment. Most families could afford that. Home ownership boomed.

Government Sponsored Enterprises (GSEs) were created, the most famous of which was called Fannie Mae (Federal National Mortgage Association). They did something unusual. They didn't offer mortgages to people themselves. Instead, they bought people's mortgages from commercial banks.

They wouldn't take just any mortgage. They only accepted those that conformed to a high-end government-insured standard set by the Federal Housing Administration. This established a reliable market for top quality mortgages and, by taking them off the banks' hands, bankers were now free to offer more loans to others, which further expanded home ownership.

In 1970, one of the GSEs – Ginnie Mae (Government National Mortgage Association) – developed a new way of funding called securitisation.

It took several of the mortgages it already owned and bundled them up into a block. It then sliced up the block and called the slices securities. It sold these securities to investors, who then received the interest on the loan payments paid by members of the public.

In 1977, the private sector decided to cash in on this innovation. The investment bank Salomon Brothers put together the first private sector securitisation of mortgages for Bank of America. Everyone seemed to win. Banks received cash for the securitisation sale. They no longer had to hold loans on their books, which meant they were not required to keep a certain amount of capital to protect them against losses. They were also freed up to offer more loans. This meant aspiring homeowners benefitted. And the investment banks made money arranging the deals.

Investors benefited, too. Property was considered a safe way to make money. Securities gave them access to the market without having to engage in the complexity of lending to an individual and working out what the chances were that they would fail to pay it back. These were highly regarded products, backed by respectable financial institutions.

Pooling the loans reduced the risk of losing money. If money was loaned to someone to buy a house, there was a chance they might not pay it back. But if lots of loans were collected together and then sliced-and-diced, the probability of loss declined. Statistically, only a few of them were likely to default, and that didn't really matter because they were only fragments of a larger block.

Not only had the risk of individual defaults been eliminated, but the financial sector believed it had engineered risk out of the entire system.

Mortgages were no longer a one-on-one transaction between a bank and a person. They were now reformulated into assets, which could be bought by investors. So the risk was no longer localised at a lending bank, it was spread thinly over the whole economy, which would lessen the impact of any shock.

Securities allowed the creation of new products to be developed for different kinds of investors. This was done by something called tranching. The securities would be sliced up again and assembled into new elaborate configurations. Risk-averse investors could buy higher tranches which paid off first and therefore had a lower risk of default. Those willing to take more risk could buy the lower tranches, which were more exposed to loss but offered a higher return.

Such riskier tranches were sometimes hard to sell. So investment banks started repackaging them into something called collateralised debt obligations (CDOs). Because of the logic of reduced risk as a result of pooling, these new vehicles could then be designated low risk, even though they came from the riskier tranches of securities.

The logic of this process was extremely seductive. Even quite risky mortgages could be recalibrated into low-risk investments by mathematical modelling.

With that logic, the machine then went into overdrive. New CDOs were created out of CDOs to create CDOs squared. When firms ran out of product, they started creating synthetic CDOs, composed not of real mortgages but of bets on other mortgage products.

The only real oversight over the process came from the credit rating agencies: Moody's, Standard & Poor's and Fitch. They were tasked with providing an assessment of the level of risk in a product. AAA was the gold standard. That designated an investment opportunity that was as close as you could get to complete safety.

The agencies were barely subject to any regulation. They had to be approved by the Securities and Exchange Commission, but once that was in place there were almost no checks on their behaviour. Until 2007, they didn't even need to publish their methodologies for assessing risk.

Investors relied heavily on credit ratings to assess the reliability of these complex products. 'The rating agencies were important tools,' Jim Callahan, a trader for the investment bank Salomon Brothers, said, 'because the people that we were selling these bonds to had never really had any history in the mortgage business. They were looking for an independent party to develop an opinion.'

But there was a critical failure of incentives at the credit rating agencies. In truth, they weren't really independent actors. They were companies. And they were being paid by the very same banks whose products they were evaluating.

The pay was very substantial. After all, their badge of quality was key to the entire endeavour. Moody's, for instance, was paid according to the size of each deal, with caps set at $500,000 for a 'standard' CDO and as much as $850,000 for a 'complex' CDO.

The methodology the agencies used was extremely weak. They had to assess two things: the probability of default in the securities and the extent to which they would combine, or 'correlate.' How likely would it be, in other words, that lots of mortgage defaults would happen to properties in different parts of the US at the same time?

But they did not look at the quality of the mortgages that were originally slapped into the securities. They barely even tried to assess correlation. 'In the absence of meaningful default data,' Moody's said, 'it is impossible to develop empirical default correlation measures based on actual observations of defaults.' Or, in the words of Gary Witt, one of Moody's team of managing directors for the CDO unit, they 'made them up.'

Given the obvious possibility of disincentives in a system where a body was rating the products of its customers, credit rating agencies clearly needed extensive government oversight. But there was almost no attempt to regulate them. Just as Greenspan had suggested, market-logic dominated. If ratings agencies handed out AAA ratings willy-nilly, the thinking went, they would lose credibility and go bust. The market would regulate itself.

Under that lack of observation, the agencies got to work. Lower tranches largely rated BBB or A from securities were repackaged into CDOs. Approximately 80 per cent would magically emerge as AAA. The machine thrummed away, converting loans into highly prized investment assets, in which the financial rewards of risky lending came with none of the downsides.

Banks started to get involved in every stage of the securitisation process. Using the freedom offered to them by the end of Glass-Steagall, investment banks like Bear Stearns and Lehman Brothers started offering consumer-facing mortgage services. Commercial banks went in the other direction, graduating from mortgage origination to securitisation, collateralisation and tranching.

They also used the securities for a different process, which would prove decisive in the events to come. They became collateral for funding from the money market.

The money market is a great pool of cash, sloshing around, searching for investment. Some of it is stowed in mutual funds, which offer wealthy clients better rates of return than a normal bank account. Some of it is in institutional cash pools, $1 billion-plus accounts filled up with cash from asset managers, pension funds or the super-rich. Managers of institutional cash pools are tasked with securing a decent return on the money.

One of the main ways this worked was through a repurchase agreement, or repo. Although a repo is a sale, it works like a loan.

Imagine a pawn shop. Someone has fallen on harsh times and needs something to tide them over until their next pay cheque. So they offer the shop their £100 watch for £90, and arrange to come back tomorrow and buy it back in exchange for an additional fee. Technically, it's a sale. In reality, it's a collateral-based loan.

Repo functioned the same way. Investment banks sold the security with a set price for its later repurchase. In doing this, they'd take a small cut to the value. So for $100 million in securities, for instance, they'd get $98 million. This was called the haircut.

This allowed the investment banks to secure funding. The transaction involved a repo rate – basically an interest payment – which would provide the purchaser with a return. The repo arrangement would then 'roll over' regularly, with the new repo rate being agreed, and the relationship would carry on.

This process became the central funding source for many investment banks. By the 2000s, the New York repo market was going through trillions of dollars a day. In 2007, half of Lehman Brothers' $691 billion balance sheet was funded by repo. For Goldman Sachs, Merrill Lynch and Morgan Stanley it was 40 per cent.

In the UK, which was even more heavily deregulated, the repo market became more complicated. 'Broker dealer' banks holding securities engaged in a process called collateral rehypothecation. This involved using the collateral as further collateral in a separate repo deal.

In the US, this was limited by regulation to no more than 140 per cent of the value of the collateral being held. But in the UK there was no limit. So investment banks – both European and American – used the looser rules in the City of London to secure up to 400 per cent collateral multiplication, adding up to around $4.5 trillion in additional funding.

Another mechanism was called asset-backed commercial paper. A bank would set up little legal child entities, called structured investment vehicles. They would then load them up with securities.

The little child entity then created commercial paper. These were effectively IOUs. Money markets gobbled them up. After all, they had the name of a large bank on them and they held securities. They seemed reliable.

The structured investment vehicle would then pay the bank back for the security with the funds it raised on the back of the commercial paper. And just like that, the bank had its funding. The commercial paper arrangement, just like repo, would 'roll over' regularly.

Commercial paper and repo were two mechanisms for the same process: the transformation of long-term consumer debt into short-term bank funding. The system converted securities into day-to-day liquidity.

Managers of cash pools lent out money to a safe institution holding decent assets and got a handsome return. Wall Street firms earned fees putting together deal after deal.

The people who ran this system, from the security industry to the regulators who were supposedly overseeing them, convinced themselves that they had eliminated risk. They believed they had spread it so thinly over the whole financial system that it had vanished.

In reality, they had done nothing of the sort. The risk existed in five separate stages of the process.

The first lay in mortgage origination. In the post-war years, lenders avoided unsafe loans because they would be lumbered with the defaults. But once securitisation took off, it wasn't even clear who the lender was anymore. The mortgages had been sliced, diced, carved, packaged and repackaged into so many incomprehensible products that no-one took responsibility for the loans at the bottom.

The second was the blocks of mortgages that formed securities. These were believed to reduce risk because it was unlikely that many mortgage-holders would default at the same time. But those models were wrong. In regions where low-quality mortgages were heavily correlated, borrowers would indeed default in large numbers.

The third was the credit rating agencies. These bodies were supposed to be assessing how risky investments were. But in reality they were too lightly regulated to achieve this reliably, and they had a financial self-interest in pleasing their customers.

The fourth was the localisation of risk. The securities industry had convinced itself that this product spread the risk of defaults around different investors and therefore minimised the impact of defaults. But the reality was entirely different. Much of the risk had actually been taken on by a small group of big financial companies, vital to the wider economy, who were themselves involved in securitisation. They possessed outsized holdings of the senior tranches of CDOs. And they had very little capital to protect themselves against potential losses, because that would have reduced their profits.

The fifth was the banks' reliance on securities to secure short-term funding through the money markets. Banks had allowed themselves to become completely reliant on repo and commercial paper for liquidity. But if those securities were suddenly devalued, the entire system would collapse.

And, eventually, that was exactly what happened.

Around the turn of the century, the mortgage business experienced a boom. It happened as the result of the deadliest terror attack in human history.

On the morning of 11th September 2001, 19 hijackers from the Islamic terror group al-Qaeda boarded four commercial airplanes flying from the northeastern US to California. They took control of the aircraft using anti-assault sprays and Stanley knives, and then directed them towards their targets – the World Trade Center in New York and the Pentagon. A total of 2,977 people were killed.

One of the most immediate effects was economic. The stock exchange did not open until 17th September and when it did so the Dow Jones industrial average fell a record 7.1 per cent. Amid fears of a recession, the Fed dropped interest rates to just one per cent. Its hope was that people would respond by refinancing their mortgages – settling the existing debt and then taking out a new mortgage at the more attractive interest rate.

It worked. The mortgage industry leapt from $1 trillion mortgages in 2001 to $3.8 trillion in 2003. The securities industry gobbled up as much as it could. By 2004, the surge had calmed, but the sector was still not sated. It needed to gorge on more mortgages.

Private issuers gave up on high-standard mortgages and started prioritising 'Alt-A' and 'subprime' – mortgages to people with low credit ratings who would struggle making the repayments.

The downpayment on mortgages, which was typically 20 per cent, was reduced. This had been possible in the past, but only if the borrower took out insurance to protect the lender. Now, that requirement was scrapped. The information required to take out a loan was also reduced, sometimes to create 'no-documentation' loans for people with fluctuating or hard to assess incomes, such as the self-employed.

People on very low incomes were offered mortgages with low initial payments, but much higher fees after a few years. Some people were simply tricked. Others allowed optimism to get the better of them. Some went in eyes-open. In the end, it made little difference. The mortgage offerer could always outsmart them. They knew exactly how it worked. They offered countless thousands of these loans. The borrower only had the one experience.

Many believed the mortgage broker was on their side. In fact this was incorrect. They were, in reality, on the side of the securitisation business.

Brokers were paid in up-front fees from the borrower, the lender, or both. One common fee paid by the lender was the 'yield spread premium,' which meant there was a more substantial payment for higher-interest loans. This created an incentive to sign up the borrower to the highest possible rate.

An analysis of a securitisation deal by the US Financial Crisis Inquiry Commission found brokers had been paid an average fee from the borrowers of $3,756 – or 1.81 per cent of the loan amount. They often also received yield spread premiums on top of that averaging $2,585 each.

Potential borrowers were flooded by advertising material promising one per cent loans, or no-money-down, or no-income-documentation mortgages. And out the other end of the Wall Street machine came securities, CDOs and synthetic CDOs.

'Securitisation could be seen as a factory line,' former Citigroup CEO Charles Prince admitted later. 'As more and more of these subprime mortgages were created as raw material for the securitisation process, not surprisingly in hindsight, more and more of it was of lower and lower quality. And at the end of that process, the raw material going into it was actually bad quality, it was toxic quality, and that is what ended up coming out the other end of the pipeline.'

By late 2005, non-traditional loans made up 59 per cent of originations at Countrywide, 58 per cent at Wells Fargo, 51 per cent at National City and 31 per cent at Washington Mutual.

It didn't take much to make the system collapse.

It started in 2005. News reports started to highlight a weakening of the real estate market. By early 2007 it was clear that prices were falling in previously booming regions and that many families, especially those with subprime loans, would fail to make their mortgage payments.

In 2007 and 2008, the credit rating agencies started to downgrade securities and CDOs. Investors panicked and market prices plunged. That was partly a fear of default. But more importantly, it stemmed from a fear that the market for securities was seizing up.

The decisive moment came on 9th August 2007. The French bank BNP Paribas announced it was freezing three of its funds. It wasn't its action which sent shock waves through the financial world, but its reasoning. 'The complete evaporation of liquidity in certain market segments of the US securitisation market,' it said, 'has made it impossible to value certain assets fairly regardless of their quality or credit rating.'

It was the death knell of an entire way of doing business. If the securities could not be valued, they could not be used as collateral. And if they could not be used as collateral, there would be no funding. That signified a general liquidity freeze: a bank run the size of the world.

In September 2007, the British bank Northern Rock failed. Savers queued up outside its branches trying to take their money out. It seemed like a replay of the Great Depression, when lack of confidence in banks had pulverised the economy. But in fact, 80 per cent of Northern Rock's funding had nothing to do with the queueing depositors. It wasn't even particularly exposed to subprime lending. Its problem was that it relied on the money markets for funding. And they were closing down.

Bear Stearns, the smallest of America's five big investment banks, followed. It had a stake in every stage of the mortgage business, from loan origination through to securitisation and sale. In late 2007, Bear Sterns lost access to the commercial paper market, so it started replacing it with repo borrowing. But even this started to falter. The interest rates were rocketing and the amount of collateral it had to post was increasing. It was getting squeezed in all directions. Then, in one brutal week, its cash ran out.

On the evening of Thursday 13th March 2008, the bank informed the Securities and Exchange Commission that it would be 'unable to operate normally on Friday.' The Fed made a $12.9 billion loan to the bank, but that simply demolished any remaining confidence.

The Fed and the Treasury Department were in a state of panic. If Bears collapsed, it might topple the $2.8 trillion tri-party repo market. Short-term lenders could end up dumping collateral on the market, destroying asset prices. 'It was heading sort of to a black hole,' Fed Chairman Ben Bernanke concluded. They hastily scrambled together a buyout by the bank JP Morgan.

Then the next domino fell. Lehman Brothers, the fourth largest investment bank in the US, was in the same position. It relied on $7.8 billion in commercial paper funding and $197 billion repo funding. Over the summer of 2008, that started to dry up.

This time Washington was intent on limiting its involvement. 'We need to talk,' Treasury chief of staff Jim Wilkinson said in an email to Michele Davis, the assistant secretary for public affairs at the Treasury. 'I just can't stomach us bailing out Lehman.'

The US government decided there would be no rescue.

On Monday 15th September, at 1.45am, Lehman's filed for bankruptcy. The Dow Jones stock market index fell over 500 points, wiping out $700 billion from retirement plans, government pension funds and other investment portfolios.

The shock rang out across the international system. For a moment, it seemed like the entire global economy might collapse. 'You had people starting to take their deposits out of very, very strong banks, long way removed in distance and risk from the guys on Wall Street,' Treasury secretary Timothy Geithner said. 'And that is a classic measure of incipient panic.'

Ben Bernanke, the Fed Chairman, felt he was staring into the abyss. 'That September and October of 2008 was the worst financial crisis in global history, including the Great Depression,' he said. 'Out of maybe the 13 most important financial institutions in the United States, 12 were at risk of failure within a period of a week or two.'

Until now, the government had largely refused to intervene. There had been efforts to make cash available and attempts to secure private purchases of ailing banks, but Lehman's collapse showed their preference was still to hang back. That position now became impossible to sustain.

On Saturday 20th September, the Treasury sent Congress a three-page document, giving it massive new powers to spend $700 billion and purchase toxic assets from financial institutions. Government would be given the leading role of clearing up the mess created by the private sector. It went to a vote on Monday 29th September.

America's elected representatives voted against the rescue package.

The markets broke down into outright panic. In a matter of hours, $1.2 trillion was wiped off the value of US businesses. The Dow Jones fell 778 points. Banks across the world were suddenly facing an existential threat and that meant that bank lending to the real economy evaporated. Sudden falls in house prices and financial markets devastated people's personal wealth.

The WTO found that every one of the 104 countries it collected data for experienced a fall in imports and exports on the back of the financial crisis. Fifty-two of the 60 countries which provided GDP information to the International Monetary Fund (IMF), an international organisation tasked with managing balance of payment emergencies, went into contraction. Between the last quarter of 2008 and the first quarter of 2009, international capital flows collapsed by 90 per cent.

The job losses trickled down society, from the top earners to the bottom. The bankers went first, but soon it was people on low incomes, especially minorities, especially the young, and especially those without a college degree. Tens of millions of people around the world were made unemployed.

The Treasury legislation was hastily rewritten and put back before Congress. It provided 'authority for the federal government to purchase and insure certain types of troubled assets for the purposes of providing stability to and preventing disruption in the economy.'

Finally, the opposition fell away. There was hardly anyone left who could pretend that 'letting things be' would work. Laissez-faire was imploding. On Friday 3rd October, the House voted 263 to 171 to accept the rescue.

The state would interfere in the market again.

It was a remarkable U-turn. After three decades of singing from Hayek's hymnsheet of non-interference, politicians and bankers changed their views overnight. An industry which had constantly broadcast the need for the state to keep out of its way was pleading for government assistance. And governments which had spent decades insisting on the inefficiency of state intervention in the markets now recognised that it was the only way to protect the broader economy.

The emergency measures introduced across the US, Europe and Britain totalled over $7 trillion.

The first major rescue operation came from the British Labour prime minister, Gordon Brown, on 8th October. He recognised that to prevent their collapse the banks needed guarantees from government. The market needed to know that the full financial might of the British state would stand behind them. They would also be offered a special provision to get rid of unsellable assets.

But in return they had to be recapitalised. This was the process of ensuring that the banks had enough money on their balance sheet to withstand further losses. It would prevent them collapsing and taking the rest of the economy with them. The money could either come from private sources, or it could come from the state, which meant nationalisation in all but name. Lloyds TSB-HBOS and RBS accepted government money and became semi-nationalised entities. Barclays and HSBC refused the offer and sought foreign funds.

Five days later, US financial authorities sat down with the chief executives of America's largest banks for an extraordinary meeting. They were offered a stark choice. Either they took government capital and got a guarantee, or they would be notified that they were undercapitalised, which would see them frozen out of the credit market.

They accepted the offer. America part-nationalised the heart of financial capitalism.

In November 2008, Barack Obama was elected president of the United States. For the US, it was a profound moment of change. A black man would occupy the White House. But in terms of economic policy there was a large degree of continuity. The emergency response had been propped by Democrat votes, and Obama surrounded himself with the old guard of deregulated markets from the Clinton era.

And yet there was one crucial appointment. Obama made the economic historian Christina Romer chair of the Council of Economic Advisers. And she was a Keynesian.

On 16th December 2008, as thick snow fell on Chicago, Obama gathered his team around him in his transition headquarters. 'Well,

Mr President,' Romer said, 'this is your "holy shit" moment. It's worse than we thought.'

The projections showed that there was an output gap of $2 trillion between how the economy should be performing and how it would perform in 2009–2010. Unless there was a stimulus, the country would be devastated.

Because of the Keynesian multiplier effect, where a dollar spent created more than its own value, the stimulus did not need to account for the whole gap. But the economy needed a decisive moment of maximum force to prop it up. Using conventional modelling, Romer said that a stimulus of over $1.2 trillion would do the job.

The advisers were aghast. No-one questioned the economics, but they couldn't stomach the politics. Congress would never accept a number so high, especially after the bail-out of the banks. So they stuck under the $1 trillion mark and hoped that special pleading by politicians in Congress would nudge up the total.

It didn't work. The final bill came in at just $787 billion. Even then, it barely squeaked through. Not a single Republican in the House of Representatives voted for it. Just three in the Senate did.

The lack of support limited the size of the stimulus and also its targets. Instead of the big totemic public works projects connected with green energy and broadband that Obama favoured, $212 billion went into tax cuts, $296 billion to boosting government programmes like Medicaid and unemployment relief, and just $279 billion was left for discretionary spending.

But despite the limitations, it performed admirably. Every reliable economic indicator found the stimulus had a positive impact. The multiplier was above 1, meaning that it limited the role of government in the economy by stimulating additional private sector activity. Some 1.6 million jobs were created a year, for four years.

What Obama was doing domestically, Brown wanted to do globally. In spring 2009, the prime minister hosted a summit of the richest 20 nations – called the G20 – in London. He had a plan:

a world stimulus, totalling $1 trillion, to apply Keynesian remedies on an international scale.

After a tense meeting, bulging with inflated egos and contradictory domestic political requirements, he squeezed it through. Countries around the world joined the US in applying domestic fiscal stimulus, including Argentina, Brazil, Indonesia, South Korea, Russia and Turkey.

'By any measure, the London summit was historic,' Obama concluded. Germany chancellor Angela Merkel agreed. 'This time the world does not react as in the thirties. This is a victory for global cooperation.'

Developed economies also experienced a Keynesian stimulus which did not need to be negotiated or arranged. It came through the automatic stabilisers that had been built into the system.

During the recession, unemployment benefits and welfare payments went up, government revenue narrowed, it had to borrow more money and the national deficit grew.

Under Keynesian analysis, this was how the system should work. Later, when the good times came again, the deficit could be reduced. But for now, the automatic stabilisers would alleviate suffering and prop up demand.

But then, just like that, it was cancelled.

The retreat back to laissez-faire involved an argument that went all the way back to Adam Smith: the need to balance the national budget.

When governments took on too much debt and their deficits became too large, the argument went, markets panicked. They started to treat traditionally safe government bonds – the IOUs issued for national borrowing – as uncertain. That drove up interest rates on borrowing, which would in turn plunge countries further into the red, trapping them in debt servitude.

This argument was given additional potency in 2010 by the publication of a research paper by two former IMF economists, Carmen Reinhart and Kenneth Rogoff, called *Growth in a Time of Debt*. It contained an alarming finding. Once public debt passed 90 per cent of GDP, it said, something happened. Economic growth slowed. The economy couldn't get out from under the sheer weight of state borrowing. Government revenue dwindled, more and more money was spent on servicing the debt, and hopes of ever paying it off vanished. The country started to sink.

But there was a problem. The calculations on the media-friendly 90 per cent marker were flawed. Undoubtedly, countries have individual tipping points, moments at which the market's lack of confidence in them paying off further debt sends them into a death spiral. But there was no evidence for a universal tipping point at a set threshold.

In fact, for wealthy and stable western countries, the reality was precisely the opposite. In a scary financial world, where even AAA private investments had turned out to be catastrophically unreliable, people craved safety. And that was available through sovereign bonds in secure countries like Germany, the UK and US. But this argument was drowned out by a chorus of demands for spending cuts.

This was the austerity programme.

With a sleight of hand, it shifted the cost of the financial crash from banks to members of the public. A crisis started by financial institutions was transferred onto welfare recipients and users of public services. The banks were bailed out and the public were bailed in.

The state of the public finances was the chief issue in Britain's 2010 general election. The campaign had an almost surreal quality. The country was facing severe problems, not least its reliance on an under-regulated financial services sector which had proven extremely volatile. But instead, debate focused on potential problems for which there was no evidence – namely the need to reduce the budget deficit.

The case for slashing public spending was weak. Britain's credit rating still held. The bond market was stable. In fact, the austerity arguments used by the Conservative party were not even about the existing financial situation. They were based on the possibility of a future decline of confidence in the bond market.

Nevertheless, within weeks, the Conservatives had taken power in a Coalition government with the Liberal Democrats and the new chancellor, George Osborne, was announcing a savage Budget that slashed government spending.

There were two areas of spending he could not touch: pensions, which were relied on by the Conservative party's elderly support base, and the National Health Service, which was politically sacrosanct. So the main cuts were reserved for local councils, who were forced into jettisoning community services.

Budgets were slashed for libraries, school services, public parks, buses and countless other services. Britain shrivelled up into itself. It became a harsher, colder and bleaker place to live. The countless small freedoms which the Keynesian revolution had brought to people – the freedom to read a book you could not otherwise afford or for poorer pupils to go on day trips – were cut down one by one, by cash-starved local councils with no other options.

As ever, the worst pain was felt by the poorest. Very little of the saving was done through tax rises. Those who used public services or relied on benefits – and especially the disabled, who were put through humiliating tests to assess their fitness for work – suffered most. Cities in the north, many of which had still not recovered from the destruction of industry in the 1980s, were hit hardest. On average, local government spending in northern cities was cut by 20 per cent, compared to nine per cent for cities in the south.

As the new prime minister, David Cameron, made clear, the cuts were not just about austerity. They were, in his words, 'something more profound.' They were ideological. He aimed to shrink the state 'permanently.'

The American austerity lobby seized on the UK experiment. Romer, the only Keynesian advising the president, was gradually frozen out of decision-making. Her recommendation, based again on conventional modelling and sensible economic calculations, was for a further stimulus. But this was politically impossible. Instead, the economic right took over.

On 2nd November, the Republicans won control of the House of Representatives in midterm elections. Obama tried to slide another mini-stimulus through before they took over, but it had to consist entirely of tax cuts, with no public spending. It was his last piece of major economic legislation. For all intents and purposes, in economic terms, the Obama presidency was over after just two years.

The consensus in Washington accepted the need for austerity. The only debate left was between Democrats arguing it should come through a mixture of tax rises and spending cuts and Republicans arguing that it should come through cuts alone.

But as painful and pointless as austerity in the UK and US was, it was not the worst example. The place where this form of free market thinking would do the most damage was Greece.

The financial crash pummelled Greece's real economy. Exports fell. Tourism declined. Tax revenue slumped. The automatic stabilisers switched on and debt rose. But there was a difference between Greece and other countries. The sudden financial shock came on top of a mountain of historic debt. If countries do face individual tipping points on debt, then Greece was approaching it.

In the years to come, when people tried to justify what came next, they would insist that Greece was borrowing excessively in the years before the crash. This helped provide a sense of moral reassurance. The feckless Greeks were getting their comeuppance.

In fact, Greece's debts went back to a troubled time in the mid-70s, when the country had shaken off a military dictatorship and remade itself as a democracy.

At the turn of the new century, Greece joined an inner core of EU member states in a new project called the eurozone. These states established a new shared currency, the euro, and a European Central Bank (ECB) to administer monetary policy. It was here that Greece made its historic mistake. But it was not overspending. It was an error of omission.

For the first time, it was able to borrow on the same terms as Germany, a country with a strong fiscal record that enjoyed low interest rates on bonds. It could have used this good fortune to consolidate – to pay back the historic debts on its balance sheet and make its tax system more efficient. It did not. It spurned the opportunity. So when the crash came, it found itself in a precarious position.

It was obvious that Greece would never be able to pay back all the debt. It stood at 115 per cent of GDP. Each year the loans were going to get bigger, demanding more borrowing. And the worse things looked, the higher the interest rate would go up on any new debt it issued, to reflect the increased risk.

Greece would be driven further and further into the ground, throwing good money after bad, unless there was forgiveness for at least some of the money it owed. This required the banks to lose a percentage of their loans – a process known as debt restructuring.

But there was an obstacle. Some €90 billion of Greece's €293 billion public debt was owned by continental European banks. And those banks were already vulnerable because they had failed to recapitalise after the 2008 crash. Europe had actually offered hundreds of billions in recapitalisation funds. But, crucially, they were voluntary. And without being forced into taking them, the banks stayed away for fear of looking weak. If Greece defaulted on its debt payments, there was a possibility that these banks would collapse, triggering a second crash.

The Greek prime minister George Papandreou visited Nicolas Sarkozy in Paris in spring 2010 to make plain Greece's peril. The French president was sympathetic. He wanted a European bail-out fund. But he would not support a restructuring of Greece's debts. French banks were highly exposed and would lose heavily.

BNP Paribas, France's biggest bank, was the largest foreign owner of Greek debt. The Franco-Belgian financial group Dexia held much less – just €3 billion – but it was in such a parlous state that it might not be able to swallow the loss.

There was also a risk that the restructuring of Greek loans could cause a loss of confidence in the whole European banking system. French banks held €500bn in public and private debts in Ireland, Spain, Italy and Portugal, all of whom were also looking vulnerable.

In Germany, Merkel had the exact opposite position. She supported restructuring the debt, but vociferously opposed any moves which would see a European bail-out fund. Domestic public opinion was strongly against German taxpayers subsidising their supposedly spendthrift Mediterranean neighbours.

Germany and France both held a piece of the puzzle – France in its support for joint European bail-outs and Germany in its support for restructuring the debt. But they were trapped in a mutual headlock. So instead they settled on an easy answer: austerity. The debt would not be restructured. There would be no joint European bailout. Instead, the Greeks would be forced to cut spending in a bid to balance their budget.

It was a punishment without purpose. Introducing austerity to Greece would make it even less likely to pay back the money. It would, as Keynes had outlined decades earlier, starve demand, and with that government revenue, which would then make it even harder to ever pay off its creditors.

The EU formed the Troika, alongside the ECB and the IMF. It loaned Greece money to pay its debts. The money was not raised by a joint European programme, but via voluntary contributions from individual nations. Nor did it come with concessionary terms. It arrived with punishing interest rates and processing fees. The money would only touch Athens briefly on its way to its European creditors.

Greece was forced to introduce the harshest austerity programme ever initiated in a modern democracy. State assets were to be privatised, public sector workers laid off, VAT ramped up and pension ages raised. In the incessant misery, a general strike broke out, bringing public transport to a standstill and triggering running street battles between protestors and riot police.

A downward spiral developed, with falling government spending causing falling demand, which led to falling economic activity. Youth unemployment surged. By 2012, half of young Greeks were out of work. Nearly a quarter of the general population was jobless. The attempt to make the debt fall as a percentage of Greece's GDP did not work, because its GDP kept shrinking. Between 2009 and 2012, it fell from €240 billion to €191 billion. Greece was being ground into the dirt.

As the months rolled past, more eurozone members entered Troika programmes, under the inexorable political narrative of austerity. First Ireland. Then Portugal. Italy looked like it was teetering on the brink. Spain was grinding to a halt. By the summer of 2012, 55 per cent of young Spaniards were unemployed.

Greece entered a cycle of bail-outs and austerity. If there was still any domestic political mandate for what was happening, it was hard to discern. The entire concept of democratic legitimacy was starting to fray at the edges. The Greek parliament had become little more than a rubber-stamping operation for austerity measures passed down by the Troika.

The main actors in the drama started behaving in increasingly dangerous ways.

Jean-Claude Trichet, the conservative head of the European Central Bank, helped drive through the austerity programme by threatening to introduce graduated haircuts on repo for bonds from lower rated countries. This would make them less attractive to banks and therefore make them even less likely to accept Greece's debt.

Then he escalated his attack. On 5th August 2011, Trichet sent a confidential memo to the prime ministers of Spain, José Luis Zapatero, and Italy, Silvio Berlusconi, making bond purchase protection contingent on massive cuts to government spending, increases in taxation and changes to labour laws that would undermine trade unions. Italy was told to privatise public services. If Berlusconi was concerned about political opposition, he was advised to use Article 77 of the Italian constitution to trigger emergency powers.

Instead of using financial mechanisms to push policy changes, the ECB was now explicitly stating the political decisions that should be made in sovereign states and then pressuring governments to use undemocratic means to achieve them, regardless of whether they had public support. Berlusconi, a self-obsessed and irresponsible leader who was prone to outbursts of hysteria, was completely reasonable when he said the letter 'made us look like an occupied government.'

Meanwhile, Papandreou was watching Greece fall into turmoil. During a military procession in Thessaloniki, anti-austerity rioters stormed the parade route, forcing the president to flee. 'Everybody was saying that the government are traitors,' he said. 'I realised the situation was getting out of control.'

He decided to take a stand. He would hold a referendum on the next deal being offered by the Troika. That decision sparked outrage from Merkel and Sarkozy. In November 2011, Papandreou was summoned to a G20 summit in Cannes. There, José Manuel Barroso, president of the European Commission, summoned his staff to his hotel room and started to discuss who could replace the Greek prime minister. The first name out of the hat was former ECB vice president Lucas Papademos.

When Papandreou arrived in Cannes, he was met with a formidable audience. Alongside Merkel, Sarkozy and Barroso was Christine Lagarde, managing director of the IMF, Herman Van Rompuy, president of the European Council, and Jean-Claude Juncker, chair of the Eurogroup of finance ministers.

Papandreou was told that there was no way he could hold a referendum on the next bail-out plan. If he was going to hold a vote, it would have to be much broader than that: in or out on eurozone membership. An existential decision. Sarkozy commanded Papandreou to go home and 'take a decision.' But as the Greek delegation left, Barroso quietly drew the Greek finance minister Evangelos Venizelos aside, and told him: 'We have to kill this referendum.'

The referendum idea was discarded and Papandreou was removed. Barroso's favourite, Papademos, was installed in his place.

European leaders then turned their attention to Italy. This was always the greatest threat of contagion. It was simply too big to fail without bringing down the eurozone.

Lagarde had a plan for a €80 billion credit lifeline alongside a monitoring programme. But the trouble was no-one trusted Berlusconi. So behind the scenes, Merkel and Sarkozy tried to get rid of him.

'The Europeans actually approached us softly, indirectly, saying: "We basically want you to join us in forcing Berlusconi out,"' Treasury secretary Timothy Geithner said. Washington was briefly tempted, but they decided against it. 'We can't have Berlusconi's blood on our hands,' he advised the president.

With or without US support, though, Berlusconi was done for. Within days, he had lost a vote of no confidence in parliament and resigned. A former European commissioner, Mario Monti, was selected to replace him. He held no elected office, so he had to be anointed 'life senator' by the Italian president.

Both cases could be justified. European leaders like Merkel were in an impossible position, facing the possible collapse of the entire eurozone project. Papandreou was playing with fire. Berlusconi was inept. If either of them had had strong support at home, they could not have been ousted.

But nevertheless, the EU had crossed a line. It had conspired to remove the democratically elected leaders of two member states and replace them with men more to its liking. The basic democratic legitimacy upon which the project rested was starting to fray dangerously.

Eventually, European policy adopted a more rational form.

After a long, rough period of inaction, with politicians pretending that Greece would be able to pay back its debts while its society disintegrated, reality finally started to shape the response.

The infrastructure of a viable rescue operation was slowly put into place. Greek debt was restructured. Bail-out funds were provided. The bond market was supported. A turning point was reached.

But the price of those four years of chaos was severe. The European project had lost its reputation for solidarity and humanity. The societies which experienced austerity in its various forms, from Britain and America to the weaker eurozone states, did not return to their former selves. They were fundamentally damaged – poorer, colder, and with a distinct sense that unaccountable elite forces worked to protect the wealthy while the poor were left to pay the price.

10. IDENTITY WAR

Liberalism had allowed itself to become associated with a puritanical form of free-market orthodoxy. So when the financial crash and austerity came, its reputation declined alongside that of the financial sector. But this was not the full extent of its problems. There was another failure it could no longer ignore.

Liberalism had a dirty secret. When it talked about the individual, it only ever seemed to be talking about heterosexual white men.

There was a hidden plot line running underneath the liberal story. It was there right at the start, in Putney, when the Levellers established early liberal principles of consent and individual freedom. Almost immediately, as soon as they got down to business, they began carving people out of those rights. Women first – that was so obvious it didn't need mentioning. Then various economic categories of men.

This pattern was replicated throughout liberal history. At every stage, certain people were excluded from the community of the free.

The moment the US Constitution was written, slavery was embedded in it. When it was abolished after the American Civil War in the 19th Century, most British liberals were in fact on the side of the pro-slavery South. They didn't consider slavery a matter of individual rights. They treated it as an issue of national self-determination.

Mill was one of the few who stood firmly on the side of the North. 'I shall all my life,' he said later, 'feel united by a sort of special tie with those, whether personally known to me or not, who have been faithful when so many were faithless.'

But on what basis could that failure have taken place? It was impossible, outside of outright murder, to think of anything that more obviously violated individual freedom than slavery. And yet that did not seem to figure in the minds of many liberals. The reason was obvious. They did not consider black people to fit into the category 'individuals.' They were excluded from the community of the free.

Even Mill himself, who was centuries ahead of his contemporaries on questions of race and gender, was not exempt from criticism. His professional life was spent as a colonial administrator at the resource-ransacking British East India Company. During that time he showed not the slightest interest in the country he was administering or any desire to visit it. The basic liberal principle of consent in government seems barely to have affected him at all. Why? Because Indians were not considered fully civilised. They did not quite count as individuals either.

The same applied to women. Despite Taylor and Mill's efforts, it took years to secure women the vote in most western countries. Even after it was achieved, most middle-class women were still trapped in the home, deprived of the education or workplace rights which would allow them to be anything other than a wife and a mother. The treatment of working-class women was considerably worse.

And then there was that other secret, playing out in Victorian London as its liberals celebrated their commitment to freedom. It was the persecution of gay men.

In 1895, Britain's most celebrated playwright, Oscar Wilde, was put on trial for gross indecency – in reality for his homosexuality. During proceedings, he was asked about the phrase 'the love that dare not speak its name,' first coined to describe gay love by Lord Alfred Douglas.

'It is in this century misunderstood,' Wilde told the court, 'so much misunderstood that it may be described as "the love that dare not speak its name," and on that account of it I am placed where I am now. It is beautiful, it is fine, it is the noblest form of affection. There is nothing unnatural about it. It is intellectual, and it repeatedly exists between an older and a younger man, when the older man has intellect, and the younger man has all the joy, hope and glamour of life before him. That it should be so, the world does not understand. The world mocks at it, and sometimes puts one in the pillory for it.'

The treatment handed out to Wilde was precisely the sort of conformist hatred of a minority group that liberals were supposed to care about. He was sentenced to two years of hard labour. When he was transferred to Reading Gaol, he was forced to stand, handcuffed, in convict dress, on the railway platform at Clapham Junction.

'Of all possible objects I was the most grotesque,' he said. 'When people saw me they laughed. Each train as it came up swelled the audience. Nothing could exceed their amusement. That was, of course, before they knew who I was. As soon as they had been informed they laughed still more. For half an hour I stood there in the grey November rain surrounded by a jeering mob.'

When he was finally allowed to write in his jail cell, a torrent of bitterness at the hypocrisy of a supposedly liberal society flowed from Wilde's pen. But it did not lead him to give up on liberalism. It led him to commit to the true expression and application of its principles.

'People used to say of me that I was too individualistic,' he wrote. 'I must be far more of an individualist than ever I was. Indeed, my ruin came not from too great individualism of life, but from too little.'

A few years later, in 1913, the English novelist EM Forster paid a visit to a gay couple, Edward Carpenter and George Merrill, in the countryside, and something happened there that inspired his next book.

'George Merrill touched my backside,' he said, 'gently and just above the buttocks. I believe he touched most people's. The sensation was unusual and I still remember it, as I remember the position of a long vanished tooth. It was as much psychological as physical. It seemed to go straight through the small of my back into my ideas, without involving my thoughts.'

He immediately set to work writing his next novel. It was called *Maurice* – a gay love story, set in middle- and upper-class Edwardian society. Forster was an eloquent advocate for liberalism. He wrote about it as intelligently and evocatively as anyone in England at the time. But in the novel, it was not the individual he celebrated. It was the idea of two men, two lovers, together.

At one point, *Maurice*'s protagonist was batting in a cricket game alongside a man he was starting to fall in love with. They were surrounded by figures from society – his friends and associates, all of whom would ostracise him if they knew about his sexuality. 'He felt that they were against the whole world,' Forster wrote. 'They played for the sake of each other and of their fragile relationship – if the one fell the other would follow. They intended no harm to the world, but so long as it attacked they must punish, they must stand wary, then hit with full strength, they must show that when two are gathered together majorities shall not triumph.'

Unlike most liberals, Forster did not see freedom in the city. He saw it in the countryside – the 'greenwood,' as he called it – a semi-mystical place, in nature, like the house where his friends had hidden away from society and its attempts to control them.

He was aware of the deeper power, beyond that of the state, which could impinge upon the individual – the power that people have over other people, the power of discrimination and prejudice, at street level, in sneers and vicious glances, of reports to the police.

Liberalism had answers for this. It was in Taylor and Mill's harm principle and their vigilance against the tyranny of the majority. But what was present in the abstract had rarely been pursued in practice. In reality, comparatively few liberals had been brave enough to argue that these principles demanded equal treatment for gay men.

Liberalism couldn't ignore these voices forever. Things finally began to change after the Second World War. The franchise was fully expanded. Free education was nearly universal. And the people who had been marginalised from society were finally in a position to make their claim.

France, Germany, Italy, Belgium, Luxembourg and the Netherlands enshrined equal pay for men and women in the 1957 Treaty of Rome. The US passed the Equal Pay Act in 1963, outlawing separate pay scales for women and men. Britain implemented similar legislation in 1970.

Firms were forced to change the way they did business. They could no longer perpetuate the old boys' network by filling vacancies through word of mouth. Now they had to advertise each post, which made it harder – although by no means impossible – to discriminate against qualified applicants.

Women gained control over their own body. In 1967, Britain significantly expanded the conditions for legal abortion. Six years later, two Supreme Court cases – Roe vs Wade and Doe vs Bolton – did the same in the US. By the late 1980s, abortion, subject to restrictions, was legal in most western European countries, as well as New Zealand, Australia, and Canada.

African Americans were starting to overturn centuries of racism. From 1954, a liberal constitutional revolution at the Supreme Court scrapped rules enforcing the segregation of races and bans on interracial marriage.

A black protest movement, involving sit-ins and long marches in the face of billy clubs and tear gas, secured the 1964 Civil Rights Act, which outlawed discrimination on the basis of race, colour, religion, or national origin. A Voting Rights Act the following year protected black voting rights. Three years later, discrimination in housing provision was outlawed.

The British parliament voted to decriminalise gay sex in 1967. Two years later, New York police raided the Stonewall Inn and sparked riots by gay men, lesbians and transsexuals. Those protests evolved into the gay pride movement which, by the end of the 20th Century, was starting to win the right for same-sex marriage and equal treatment.

These changes did not achieve equality in western countries. Even today, prejudice and discrimination continue – in pay scales, in treatment under the justice system, in police brutality, in abuse on the street, in exclusion from senior positions in politics, the media and business. But they finally began the process of rectifying it. It was the start, not the end, of the battle.

It is impossible to quantify the loss of freedom that racism, sexism and homophobia have caused over the centuries. Countless black people were killed, enslaved, or brutalised because of it. Countless women lived lives devoid of meaning and agency. Countless lesbians and gay men were spat at, or beaten up, or trapped in a mimicry of life where they could not express their true self. In many cases, people who called themselves liberals were responsible for this oppression. In others, they turned a blind eye, because these people didn't count.

But when these discriminated-against groups rose up in the post-war period, they did not reject liberal values. They showed true commitment to them, rather than selective application. Their campaigns were based on individual rights, liberty and reason.

Those battles brought back the question of belonging and asked searching questions of liberalism's relationship with group identity.

Two definitions of the group emerged. The first was based on oppression. The battle for equal rights demonstrated what should have anyway been obvious by the time of the Dreyfus Affair. Even if people didn't see themselves as a member of a group, they were often treated as if they were one. Regardless of whether a Jewish person in France in 1906 strongly associated with being Jewish, others strongly thought of them in those terms. Regardless of whether a black man in Alabama in the 1950s thought of himself as black, others most certainly did. And therefore the group existed.

When people said they wanted to stand up for women, they were not talking about a desire to promote humans born with a certain biology. They were talking about a class of people who faced oppression because of how others saw them. They were members of the group 'women' because they all faced the same restrictions.

Secondly, there was also a more active and positive view of group identity. Oppressed groups often had pride in their identity. They embraced the very categories that had been used to smear and denigrate them for centuries.

This corresponded to Orwell and Berlin's work on belonging, where the group could be a positive place of self-identity. For Orwell and Berlin, this was primarily about national identity. But the same arguments applied to those with marginalised identities.

As it happened, Berlin himself was not especially sympathetic to this idea. 'Yes, I know,' he said dismissively. 'Black studies, Puerto Rican studies, and the rest.' But in fact it was his work that recognised belonging as a core part of the human experience. There was no reason it should be limited to national identity.

Liberals after Berlin took his vision further than he was prepared to do. They started applying his ideas to groups based on sex, gender, skin colour, sexuality, religion, language, nationality, and more. There are no truly satisfactory terms for this mixture of culture and identity, but the best is probably 'marginalised.' These are groups who are distinct from the dominant culture in a society. Usually, they are a minority, but that's not always the case. Women often make up a majority and are still under-represented in leadership positions.

People could find meaning in these groups, whether it was through a sense of community, or heritage, or a shared history of struggle, or music, dress, cuisine. It could enrich their lives. That might simply be about lifestyle and self-identity, but it could also be political, in the same way that Orwell found political meaning in the English love of a cup of tea. And that was precisely what many marginalised people did, through phrases such as 'black is beautiful,' or the development of queer culture.

Liberal pluralism did not just tolerate this type of group identity. It welcomed it as part of the expression of different ways of life and people's authorship over their lives.

In the years after Berlin's pluralism theory, and especially from the 1980s, liberal philosophers started to build a picture of how such group identity worked. It was a delicate and difficult task: a historic compromise between two extremes of political philosophy.

On the one hand was pure universalism. This viewed human experience and conduct as full of commonalities. Cultural deviations were ephemeral, transitory issues – a detritus of superficiality that was not worth bothering with.

Orwell and Berlin had shown that this was false. People did not act like that. Any liberalism which tried to claim they did was misguided. And any which tried to force them to would become tyrannical.

On the other hand was cultural relativism, which was worse than false. It was the abyss, the terrible shadow which loomed large over any mention of identity.

Cultural relativism arguably went back to Ancient Greece, but it found expression during the 18th Century with the work of the German philosopher Johann Gottfried von Herder and in the early 20th Century through anthropologists like Ruth Benedict. In the late 20th Century it was given a powerful new lease of life on parts of the activist left through postmodernism – a collection of theories which rejected 'grand narratives.'

Relativism viewed cultures as if they were internally pure. They were homogeneous blocks of humanity with an essence, a fixed set of characteristics, which spoke with one voice. They were, in effect, disconnected territories, between which there could be no shared communication or shared values.

Under this view, no culture was any better or worse than any other. None could judge what went on in another, because there were no universal values to do so. Culture itself was its own moral authority.

If cultural relativism was true, even the most despicable acts could be justified on the basis that they were culturally appropriate. The conclusions it came to, much to the horror of its left-wing defenders, were invariably very right wing. What opposition could there be to imperialism, for example, if it was a genuine cultural practice? Why oppose Nazism? To accept relativism was to submit to atrocities at the extreme of the human condition.

Berlin himself had teetered close to cultural relativism once or twice, but then he pulled back. It was wrong, he realised, to treat cultures as complete and self-contained, with thick insurmountable boundaries. That was a vision of cultures as 'impenetrable bubbles' or 'windowless boxes.'

Berlin recognised that relativism wasn't just false on pragmatic grounds. It was also essentially false as a description of human life. Universality does exist – not just in theory, but as a point of objective fact. All cultures have a belief in key values like freedom, equality, justice and belonging, even if they express them in different ways, estimate them to different degrees and apply them to different groups.

Among those universal values is empathy – a capacity to imagine what things are like for others, to find the commonality between people as well as the distinctions. This was what provided the windows into the cultural boxes.

Relativism also presumed people were much more rigid than they really were. In reality, individuals have various identities – parent, child, spouse, a lover of your continent, your country, your city, and much more besides. Each of these identities had its own multiple cultural sources. No single culture defined an individual. They contributed to them, but they did not encapsulate them.

This was the area in which liberals went to work. Chief among the thinkers processing these issues were Will Kymlicka, who set out a liberal theory for multiculturalism, Chandran Kukathas, who rejected it on laissez-faire grounds, Brian Barry, who agreed with neither of them, and Susan Moller Okin, who critiqued it on liberal feminist grounds.

One of their key disagreements was the extent to which the state should actively support marginalised groups.

Take positive discrimination. This is the tactic of introducing unequal treatment in order to improve the condition of people who face unfair disadvantage, for instance by favouring female applicants for senior positions in business or politics.

For some liberals, this was intolerable. The use of unequal law to favour a group was a step too far. It treated people on the basis of their group membership rather than as individuals.

For others, it was a way to achieve equal status for individuals. The starting position of society was stacked against marginalised groups. They had reduced access to education, faced greater material barriers, and experienced widespread discrimination. As a temporary measure, positive discrimination could rebalance those odds.

Barbara Babcock, the first woman to serve as an assistant attorney general in the US Department of Justice, made the case well when she was asked how she felt about getting a job because she was a woman. 'It feels better,' she replied, 'than being rejected for the position because you're a woman.' Her point was that men often enjoyed positive discrimination. It was just never acknowledged.

Another issue concerned exceptions in law on the basis of religious membership. Was it right, for instance, to exempt Sikhs, who wear a turban, from legislation requiring the wearing of motorcycle helmets?

Some liberals felt it was not. The Sikh had not been stopped from riding a motorcycle. He was deciding not to because of his religion. That was his personal choice and it was not the state's job to cater for him when constructing road safety policy.

Other liberals felt it was. In line with Berlin's injunction that conflict over values should be eased wherever possible, they wanted to reduce the private challenges people faced, especially when it came to religious membership and societal participation.

But the fiercest debate raged over what to do about conservative religious cultures that limited the freedom of their members. Taylor and Mill had encountered this problem in the case of Mormon polygamy. Liberals, they believed, had to allow people to live illiberal lives, anything else was a kind of tyranny. They had recommended a solution of entry and exit checks – a need for the liberal state to ensure that people entered these arrangements willingly and were able to leave when they wanted.

The blossoming of cultural diversity in the 20th Century threw up many more examples. Jehovah's Witnesses, for instance, believed it was against God's will to receive blood and sometimes tried to exclude their children from necessary medical procedures. The Pueblo Indian community in the US denied housing benefits to Christian converts. An Old Order Amish community, which wanted to live apart from mainstream American life, won the right to take its children out of school at the age of 14 instead of 16, in order to limit their awareness of the outside world.

But the most common and pernicious limitations on freedom within religious groups were inflicted on women. Examples included female genital mutilation, in which the clitoris is either removed or mutilated to deprive a woman of sexual pleasure in adulthood, polygamy, forced marriage – including rape victims being made to marry their attackers – and punishment for bringing dishonour against the family.

Liberals had different instincts about how to solve these problems. Tellingly, the debate mirrored that over economics, with hands-off laissez-faire liberals disagreeing with those who wanted a more active state.

The former camp argued that the state should simply ensure that people had the formal right to exit illiberal communities. Getting any more involved than that was overstepping its bounds. Most liberal feminists wanted much more extensive action.

Conservative religious communities, they said, started inculcating women with notions of servility when they were young, through the social authority of father figures, backed by the complicity of older women. Once that damage was done, it was impossible for girls to become the kind of confident autonomous women who would be prepared to leave their community. They wanted an activist state that ensured young women were given the tools to make truly free choices.

There was also disagreement about what to do about illiberal cultural institutions. What was the liberal response to the Catholic Church's refusal to ordain female priests, for instance? Was it entitled to continue as it wished? Or did the state have a duty to force it to reform, or at least remove tax exempt status?

These were difficult questions and the debate did not offer easy answers. The disagreements were occasionally very heated, but the liberals on both sides were united by a common sense of values. They recognised a central moral fact: that authority lay with the individual. This was the crucial principle that gave clarity to the whole endeavour. Groups did not matter on their own terms. They mattered only insofar as they mattered to the individual.

Because most individuals did think they mattered, groups should be respected. But that respect ended where the group tried to limit individual freedom. Cultural diversity and identity were ruled over by the great meta-values of liberal thought: freedom of choice, reason, autonomy and moderation.

And yet, as the years wore on, the liberal debate was overshadowed. For perhaps the first time, liberals found that they were talking increasingly to themselves, with little impact outside of academia. They were being ignored.

Liberalism was no longer at the centre of political debate. Its place had been taken by a new form of political thought: identity politics.

And that school had its own heritage, its own way of doing things, which rejected liberalism's commitment to the individual altogether.

The process that created identity politics began in the 1960s and 70s, when campaigners on the left started to ask some searching questions of liberalism.

What exactly was this thing called the individual? Liberals had an easy answer. The individual was everyone. The whole point of the individual was to create a set of political rules that treated people as moral equals. It was a category that stood for universal humankind.

But if that was true, why did the entire practice of liberalism appear to refute it? Why did it take so long for women to enter the conversation? Why were black people excluded from it? Why were lesbians and gay men seemingly outside of its remit?

Maybe the individual wasn't everyone after all. Maybe when liberals said 'individual' what they actually meant was heterosexual white men.

And who were these liberal theorists exactly? They were mostly heterosexual white men.

Campaigners started putting two and two together. It wasn't hard. The conclusion was near-inescapable. Liberalism wasn't about freedom. It was about freedom for heterosexual white men.

This critique was called standpoint theory. It was one of the most important ideas in 20th-Century politics. As soon as it was expressed, it changed everything.

Standpoint theory was a form of epistemology which stated that our knowledge of the world was dependent on the social context in which it was learned. If you were a white man, with the experiences of a white man, your view of freedom would be that of a white man. You would prioritise things like free speech, and maybe property rights. You probably wouldn't prioritise office harassment, or racial discrimination in employment contracts, or domestic violence.

Standpoint theory was more than a political argument. It went to the heart of the human ability to process reality. It suggested that people's imaginative capacity was limited. When they thought about the world, they went through their own experiences and then projected them out as if they were universal. But they weren't. They were just their experiences.

Given the history of liberalism, this theory seemed convincing. Liberal theorists had spent generations talking about universally applicable ideals that had been applied only to the segment of the population that looked like them.

Until the 1960s, feminism – the belief that men and women should be equal – had mostly been grafted on to existing political theories, like liberalism and Marxism. When its first completely indigenous system of thought emerged, it was called radical feminism. And it used standpoint theory to launch a devastating critique of liberalism.

Under this view, liberalism had conspired to allow the oppression of women through a two-stage process: silencing and classification.

The silencing started in school. Feminist researchers in the US discovered that both male and female teachers, across all age groups, from kindergarten to college, were more likely to pick boys than girls to answer questions in the classroom. The researcher Peggy Orenstein found this approach reduced girls' willingness to speak at a very young age. It then continued into adulthood: across various cultures, from England to Japan, women were encouraged to be demure as a prerequisite of ladylike behaviour.

Society understood, on some deep unspoken level, that if women talked they could provide their own accounts of the world. Their silence was a prerequisite of their control. This left men free to define the parameters of the political world and present them as universal.

Secondly, there was classification. Political thought had been cut in two throughout the history of ideas. There was the public world – the world outside the home where politics was conducted. And then there was the private world, the world inside the home, a place of family loyalties and comfort – slippers and a dog snoozing by the fire. It was defined as non-political.

Women were relegated to the second. So all their concerns – the right to vote, or work, or keep property, or be safe from domestic violence – were quarantined outside of political debate.

This was why liberalism had taken so long to apply its critique of power to the restraints faced by women. They had been designated out of pertinence. Liberalism consequently built up a political system that was ostensibly about general freedom, but was in fact about men's freedom.

In order to tear down the system of male domination, women in the radical feminist movement needed to speak out. And they did so with a phrase that was startling in its simplicity and implication: the personal is political.

All the things that had previously been ignored as 'private' were now primed for discussion: every wolf-whistle in the street, every bit of housework that the wife did instead of her husband, every lazy assumption about male sexual desires. And there, from the ground up, by politicising what had until then been considered irrelevant, a new world would be built that was suitable for both genders.

But radical feminists didn't trust liberals with this project. 'Anyone who has listened closely to academic feminists,' the author Jennifer Nedelsky wrote in 1989, 'will have heard this undercurrent of rage at all things liberal.'

The problem wasn't just about past failures. It was conceptual. Radical feminists didn't feel the individual was a useful unit of analysis.

The relationship between radical feminism and liberalism was a lot like the one liberalism had with Marxism. Marxists had looked at what liberals called a transaction – a business owner hiring a labourer, for instance – and reinterpreted it as an example of class oppression. Radical feminists looked at what liberals called interpersonal relationships and reinterpreted them as part of a system of gender oppression.

This was class war, along gender lines – not a collection of individual power relations that needed to be recalibrated. Under this analysis, liberalism was at best naive and at worst complicit.

A second flank was opened up against liberalism on the grounds of ethnicity. If standpoint theory was true, then liberalism's claims of universality were no more than a form of ethnocentrism – the evaluation of one culture according to the assumptions of another. Liberalism claimed to project norms that could apply to all humanity, but were in fact culturally specific to the West.

In this view, imperialism was not just something that happened to coincide with the advent of liberalism in the late 17th Century. They were the same project. Locke's account of property acquisition, for instance, had legitimised colonialism. By acting as if European forms of agriculture were what constituted the proper cultivation of natural resources, it allowed western countries to treat aboriginal people as being in a state of nature, with no property rights, and thereby justify the appropriation of their resources.

If liberal values were pertinent at all, it was only to certain cultures, at certain times. They had no more moral force than any other way of looking at the world.

For many campaigners, liberalism became irrelevant the moment that standpoint theory was accepted. It was the product of predominantly heterosexual white men and therefore those were the only people it was pertinent to.

This was the moment that liberalism and social justice movements got divorced.

That was a tragedy for both camps. The uncomfortable truth, which almost no-one could accept, was this: liberalism needed standpoint theory and standpoint theory needed liberalism. Without each other, they became poorer and more narrow-minded versions of themselves.

The strict interpretation of standpoint theory was dangerous. It veered too close to relativism. It seemed to write off any capacity for empathy or emotional imagination. It could not explain, for instance, why someone like John Stuart Mill would care about women and strive to liberate them. It provided no justification for why people of one background often stood in solidarity with those from another.

But a more moderate interpretation of standpoint theory provided a corrective to liberalism's historic failures. It would acknowledge that people brought their social context to politics while rejecting the idea that they were forever to be a prisoner of that social context.

Its moral lesson for liberalism was therefore quite simple. Lived experience was a data point. If liberalism listened to people, if it searched out the full range of human experience, it could discover and address restraints on freedom that it hadn't previously identified. That required a degree of inquisitiveness and humility that was historically lacking.

The things they heard would also reveal whole new concepts that liberals had never really thought about before.

One of the core notions of radical feminism was the idea of a separation between sex and gender – where sex was the biological form of man and woman and gender was the social expectations and constraints society projected onto them.

That distinction opened up whole new territories of liberty. For centuries, women were told to act in a ladylike way – meek and submissive – and to avoid dangerous jobs or scientific work. Men were told to be tough and physical, to play sports and avoid caring professions. Once you started breaking that down, those socially enforced straitjackets fell away with them, in a manner that was as liberating for men as it was for women.

Men too could be gentle and caring, they could allow themselves to feel more and not have to hide their emotions to demonstrate manliness. Women could enter professions they had been barred from or never considered. They could express competitive urges in sport or work, decide if they wanted to prioritise career success over childcaring. Everyone could break free of the vacuous binary of manliness and femininity that had trapped humans for centuries.

Similar opportunities were offered by queer theory, which was demolishing the monolithic nature of terms like heterosexual and homosexual and suggesting that human sexuality was fluid and ever-changing. People didn't have to define themselves with these terms, or feel a need to constantly prove them. They could be whatever they wanted.

How much human misery, over how many centuries, had centred on the demands of insisting people were either 100 per cent heterosexual or 100 per cent homosexual? How many people silently suffered, too afraid to confess their feelings, under the terrible weight of that false choice? And now here was a theory that was offering liberals a solution.

This was a whole new arena of human flourishing through free choices, without the anchored-down simplifications of old brute categories. It was rich, fertile terrain for liberalism, which it proceeded to almost completely ignore.

Liberalism's lack of interest in these ideas made it weaker and narrower. It lost contact with whole parts of the left. And more fundamentally, it was cut off from the people it should have been fighting for. A political philosophy grounded in individual freedom was being rejected by many of the people who stood to gain the most from it.

But the damage was not one sided. The divorce hurt movements for social justice too. With liberalism drifting away, there was no-one to point out the hazards of group politics.

The truth was, there was something terribly dangerous about standpoint theory. If interpreted in a strict way, it suggested that groups were homogeneous. By saying that someone's views were defined by their social context, standpoint theory implied that everyone in that social context thought the same way. It robbed people of their individuality.

This same problem also operated on the group's external boundaries. By making information processing dependent on identity, strict standpoint theory rejected the human capacity for empathy. It suggested that groups had hard shells and were utterly distinct and separate from each other.

And that's when the abyss opened up again. This was relativism: the homogeneous inside and the blocked-off outside. Orwell's nationalism. Berlin's windowless boxes. Monolithic uniform blocks of humanity, unable to talk to or understand one another.

Most academics and activists in social justice movements recognised this danger. 'Cultural identity is not a fixed essence, lying unchanged outside history and culture,' Stuart Hall wrote in *Cultural Identity and Diaspora*. 'It is not some universal and transcendental spirit inside us on which history has made no fundamental mark.' Writers could feel the shadow of cultural relativism looming behind them. They would constantly emphasise the need for identity to be 'relational and intersubjective,' acquired through 'dialogical relations' in a 'negotiation' or 'dialogue.'

But no matter what they did, they could not make the shadow go away. Because without a constant reminder of the absolute moral primacy of the individual, there was no way to properly articulate the danger.

The result of this failure was that the powerful within a group began speaking in the name of the powerless. That process happened in two ways: on the right and the left. On the right, it meant that older traditional figures in marginalised groups took control. On the left, it meant that progressive academics and activists secured an unchallengeable moral right to speak on behalf of everyone else.

The first glimmer of what would come actually occurred back in 1851, at a women's rights conference in Akron, Ohio. A group of men had interrupted the speakers on stage to claim that women were too delicate to take on political activity.

A black woman named Sojourner Truth rose from the audience. She had been born a slave in 1797, spent her youth being beaten and mistreated, and then escaped in 1827 to become an itinerant preacher.

The men didn't want her to speak. And neither, in all likelihood, did the white women, who made up the majority of the audience. Many women's rights campaigners at the time feared the presence of black women would damage the suffrage movement. But Truth spoke anyway. And the things she said would become a cornerstone of political thought in the 20th and 21st Century.

'That man over there says that women need to be helped into carriages, and lifted over ditches, and to have the best place everywhere,' she said. 'Nobody ever helps me into carriages, or over mud-puddles, or gives me any best place. And ain't I a woman? Look at me. Look at my arm. I have ploughed and planted, and gathered into barns, and no man could head me. And ain't I a woman? I could work as much and eat as much as a man – when I could get it – and bear the lash as well. And ain't I a woman? I have borne 13 children, and seen most all sold off to slavery, and when I cried out with my mother's grief, none but Jesus heard me. And ain't I a woman?'

Even now, this passage still feels immediate and full of moral clarity. In reality, the 'ain't I a woman' refrain was added later, but that does not lessen its force. Truth used her own life experience to discredit the homogeneous generalisations that were applied to women. She did it in response to men's criticism of the suffrage movement, but actually the greatest impact was on feminists themselves.

From a black woman's perspective, the feminist campaign for women to be able to work was a cruel joke. They had worked. They had been forced to work by slavery. And then even after slavery ended, they were still disproportionately likely to work, often as domestic help. Black women weren't treated as gentle and delicate. Nor were they treated as chaste and virtuous. They were portrayed as sexually immoral and constantly available – a legacy of their repeated assaults during slavery. When white women in the suffrage movement stood up and claimed to speak on behalf of all women, it was quite clear they did not.

Feminism had reduced all political struggle to the structural oppression of women. The anti-racism movement had reduced all political struggle to structural oppression of black people. That ignored individuals who did not fit neatly into those binary categories. They had been marginalised by movements dedicated to giving voice to the marginalised.

That cry to be heard took on a distinctly modern form in Massachusetts in 1974.

A network of black lesbian feminists had helped form the Boston chapter of the National Black Feminist Organisation. But even breaking the group down on race and gender lines wasn't enough to address the prejudice they faced. Once the chapter was established, they discovered homophobia in their ranks.

So they broke off and formed something new: the Combahee River Collective. 'Combahee was really so wonderful because it was the first time that I could be all of who I was in the same place,' founder member Barbara Smith said. 'That I didn't have to leave my feminism outside the door to be accepted as I would in a conservative black political context. I didn't have to leave my lesbianism outside. I didn't have to leave my race outside, as I might in an all-white-women's context where they don't want to know all of that. That is what Combahee created, a place where we could be ourselves and where we were valued.'

Over the late 1970s, the group held regular retreats for black lesbian feminists to sit, debate and formulate their positions. In 1977, it published the Combahee River Collective statement.

At its heart, it was a rejection of binaries. The statement was not making a political claim against gender oppression as women, or against racial oppression as black people, or even against homophobia as lesbians. It was making a claim against all of them, from victims of all of them.

'We realise that the only people who care enough about us to work consistently for our liberation are us,' the statement said. 'Our politics evolve from a healthy love for ourselves, our sisters and our community which allows us to continue our struggle and work.'

It communicated a single, damning truth: no-one had ever really cared about women like them. To even say you were representing black feminist lesbians would have prompted derisive laughter in most of society in the 1970s and still would in many parts today. Mainstream political debate hadn't cared about black feminist lesbians. Liberalism hadn't cared about them. Even the movements set up to challenge racism or sexism hadn't cared about them.

It was an act of rebellion against the white women who had claimed to represent them as women and failed, and the black men who claimed to represent them as black people and failed. Their groups were homogenised in a way that erased their experiences.

This could have been the moment when liberalism emphasised the freedom of every individual in such marginalised groups. But it was not. The authority of the group was all there was to work with. So instead the group splintered into smaller and smaller units to ensure consistent internal characteristics. And that was the moment identity politics properly took form.

'We believe that the most profound and potentially most radical politics come directly out of our own identity,' the statement said, 'as opposed to working to end somebody else's oppression.'

From its origin at the Combahee River Collective, identity politics slowly became more dominant on the radical left in the US. Organisations were established representing the ignored sub-categories within marginalised groups: Asian Women United, Women of All Red Nations, the National Black Women's Health Project.

A similar process was taking place in Britain at the level of local government. It began in Brixton, south London, in 1981. It was the depths of recession. Brixton was an area with a large African Caribbean population, which experienced particularly high unemployment and crime. On 6th April, the police launched Operation Swamp 81. They flooded the area with plain-clothes officers and started stopping and searching mostly young black men.

After a few days of ever-increasing tension, a confrontation broke out. Anything could have set it off, but as it happened it was confusion over the fate of Michael Bailey, a young black man who had been found with a four-inch stab wound. Over 200 young people – black and white, but mostly of Afro-Caribbean heritage – turned on the police. Officer responses were stepped up and soon there was a full-scale riot.

By the time it was over, hundreds of cars and vans – predominantly police vehicles – had been torched and many were injured. The disturbance soon spread out from Brixton across all of London, to Peckham, Southall, Wood Green, Finsbury Park, and Notting Hill, and then to other major cities in England.

Thatcher's government was known for its commitment to ramming through hardline policies, but its response to this incident was surprisingly pragmatic. It decided that it needed to engage with ethnic minority communities and especially to direct funding at voices of moderation within them. 'If they don't deliver,' George Young, the UK's first minister for race relations said, 'people will turn to the militants.'

A home affairs select committee report that year encouraged local authorities to 'make as much direct contact as possible with ethnic minorities.' The Conservative party was treated with suspicion by even the most moderate of ethnic minority political leaders, so most of the work fell to councils under Labour control. Chief among them was the left-wing Greater London Council.

Under its leadership, it began to formulate the identity politics of the Combahee River Collective into an official programme of local government funding. It started dishing out money. The Ethnic Minority Unit gave over £2.3 million to 247 groups in 1983/84, rising to £6.2 million to around 300 groups five years later. More funding was available through other institutions too, including the police committee, the enterprise committee and the arts and recreation committee.

Most of these communities urgently needed the investment. But there was something unusual about the way the money was distributed. It was not done on the basis of need. It was done on the basis of identity. The council set up race-relations units and arranged consultations with 'community representatives.' These figures were expected to encapsulate the views and desires of everyone in their ethnic or cultural group.

'Race relations' was a new name for what had until that point mostly been an anti-racism agenda. But the task of eradicating racism was not actually part of the programme anymore. There had been a subtle shift. Policy was now aimed, in the words of Gita Sahgal and Nira Yuval-Davis of the Southall Black Sisters group, who were troubled by what they saw, at 'preserving the "traditions and cultures" of the different ethnic minorities.'

This blueprint was eventually copied by various local governments. In 1985, black, white and Asian youths clashed with the police in riots in the Handsworth area of Birmingham. The city council emulated the Greater London Council strategy. It created nine 'umbrella groups,' based on faith and ethnicity, to represent communities and distribute resources. They included the African and Caribbean People's Movement, the Bangladeshi Islamic Projects Consultative Committee, the Birmingham Chinese Society, the Council of Black Led Churches, the Hindu Council, the Irish Forum and the Vietnamese Association. These representatives had not been elected. They had no mandate from which to act as figureheads for the varied views of the people they were supposed to represent.

As soon as this left-wing view of identity had been initiated, it began to have very conservative consequences. The self-selected representatives were usually drawn from older, male, reactionary figures in the community – typically those involved in local business and religious worship.

They now had enormous power. They acted as the communications channel between government and the public. And more than that, they were the financial distribution points from the local council to the community.

The idea of a fixed group identity was being injected directly into local government. These authorities told people that they were fundamentally different from each other on the basis of their heritage, skin colour, or faith, and that they were homogeneous with other people of that group.

That message hit home. It created the incentives for a particular kind of self-identification. If you wanted to get a new community centre, there was no use trying to highlight the social need for one. It was more effective to brand it as an Asian or African-Caribbean community centre. People soon began to internalise these requirements.

The process could be seen quite dramatically in Bradford, which operated a similar initiative. In 1981, Bradford city council decided that it had 'no direct knowledge of Asian needs and requirements,' so it adopted the Greater London Council approach: a 12-point race relations plan making clear that every section of the city had an 'equal right to maintain its own identity, culture, language, religion and customs.'

In the same year, it set up the Bradford Council for Mosques, with six founding members representing various Islamic sects and traditions. The Council received initial grants for its headquarters and funding for mosque-based social projects, including two centres for the elderly, and Muslim youth and community centres.

This was supposed to represent the 'Muslim community,' although even that term highlighted the manner in which the system helped its most conservative elements. Many people of Pakistani or Bangladeshi heritage did not relate strongly to the word 'Muslim.' They happened to be Muslim, but it was not the way they primarily defined themselves. Some said Pakistani, or Bengali, or Kashmiri, or Asian, or simply British. But now the mosque was made the voice of the community, through which individuals communicated with the world.

What about a young lesbian teenager in the Asian community? She was now represented by the conservative older men in the Council for Mosques structure, many of whom denied her existence. What about an atheist, or one of the many Muslims who was equally happy in the mosque and down the pub? They too were notionally represented by the religious authorities.

'What we wanted from the council,' local businessman and mosque chairman Sher Azam later told journalist Kenan Malik, 'was their support for our efforts to make sure that our children were not lost to our culture or Islam. We were worried that they had become so Westernised that they no longer saw themselves as Muslims or wanted to practise their faith.'

This approach soon went national. In March 1994, the Conservative home secretary Michael Howard made it clear that he would like there to be a Muslim 'representative body' to communicate with central government. By November 1997, the Muslim Council of Britain was formed.

The Council didn't really represent anyone. In 2006, after nearly two decades of activity, an NOP poll for the Policy Exchange think tank found just six per cent of British Muslims thought it represented their political views. 'Who elected them?' one respondent asked. 'Who put them there? I don't even know who they are.'

This process was repeated in many western countries. In Denmark, for instance, the liberal Muslim MP Naser Khader objected to the way the prime minister kept acting as if conservative Islamic figures somehow embodied their community. 'Nobody listened,' he said. 'The government thought if they talked to someone who looked like a Muslim, then they were talking to real Muslims. I don't look like what they think a Muslim should look like – I don't have a beard, I wear a suit, I drink – so I'm not a real Muslim.'

All the abstract dangers of identity politics were quickly becoming real. Individuals within marginalised groups were being airbrushed out of existence. Self-selecting leaders were able to present themselves as representatives of a homogeneous group, as the projection of its general will, when they had no legitimate claim to do so. The most conservative elements of political thought were able to define a community. And people were encouraged to see themselves as fundamentally different from other groups, even in conflict with them.

By the late 1980s, identity politics had established itself as a respected area of academia, due in large part to the work of Kimberlé Crenshaw, an American legal scholar. Crenshaw recognised something important: that discrimination intersects. Different forms of oppression can operate on someone at the same time to create a unique form of disadvantage. And she started looking at the point of that interaction, the spaces where multiple forms of prejudice overlapped.

She published two academic articles which were crucial to this new area of study: *Demarginalizing the Intersection of Race and Sex* in 1989 and *Mapping the Margins* in 1991.

They were rigorous, had a sophisticated theoretical framework and came wrapped in a detailed understanding of discrimination case law. They challenged some of the enduring simplifications of identity politics and brought a sense of scholarly respectability to what had until then been a fairly haphazard activist initiative. This was called intersectionality.

'Black women can experience discrimination in ways that are both similar to and different from those experienced by white women and black men,' she wrote. 'Black women sometimes experience discrimination in ways similar to white women's experiences; sometimes they share very similar experiences with black men.

Yet often they experience double-discrimination – the combined effects of practices which discriminate on the basis of race, and on the basis of sex. And sometimes, they experience discrimination as black women – not the sum of race and sex discrimination, but as black women.'

Crenshaw was bringing a welcome dose of complexity to what had been binary opposition around race – white/black – and gender – man/woman. Intersectionality argued that people's lives were formed from multiple axes of social division, which worked together and influenced each other. They included not just race and gender, but also class, sexuality, disability, ethnicity, nation, religion and age.

Examining anti-discrimination legislation, Crenshaw showed how black women were ignored by a legal system that was designed to prevent racism and sexism, but not their own unique form of disadvantage. Her approach helped to make the group identity discussion much more complex and ensured there was a focus on those who were marginalised within groups.

But this was not a rejection of identity politics. It was an attempt to make it more sophisticated. Like the Combahee collective before her, Crenshaw believed there was something valuable in a political commitment to identity.

She compared two statements: 'I am a person who happens to be black' and 'I am black.' The first implicitly emphasised the idea of universal humanity, of a demand for rights on the basis of moral equality regardless of identity. It put the individual first and the identity second, as a kind of circumstantial irrelevance. The second was different. It was proud. It put identity first.

'"I am black" becomes not simply a statement of resistance,' she said, 'but also a positive discourse of self-identification, intimately linked to celebratory statements like the black nationalist "black is beautiful."'

For the time being, Crenshaw concluded, this was a more effective way to proceed. 'At this point in history, a strong case can be made that the most critical resistance strategy for disempowered groups is to occupy and defend a politics of social location rather than to vacate and destroy it.'

This was still compatible with liberalism's positive view of group identity. But it had a different effect, because identity politics was not guided by the notion of the individual. Moral authority had been placed instead on the group identity without any countervailing force to protect its individual members.

In the case of British local government policy, this had allowed conservative forces to claim leadership. But in this academic and activist context it handed it to left-wing campaigners.

Who got to speak for these identity groups? On what basis did they have that mandate? Did people have to have that identity – of being black, or a woman, or a gay man – or could they choose to discard it? Could they refuse to be defined in that way? What actually was the political content of the identity, beyond a general desire for liberation? Was there agreement on what constituted liberation, or on the tactics for how to achieve it? How was that decided? What happened to the people who associated with that identity but did not agree with whatever they concluded?

The response to these questions was typically that these issues would be worked out in a dialogue. But that raised the question of how that dialogue would take place. In reality, almost by definition, that dialogue took place between those who already agreed with identity politics, in whichever forum they were using.

Campaigners became the leadership class of the group.

The first problem identity politics faced was what to do with its critics. Many campaigners began to treat challenges to their opinion as an act of 'violence.' Statements were collected around universities, activist movements and newspapers in which it was claimed that the presence – either in person or writing – of those who disputed identity politics made its members feel unsafe.

This was a logical consequence of the group identity. If the individual was defined by the group, then it followed that any political attack on the group was an attack on the individual. The two things became indistinguishable. The notion that the personal was political now took on a grim new form, in which political speech was equivalent to personal victimisation.

In most cases, identity campaigners maintained the censorship threshold of inciting violence that Taylor and Mill had used in *On Liberty*. But the standards by which that threshold was reached dropped precipitously, from actual physical violence to the notion that critical arguments were themselves a form of assault.

A more difficult issue emerged over what to do about critical voices from within the identity group. This, for any political movement based on identity, was a profound problem, because people with the same identity would have different views. Some, for instance, would have more conservative opinions than others. This was precisely the sort of difficulty Lenin had faced with the proletariat. Now it rose again in a markedly different form.

Feminists were well aware of this problem and addressed it under the term 'adaptive preference.' This described situations where people with few choices learned to become satisfied with those they had. Their ambitions shrank to fit their smaller horizons.

Some feminists saw the greater tendency of women to value caring roles, both within the home and professionally, as an adaptive preference born of limited historic opportunities. Others believed that some women's tolerance of sexual harassment, like wolf whistles in the street, were part of the same pattern. It was a tendency that was consistently associated with older women, who sometimes learned to accept and even cling to the more limited options they had during their formative years.

Similarly, many people in marginalised racial groups held views that were not radical and were in fact highly conservative.

There were two ways to deal with this problem. The first was the Marxist approach of accusing the dissenting individual of false consciousness – they had not grasped the authentic collective identity. They did not really know or understand what they were saying. They were too distorted by the power that had been inflicted upon them. Identity politics leaders would have to speak for their identity group and tell its members what their authentic social self really thought.

The second was to strip the person of their identity altogether and claim that they were not really black, or not really gay, or not properly a woman, because if they had been, they would not have held those opinions. This second approach, which on the face of it was absurd, became quite common. When Peter Thiel, the gay Silicon Valley billionaire, expressed support for the Republicans in 2016, he was soon told that he was no longer entitled to his sexual identity. 'By the logic of gay liberation, Thiel is an example of a man who has sex with other men, but not a gay man,' the writer Jim Downs wrote in *Advocate* magazine, 'because he does not embrace the struggle of people to embrace their distinctive identity.'

When an Asian politician called Sajid Javid became British home secretary in a Conservative government, it provoked a similar response. Social media accounts on the left quickly began to question his identity, often with the racial slur 'coconut' – meaning brown on the outside, white on the inside. 'When I refer to Sajid Javid as a coconut, I am not referring to his skin colour,' the comedian Shazia Mirza said on the website *Boundless*. 'I am referring to his lack of loyalties and patriotism towards a group of people from the same background.'

Javid compared the abuse he received from the left to that from the far right. 'I get it from the far left, including lots of Asians, who say: "He's not brown enough." I get it from the right, and the far right in particular, saying: "He's too brown." They believe, whether they are coming from the far left or far right, that someone's colour should define who they are – or their background, their faith, or something, that characteristic, rather than the content of their character.'

The identity to be found in the group was, by definition, based on what made it different to other groups, not what they had in common. It involved a search, in the words of black power activist Julius Lester, for 'a recognition of those things uniquely ours which separate ourselves from the white man.'

Instead of a search for the commonality in humankind, a quest was undertaken for the precise opposite. 'The demand is not for inclusion within the fold of "universal humankind" on the basis of shared human attributes,' the feminist sociologist Sonia Kruks concluded, 'nor is it for respect "in spite of one's differences." Rather, what is demanded is respect for oneself as different.'

This was not accidental. By placing moral authority on the group rather than the individual, identity politics had cemented difference as a key attribute of human society.

The walls dividing groups soon became much thicker. A new notion emerged, called cultural appropriation. It described the use of a culture's ideas, intellectual property, traditions, symbols, artefacts, genres, rituals, or technologies by members of another culture without permission. That included things like cuisine, dance, dress, language, music, traditional medicine and religious symbols.

Under liberal thought, especially Constant and Mill, the mixing of people, cultures and ideas was considered to be intrinsically good. There was a fundamental underlying belief that by mixing ideas, greater truths could be discovered. And indeed on any typical cultural account of civilisation, collaboration and cross-fertilisation propelled the evolution of all the great pleasures of life, from music to recipes.

But under identity politics, culture was increasingly becoming a battleground where hermetically sealed groups could not share ideas. In May 2017, a local Portland website ran an interview with two white women who had set up a burrito food truck after enjoying the food on holiday in Mexico. 'I picked the brains of every tortilla lady there in the worst broken Spanish ever, and they showed me a little of what they did,' one of them said.

Within hours, the website was overwhelmed by angry comments. 'This article is a clear example of how media perpetuates and reinforces racism and white supremacy, brandishing it as "fun" and "innovative,"' one read. A so-called 'shit list' of 'white-owned appropriative restaurants' was published online, listing 60 restaurants in the area owned by white people serving ethnic cuisine. A local newspaper, the *Portland Mercury*, linked to the list and called it a 'who's who of culinary white supremacy.' Within 48 hours, after at least 10 death threats, the two women closed the food truck.

Debates over cultural appropriation started to take place almost daily, usually on trivial matters and yet involving grave accusations of racism. The American reality TV star Kim Kardashian West was criticised for wearing her hair in braids. A white American teenager who posted a photo of herself in a prom dress in the Chinese qipao style received thousands of abusive tweets.

Campaigners insisted that the prohibition only held when the dominant culture appropriated an item from a marginalised culture, but in fact the attacks were far broader. The singer Bruno Mars – of Jewish, Puerto Rican and Filipino heritage – was accused of appropriating 'black music.' The Trinidad and Tobago-born rapper Nicki Minaj was accused of appropriating Chinese culture when she performed her song 'Chun-Li' on the US TV show *Saturday Night Live*.

The cultural appropriation argument contained a grain of truth. Cultural mixing is frequently unequal and, historically, has often taken place as a result of war or colonialism. Even in peacetime, racism and inequality have tended to scar cultural exchange. It was because of racism, for instance, that the black pioneers of rock and roll were ignored, in favour of the white Elvis Presley.

But the problem had been mislocated. In those instances, the issue was the racism, not the sharing. 'The problem is that if The

Beatles tell me that they learned everything they know from Blind Willie Johnson,' the poet Amiri Baraka said, 'I want to know why Blind Willie is still running an elevator in Jackson, Mississippi. It's that kind of inequality that is abusive, not the actual appropriation of culture because that's normal.'

Cultural appropriation's view of culture as a form of territory, from which things could be stolen, had several implications. The first was that cultures were singular and fixed, rather than various and evolving. Appropriation could have 'corrosive effects on the integrity of an exploited culture,' the writers Bruce Ziff and Pratima Rao argued, because 'tears can appear in the fabric of a group's cultural identity.' This idea of degradation suggested that a culture's natural state was pure and bounded.

The second went back to the issue of leadership. If culture was a kind of territory, and appropriation was borrowing without permission, then it followed that there were gatekeepers: people who could decide when it was and was not appropriate.

Standpoint theory provided that gatekeeper status. People's entitlement to adjudicate on cultural borrowing derived from their identity. But once again, it faced the problems it always faced: that people did not necessarily agree simply because they shared an identity.

In 2014, London's Barbican Centre tried to stage a show called Exhibit B, in which motionless black performers were exhibited as artefacts. It was based on 19th-Century freak shows, with the intention of exploring and addressing slavery, colonialism and modern-day racism.

Protests erupted and it was closed down. The actors involved put out a statement stating that 'we are proud to be black performers in this piece,' which they described as 'a powerful tool in the fight against racism,' but their voices were discounted. 'Black artists do not have the authority to define what is and is not acceptable,' the sociologist Kehinde Andrews said during a debate with one of the performers. This raised the question of who did have that authority.

In truth, the gatekeepers were the academics and activists who demanded the closure. 'When all is said and done, the racial outrage is about protection of the boundaries of racial authenticity as the exclusive property of the guild of Racial Spokespersonship,' concluded Adolph Reed, professor of political science at the University of Pennsylvania.

The activist control over politics that was expressed in these identity disputes mirrored the control that identity politics had given conservative male figures in the UK. The process was identical. It served to strengthen the powerful within a group. In this case, that meant those of a particular political persuasion who had been sufficiently educated to take part in the debate, which was conducted in esoteric terms using academic and occasionally impenetrable terminology.

But it also did something more pernicious than that. It started corroding the notion of human empathy.

Under Berlin's pluralism, empathy and universal values made cross-cultural communication possible. But under cultural appropriation, that capacity was dismissed.

In 2017, a painting called *Open Casket*, by the artist Dana Schutz, was included in the Whitney Biennial Exhibition in New York. It was based on a photograph of the body of Emmett Till, a 14-year-old African American murdered by two white men in Mississippi in 1955. The exhibition also featured a painting by the artist Henry Taylor titled *THE TIMES THAY AINT A CHANGING, FAST ENOUGH!* which depicted Philando Castile, an African American man shot dead in his car by police in 2016.

The latter painting caused no controversy, but *Open Casket* did. The reason was that its creator, Schutz, was white while Taylor was black.

Protests were held outside the exhibit. The artist Hannah Black wrote an open letter to the museum's curators calling for Schutz's painting to be destroyed. 'The subject matter is not Schutz's,' she said. 'White free speech and white creative freedom have been founded on the constraint of others, and are not natural rights. The painting must go.'

This attack suggested that only people of a certain identity could feel any commonality with those of another. 'What started as a thoughtful post-colonial critique of certain types of imperial texts,' the novelist Kamila Shamsie said, 'somehow became a peculiar orthodoxy that essentially denies the possibility of imaginative engagement with anyone outside your little circle.'

The attack on empathy was more severe than any of the other restrictions imposed by the theory of cultural appropriation, because it centred on the quality that could give rise to human commonality in the first place. It was therefore natural that one of the main battlegrounds against appropriation was the novel, the art form that was perhaps most capable of allowing someone from one culture to imagine what it was like to be from another. Increasingly, authors were told to restrict their writing to people who were fundamentally like them – racially, sexually, culturally and nationally.

The writer Zadie Smith, of half English and half Jamaican heritage, offered the most cogent defence against this assault, in a discussion of *Olive Kitteridge*, a novel by Elizabeth Strout which featured characters whose experiences were far removed from her own, in the coastal town of Crosby, in the US. In doing so, she reached out beyond the subject of literature to the basic capacity for human empathy.

'What do I have in common with Olive Kitteridge, a salty old white woman who has spent her entire life in Maine?' she wrote. 'And yet, as it turns out, her griefs are like my own. Not all of them. It's not a perfect mapping of self onto book – I've never met a book that did that. But some of Olive's grief weighed like mine. I am fascinated to presume, as a reader, that many types of people, strange to me in life, might be revealed, through the intimate space of fiction, to have griefs not unlike my own. And so I read.'

There was a willing audience for the message of the new left-wing identity politics. It was right-wing identity politics.

For a new breed of nationalist, the broad outlines of the argument seemed perfectly natural. Humanity was split into homogeneous blocks of strictly bounded identity. Those groups were defined by their competition and incompatibility. They just happened to be in a different group: the dominant one.

Right-wing identity politics was on the move in the wake of the financial crisis. It had changed markedly over the 20th Century. It learned how to put on a more respectable face for mainstream attention.

It was not fascist. It was not totalitarian. It did not seek full control over every aspect of people's lives. It did not try to stop elections. It was rarely explicitly racist. It made the leap which all successful political movements must take: learning where to compromise and where to stand firm.

It had largely given up on the notion of biological superiority in race, or at least in expressing it out loud. Instead, most nationalist thought had adopted a new idea, derived from a quasi-fascist group called the New Right in France during the 1960s and 70s. It was called ethnopluralism.

This was a cultural argument, rather than a biological one. It stated that ethnic groups were no longer to be considered superior or inferior. There was no hierarchy. But they were distinct. If they mixed together, they would damage each other.

Humankind was unsuited to living alongside other cultures. People were only able to flourish within the society of their ethnic heritage. Multiculturalism was therefore a crime against the human condition. Diversity was an act of violence against the self.

In truth, racism was never far from the surface. The New Right never seriously suggested that other cultures were really equivalent to their own or better in any particular area. The language used to describe immigrants was relentlessly negative and centred on their threat to the domestic population.

But this twist gave nationalists an inbuilt intellectual defence. Immigrants were criminals and rapists, they insisted, but this wasn't because they were morally inferior. It was because they were living outside of their natural context.

The ethnopluralist view allowed the nationalist right to deracialise their rhetoric. It won them a place in mainstream debate that had previously been denied to them. They used that status to pursue the classic nationalist position: the nation was homogeneous. It was pure. Any new additions were an infection.

Crime was racialised. Any criminal act perpetrated by the indigenous population was ignored, but any committed by an ethnic minority was sensationalised. As the years went on, crime was redefined so that nearly all criminal activity was portrayed as committed by minorities or immigrants.

But these new arguments, which were, to all intents and purposes, identical to fascism's hatred of minorities, were no longer branded racism. They were now nativism: the belief that states should be populated exclusively by members of the native group.

The terror attacks on the US on 11th September 2001 delivered a crucial turning point in the narrative. They provided a villain. All the various abstract ideas of nativism could now be encapsulated in the image of the suicide bomber, looking to enslave the West.

In many ways, 21st-Century Muslims took the role that Jews took during the Dreyfus Affair. They could be portrayed as capable of global conspiracy and yet simultaneously as crime-crazed thugs and rapists.

As ever, the caricature made no logical sense. How could a group with the latter characteristics be clever enough to accomplish the former? But as before, that did not matter and was in fact useful. It meant Islam could be blamed for everything, from petty crime on the street to national humiliation on the global stage.

To properly establish themselves, nationalists needed to convert economic anxieties into cultural anxieties. They addressed the effects of laissez-faire – from the death of industry in the 80s to austerity in the 2010s – in the language of nativism.

This offered access to a massive new pool of support. A whole swathe of the western world had been left behind by the indifference of the market, from the post-industrial towns of northern England to the Rust Belt of former manufacturing states in the US. Nationalism presented itself as the solution. And it did so with a socio-cultural narrative for socio-economic problems.

The immigration debate, for instance, was rarely framed as pure nativism. It was purposefully intertwined with economic concerns. Immigrants were coming to steal people's jobs, or their benefits, or to put a strain on housing or public services. The immigrant offered a perfect symbol of industrial decline and reduced job security. They could encapsulate a variety of complex problems, with various causes and effects, in the same way that the Jew could encapsulate the reasons for France's difficulties during the Dreyfus Affair.

For many millions of people, especially men previously working in unsustainable or non-competitive industries like coal or parts of manufacturing, economic decline had robbed them of their status. Unemployment had not just had an economic impact. It had destroyed self-worth.

Nationalists gave them a simple and compelling message. Those who had been left behind did have status. It was the status of their country, their gender and their race – all the things that could never be taken from them. The ethnic minorities and upwardly mobile women who were now laying their claim for fair treatment were dismantling the natural social order. It was time to fight back.

It proved to be powerfully effective. Across Europe and America, the popularity of nationalist politicians soared.

In some countries, like Poland under the Law and Justice party, nationalists were able to seize control of the government. In others, like Austria under the Freedom Party and Greece under the Popular Orthodox Rally, they became minority partners in a coalition with a mainstream party. In others, like the Netherlands under the Party for Freedom, nationalist parties supported minority mainstream governments in return for policy concessions on immigration and other issues.

But even where countries were not formally ruled to any extent by nationalists, they seemed to fall under their influence. They could dominate media coverage and dictate the political agenda from opposition.

Nationalism exploded into countless organisational variants outside of party politics. They ranged from the media-friendly Generation Identity group in the US, to so-called alt-right networks online, to street movements like the English Defence League in the UK or Patriotic Europeans Against the Islamisation of the Occident (Pegida) in Germany, to lone-wolf terrorists like Anders Breivik, who murdered 77 people in Norway.

Groups and individuals like these had historically struggled to convince white people that they were engaged in a culture war against minorities. But now left-wing identity politics seemed to accept their narrative and was, in its own way, substantiating it.

'It is the left that has been most active in racial consciousness formation,' the far-right campaigner Richard Spencer wrote on the white supremacist website *Radix*. 'On campus, they have created not only African-American Students Association but Asian Students Associations, that is, racial consciousness where little cultural commonality existed. Leftists are engaging in the kind of ideological project that traditionalists should be hard at work on.'

Whole sections of the internet, centred primarily around popular forums like Reddit and 4chan, came to be populated by angry young men claiming to represent their own white male heterosexual identity.

A so-called 'manosphere' developed which routinely described all women as 'worthless cunts' and 'attention whores.' A subgenre of YouTube videos emerged attacking feminism, in which the comment section would typically fill up with comments branding women as worthless, stupid, lazy, shallow, and deserving of violent retribution. Separatist groups such as Men Going Their Own Way urged men to avoid all contact with women.

At the heart of it was a website called Breitbart, which operated as base-camp for the alt-right. It was described, even by fellow travellers like the commentator Ben Shapiro, as 'pushing white ethno-nationalism as a legitimate response to political correctness.'

The new nationalism was extremely multifaceted and diverse. It spanned from lonely internet users to presidents, from terrorists to respectable politicians.

But in all guises it shared these central political ideas. The people were homogeneous. They were in a struggle against the elites. Immigration had to be stopped. There was no truth except for tribal identity.

This was how the culture war began. It was the product of identity groups, on left and right, with no notion of the individual and no acceptance of shared values.

In 2017, an event took place in Evergreen State College in Washington that seemed to encapsulate this new kind of politics. The university had a tradition, going back decades, of a Day of Absence during which ethnic minority students would stay away from campus in order to highlight their contribution to the college. But in 2017, organisers decided to flip the arrangement around. Instead, white students and staff would be asked to stay away from the campus.

This stepped over a line for Bret Weinstein, a biologist and evolutionary theorist teaching at the college. 'There is a huge difference between a group or coalition deciding to voluntarily absent themselves from a shared space in order to highlight their vital and under-appreciated roles and a group encouraging another group to go away,' he wrote. 'The first is a forceful call to consciousness, which is, of course, crippling to the logic of oppression. The second is a show of force, and an act of oppression in and of itself.'

The email was widely circulated. Shortly afterwards, during a protest at the university, students took a detour to confront him in his classroom. They called him a racist and a white supremacist.

He tried to engage in debate with them. 'I listen to you and you listen to me,' he insisted. 'I am talking about terms that serve the truth.' A student replied: 'We don't care what terms you want to speak on. This is not about you. We are not speaking on terms of white privilege. This is not a discussion, you have lost that one.'

The protests took over the entire university, leading to an extraordinary public meeting between hundreds of angry students and the college president, George Bridges. Several students jabbed their finger in his face and screamed at him. Critical voices were silenced. One black student rose during the meeting to encourage her classmates to allow Bridges to speak. 'I want to hear what he has to say,' she said. But she was drowned out by boos. 'These are the lost ones,' another said. 'The lost ones are rising. Pay no attention.'

Those who did not reflect the authentic self of the group were silenced. Only afterwards did critical students feel able to speak out. 'I wasn't against Bret and I was against their methods and the protests,' one mixed-race student said. 'I was deemed a traitor. They explained that we are trying to give voice to those who don't have a voice. I thought it was very ironic. The people who were telling me that they wanted to give a platform for minorities to speak weren't listening to mine. It creates a campus where you're just really scared to say anything, so you just keep your mouth shut.'

Then the right-wing identity politics counter-attack took place. Weinstein appeared on the conservative TV channel Fox News, under a segment entitled 'Campus Craziness.' Right-wing media outlets in the US and UK were starting to obsess over student free speech stories, as an example of what they called 'generation snowflake.' The channel misrepresented the controversy, running a banner which erroneously suggested that the Day of Absence initiative ordered 'All White People Leave Campus OR ELSE.'

The response was instantaneous. Alt-right accounts directed hundreds of phone calls, anonymous texts, emails, social media attacks and death threats at students and faculty at the college. 'You radical bitches need to rein your asses in,' one email read. 'The days of anti-white male hatred, intolerance and bigotry are over.'

Soon an anonymous caller said he was on his way to 'execute as many people on that campus as I can get a hold of.' The school was evacuated for three days. Alt-right and white supremacist groups gathered outside under the banner of a so-called Patriot Prayer group.

'As someone who's monitored white nationalist activity for the last 25 years, I can state without reservation that the evidence of dangerous far-right activity is incontrovertible,' Devin Burghart, president of the Institute for Research and Education on Human Rights, said. 'The flags, banners, hats, T-shirts and other paraphernalia in the crowd represented a melding of white nationalists and alt-right activists with far-right paramilitaries.'

That in turn confirmed the worst fears of the students about what free speech entailed. 'When we're dead,' one of them said, 'when people die, and you're sitting here like: "We'll at least they got to practice their free speech." I'm so sorry about it, your free speech is not more important than the lives of black, trans, fems and students on this campus.'

What went on in that campus was not an isolated incident. It was a case study in a kind of political debate that spread across society – online, in newspapers, on morning television, in election campaigns, even the corridors of power.

In that titanic struggle between two warring sets of tribes, liberalism was simply an afterthought. One by one, its principles were made irrelevant by a new political culture. There could be no compromise. There could be no step-by-step decision making, or reason, or objectivity. There could be no individuals. There was only the group.

This was no longer the politics of how to change the world. It was the politics of who you were. And that was a zero-sum game.

11. ANTI-TRUTH

The individual and reason had been born as twins in Descartes'
Cogito. One was the unit of analysis, the other the language it
used to communicate. But quite suddenly – just as liberalism was
facing multiple threats from the resurgence of nationalism, the
rise of identity politics and the after-effects of the financial crash
– people's ability to use reason diminished. The notion that there
was a commonly accepted set of facts about the world and an agreed
way of assessing them came under intense challenge.

The key to understanding what happened lay in a strange
moment in the past: a remote outpost, populated by scientists and
warring children, in 1950s Oklahoma.

The outpost was being run by one of the great figures in social
psychology, Muzafer Sherif. He had become obsessed with a single
subject: how quickly humans could descend into tribalism and
what, if anything, could pull them out of it.

This led him to create a series of extremely unusual sociological
experiments, in which researchers would run summer camps
for young boys, create the conditions for group conflict, record
the way they behaved, and then try different ways to repair the
relationships.

In 1954, his team of researchers found an isolated 200-acre
camp completely surrounded by the Robbers Cave State Park that
was ideal for the experiment. The nearest town, McAlester, was
40 miles away. Heavy foliage meant the camp could not be seen
from nearby roads. Signs saying 'Keep Out' and 'Restricted' were
erected on the surrounding fence.

Most importantly, the terrain of the camp meant he could keep two groups of boys there without them realising the existence of the other group. This was key to the whole endeavour. Sherif wanted to spend the first week of the three-week study with each group developing its own identity. He predicted this would power the aggressive social responses which followed when they finally discovered the other group.

The camp was perfect for this purpose. It had two cabins, which were beyond the sight or hearing of each other. There were duplicate facilities for swimming and other camp activities. The only place both groups would use was the mess area where they would eat, but the timing of meals could be staggered to prevent any evidence emerging of the other set of boys.

Then he had to select the participants. He wanted 22 11-to-12-year-olds, from middle-class Protestant families living in Oklahoma City, who didn't know each other. It was vital that they were as culturally and socio-economically similar to each other as possible. But he also needed them to have no pre-existing relationships that could influence the groups' behaviour.

Sherif's researchers stood in the playground of participating local schools and observed the pupils playing in their natural environment. Once they found suitable individuals, they delved into their school records and conducted interviews with teaching staff. A file on each boy was composed with their IQ, school grades, social attitudes, popularity and 'membership in school cliques.'

Then they visited their parents. Sherif told them he wanted to give the boys 'a wholesome cooperative living experience which will prepare the youngsters for better citizenship and to be leaders in their communities.' No mention was made of the real purpose of the experiment.

After 300 hours of selection Sherif whittled down the list to 22 'experimental subjects,' who would be split into two groups of 11 each.

His plan was split into three phases, each lasting a week. In the first, the two groups would be kept apart and watched for how they developed a group identity. Towards the end of the week they would slowly be given evidence of the existence of the other group.

In the second week a series of competitive games would be held, in which the groups challenged each other to baseball, a tug-of-war and speed trials for erecting tents. Winning them meant you received a prize, losing meant you got nothing. This was supposed to replicate the kind of contests for resources and political power that typified group dynamics in the real world.

In the third and final week, the two groups would be brought back together, first by being given a shared space in which there was no competitive element and then by facing seemingly natural challenges which required their cooperation to defeat.

The bus arrived to pick up Group One on 19th June 1954. Sherif could hardly believe how quickly a group identity started to emerge. One boy had arrived late at the first stop and the delay allowed the four already on board to develop an embryonic clique. Before the bus had even arrived at the camp, they asked if 'us south-siders' could stay together and chose neighbouring bunks.

Group Two was picked up the next day. For the first few days, the two groups were kept apart doing a variety of activities, like canoeing and swimming. But toward the end of the week, the 'subjects were allowed to discover definitely that there were two groups in camp.'

On the sixth day, three members of Group One found paper cups belonging to Group Two at their hideout. They instantly became angry that 'outsiders' had been there. The next day they were 'allowed to wander within hearing distance' of the other group as they played on the baseball field. Their immediate reaction was to 'run them off' and 'challenge them.' One of the group instantly started to cry.

The next morning they changed some of the features of the baseball field. 'Now this is our diamond,' one of them said. The other areas of the camp were also classed as their territory. They spoke aggressively of 'our Upper Camp,' 'our Stone Corral' and warned that the other group 'better not be in our swimming hole.'

Group Two was demanding to know if the other group had a name. The researchers, who were disguised as camp caretakers, would not tell them. They decided to come up with one for themselves: The Eagles. They formulated plans to make a flag and adopt a song one of them had sung on the bus as their anthem.

Group One settled on the name Rattlers, after coming across several rattlesnakes at the camp. They were also developing their identity in other, deeper ways. The most influential boy in their clique hurt his toe one day but did not mention it until it was discovered at bedtime. This started a social norm of being 'tough.' Boys who injured themselves after this incident did not cry and often continued to engage in strenuous activity.

Swearing was also met with strong group approval, much more so than in the Eagles group, where the boys encouraged each other to be 'good sports' and refrain from bad language.

Finally, at the end of week one, the presence of the other group was definitively announced by camp caretakers. Immediately the Rattlers demanded to be allowed to challenge them. Sherif's team devised a tournament that would involve competitive activities like baseball, tug-of-war and treasure hunts. They would be given highly desired rewards for winning, such as medals and knives. Sherif struggled to hold off demands that competition start immediately. 'Delaying Stage 2 became increasingly difficult,' he wrote.

On the baseball field, the Rattlers devised their own flag, put it behind the backstop, and erected a 'Keep Out' sign. Both tribes had by this stage developed an almost sacred approach to their flag. One Eagle stated that it 'shall never touch the ground.'

The next day they set eyes on each other for the first time, as they both arrived at the baseball field for their first competition. The Eagles approached with their flag on a pole singing their anthem. For a moment the two groups stood and looked at one another, then one of the Eagles called a Rattler a 'dirty shit.' This was their first communication. The Rattlers picked on one Eagle boy in particular, calling him 'fatty.' As the game wore on even those boys who had encouraged good relations between the group started hurling insults.

For the first time, the two groups ate in the mess hall together. They continued to shout names at each other and started singing derogatory songs. Several members of the Eagles asked not to have to eat with the Rattlers. After dinner, they went outside for their second contest – tug-of-war – which the Eagles lost.

The Rattlers marched off celebrating their victory, but they forgot their flag, which was still on the baseball field. Craig, the Eagle group leader, pulled it down. For a while they tried to tear it up before someone suggested they burn it. One boy found matches. They then set fire to the flag and attached the remnants back to where it had originally flown. 'This flag-burning episode,' Sherif wrote, 'started a chain of events which made it unnecessary for the experimenters to introduce special situations of mutual frustration for the two groups.'

The Rattlers found their burned flag the next morning and a fist fight broke out. Eventually – it's not clear from the notes exactly how long they would allow these fights to go on for – staff intervened to stop the fighting, but the altercations would start again at regular intervals. After just one day of contact, the groups were effectively at war.

That afternoon, the Rattlers plotted a raid on the Eagles' dorm. The leader, Mills, set a time of 10.30pm. They darkened their face and arms in imitation of commando paint, approached the other side of the camp, broke into their dorm, turned over their beds and stole their clothes and comic books.

Once the Rattlers retreated back to their own camp, they turned one of the pairs of jeans they had taken into a new flag. They attached it to a stick and scrawled over it: 'The Last of the Eagles.'

The Eagles started a retaliatory raid the same evening, but they were stopped by research staff when they saw the boys putting rocks in socks to use as weapons. Instead, they waited until the next morning, when the Rattlers were eating breakfast. Then they armed themselves with sticks and bats and raided their dorm, turning over beds, covering it with dirt and throwing possessions around. Camp supervisors had to again intervene to prevent further violence.

This series of tit-for-tat fist fights and raids went on for days. Sherif's second stage had reached its natural endpoint: deep and abiding hatred. Neither group would have anything to do with the other. Sherif noted how 'derogatory terms for the out-group had become standardised.'

The researchers now attempted to bring the two groups together. First they tried to reduce the animosity by having them share time together in a non-competitive structure, but this proved almost impossible. The boys felt 'positively insulted' by the idea.

Eventually, Sherif introduced his hypothesised solution, a series of experiments in which problems were created that would require cooperative solutions. A large water tank that supplied the camp was blocked off, requiring the two groups to work together to fix it. A tug-of-war rope was used to move a truck, needing the strength of both sets of boys to get it going.

It was mostly successful. The group identities of the Rattlers and Eagles were still set in place by the end, but Sherif reported that they were intermingling and even occasionally offered friendly farewells when they were dropped off back home.

Sherif's experiment was intended to test whether competition for resources triggers group conflict, but it hinted at something broader – something fundamental in the human personality, a driving force deep in our psychology. We are instinctively prone to forming groups. This mechanism is so strong it can make us see things which are not there and think things which we know to be untrue.

In 1951, a pioneering social psychologist called Solomon Asch set out to test how strongly we will conform to the views of the group. He devised an incredibly simple study. Eight male college students were invited into a room and given two sets of cards. Card one had a set of three lines on it: one short, one mid-length and one long. Card two had just one line. They were then asked which of the lines on the first card was the same length as on the second. This process was to run for 18 rounds.

It was very basic. The lines were not remotely similar. Anyone could see what the right answer was. In a control test ahead of the experiment, the error rate was below one per cent.

The eight students went into the room. But in reality, only one was a college student – the other seven were actors. They were lined up ahead of the experimental subject so that he would see all but one of them give their answers before he gave his.

These seven actors were given detailed instructions about how they should behave. For the first two rounds they would all say the same obviously right answer. Then, in the third round, they would all give the same wrong answer. They would do this again for 11 of the remaining 15 rounds.

The aim of the study was to see how this kind of social pressure would affect the one genuine student in the room. When everyone in a room was saying something that was visibly and demonstrably wrong, did people stick to what they knew was true, or did they shift their position in line with the group? What does it take to make us veer from reality?

The results were startling. In over a third of cases – 36.8 per cent – the test subject swung with the group.

After a series of post-experiment interviews, in which the subjects were told what the experiment was really about and how it worked, Asch categorised those who went with the group into three categories.

The first felt self-doubt and lacked confidence. Asch said they experienced a 'distortion of judgment.' The second felt the group was wrong but answered with them so they could appear normal. They were said to be suffering from 'distortion of action.' Interestingly, even many independent-minded types who stuck with their own answer later acknowledged a feeling of intense pressure to conform. 'I do not deny,' one said, 'that at times I had the feeling to go with it, I'll go along with the rest.'

The third category experienced 'distortion of perception.' They did not even consciously recognise that they were wrong or that something strange was happening. They literally saw the line as longer or shorter, depending on what was necessary to stay in the group. Their perception of the world had apparently shifted in order to satisfy social pressure.

In the late 20th Century, a new form of technology developed which intensified group dynamics and threatened to drive them out of control. It began in the CERN research facility in Switzerland in 1989, where physicists were trying to work out a way to share information between them about their experiments.

A British computer scientist called Tim Berners-Lee, had an idea, which he called Mesh. A new kind of technology called hypertext allowed him to link documents together, so that a highlighted word could be selected by a user and take them to another document containing further information. The documents could then be stored on several servers, which were interconnected, so they were readily available for everyone to read.

'Vague but exciting,' his boss scribbled on top of the proposal. In 1990, Berners-Lee began to write the code for it. This time he came up with a name that showed precisely the right amount of ambition: World Wide Web. Its growth was extraordinary. In 1993, just one per cent of the world's information flowed through the web. By the year 2000 it was 51 per cent. By 2007, it was 97 per cent. Electronic mail, instant messaging, forums, online shopping and blogs soon became widespread. As the internet developed, communicating with colleagues from home got easier and shopping slowly became more convenient.

But it was only in the mid-2000s that it became clear how fundamentally the web would change politics. The key development was called Web 2.0. Instead of just reading content, users would be able to generate it themselves.

The social networking site Facebook went online in 2004. At first it was only available in Harvard, where its founder Mark Zuckerberg was studying, but by 2006, it was open to anyone over 13 years old. It now has 2.6 billion active users. Facebook also owns the WhatsApp messaging service, with two billion users, Facebook Messenger, with 1.3 billion users, and the photo-sharing app Instagram, with over one billion users.

Twitter went online in 2006, with a single message: 'just setting up my twttr' – from Jack Dorsey, a New York University undergraduate. It would allow users to post short messages, in no more than 140 characters, to their followers. It grew exponentially. There were 400,000 tweets posted per quarter in 2007. By 2008, it was 100 million tweets. By February 2010, Twitter users were sending 50 million tweets a day. In 2020, the number was close to 500 million.

YouTube, a site which allows users to watch and upload video content, went online in February 2005. In November, a Nike advert became the first video to hit one million views. By the end of the year, the site was receiving eight million views a day. It was soon taken over by Google. Users now upload eight hours of footage every second, in 76 different languages.

Very quickly, these tech companies attained a degree of power and influence over human communication which arguably has no parallel in human history. Some 3.4 billion people now use the internet. In the average North American household, there are 13 internet-connected devices. Users check their phone about 150 times a day and touch them over 2,600 times a day. Most Americans get their news from Facebook and Twitter.

At the start, it really did seem as if social media might lead to a new, empowered politics, one in which the individual was equipped to take on the state.

When combined with smart phones – web-surfing mobile computing devices with cameras – it offered something which had never previously been possible: cheap access to media-creation and distribution technology.

People who could not afford professional video cameras in the analogue age, or who would not have been invited into a broadcasting studio, were now able to shoot video on their phone, upload it to the internet, and reach millions of people. The financial obstacles to media creation and promotion had been removed. Similarly, anyone could be a publisher, simply by switching on their phone and typing in their thoughts.

This had a powerful effect, especially in dictatorships. Social media was a direct threat to the ability of despots to control the flow of information. Until now, they could make sure that the content which went out from national TV studios and was printed in newspapers suited them. Social media changed all that. It democratised information.

On 17th December 2010, a Tunisian street vendor named Mohamed Bouazizi set himself on fire in a protest against police harassment. It was captured on a camera phone, uploaded to social media, and spread around the world. Huge protests broke out. Within days, President Zine El Abidine Ben Ali had been overthrown.

The video kept spreading. Political demonstrations broke out in Egypt against the dictator Hosni Mubarak. Up to two million people protested in Cairo's Tahrir Square, many of them mobilised by social media. Those who were killed by security forces were celebrated in Facebook pages, which then themselves became focal points for resistance and organisation. The government eventually became so alarmed it tried to cut off the country's internet access, but it was too late. Mubarak was toppled, just like Ben Ali before him.

The 'Arab Spring' spread from that initial spark by a Tunisia street vendor to Algeria, Bahrain, Iraq, Jordan, Kuwait, Lebanon, Libya, Morocco, Oman, Sudan, Yemen and others.

For a brief moment there was a surge of optimism that this new technology might make despotism impossible. But that proved too optimistic. The revolution in Libya degenerated into chaos, sadism and despair. In Syria, the dictator Bashar al-Assad, with help from Russia's nationalist president Vladimir Putin, managed to hold on to power by murdering hundreds of thousands of his people.

As the dreams of the Arab Spring faded, the optimism about social media seemed to fade with them. Alongside its capacity for resistance against power, it demonstrated other previously unforeseen qualities. It super-charged the human instinct around group identity and undermined our capacity to process information.

Taylor and Mill had outlined the way that debate should operate in a free society. It required people to think for themselves, evaluate information rationally, be confident enough to seek out the strongest arguments against their position and humble enough to recognise where they might be wrong.

This required autonomy – an 'inward domain of consciousness' that allowed for genuine 'liberty of thought and feeling.' There had to be a space within people – a calm, protective barrier against outside influences – for contemplation.

This was always a struggle. As with most of Taylor and Mill's ideals, it was an aspiration. But when social media emerged, it seemed to recede altogether from view. And that happened for a quite simple reason. This technology was not designed to encourage rationality or independent judgement. It was designed to keep people constantly engaged. It prioritised methods it had learned from the advertising industry: a remorseless focus on maintaining user attention and the use of subconscious prompts in the emotional vulnerabilities of the human brain.

One of the reasons for this was that many of the companies people thought of as 'tech firms' were actually advertising companies. Around 90 per cent of Facebook and Google's revenue came from selling advertising.

Social media sites and their users agreed a mutually beneficial pact. It was contained in a screed of text listing the terms and conditions. The service was provided for free in exchange for data on the user's behaviour. An app for your privacy. The information was collected from the user and used to sell advertising.

Advertising as an industry developed during the great modernising shift, between the death of Mill and the advent of the First World War. At first it merely told people about what was on sale and where to buy it. But in the 20th Century, it became less about information provision and more about the shaping of desires. The industry began to take a more active role in the formulation of people's aspirations.

Advertisers understood that human beings – rushing to work, caring for a baby, visiting their parents – often didn't have the time to sit and rationally decide what they wanted. Instead, they were susceptible to subconscious automatic behaviour. Their brains tended to follow certain pathways, which could be exploited for commercial gain.

This is why products are often priced at £4.99 rather than just £5, say, or £799 instead of £800. Someone who took the time to think about the difference rationally would recognise that it was negligible. But the hurried, automatic part of the brain places undue priority on the first number it sees. Nearly everyone knows this is true, and yet nearly everyone is vulnerable to it.

For a long time, this effect was relatively contained. Advertising took place within limited spaces in people's lives. There was an advert in the newspaper, but they could skim over it. It came on during a television show, so they waited for it to end. It was plastered over a billboard, but they passed it by. Even when people chose to pay attention to the adverts, they were at least aware that someone was trying to influence them in a certain way. They knew they were experiencing advertising.

Advertisers, on the other hand, could not be sure that their adverts had been effective. Of course, certain campaigns would lead to increased sales of a product and that was unlikely to be coincidental, but there was little concrete information on the link between an individual advert and consumer behaviour.

The internet changed that. It provided a massive amount of data showing almost every aspect of consumer behaviour. It could show which pages people viewed, in which order, what terms they searched for and when, what their interests were and what device they were using when they searched them out. It could follow them, from the point they clicked on an ad, to the selection of a product, to the page at which they inputted their payment details and 'benchmark' that data against the performance of their competitors.

A powerful new infrastructure of analysis grew, using websites such as Google Analytics, Omniture and Coremetrics, to collect and evaluate user data. It had its own vocabulary to assess the most cherished behaviour of all: engagement. Measurement centred on the number of clicks, page impressions, time on site and bounce rate – the percentage of users who left after visiting just one page.

This was the information and design system of advertising online. But increasingly it also became the status quo for non-advertising too.

Social media companies could make more money on advertising when they captured the maximum amount of user time and attention possible. And that task demanded that they themselves behave like advertisers.

Companies hired vast teams of highly intelligent young people to work out how to satisfy this goal. Thousands of tests were run with millions of users to tweak the experience, covering everything down to the smallest details, from fonts to images to hues. All of it was geared towards that one central aim: maximising time and attention. Keep them clicking. Keep them scrolling.

A video ended and then another one started automatically. Someone liked a post the user had written and a red indicator appeared on the top right of the screen. The use of visible numbers was prioritised – from friend requests, posts and interactions – all carefully designed to make people respond to them and push them to return to the site, over and over again, several times a day.

The Facebook 'like' function, which let users show they enjoyed a post, was described by Sean Parker, the company's first president, as a 'social-validation feedback loop.' It was, he said, 'exactly the kind of thing a hacker like myself would come up with, because you're exploiting a vulnerability in human psychology.'

One of the key tools used in this process was that of variable rewards. It was the basic psychological driver behind slot machines in the gambling industry. When you randomised the reward schedule for a particular action, the user took that action more regularly.

Twitter and Facebook displayed infinitely scrolling news feeds that could be pulled down to be refreshed, just like a slot machine. The repeated use of red indicators and notifications made users come back time and again to see who had responded and what they had said .

The slot machine variable reward function made people spend more money. The social media variable reward function made them spend more time. And people kept spending the time. A tsunami of information started to overwhelm their lives. Drag, scroll, click, repeat. On every device. All the time. Friend requests, likes, Facebook posts, tweets, retweets, WhatsApp messages, blogs, video clips, memes, gifs, real news, fake news, audio clips. An endless incessant wall of noise which users kept returning to, several times an hour, every day, all the time.

Humankind's basic relationship with the world – the way it received news, discussed politics, bought things, socialised, heard music, celebrated birthdays, communicated with parents, and accessed entertainment – was suddenly sucked into an advertising model which pulled every psychological trick it could find to encourage further engagement.

The internal space that Taylor and Mill demanded started to shrink. Calm, properly contemplated rationality was alien to the advertising model. It operated instead in the world of emotional automaticity – desire and reward.

People lost the time they needed to think, to define and pursue their goals, to reflect, to remember, to reason. Instead, they were flooded with information. And that allowed their instincts to take over their rational decision-making.

Two qualities encouraged engagement more than any others: tribalism and emotions.

Facebook knew its users better than they knew themselves. They had told the company everything about themselves, by accident, over the countless hours they had spent on the site. They had liked pages revealing their interests, their friends, their job, their age and their leisure activities.

The company combined this information with that contained by data brokerage firms like Acxiom, on up to 200 million active consumers worldwide, covering their sex, race, weight, height, health, relationship status, politics, education, purchases and holidays, all of it analysed and cross-referenced to maximise advertising efficiency.

Facebook then used algorithms – a set of instructions for solving a command – to predict and shape its users' behaviour. The process was replicated by the full range of social media sites and apps.

It was a project unlike any other in human history. By the time it was done, users' lives started to become programmed by the algorithms. They listened to music, read news, bought products and even dated people chosen for them by the algorithm.

In 2011, Michal Kosinski, a psychologist at Cambridge University, made a startling discovery about this information. He and his team developed personality tests, put them on Facebook and asked people to fill them in. Millions did. Then they cross-referenced the personality test scores with their Facebook likes.

Using the results, Kosinski developed an algorithm that could compute the personality of Facebook users who hadn't even taken the test. It could predict extremely intimate information – people's sexuality, ethnicity, political views, personality traits, happiness, intelligence, and even whether their parents were separated – from which TV shows, books and magazines they said they enjoyed on Facebook. The results were staggeringly accurate.

'Obviously if you like Lady Gaga on Facebook, I can tell you like Lady Gaga,' Kosinski told the journalist Jamie Bartlett. 'What's really world-changing about those algorithms is that they can take your musical preferences or your book preferences and extract from this seemingly innocent information very accurate predictions about your religiosity, leadership potential, political views, personality and so on.'

To advertisers, this was data gold. It would allow them to rebuild the basic architecture of the user experience in a way that was most likely to engage them. To online firms, it meant that the world around the user could be shaped in a way they responded to most consistently.

Many people were unaware of this change. They continued to assume that the online world was like the real physical world, where different people shared communal space with each other. When two people of different cultures and political viewpoints walk past each other on the street, they exist in the same place, see the same buildings and cross the same roads.

What was happening online was something altogether different. The shared objective world was gone. People were living in a virtual world that reflected back their own subjective self. The news they saw, the products that were advertised, the views they came across, the advertising they clicked on – all of it was tailored around an algorithm's assessment of their identity.

The same applied to politics. People online were already prone to selecting the people they followed according to their bias. But the architecture of the online world drove that inclination even further. The sense of common humanity, or universal values, or national debate, or shared identity, began to recede. It was replaced by a personalised experience based on categories of identity. And those categories perfectly matched the groups given moral authority by identity politics.

When people began to realise this trend, they gave it a label: the echo chamber. It referred to an online space where a tribe would increasingly talk only to itself. But in fact this phrase was too modest. Echoes fade. These new tribal territories were more like feedback loops, in which messages contained did not fade, but increased in volume, becoming ever more extreme. This made identity ever more pivotal to people's assessment of politics, and demanded strict adherence to increasingly radical statements about that group's principles.

Nowhere was this process more evident than on YouTube. It quickly became the most popular social network in the US, with far more users than there were viewers for cable news. And those users were subject to an algorithm that seemed to push them towards ever more extreme material for their political tribe. This was chiefly because of its recommendation engine, which presented a viewer with options for what they might want to watch after they finished a video.

The YouTube algorithm was not based on how to make sure people came across alternate views so that it could preserve the health of liberal democracy. It was based, like that of other social media operations, purely on engagement. Initially, the website grounded it in 'clicks to watch,' but it then pivoted to 'watchtime.' Whatever got people watching longer was what mattered.

The political effect was potentially very far-reaching. If someone clicked on a left-wing video and watched it to the end, the recommendation engine would provide more left-wing videos. Out of the options, the user might pick one. Once they did so, their choices were again narrowed, on the basis that the algorithm presumed the user had made an active choice for more left-wing content. Videos which were more edgy or shocking, which triggered more of an emotional response, provoked more engagement and were therefore prioritised in recommendations.

An academic study in August 2019 tried to assess the extent of this development. It was the first large scale quantitative audit of its type. The researchers identified three online right-wing communities, each one more radical than the last.

The 'Intellectual Dark Web' discussed issues like the connection between race and IQ, but self-identified as a community of people willing to address controversial subjects rather than necessarily endorsing them. 'The Alt-Lite' flirted with far-right concepts, but denied being openly in favour of white supremacy. 'The Alt-Right' were out-and-out white supremacists.

The researchers looked at the direction of travel users took between these groups. They analysed 330,925 videos posted on 349 channels, processed over 72 million comments, and assessed over two million video and channel recommendations. They compared their findings with results from mainstream media channels without content from the right-wing culture war.

Videos on all three right-wing sites received more comments than those on mainstream media. And the more extreme a video was, the more engagement it received. Fewer comments were posted on the milder content on the Intellectual Dark Web and the Alt-Lite sites than the videos on the white supremacist Alt-Right sites – which, in 2018, reached a high of one comment for every five views. Those comments were almost uniformly supportive of the videos. One check of 900 randomly selected comments showed that only five could be interpreted as criticisms.

The study also suggested that people worked their way through the three groups, typically starting in the Intellectual Dark Web and ending up in the much more extreme white supremacy material from the Alt-Right.

The findings were not definitive, because demonstrating causation was difficult, but they were troubling. 'We find strong evidence for radicalisation among YouTube users,' the authors concluded. 'The study suggests that the pipeline effect does exist, and that indeed users systematically go from milder communities to the Alt-Right.'

If the conclusion was true, it wasn't restricted to the right. It was happening across the political spectrum. And as people's information about the world was increasingly filtered to reflect what they already thought, they started to react with shock and outrage at any information that did not fit their world view.

This was useful to social media sites, because outrage was one of the most effective mechanisms for encouraging engagement. Alongside tribalism, the promise of an emotional response was the chief predictor of engagement. One study of 100 million shares on Facebook found that the top performing headlines used phrases like 'shocked to see,' 'freaking out' and 'make you cry.'

On websites like Twitter, that promise of a strong emotional response typically came through the reaction of other users to something controversial.

In 2013, Justine Sacco, a corporate communications director, sent a sarcastic tweet about the way that white people in the West felt immune from disease and poverty. 'Going to Africa,' she wrote, as she killed time in Heathrow airport. 'Hope I don't get AIDS. Just kidding. I'm white!' She sent it to her 170 followers.

Before her plane even landed, she was the number one worldwide trend on Twitter. Hundreds of thousands of people online had deemed her a racist, rather than someone making a poorly judged joke. Her employer made it clear that she would not be staying in her job for long. 'This is an outrageous, offensive comment,' it tweeted. 'Employee in question currently unreachable on an intl flight.'

Thousands tuned in to watch her flight as it crossed the ocean, so they could savour the moment when she had internet reception again and learned what had happened. Twitter users adopted a hashtag – a category identifier which allows people to follow messages on a certain topic – #HasJustineLandedYet, which trended worldwide.

'Oh man, @JustineSacco is going to have the most painful phone-turning-on moment ever when her plane lands,' one said. Then: 'We are about to watch this @JustineSacco bitch get fired. In REAL time. Before she even KNOWS she's getting fired.'

Their predictions were correct. She lost her job. Her life was destroyed. Workers threatened to strike at hotels she planned to visit. Her own family distanced itself from her, telling her she had tarnished their name. She was ostracised.

In July 2015, a dentist from Minnesota went hunting in Zimbabwe and killed a lion named Cecil. He wounded the animal with an arrow and then finished it off, about 40 hours later, with a rifle shot.

The outrage crackled across social media. Celebrities posted his home address. Crowds appeared outside his office to chant 'murderer.' The outside of his house was vandalised with the phrase 'lion killer.' Internet activists posted falsified one-star reviews for his business. He was ruined.

Those were the early days. Sometimes, as in the case of the dentist, the person had done something reprehensible. Sometimes, as in the case of Sacco, they had just made a poorly judged joke. Sometimes they really hadn't done much wrong at all.

In the years which followed, online shaming became a daily event. It was like a reputational human sacrifice ritual. Every day, someone had to be destroyed by the internet.

In many cases, the people who suffered the ritual were lambasted for years. They were sacked from their jobs and never allowed to say anything online without being reminded of whichever misguided tweet they'd sent. Many developed a form of trauma from the episode.

Moral outrage was the perfect political expression of social media's dual prioritisation of emotion and tribe. A desire for anger was the primary cause for engagement. It served to make a tribal member feel superior simply by virtue of being in the tribe.

Saintliness was demonstrated by viciousness. By disparaging the supposed racist, the supposed animal murderer, the supposed metropolitan elite, the user could better demonstrate their own virtue. And that applied equally to those within their identity tribe. In fact, it worked better like that. If someone of high virtue was being shamed, it showed that the denigrater was even more virtuous. This drove the criteria for authorised public shaming remorselessly down, until no-one was safe.

This daily moral outrage was a modern version of Taylor and Mill's fear of the mob, of the catastrophic effect of majority rule on the minds of the eccentric and the unusual. It policed impure political thoughts, creating a climate of fear, shared by everyone, that they would be next, if they framed a thought on race, or sexuality, or identity, or politics, in anything but the most anodyne and inoffensive way.

But even though it was loud, it was profoundly unproductive. The early days of social media had involved some degree of moral outrage too. It had motivated those watching the self-immolation of Mohamed Bouazizi to act. But the new breed of moral outrage was not intended to galvanise political organisation. It was intended to demonstrate moral superiority.

This completely inverted Taylor and Mill's insistence that people search for the strongest possible example of their opponent's argument. Instead, the moral outrage function sought out the weakest and extreme version of the counter-argument, which it could then twist into an encapsulation of their general position.

In fact, it was difficult to think of any forum for political debate that was further removed from that suggested by Taylor and Mill. Twitter seemed to militate against any constructive discussion. Exchanges were brief and emotionally heightened. Because of their highly public quality, they encouraged people to argue in a way that stirred their own side rather than seeking to understand the other. And they took place in a depersonalised manner, without either participant being able to see the face or ever having to meet the other, so that all standard social rules about civility could be discarded.

The result was call-out culture – a form of public shaming in which those who made so-called 'problematic' statements were subject to a tidal wave of abuse and performative outrage and then simply 'cancelled.' This involved a mass unfollowing of the individual and a boycott of their existence, so they could never be heard of again.

They were made to disappear. The idea their minds could be changed through argument, or that they might be right about some things and wrong about others, or that in their falsity some truth might nevertheless exist, was so alien as to be incomprehensible.

Orwell's vision of the nationalist tendency – the group's avoidance of challenging information and celebration of confirmatory information – now ran rampant. The notion of doubt faded away. In its place came a sense of fevered moral certainty.

The idea that truth was something people needed to find, something to be searched for amid the clutter and noise of human error, something to reach for through debate, became old fashioned. It was a Victorian relic.

This phenomenon was not externally imposed. It was the consequence of social media incentives and human psychology. But the situation became particularly dangerous when the state got involved.

The test bed was Ukraine in 2013, when the country was trying to decide between two very different futures. The government had initialled an Association Agreement on regulatory harmonisation and trade with the EU that could open the door to future membership. But Russia was offering a separate customs union deal, which would bring it back into its sphere of influence.

Putin informed the government that any agreement with the EU would be a 'suicidal step,' which would be met with sanctions. Then, on 21st November, he added an incentive. If the country rejected the EU agreement and joined the Russian customs union, he would provide a gas contract on concessionary terms and a $15 billion loan. The Ukrainian president, Viktor Yanukovych, took the deal.

The reaction was instantaneous. Crowds gathered in Independence Square in the capital Kiev. At first, just a few hundred came. Then, as the days wore on, more joined them. They protested during the day and slept there at night. Yanukovych ordered his riot police to disperse them, but it didn't work. Over the following weeks, hundreds of thousands of people arrived at the square. It was a revolution.

Talks brokered by France, Germany and Poland saw Yanukovych offered the protection of the presidency until a new election could be held at the end of the year. But he was nervous, remembering the savage treatment handed out to Colonel Gaddafi in Libya three years earlier, and fled to Moscow. Just like that, the regime was gone. A provisional government took over and made it clear it would be signing the deal with the European Union.

Ukraine was slipping from Putin's grasp, so he took action. The manner in which he did so would go on to define the disinformation tactics he went on to use across the globe.

In the early morning of 27th February 2014, the so-called 'little green men' appeared. They emerged as if from nowhere, outside the regional parliament in Simferopol, the capital of Ukraine's Crimean Peninsula. They were masked commandos, wearing green uniforms similar to that of the Russian military. But they bore no insignia or identifying marks. There was no way to tell what they were. They were walking deniabilities.

The next day they took the nearby Simferopol airport. 'There are no troops whatsoever, no Russian troops at least,' Russia's ambassador to the EU insisted. Then they blockaded Ukrainian soldiers inside their bases. 'Those were local self-defense units,' Putin said.

No war was declared. No Russian soldiers ever officially crossed the border. Russia was both there and not there. On 16th March, a referendum was held – deemed illegal and illegitimate by most of the international community – in which more than 96 per cent of the population apparently voted to join with Russia. And then Putin annexed the Crimea.

From there, the little green men swarmed outwards over the east of Ukraine. Pro-Russian separatists took control of government buildings in major cities like Donetsk and Luhansk.

This was how the anti-truth invasion of Ukraine began. From that moment on, the country was simultaneously at war and at peace. It was fighting Russia and yet it was not. It was caught outside the world of formal reality.

The physical invasion was the first sequence in a three-stage anti-truth operation. Stage two focused primarily on television. Kremlin propaganda was beamed out relentlessly to people in eastern Ukraine through channels like Channel One Russia, RTR Planeta, Russia 24, NTV and Vesti.

There were a handful of key messages. The most prominent was that Ukraine was being run by a 'fascist junta.' Russian TV focused almost exclusively on Right Sector, a Neo-Nazi group that had joined the pro-West demonstrators. It was a nasty organisation, but its leader, Dmytro Yarosh, had never held a government job and only received 0.7 per cent of the vote in the presidential elections in May 2014. He was a speck in the revolution. Russian propaganda made him out to be its personification.

Other key propaganda messages were that Kiev was now under American control, that the government was violently Russophobic and that it was sending armies to terrorise the east and ban the Russian language.

None of this bore the remotest connection to reality. But it worked more effectively than Moscow could have dreamed. Many eastern Ukrainians would repeat the messaging almost by rote.

Stage three of the operation was entirely focused on social media. It began on 17th July. During fierce fighting in the east, pro-Russian forces made a devastating mistake. They saw a plane, assumed it was Ukrainian and shot it down using a surface-to-air missile. It turned out to be Malaysian Airlines flight MH17 from Amsterdam to Kuala Lumpur. All 298 people on board died.

The international outrage was fierce. It was immediately obvious that the only place separatists could have secured the anti-aircraft missiles was Russia. Later reports by data analysts and the official investigation confirmed this. Putin was now in a precarious position, so he unleashed a new tactic: troll warfare.

Trolls are people who post incendiary and distracting content online in a bid to disrupt any kind of meaningful discussion. For some time, the Russian state had been building up a troll army in order to exploit this development. They were based in troll factories, establishments hosting dozens of workers paid to produce and disseminate angry and deceptive material on the internet.

Vitaly Bespalov, a young unemployed liberal journalist, found himself so desperate for work that he accepted a job offer from one of them. He later quit in despair and described the workplace to the foreign correspondent David Patrikarakos.

It was based in a drab four-storey building on Savushkina Street in St Petersburg. On the first floor was the media holdings department – around a dozen Russian and fake Ukrainian websites, with a workforce of around 60 people. They were mainly young, aged between 25 and 30. They weren't grey men in suits – they had been picked for their ability to navigate the online environment like a typical digital journalist or social media user.

Most of the pieces on the websites aimed to discredit the Ukrainian army and valourise the separatists. But they did not do this merely by reputational propaganda. They often did it by denying that certain events had taken place. If the Ukrainian government took control of an area, for instance, they would write an article insisting it was a lie.

On the second floor was the social media department, where people created memes and cartoons to spread online. These were basic, but highly effective, travelling quickly on social media. One showed a photo of an angry-looking Obama with the caption 'we don't talk to terrorists' next to another with him smiling which said 'we just sponsor them.' Another showed Obama looking tearful with the caption: 'I want to start a war but none of my friends will join me.'

On the third floor were the bloggers, writing fake accounts from supposed eastern Ukrainians about the things they had seen or experienced, like a lack of food or electricity. Sometimes they also wrote fake blogs from Americans complaining about Obama. Often the websites on the first floor would write a story about the blogs produced on the third floor as evidence of what was really happening in Ukraine. The fourth floor was the commenting section, where people would post opinions friendly to Moscow on websites like Facebook and YouTube.

Within hours of MH17 going down, the troll operation went into overdrive. Thousands of pro-Kremlin trolls started commenting online trying to dispel the reality of what had happened. Other unpaid pro-Kremlin figures, both in and out of Russia, joined in, aggressively parroting the narrative. Conspiracy theories were deployed to blame the Ukrainian government for firing on the plane, or the Americans. They threw it out wherever they could, smattering it all over the internet.

It was not effective in convincing many people outside of Russia or east Ukraine. But that was not the purpose. The aim was in fact twofold. Firstly, it would give Moscow a spreadable narrative in which it could maintain its innocence. And secondly it would confuse people. It would smudge reality, sow doubt, churn out as much disinformation as possible and hope the noise cancelled out the facts.

The Ukrainian disinformation campaign worked as proof-of-concept for Putin. He now turned his attention to his opponents in the West. Using the same tactics, he could try to achieve similar results in countries like Britain and the US.

From the end of 2014, the proportion of English, as opposed to Russian, language tweets from Kremlin fake accounts started to increase dramatically. By 2016, English and Russian language tweets were in roughly equal numbers. The tactic was now fully internationalised.

The operation was not fixed on Twitter. It was intended to work across platforms. Moscow would set up certain branded outlets, on various political topics, intended to reach different sets of internet users, then establish them on Twitter, Facebook, Instagram and YouTube. This gave an impression of editorial legitimacy. It also allowed it to use one social media site to complain if an outlet had been suspended by another platform.

It was effective. Between 2015 and 2017, over 30 million users shared Russian disinformation content on Instagram and Facebook accounts alone. They liked them. They commented on them. They spread them.

The content was not uniform. It was carefully tailored to motivate the different identity groups on social media.

Some of this was done by advertising. Facebook's identity segments allowed Russia to pick out and target audiences for their messages based on race, ethnicity and identity. African Americans who had shown interest in black identity or the prison system were separated out and targeted with specific campaigns. Conservative voters who had shown interest in supporting veterans, patriotism or gun rights were targeted with different ones.

These ads were bolstered with organic posts – content written and put on social media by Russia's troll army. The purpose was to drive users towards the dedicated Facebook or Instagram page of the brand they had set up. They often did this in a way that was only loosely political. Much of the content tapped into existing narratives within the community they were targeting. Posts on supporting veterans were aimed at conservatives, while posts on black pride were aimed at African Americans.

The most shared Russian disinformation Facebook post between 2015 and 2017 was an image of Yosemite Sam, the adversary of Bugs Bunny in the Looney Tunes cartoons, with two guns drawn and a confederate flag behind him. The text read: 'I was banned from television for being too violent. Like and share if you grew up watching me on television, have a gun, and haven't shot or killed anyone.' It was aimed at conservatives.

The most liked post on Instagram was an image of eight female legs of different skin tones, starting with white and ending with black. It read: 'All the tones are nude. Get over it.' It was published with hashtags like #blackandproud and #unapologeticallyblack and targeted at African Americans.

These and other memes drove users to pages created by the disinformation campaign. And it was here that the real work of manipulating different identity groups was done. The pages had two primary functions: They would seek to divide communities against each other, and they would tailor specific incentives to each group to try to secure Russia's optimal outcome in elections.

The pages stoked outrage and anger over pre-existing issues dividing Americans. Conservatives were given content pitting immigrants against veterans, or pushing an anti-Muslim, or anti-Obama, agenda.

African Americans were delivered content focusing on police violence against black people. The Russian-created Black Matters page, for instance, which described itself as a 'fast-growing group of online activists,' put out a message saying: 'Cops kill black kids. Are you sure that your son won't be the next?' When it was eventually caught by Facebook and closed down, its Twitter account accused the company of 'supporting white supremacy.'

In reality, all these accounts were being maintained by people in the same building. Analysis of the Russian disinformation campaign based on evidence provided to the Senate select committee on intelligence found many of these messages came from an identical IP address – a unique number linking online activity at a particular location. In some cases, accounts aggravating different groups against each other were being run from the same computer.

On 21st May 2016, two opposing protests took place outside the Islamic Da'wah Center in Houston, Texas. One was organised on Facebook to oppose the centre by a group called Heart of Texas and the other to support it by a group called United Muslims of America. Many people saw the posts and attended, on both sides. The two demonstrations eventually descended into confrontation and verbal attacks. In fact, both protests had been organised by the Russian disinformation operation.

But there was one crucial distinction between the content aimed at conservative Americans and other groups. Conservative Americans were encouraged to vote, in order to boost America's nationalist movement. Other groups were encouraged not to vote.

African Americans and other minorities groups were provided with material which aimed to increase their distrust of US institutions, boycott the political process and discourage them from voting. 'NOT VOTING is a way to exercise our rights' the Russian brand Blacktivist posted on 3rd November 2016.

Arguably, the more innocuous posts appealing to group narratives were more pernicious than the outright divisive content. If something that harmless, and even inspiring, could be from Russian propaganda units, then anything could be. It became impossible to trust any piece of information at all.

Russia's aim was not limited to a specific political outcome. It was something more general: to convince the world that nothing could be relied on, that nothing could be guaranteed as true.

'Look,' the troll worker Bespalov said, 'my parents use the internet. They used to read these sorts of comments and articles, to look at the memes and cartoons, and they used to believe them – like so many other people. Now they know it's probably almost all fake. Now no-one believes anything anymore.'

The capacity of truth to offer a defence against power, articulated by Orwell in *Nineteen Eighty-Four*, was crumbling away. Nothing was certain anymore. Nothing could be relied on. And even if it could, many would ignore it as inconvenient. Descartes' demon had come back to life.

12. THE NEW NATIONALISM

Liberalism had been weakened by the financial crash, the rise of identity war and growing misinformation. Then, in 2016, nationalism punched through its defences with breakthroughs in Britain and America.

For many people, this was the start of the nationalist takeover. But in fact its momentum had been building for years.

Hungary's leader, Viktor Orbán, had blazed the trail. He demonstrated how a nationalist agenda could create a narrative of division, amass vast executive power, and subvert and manipulate democracy.

Orbán's ascent had begun a decade earlier with an audio recording that changed the direction of Hungarian politics. In 2006, comments from the Socialist prime minister, Ferenc Gyurcsány, to party members were secretly taped and released to the public.

'We have fucked it up,' Gyurcsány could be heard saying. 'Not a little but a lot. We have obviously lied throughout the past one and a half to two years. It was perfectly clear that what we were saying was not true. We did not do anything for four years. Nothing. I had to pretend for one and a half years that we were governing. Instead, we lied in the morning, at noon and at night.'

It is hard to think of any political communication, in any country, in living memory that had a more devastating impact on an incumbent leader. Gyurcsány had shredded his reputation and that of the Socialist party. Riots erupted in the street, but he struggled on in power for several more years.

Then the financial crisis hit. The collapse of the banking system battered eastern Europe. Before the crisis, around $50 billion of investment flowed into the region every quarter. In the last quarter of 2008, that had reversed into an outflow of $100 billion. Domestic currencies plunged and the cost of servicing international loans spiralled. In a matter of weeks, many Hungarian families saw their mortgage or car loan bills surge by 20 per cent.

Hungary was forced to seek an emergency package from the IMF and EU. The terms were actually relatively generous, but public opinion inside the country viewed it as a humiliation. Nationalists branded the requirements attached to the loan an act of neocolonialism. They compared it to the Treaty of Trianon after the First World War, when Hungary was stripped of two-thirds of its territory.

Orbán, the leader of the far-right Fidesz party, took the spoils. He swept into power in 2010 with two-thirds of the parliamentary seats – a super-majority that allowed him to do almost anything he wanted. And what he wanted was to destroy liberalism in Hungary.

'My position is that what we are experiencing now is the end of an era,' he said in 2015, 'a conceptual-ideological era. Putting pretension aside, we can simply call this the era of liberal babble. This era is now at an end, and this situation both carries a huge risk and offers a new opportunity.'

In Orbán's world view, liberal societies faced a threat that they would not be able to withstand. That threat was immigration. 'Mass migration is like a slow and steady current of water which washes away the shore,' he said. 'It appears in the guise of humanitarian action, but its true nature is the occupation of territory.'

He delivered a fairly typical example of the New Right's narrative, which was itself a diluted version of the fascist notion of the corrupted volk. The people were pure and homogeneous. They had been polluted by outside forces. The primary threat came from immigrants, and particularly Muslim refugees.

'There is no cultural identity in a population without a stable ethnic composition,' Orbán said. 'The alteration of a country's ethnic makeup amounts to an alteration of its cultural identity.'

Europe, he claimed, was being 'de-Christianised' as part of a global elite conspiracy to create a 'new, mixed, Islamised' society. This plot was masterminded by two forces. The first was the European Union and the second was George Soros, a Hungarian Jewish financier whose Open Society Foundations supported liberal organisations around the world. The caricature of Soros had echoes of the demonisation of Dreyfus – Jewish, rootless, and operating to undermine the state.

Most damagingly of all, Hungary was able to do all this while remaining a member of the European Union. It sidestepped Europe's half-hearted efforts to restrain it and demonstrated something disturbing. The EU was very good at getting states to become more liberal when they were trying to join, but once they were inside, it did not stop them sliding into authoritarianism.

The moment he got into power, Orbán and his colleagues in Fidesz started dismantling Hungarian democracy. Without consulting the public or opposition parties, Fidesz wrote and passed a new constitution. The constitutional court, which had significant powers to hold Orbán back, was neutralised. The new constitution prohibited it from overturning anything voted on in parliament, where Fidesz held total control. When the court tried to hit back by striking down some of the government's laws, Fidesz simply wrote new legislation directly into the constitution through amendments.

Then the party reformed parliament to make sure the super-majority could never be undone. The number of members of parliament was significantly reduced. This ensured Fidesz's control was maintained even if its popular vote went into decline. Four years later, in 2014, it won 133 of the 199 seats in parliament with just 44 per cent of the vote.

Constituency boundaries were redrawn to make them more favourable to the party. The geographic limits of voting areas were rejigged so that supportive voters would outnumber liberals.

Constituencies like District One in downtown Hungary, for instance, were redrawn to include the Castle area, which had a more conservative demographic. Now these seats, too, would fall to Fidesz.

Orbán offered full voting rights to the Hungarian diaspora in neighbouring Romania, Slovakia, Serbia and Ukraine. This was presented as an act of national solidarity that showed his loyalty to the Hungarian ethnic group. In reality it was a much more prosaic example of electoral manipulation. Hungarians in the West overwhelmingly voted against Fidesz and were forced to vote in person at embassies and consulates. Hungarians in the newly included countries, who overwhelmingly supported Fidesz, could vote by post.

With his position in power cemented, Orbán adopted a three-pronged programme of executive control: croneyism, societal infiltration and nationalist propaganda. These elements were not fully distinct. Each one served to support the others. Every policy had at least a dual function, utilising one aspect of the system to bolster another.

Across society – from the media to think tanks – Orbán initiated a shadow system composed of parallel power structures. These were funded by a complex network of clients, who articulated his anti-liberal ideology, built up their status and then ultimately closed down and replaced the existing civil organisation. Through this technique, he slowly absorbed liberal institutions until they were under Fidesz control.

The party tried to avoid international condemnation. Journalists were not arrested. Judges were not thrown in jail. Free speech was allowed everywhere. But life was slowly squeezed out of the free press, the courts, academia and civil society.

Fidesz had already been waging a long and successful campaign to control the media. It started buying up media outlets in the mid-

1990s, via Orbán's childhood friend and close ally Lajos Simicska. In 1994, Simicska took control of Mahir, a state-owned media company, and Hírlapkiadó, a large publishing company, which owned the rights to a major newspaper. The pair then used tax-loopholes to save up the money required to found Fidesz's first daily newspaper, *Napi Magyarország*. It was here, in the early days, that Orbán and Simicska first formulated their propaganda strategy. First they bought out an entity, then they shifted its editorial stance to a pro-Orbán position, and finally they boosted its finances with advertising from their other business interests.

During Orbán's first stint as Hungary's prime minister between 1998 and 2002, he and Simicska installed an ally as director of the state-owned bank, Postabank. The bank then purchased the publishing rights to *Magyar Nemzet*, the country's largest daily newspaper, and installed two Orbán allies to run it. In a taste of what was to come, the paper was flooded with advertising from state-owned companies.

When Orbán was ousted in 2002, Simicska took over *Hír TV*, Hungary's first news TV channel, and began churning out the same Fidesz propaganda as *Magyar Nemzet*. The next step was radio. Once he was prime minister again in 2010, Orbán killed off the advertising funding for the *Neo* station, which was controlled by the Socialist party, until it went bankrupt, leaving just the Fidesz-controlled *Class FM* out of the main stations.

With a grip on big newspapers and television and radio televisions, Orbán was moving towards gaining control of the media. His network of oligarch allies bought out media entities in a wave of purchases – from national and local newspapers to websites to TV stations. Once they were purchased, they were either closed or turned into Fidesz mouthpieces. Influenced by the government, they pumped out a relentless stream of brutal anti-immigrant propaganda, day after day. The typical image, used repeatedly in influential tabloids like *Lokál*, was of an attractive white woman beside a pixellated image of a dark skinned man who had just assaulted her. The messages were always the same: hatred of immigrants, hatred of the EU, hatred of Soros.

Editorial coverage generated only half the propaganda. The rest was disseminated by state advertising, which simultaneously stuffed the pockets of friendly oligarchs. Orbán loyalists were given key positions in state advertising and then quadrupled funding in real terms to $300 million a year.

In 2017, the government initiated a so-called 'national consultation' on a plan by Soros for free immigration to Hungary. The plan never existed, but the pretence allowed Orbán to channel €40 million to friendly outlets which churned out anti-semitic tropes about a cosmopolitan international Jewish financier trying to undermine the nation. Posters depicted Soros smiling, with the words: 'Don't let Soros have the last laugh.' Some were defaced with graffiti reading: 'Stinking Jew.' A Fidesz MP put up a photo on Facebook of a dead pig, its skin seared black, with the phrase: 'This was Soros.'

Again, the operation combined several goals. It enriched Orbán's cronies, funded more propaganda, maintained his grip on the press and helped wipe out any remaining independent newspapers. Outlets controlled by Fidesz were awash with advertising contracts. Those that were not were starved of them. They either folded or found themselves so financially vulnerable that they could be bought out by the oligarchs. Croneyism was serving the nationalist agenda and the nationalist agenda was serving croneyism.

But, eventually, as Orbán tightened his grip on power, his associates started to lose theirs. In 2018, just days after winning his third consecutive two-thirds majority parliamentary election, Orbán moved decisively against Simicska and dismantled his media empire. Then loyal oligarch owners, in an act of benevolence unusual in a functioning democracy, donated 476 media outlets to a new government-run body: the Central European Press and Media Foundation. Orbán now assumed direct control of the majority of the country's major media assets, from cable news, to internet sites, to tabloid newspapers, to sports papers, to the regional press, to lifestyle magazines, to radio stations.

A few independent outlets survived, with their remaining journalists being branded enemies of the people. Their existence offered plausible deniability. Whenever anyone questioned him, Orbán could point out that free speech was legal in Hungary. Everyone was free to say whatever they wanted. It was true and yet simultaneously meaningless, because he controlled the flow of information. He had found a way of silencing dissent – not by law, but by funding.

Orbán simultaneously went to war against the other institutions restraining government. He got rid of independent-minded judges. Fidesz established a new body, the National Judicial Office, with extensive powers over judicial appointments, and placed loyalists in charge. The judiciary was purged of anyone who might stand up to Orbán. The older, respected judges, who might have the confidence to rule against the government, went first. A new rule forced any judge aged over 62 to retire. At a stroke, the most senior judges were removed. Positions were given to party loyalists in their place.

In a rare intervention, the European Union brought a case against Hungary at the European Court of Justice. The EU did not challenge Orbán's descent into autocracy, but instead took issue with his use of age discrimination against the judges. Orbán lost the case, but he proved to be an astute and legally literate opponent. He was highly adept at bending the rules just enough to stay on the right side of the law while making sure that his agenda marched forward as planned.

He set a new retirement age for judges of 65, to be phased in over a 10-year period, with reinstatement or compensation for those who had lost their jobs. It seemed like a capitulation, but in reality the prime minister and his supporters had won. Fidesz argued that firing the new recruits who had filled the judicial vacancies caused by the purge would breach their employment contracts. So instead the sacked judges, most of whom were from the high courts, were offered small roles in the provinces, in the full knowledge that they were unlikely to accept them. A 2015 report by the International Bar Association's Human Rights Institute found most of them never did. They accepted retirement and Orbán got his way.

Then he turned on scientists. The Hungarian Academy of Sciences had a proud heritage going back to 1825 and received the bulk of scientific research funding. But independent scientific research posed a threat to Orbán's narrative. Any objective assessment of Hungary's ethnic composition, for instance, would find that it was incredibly diverse. So the academy was brought under state control.

The same thing happened to historians. Orbán viewed the research undertaken by the independent and well-respected 1956 Institute to be against his monocultural narrative, so he absorbed it into the government-run Veritas Historical Research Institute and Archive.

Other non-government organisations (NGOs) were simply hustled out. Orbán created a network of absurdly-titled 'government NGOs,' which expanded until they comprised about two-thirds of the sector. They spewed out weakly researched pro-government findings on Orbán policy priorities, like the need for higher reproduction rates among ethnic Hungarians to prevent the economic need for immigration.

In education, a new body, the Klebelsberg Institution Maintenance Centre, was given authority over primary and secondary schools. It ensured that every head of every school would be a Fidesz loyalist. In primary schools, non-Fidesz principles were removed from their position, to be replaced by obedient party men. The curriculum was changed to reflect Orbán's nationalist narrative. From the eighth grade, in the words of one textbook, pupils were taught that 'it can be problematic for different cultures to coexist.'

Government-appointed figures were installed at the head of the opera and in charge of literary museums. Even the position of editor of a cooking magazine was reserved for a Fidesz loyalist.

Orbán had not tried to control every aspect of the individual's behaviour. People were still free to say and think what they wanted. Instead, he controlled every aspect of the nation's institutions and its civil structure. And that created an eerie silence in Hungary. No independent power could restrain or challenge the state. Publication of critical information was scant and protests were few. Orbán had killed off anything which could threaten him.

Orbán called Hungary an 'illiberal democracy.' The European Parliament's centre-left grouping, the Progressive Alliance of Socialists and Democrats, described it as 'the first dictatorship in the EU.'

The nationalism that took hold around the world in the wake of Fidesz's victory was not as extreme as that in Hungary. It did not exert the same degree of manipulation and control, and in many cases, the leaders who pursued it distanced themselves from Orbán. But his approach provided the broad storyline that would be told around the West: the people versus the elite, the fixation on immigration as a threat to the country, the denigration of the global rules-based order and the subversion of domestic institutions in a bid to undermine the separation of power.

In the UK, nationalism entered government by being absorbed into the ruling party. Unlike Hungary, this did not happen by ideological conviction or structured takeover. It was a typically British example of practicalities, accidents and political opportunism.

It began with a man called Nigel Farage. He was a fairly standard reactionary politician, with a canny ability to stay just on the right side of acceptable opinion, who had for years carved out a political career as the leader of the UK Independence Party (UKIP) demanding Britain leave the EU and limit immigration.

Farage was at once staggeringly successful and an abysmal failure. On each of the seven occasions he stood for parliament – five general elections and two by-elections – he was defeated. But he was able to wield disproportionate influence on the Conservative party from outside Westminster, by posing a threat on its right flank. A dynamic developed in which the Tories were forced to adopt ever-more hardline positions in order to reduce his appeal to their voter base. This process culminated in 2013, when Conservative prime minister David Cameron promised to hold a referendum on Britain's membership of the EU if the party won an outright majority at the next general election.

It was a short-term calculation, motivated predominantly by an attempt to limit UKIP's share of the vote in local elections later that year. But its effects were historic. It would toss a grenade into the system of international institutions and dismantle age-old assumptions about the moderate nature of British political debate.

Over the course of the ensuing referendum campaign, through a strange kind of political osmosis, the nationalist politics of UKIP seeped directly into the mainstream Conservative party.

At first it seemed as if there might be a formal barrier to prevent this kind of contamination. The movement to leave the EU was split in two, between a Farage-dominated camp called Leave.EU and an official mainstream campaign called Vote Leave.

Vote Leave was expected to be more respectable, to deliver a traditional eurosceptic message focused on loss of sovereignty. The man at its head was called Dominic Cummings. He seemed to be a fairly typical political figure, with a track record working in the education department during the Conservative government. But in fact he was something altogether different. Cummings was prepared to break all the unspoken rules and principles of political conduct. His thinking was not really conservative at all. Instead of preserving traditional structures, he seemed motivated by a desire to destroy and remould them. His world view corresponded neatly with the identity war. Anti-immigration, anti-European voters were, in his mind, a true expression of the people. Pro-immigration, pro-European figures were simply members of an elite conspiracy determined to thwart the people's will.

Cummings attracted two key figures from the mainstream, respectable right to front Vote Leave. The first was Boris Johnson, a jovial and self-interested Conservative who had once been mayor of London. Johnson had no ideology to speak of and indeed appeared to have no convictions whatsoever other than the centrality of his own advancement. Certainly he was not ideologically committed to Brexit or nationalism. If the wind had blown another way – as it had when he was mayor of London – he would have pursued an inclusive pro-European message for Remain. But that was not the way the wind blew.

The second was Michael Gove, who had nurtured Cummings' career while he was education secretary. He was intelligent and ambitious, with an ostentatious sense of manners that served to conceal a mercenary inner disposition.

Before their arrival, the Leave campaign was mostly made up of fringe eurosceptics. But Johnson and Gove's entrance changed everything. They brought respectability and gravitas to what had until then been a haphazard initiative.

In contrast, Leave.EU was expected to veer off into anti-immigrant rhetoric, using racialised messaging on freedom of movement to appeal to its base. This was thought to offer considerable advantages to the official Vote Leave campaign. The UKIP leader would bring in roughly the quarter of the population who held very right-wing anti-immigrant views. Cummings could then keep the hands of Vote Leave clean and offer a more professional mainstream proposition, fronted by Johnson and Gove, for voters in the centre and centre-right.

Farage played his part as expected. On 16th June 2016, just days from polling day, he unveiled a poster that plastered the phrase 'Breaking Point' over an image of hundreds of dark-skinned refugees. The one white face in the crowd was covered up by a block of text. The message was clear: although free movement only applied within the EU and had nothing to do with asylum policy, a vote for staying in the EU would introduce an army of dark-skinned refugees into the country. It was a classic Fidesz-style campaign. In fact, Orbán used the same image two years later.

But troubling as many people found it, this behaviour had at least been anticipated. What no-one expected was what happened to the Vote Leave camp. Instead of soft-pedalling on immigration issues, the official campaign started pumping out alarmist messages about swarms of immigrants arriving in the UK from Turkey. It used Facebook identity segment advertising to convince many voters that Turkey's 76 million inhabitants were about to join the EU, securing freedom of movement and the right to enter Britain. It played on the standard nationalist trope linking immigration with crime by stressing that 'the government will not be able to exclude Turkish criminals from entering the UK.'

Another ad grasped even further around the globe. One was put out showing a map of Europe with Turkey on one end and Britain on the other. A large arrow joined them, indicating immigration flow. Large text then singled out Syria and Iraq, implying that they would somehow also secure access to free movement, bringing a wave of Muslim refugees into the country.

As the campaign went on, people noticed that something had changed, but it was hard to pin down exactly what. It wasn't that there were lies taking place. Politicians had always issued misleading comments. It was something more than that. The truth seemed to be losing any kind of foothold in the debate at all.

Until now, there had been a cultural check on the extent to which politicians could mislead the public. They believed that if journalists and independent organisations said they were wrong, and especially if they said they were wrong repeatedly, it would damage their political career. This dynamic relied on the notion of shame. Most people presumed it would continue indefinitely as a basic fact of civilised political society. They had not asked themselves what would happen if that sense of shame disappeared.

Cummings' core realisation was that the conventions on truth-telling no longer applied. A war in Iraq, launched on the basis of a series of falsehoods by the UK and US governments in the years after the September IIth attacks, destroyed people's trust in government communication. The financial crash took away their faith in financial institutions, business leaders and even the notion of economic fairness. A scandal over MPs expenses in 2009 did profound damage to the reputation of elected representatives. A row over phone-hacking by journalists in 2011 accomplished the same for the media. By the time of the referendum, British institutions had largely discredited themselves in the public's eyes.

Policy institutes, economists, trade bodies, statistical authorities and journalists were now considered part of the elite, a metropolitan grouping which was geographically and culturally distant from people's real communities. Their attempt to check facts could therefore be safely ignored. People didn't care what they said anymore. Fact checks no longer caused the political damage they once did. And in fact it went further than that. Through the canny use of misleading information, they could be turned into a broadcast system for the very falsehoods they were supposed to refute.

The Turkish immigration claim, for instance, was a lie. Turkey had its own nationalist leader in the form of Recep Tayyip Erdogan and had never been further from EU membership. But even if it did get to the point of being accepted, Britain had the power to veto it. When the armed forces minister, Penny Mordaunt, who was campaigning for Vote Leave, was challenged on this during a television interview, she simply replied: 'No, it doesn't. We are not going to be able to have a say.' This claim was quickly refuted, but those refutations did not end the arguments about Turkish membership – they simply promoted it to a wider audience.

Cummings then deployed a lie which would go on to define the campaign: 'We send the EU £350 million a week. Let's fund our NHS instead.' The figure was incorrect. It did not include the rebate negotiated by previous British governments, which reduced the UK's budgetary contributions, and it excluded financial flows from Europe back to Britain. The UK Statistics Authority said it was 'misleading and undermines trust in official statistics.' But that didn't matter. The fact checks were ignored while the misleading claim was promoted. 'Sometimes we said "we send the EU £350m" to provoke people into argument,' Cummings wrote. 'This worked much better than I thought it would.'

These two lies on Turkish immigration and EU funding were crucial to the Leave campaign. Cummings found the £350 million statement played a decisive role with all his voter target groups. It 'was clearly the most effective argument not only with the crucial swing fifth but with almost every demographic,' he said. 'Even with UKIP voters it was level-pegging with immigration.'

The campaign then adopted a secondary attack on fact-checkers. Not only would it use them to republish its erroneous information, it would rebrand their efforts to establish the truth as an attack on the people by the elite.

On 3rd June 2016, Michael Gove appeared on Sky News for an interview. He was told that the Bank of England, the Institute for Fiscal Studies, the IMF, the Confederation of British Industry and most trade union leaders all thought that Britain would be worse off outside of the EU. Why should people believe him over them?

'I'm not asking the public to trust me,' he replied. 'I'm asking the public to trust themselves. I'm asking the British public to take back control of our destiny from those organisations which are distant, unaccountable, elitist and don't have their own interests at heart.'

It was a crucial moment. Gove was, as ever, unfailingly polite. He came across as a standard moderate British Conservative politician. But the logic of his argument was pure Orbán. He wasn't debating the evidence. He was rejecting the idea that independent economic analysis could exist and portraying those who cited it as enemies of the people. 'I think the people of this country have had enough of experts, from organisations with acronyms, saying that they know what is best and getting it consistently wrong,' he added.

In other areas, Vote Leave sidestepped the mainstream debate altogether. Social media advertising allowed the campaign to target its messaging in a medium where fact-checking was largely impossible. Facebook's identity segments could now achieve what mainstream debate had always prevented: a completely bespoke information ecosystem for different tribes of voters. Firms like Cambridge Analytica, which claimed its behavioural algorithms could predict the personality type of every single adult in the US, were employed to advance the campaign. Messages were extensively A/B tested, trying out different wording and images and seeing which ones took off. They were then micro-targeted at voters.

Since the development of the franchise in the second half of the 20th Century, electoral politics in Britain had been based on broad electoral appeals that could maintain a large alliance of voters. This encouraged politicians to avoid divisive rhetoric and instead appeal to what united the public. But advertising to discrete groups of voters on social media demanded a completely different approach. It rewarded those who zeroed-in on the instincts of a particular tribe. Policy was not necessarily the best way to do this. Emotional nudges, primarily through the affirmation of cultural values, were more effective.

This meant that voters were no longer getting the same messages during election campaigns. And in fact they didn't even know what messages other people were getting. The idea of a common policy debate, with commonly accepted facts, started to disappear.

These techniques were deployed amid a political debate which had already deteriorated in the face of the identity war. The referendum campaign was never really about the EU or its comparative advantages and disadvantages, any more than the Dreyfus Affair was about the evidence of a soldier's guilt. It was a symbolic culture war in which information was processed by virtue of whether it corresponded to someone's tribal identity.

On 16th June, hours after Farage's Breaking Point poster had been unveiled, events reached a tragic crescendo. At 12.53pm, just before she held a constituency meeting in West Yorkshire, the Remain-supporting Labour MP Jo Cox was shot three times and stabbed repeatedly by a far-right terrorist. As he killed her, he shouted: 'This is for Britain. Britain will always come first.'

The Brexit campaigns feared the assassination would lose them support, but it didn't. A week later, Britain voted to leave the EU.

The days after the referendum were defined by absence. Everyone could see the status quo was gone. The political class was discredited. Cameron, who had called the referendum and campaigned on the Remain side, resigned that morning. Nearly all the mainstream political parties – the Conservatives, Labour, the Liberal Democrats, the Scottish National Party, Plaid Cymru, the Greens – had backed Remain and been defeated. In a parliament of 650 MPs, just 159 had supported Leave.

For a few months, chaos reigned in Westminster. Then a new Tory leader emerged through a party leadership contest. Her name was Theresa May. On the face of it, she was a strange fit for the new era. She had been home secretary for six years in the old regime. She had campaigned – albeit half-heartedly – for Remain. But she had one quality which made her suitable for the changed face of British politics: she was an avowed opponent of immigration.

May's problem, and indeed that of the country, was that the anti-truth rhetoric of the referendum campaign now had to be translated into policy that functioned in objective reality. Leaving the EU was an extremely complicated endeavour, which would require acute sacrifices, either to political principles, or economic performance, or both.

Over nearly half a century of membership, Britain's legal and trading arrangements had become completely entwined with

Europe. People and products flowed freely across borders. Three million Europeans lived in Britain and over one million Brits lived in the EU. British businesses had become so used to the hassle-free arrangements of the European project that many industries – including car manufacture, aerospace engineering, financial services, food processing, chemical production and pharmaceuticals – relied on just-in-time production processes which assumed there would be smooth and simple trade.

The Leave campaign had promised that Britain would regain full sovereignty, taking back all decision-making powers from Europe, but it also insisted that Brexit Britain would become a wealthier country. This was one of the central falsehoods of the campaign. In fact, the trading arrangements Britain enjoyed were dependent on the European customs union and single market, where sovereignty was shared.

Britain had the option of staying in the single market and customs union outside of Europe, but it would still have to abide by its rules. It had to make a choice: commit to full sovereignty and take the economic hit, or abandon the aim of full sovereignty and maintain the economy.

In October 2016, May walked onto the stage of the Conservative party conference. She told delegates: 'We are not leaving the European Union only to give up control of immigration again. And we are not leaving only to return to the jurisdiction of the European Court of Justice.' Freedom of movement was a requirement of single market membership, while the European Court of Justice oversaw the customs union. In two sentences May had confirmed the most radical economic policy in the history of modern British politics: Britain was clearly pulling out of both.

This was the moment when nationalism was absorbed into the bloodstream of the Conservative party. It was not an ideological matter. It was a question of practicalities. This was seen as the most sensible path to follow given the referendum result. But regardless of the motivation, the policy implications were undeniable. The reduction of immigration now took precedence over any other policy agenda. The prime minister of Great Britain was prepared to detonate the country's trading arrangements in order to halt the arrival of foreigners.

This central policy agenda was propped up by nationalism's cultural architecture. The victory of the Leave campaign was not seen simply as a confirmation of the need to leave the EU. It was accepted more broadly as a new political consensus. The people versus the elite became the default narrative of government communication.

May made it clear what this entailed. 'If you believe you're a citizen of the world,' she said, 'you're a citizen of nowhere. You don't understand what the very word "citizenship" means.' She made those remarks when condemning tax avoidance, but the message resonated much further than that. The Conservative government was entering the identity war.

The people versus the elite framing provided, as it had done historically, a tremendous amount of leeway to the executive. It allowed the British government to reject any argument against its position as a betrayal of the will of the people and provided a rhetorical vehicle by which it could silence dissent.

Since the English Civil War and Glorious Revolution, sovereignty had rested with parliament. The government ruled on the basis of parliament's support and within the restraints of the courts. But now a new mandate took precedence: the people's will, as expressed through the referendum result.

The first salvo came over Article 50, the legal mechanism for leaving the EU. May attempted to trigger it unilaterally without consulting parliament. She was challenged in the Supreme Court by a Guyanese-British businesswoman called Gina Miller, who argued that, constitutionally, parliament must take the decision. The court ruled against the government. It was the first time a liberal institution had stood its ground in the wake of the referendum result.

The reaction was instantaneous. The *Daily Mail* newspaper published photographs of the three judges who heard the case under the headline: 'Enemies of the People.' The upmarket *Daily Telegraph* ran the headline: 'The Judges vs the People.' The Lord Chancellor, Liz Truss, whose role was to protect the independence of the courts, refused to condemn the coverage.

The death threats started arriving. Rhodri Philipps, the 4th Viscount St Davids, offered £5,000 for anyone who would run Miller over. 'If this is what we should expect from immigrants,' he said, 'send them back to their stinking jungles.'

Once Article 50 was triggered and the negotiations got underway, May attempted to eradicate any meaningful contribution from parliament on the details of the exit deal. She offered MPs only two choices: either support the deal, or fall out of Europe with no deal after the two-year Article 50 time window expired.

In reality, this was no choice at all. Leaving with no deal would sever all connections with the continent overnight. Citizens' rights, the legal basis for trade, security cooperation, the rights of airplanes to fly, even the import of radioactive isotopes for cancer treatment – all would have vanished at a stroke. But once again, the liberal system held firm. In a protracted series of parliamentary skirmishes, with amendments and counter-amendments whizzing across the chamber like bullets, the House of Commons managed to secure the right to a meaningful vote on her deal.

That deal had now finally developed into something which reflected the tortuous reality of leaving the EU. In effect, Britain would exit the customs union and single market, but otherwise wanted to maintain the closest possible relationship.

The emergence of a deal was a crucial moment in the public debate over Brexit. It was the first time that the rhetoric of the referendum campaign met reality. As soon as it happened, everything fell apart. Ministers quit. Conservative MPs revolted against their government. In a series of three humiliating votes, the Commons rejected the deal. In May 2019, her voice cracking with emotion, May stood outside Downing Street and confirmed she was stepping down.

May's defeat precipitated another flight from reality. In the ensuing Conservative leadership contest, members penalised candidates who recognised the difficulties of Brexit and rewarded those who denied them. Boris Johnson walked into Downing Street. His approach to the issue was summarised by a mantra, which would be repeated over and over again in the months to come: Get Brexit Done.

Johnson was no more a nationalist than May, but it was expedient to accept Cummings' agenda – politically, culturally and methodologically. So instead of just emulating Vote Leave's approach, as May had done, Johnson went a step further. He installed its operation at the heart of government. Cummings was made senior adviser, the power behind the throne. Gove was put in charge of no-deal preparations. The Cabinet was selected exclusively on the basis of its commitment for Brexit and its loyalty to the Johnson-Cummings partnership. The Tory party was purged of any remaining moderate figures – those who could not bring themselves to support no-deal. Almost overnight, some of the most respected and experienced politicians on the British centre-right were removed from the parliamentary party.

One of the Vote Leave government's first moves was to suspend parliament. On the morning of 28th August 2019, with just two months to go until the Article 50 deadline, the prime minister initiated a prorogation.

The Speaker of the Commons, John Bercow, branded the move a 'constitutional outrage,' but he was powerless to stop it. In the early hours of 10th September, for the first time in the modern era, parliament was suspended against its will.

Once again, the liberal system fought back. Miller took another case to the Supreme Court, amid more death threats and racial abuse. It ruled that the prorogation was unlawful. Parliament returned. Despite strong pressure, the institutions were holding firm in a way they had not in Hungary.

Johnson proceeded to negotiate his own Brexit deal. In doing so he made an extraordinary concession: he accepted a customs border between the British mainland and Northern Ireland. This had once been considered politically impossible because it would divide the UK's territory. May had insisted that 'no UK prime minister could ever agree to it.' Johnson himself had said that 'no British Conservative government could or should sign up to any such arrangement.' But he now pursued the strategy he had once disparaged.

Instead of arguing for this change in direction, however, he adopted a different approach. He denied it existed. Contrary to expert conclusions, against all evidence, and at odds even with the stated opinion of his own Brexit department, Johnson repeatedly insisted there would be no customs checks in the Irish Sea. For many British voters, this an esoteric policy matter. But it marked a significant moment in the development of British political discourse. The Brexit deal, which would define the UK's economic and political status for a generation, now existed in two realities simultaneously: that of the black-and-white legal text and that of the public-facing communications strategy. Government rhetoric had abandoned reality.

Just as May had done, the Vote Leave government used the people versus elite narrative to defend itself from scrutiny. Any potentially independent power source outside of Downing Street was attacked. Parliament and the courts were branded bastions of the establishment. The civil service was targeted for aggressive reform. Cummings loyalists were installed in government departments. When the chancellor, Sajid Javid, refused to accept their presence, he was sacked.

The Vote Leave government moved decisively against the media. Downing Street refused all Channel 4 requests for interviews with Cabinet ministers. A blacklist of supposedly hostile journalists grew to include senior reporters from the BBC and Sky, alongside two of the most popular morning current affairs shows, ITV's *Good Morning Britain* and Radio 4's *Today* programme.

On 12th December 2019, the Conservatives won a general election with a majority of 80. Immediately afterwards, Johnson branded it 'the people's government' and floated plans to weaken the BBC, restrict the role of the courts, limit the capacity of individuals to legally challenge the state through judicial review, and leave the European Convention on Human Rights.

Just over a month later, on 31st January 2020, Britain left the EU.

That evening in the European Parliament, as the clocks counted down to the moment of departure, politicians from across the continent held hands, many of them weeping, and sang the Scottish song Auld Lang Syne. Above them, in the upper levels where he sat as an MEP, Farage waved a tiny plastic British flag.

⚡

After Britain voted to leave Europe, the nationalist wave surged across the Atlantic.

The White House was the point at which the world changed. Even in an age of relative decline, America remained the most powerful and influential country on earth. It was the primary author of the rules-based international system. It was the country, out of all the liberal states, which defined itself by immigration. If it fell to nationalism, it would signal that we were entering a new era.

And then a man emerged who could achieve precisely that. His name was Donald Trump.

Many people associated Trump and Johnson closely together. They both took leadership positions in their respective nationalist movements. They both lied incessantly. They both lacked intellectual consistency. And on a personal level they seemed to recognise that their projects were complementary to each other. But in fact the differences between them were subtle, counter-intuitive and important. Unlike Johnson, Trump was a committed nationalist and had been all his life.

The target of his resentment changed – from Japan in the 1980s to Mexico in the 2010s. But the basic approach was always the same – a demand for America to come first and a suspicion and resentment of foreigners. He was less intelligent than Johnson and unable to place these positions within any kind of coherent ideological framework, but his instincts were reliably and uniformly racist, xenophobic and aggressive, like a ball covered in shattered glass.

Trump's approach to politics developed through a career in reality TV. He'd starred in a programme called *The Apprentice*, in which contestants vied to work for his real estate companies. When on set he was adept at noticing what drew a reaction from the film crew, assuming it would land with the audience, and repeating or emphasising it in later episodes.

He adopted that sense of intuition while mulling over a potential presidential run. As he went around the country making speeches, Trump found that an anti-immigration message worked. And the simpler and more brutal it was, the better.

In 2013, Trump made a speech to the Republicans at the Conservative Political Action Conference in Washington, in which he outlined the themes that would go on to define him – the threat of a rising China, the possibility of 11 million 'illegals' being able to vote, and a decline in manufacturing. 'You're on a suicide mission,' he told the delegates. 'Our country is a total mess – a total and complete mess – and what we need is leadership.'

In the audience was Steve Bannon, the executive chairman of the white nationalist website Breitbart. Bannon liked what he saw in Trump and in particular the unquestioning adulation he could produce in many voters.

He reported the speech back to two men who would be crucial in allowing Trump to deliver on his agenda. The first was Jeff Sessions, a Republican senator from Alabama, who had been fighting a battle against immigration for years. The second was his top aide, a man called Stephen Miller.

Miller was a young man, who came from a wealthy family in southern California. His own great-grandfather was an immigrant to the US after fleeing the anti-Jewish pogroms in Belarus in 1903, but he had grown up with a fierce hatred of diversity and immigration. Even during his teenage years at Santa Monica High School, he would bitterly complain about the announcements being made in English and Spanish for the 30 per cent Hispanic student body.

His anti-immigrant agenda was not made of jagged instinctive pieces, like Trump's. It was pure missionary zeal. While working for Sessions, he had spent half his time drafting speeches against Obama-era immigration policy and the other half side-lining as a source for Breitbart, sending the website a constant flurry of information that it turned into stories.

Miller and Bannon were both conspiracy theorists. To them, the separation of powers was in fact the functioning of a 'deep state' that aimed to thwart the will of the people.

This team was able to mould Trump's impulses into something resembling an ideological proposition. It was much more aggressive and ideological than the Brexit lobby in the UK. The Vote Leave campaign had dabbled in racial propaganda, but neither May nor Johnson believed in that approach. They were prepared to exploit nationalism insofar as it was useful but generally avoided anything with racist overtones, focusing instead on questions of sovereignty and immigration, where the latter primarily concerned white eastern Europeans.

Trump's team, by contrast, traded in racist rhetoric from the very beginning, tapping in to a long American history of racial hatred and paranoia dating back to slavery. Racism was laced into every aspect of the project. Trump's election slogan – Make America Great Again – was noticeable for the final word. It harked back to the past – the days before a black man had occupied the White House and before the campaigns for equal rights in the 1960s. This rhetoric allowed him to combine older sentimental voters wanting to go back to the 1950s with the angry young nationalists online.

Bannon, Miller and Sessions' plan for Trump was policy-orientated. They wanted to use him to deliver nationalist government to America and then export it to the world, bolstering his half-formed prejudices and emotional outbursts with a coherent political edifice.

But even if that project failed, a Trump campaign for the presidency could make huge progress in their broader cultural agenda. Trump lacked any notions of civility or decency. He was not reliant on the mores of a political age in which politicians tried to build a large cross-section of support. He was of the Facebook political age, the era of identity segments. He was prepared to campaign by turning people against one another and delivering precisely the rhetoric which his target tribe wanted to hear.

The wall started life as a fence. Trump first mentioned it in January 2015, in an event in Iowa called the Freedom Summit. 'We have to build a fence,' Trump told the crowd, 'and it's got to be a beauty. Who can build a better fence than Trump? I build. It's what I do. I build. I build nice fences. Fences are easy – believe me.'

It went down well, so four months later, at an event by the Texas Patriots, he upgraded the idea. There was a rampaging hostile army across the border and liberals were too weak to keep them out, he insisted. 'These are people – and some are very fine, I'm sure – but they're sending their killers, their rapists, their murderers, their drug lords. This is what we're getting. One thing I can tell you – I'm a great builder. I would build the greatest wall that anybody's ever seen.' The crowd loved it. And Trump loved that they loved it. It became the central idea of his presidency.

The wall defined Trump. It provided an easily comprehensible symbol of control, one which wasn't restricted to keeping out immigrants. It echoed out to Trump's message on trade and manufacturing. The country could be closed off to competition. The people who had been left behind by manufacturing decline could be insulated from the ravages of the economy. It shrank down the sense of anxiety over diversity and laissez-faire liberalism into a single, practical emblem.

The wall also contained a broader message. It suggested that complex problems had simple solutions. All you needed was common sense and the will to achieve. Reality would then fall in line behind you.

This fixation on simple solutions bolstered the notion of the deep state. Once you accepted that the world was simple, it followed that any obstacle to the implementation of a solution did not come from its inherent complications but from an internal conspiracy – a plot by the elite to undermine the people's will.

On 16th June 2015, when Trump announced his presidential bid on a flag-lined stage, he made the wall the centre-piece of his campaign. 'The US has become a dumping ground for everybody else's problems,' he said. 'When Mexico sends its people, they are not sending their best. They are sending people that have lots of problems. They are bringing drugs, they are bringing crime. They're rapists. And some, I assume, are good people.'

As soon as he said it, Bannon knew what he had. 'That's the soundbite,' he said. This was an opportunity not just for policy change, but to undermine the basic standards of anti-racism in political discourse. 'They're going to go full meltdown,' he said. 'Nobody's ever talked like this. People don't talk like this – you can't. This is the way you cut through.'

He was right. At first, the world reacted in the old way. Corporate America backed away. Broadcasters NBC and Univision dumped Trump's *Miss USA* and *Miss Universe* programmes. The Macy's department store cancelled its line of Trump-branded menswear.

But it didn't matter. Or if it did, it was useful. Some polls had Trump in eighth place in the Republican race before he gave the speech. Within weeks he was at the top.

At his election rallies, Trump would whip the crowds into fury, warning them that the media was working with the Democratic party as part of a 'global conspiracy.' Any story about his behaviour, such as audio recording of him admitting he had assaulted women, was the result of 'the corrupt media doing everything in their power to stop this movement.' Press contingents of around 20 journalists would stand in a hall surrounded by 15,000 people as they chanted abuse at them. Many feared for their safety.

And not long after that, Trump was the president of the United States.

From the very start of his time in the White House, Trump exploited the people versus the elite narrative, using the classic nationalist technique of turning economic anxiety in the wake of the financial crash into a nativist political programme. In his inaugural address on 20th January 2017, flanked by the grandeur of the American capital, he said: 'For too long, a small group in our nation's capital has reaped the rewards of government while the people have borne the cost. Washington flourished – but the people did not share its wealth. Politicians prospered – but the jobs left, and the factories closed. The establishment protected itself, but not the citizens of the country.' There could only be one logical conclusion. 'Our plan will put America First. Americanism, not globalism, will be our credo.'

The lies started immediately. In the days before his inauguration, Trump boasted there would be 'an unbelievable, perhaps record-setting turnout.' In the end, it was a subdued affair, far less full than for the inauguration of Obama eight years earlier and with several empty areas on the parade route.

The next morning, the president personally demanded that the director of the National Park Service produce aerial photographs of the crowds. A government photographer was then asked to doctor the images to cut out the empty spaces. When the White House press secretary, Sean Spicer, briefed the press on the event, he insisted it was 'the largest audience ever to witness an inauguration, period,' and accused the media of downplaying its size to 'lessen the enthusiasm.' The comment on audience size was subsequently refuted, prompting Trump's spokesperson, Kellyanne Conway, to say that Spicer had merely used 'alternative facts.'

It was an absurd, almost comically egotistical series of lies, but it had a purpose. The Trump administration used deceit to distract opponents and evade policy scrutiny. By constantly churning out falsehoods, Trump could ensure that the media's ability to focus on one story was severely diminished. There would be a debilitating wave of constant news, and constant misleading statements, so that everything was eventually drowned out. 'The Democrats don't matter,' Bannon said. 'The real opposition is the media. And the way to deal with them is to flood the zone with shit.'

By the summer of 2020, Trump had made over 18,000 false or misleading claims. During 2018, he averaged 15 erroneous claims a day.

He lied about big things and small things. He lied about damaging stories, like the payments his attorney said he authorised to silence women alleging affairs with him. But he also lied, pointlessly, about events which would have otherwise portrayed him in a favourable light. At a well-attended rally in Tampa, Florida, for instance, he declared that 'thousands of people' could not get in and were watching outside on a 'tremendous movie screen.' That crowd was there – his rallies were always well attended. But the numbers were not that big and the screen did not exist.

Nor did the wall with Mexico. Just like Vote Leave, which had struggled to live up to the glib promises of the campaign trail, Trump found his encounters with objective reality bruising. When he got into office, he could not secure the funding for the wall because his relentless tribalism made Democrats unwilling to work with him and even rank-and-file Republicans were reluctant to support the idea.

He started by insisting that the wall be built from concrete. Officials spent months trying to convince him otherwise. Concrete was very easy to break and it prevented border authorities from seeing what was on the other side. So he decided it should be steel bollards.

'But it's got to be the bollards right next to each other,' he said. 'Just the bollards.' At the top of the bollards would be spikes, so people could not climb over them. He wanted the tips painted black so they would heat up in the sun.

He would constantly talk of the beauty of the wall. This was his idea of beauty. A structure which would keep immigrants out, which would pierce and tear their skin, which would cut them, or burn them.

With the people versus the elite agenda in place and a torrent of lies spilling from his lips, Trump went to war with domestic institutions.

Court rulings which went against the president were treated as an attack by the deep state, both by the administration itself and its outriders in the media. Sean Hannity, a presenter on Fox News who would dine with the president in the White House, said: 'All of this is happening because of the deep state. It's now the deep state gone rogue. The deep state against the American people.'

Like Orbán, Trump's sabotage was not limited to the courts. He also went after scientific bodies, particularly over the issue of climate change, which he insisted was a hoax perpetrated by China 'in order to make US manufacturing non-competitive.'

Trump's new chief of the Environmental Protection Agency denied any link between CO_2 and climate change. Another climate change conspiracy theorist, Jim Bridenstine, was appointed to head NASA, the world's most important space agency.

Even the independent, Republic-headed Congressional Budget Office, which produced data-heavy assessment reports on the economic impacts of policies, was branded part of the deep state. When it provided a cost and impact assessment of a short-lived Trump health-care proposal in 2017, the White House branded it 'little more than fake news.' Gingrich said: 'Here's the Congressional Budget Office as part of the deep state doing a hit job on the Senate Republicans.'

Bob Mueller, the FBI special counsel put in charge of investigating Russian disinformation interference in the election results, was branded the tip of the 'deep state spear.' Trump retweeted a rant by Hannity saying the investigation showed the deep state was 'a clear and present danger to this country and to you.'

The attack on the institutions also took place at the international level. In November 2017, a celebration was held to mark the 70th anniversary of GATT, the WTO's core treaty. Trump declined to attend. Instead, he travelled to the studio of Fox News and made a pointed threat. 'The WTO was set up for the benefit of everyone but us,' he said. 'They have taken advantage of this country like you wouldn't believe.'

Trump picked up the thread of three long-held American complaints about the WTO and used them as an excuse to try and kneecap the organisation. He adopted a very simple and potentially ruinous procedure: America's national veto on appointments to the appellate court. The court was supposed to consist of seven members, who sat for a set period of time. Once their period finished, they were replaced by new ones.

Under Obama, America had behaved aggressively on individual appointments, including in one instance unseating a South Korean jurist whose rulings had gone against the US. But Trump now massively escalated this approach. He did not target individual members. He acted to sabotage the system as a whole. He introduced a blanket block on all new appointments or reappointments.

The crucial number was three. In order for the court to adjudicate on a dispute, it required three members. As Trump kept vetoing, and more members kept reaching the end of their term without being replaced, the numbers dwindled. He was strangling it to death.

The calculation was simple. Once the court ceased operating, countries would simply take matters into their own hands. There would be no alternative – the appeals process would have collapsed. And then the world would return, by virtue of operational reality, to the previous informal model in which it was much easier for powerful countries to get what they wanted.

On 10th December 2019, the terms of two of the three remaining members finally expired. The appellate court lost its ability to function.

Trump simultaneously pursued a second front of attack. He created a trade war, on a scale the world had not seen since the tit-for-tat tariff conflicts of the 1920s. And by doing so, with little regard for the WTO and no restraint in his actions, he showed how powerless the international liberal institutions were when faced with unbridled economic nationalism.

The primary target was China. Trump had been spoiling for a fight with the country since the 1980s, when it and Japan began to perform strongly in the auto industry.

At the heart of his animosity was a basic, almost childlike, error. He thought trade was a zero-sum game. He could not conceive of a negotiation between two individuals in which one was not the loser. The entire notion that partners could have a mutually advantageous interaction was alien to him.

The existence of a trade surplus – where one country sells more to its partner than it sells to them – was redefined as triumph and a trade deficit was redefined as national humiliation. China sold more to the US than the US did to it, so Trump went after it.

Again, reality could not intervene. Americans are on average vastly wealthier than their Chinese counterparts, with easy access to credit and a fondness for consumption. The trade deficit was not in itself a problem – it simply meant one country wanted to buy more material goods.

Trump introduced new tariffs of three per cent on imports of Chinese parts. Companies passed most of the costs onto the consumer, but the difference was hard for an average shopper to spot. Then phase two started. It began to hit consumer products themselves, the types of items most Americans owned: toys, clothing, shoes, smartphones, video games, consumer electronics. By the end of 2019, there were tariffs on nearly every product America bought from China, adding up to 20 per cent of America's total imports. China responded in kind, with a retaliation that eliminated soybean farmers' access to their market. Trump bought off the sector off with billions of dollars of taxpayer subsidy, but it was a short-term strategy – he would not be able to do the same for the consumers who would see prices rise as a result of his tariff war. Then China placed retaliatory tariffs on virtually all products from the US. The relationship became more toxic by the day.

Trump also moved against trading agreements. He announced plans to pull out of the North American Free Trade Agreement (NAFTA) between the US, Canada and Mexico – a continental trading system that was bringing the three countries together. Three days later, he withdrew from talks on the Trans-Pacific Partnership (TPP). A deal which had been worked on for years between the EU and the US, called the Transatlantic Trade and Investment Partnership (TTIP), was left dead on the table.

The NAFTA deal was just about salvaged. The countries in TPP carried on without the US. But the message was clear. Decades of American commitment to multilateral trade had been put into reverse. Liberalism's commitment to trade as a safeguard against war was being destroyed.

The enlightened self-interest of the post-war US, which recognised that global free trade underpinned by a rules-based order would be to its material benefit, was gone. It was replaced by a dog-eat-dog world in which Trump calculated that he could use America's size to bully other countries into submission.

The US made a cursory effort to pretend it was following WTO law by stating that its tariff attacks, which plainly broke Most Favoured Nation rules, were legal under Article 21 of the GATT – an exemption allowing states to step outside the rules for reasons of national security. But there was a problem: the tariffs had nothing to do with national security.

The creaking engine of WTO dispute resolution spluttered into action, but it was slow. It could not promise any resolution for several years. Many people at the WTO thought that might actually be the lesser of two evils, because they really had no idea what to do with the case if it was resolved. If the WTO found for the US, any country could use the national security exemption at any time, making the whole system worthless. But if it found against the US, Trump would probably storm off and leave the organisation, depriving it of one of the world's most important trading nations. Whatever happened, it would be severely, perhaps fatally, weakened.

In a sense it didn't matter. Trump had already shown that the international rules didn't matter to him. He had sent a signal to every other nationalist that they could do whatever they wanted. Simply by virtue of acting, he was creating the world he wanted. The size of the US, in terms of trading clout and political authority, meant that any action it took became a new norm.

The liberal world order was falling down. Orbán was undermining the EU from within. Britain was undermining it from without. And Trump was humbling the WTO. Decades of delicate construction work were being dismantled.

Inside these countries, the same process was undermining the institutions which kept executive power in check. Parliaments, the judiciary, civil society, the press. All were under sustained attack.

And at the core of the programme, in its engine room, the real work was being done which made all the other projects possible. The notion of objective truth was being eradicated. The concept of the individual was being subsumed into the people.

13. THE OTHER

One morning in July 2011, Pietro Bartolo saw something no-one should ever see.

He was a doctor on the Italian island of Lampedusa, where boats full of migrants regularly washed up on the shore, carrying Tunisians, sub-Saharan Africans, Libyans and others – fleeing war, or violence, or economic and societal collapse.

Over the years he'd helped countless migrants off countless rickety boats, but this time something was different. Instead of looking fatigued and dehydrated like usual, the passengers were traumatised. 'Problem in the hold,' someone said to him as they stumbled onto the land. But it wasn't a hold. It was a freezer for storing fish.

Too many people had been on the boat. When it looked like it might capsize, the smugglers ordered people down into the freezer to maintain its stability. Other passengers were forced to sit on the hatch at gunpoint so the ones below couldn't get out. And down there, in the dark, they suffocated to death.

'I found myself in a chamber of hell,' Bartolo said. 'The hold was paved entirely with corpses. I had been walking on dead bodies. Innumerable young bodies. They were naked, piled on top of each other, some with limbs intertwined. The walls were scratched and dripping with blood. Many of the young dead people had no fingernails.'

It was only the beginning. As the years wore on, the numbers of people trying desperately to get into Europe soared. The Arab Spring had degenerated into a charnel house in Libya and Syria.

Iraq was still unstable from the war. In Africa, climate change and economic and social disintegration had driven thousands from their homes in search of safety and security.

By 2015, there were 150,000 people a year taking boats across the Mediterranean Sea from Libya to Italy. Around 2,300 a day were using an alternate route in the Aegean Sea from Turkey to Greece. In total, 1.3 million people claimed asylum in the European Union that year.

People were dying in their thousands. Some 3,261 migrants lost their lives trying to reach Europe by the Mediterranean in 2014. Another 3,285 died in the Med in 2015, along with 806 deaths in the Aegean Sea.

The disasters kept repeating, a drumbeat of death sounding out across the continent. In October 2013, a boat sank off the coast of Lampedusa, killing over 360 people. In August 2015, police in Austria found an abandoned lorry with 71 men, women and children inside in an advanced state of decomposition. They had suffocated.

On 2nd September 2015, a three-year-old boy named Alan Kurdi drowned, along with his mother and brother, on the journey from Bodrum in Turkey to the Greek island of Kos. A photograph showed his body washed up on the shore, limp, face down in the water. It was reproduced all over the world: a testament to the scale of human tragedy.

At the start, people were heartbroken. From 2013 to 2014, the centre-left Democratic party government in Italy set up a search-and-rescue operation called Mare Nostrum, which saved over 150,000 lives at sea. A small navy of charity-funded rescue ships, operated by NGOs, took to the waves, scouring the water for people who needed help. People called them the 'angels of the sea.'

European nationalists were disarmed by the outpouring of grief. Then, on 21st September 2015, just days after Kurdi's body had been found, Viktor Orbán in Hungary took a stand. 'Immigrants are now not just pounding on our doors, but are breaking them down on top of us,' he told the Hungarian parliament. 'Not just a few hundred or thousand, but hundreds of thousands – indeed, millions – of migrants are besieging the borders of Hungary and Europe. What is happening now is an invasion. We are being invaded.'

He seemed like an anomaly, an aberration. European leaders distanced themselves from him. But in fact Orbán won the debate. He stood stock still and the continent shifted to his position.

This was indicative of nationalism's broader success. In country after country – some run by nationalists, some by mainstream politicians terrified of losing to them at the polls – immigrants were targeted. They became the chief victims of the nationalist advance.

Sometimes they were refugees, like the people drowning in the Mediterranean. Sometimes they were economic migrants, searching for a better life. Sometimes they were simply someone who fell in love with a person in another country. In each case, they were treated as a kind of social pollution: a corruption of the people. In an age of walls, they were an aberration. Their rights were abused. Their freedom was stripped from them. They became a number.

Internationalists in Europe, led by politicians in Germany and Sweden, argued that the crisis demanded the best of liberal values: an understanding of shared humanity, a defence of the post-war Refugee Convention, a commitment to human rights and a sharing of the burden within Europe.

'The German constitution and European values require the protection of people's dignity,' Merkel said. 'That means not only the dignity of people in Germany but it also means a global understanding of the dignity of people.' She opened up Germany's borders to hundreds of thousands of refugees.

Europe's nationalists urged the EU to go the other way. The Visegrád Group of the Czech Republic, Hungary, Poland and

Slovakia – the very nations which had benefited from expansion to the east – started closing their borders. They rebranded the humanitarian crisis as a national security issue.

In fairness, the rules on the acceptance of refugees were flawed. Under the EU's Dublin Convention, asylum seekers had to apply for refugee status at the first safe country they reached. But this didn't reflect the geographical reality of the situation. The boats were not evenly spread across Europe. Most were landing in Italy and Greece, who struggled to handle the pressure of such a large influx of people.

This was an issue that went to the heart of the European project. It was the first test since the eurozone crisis of the EU's values of countries acting in solidarity and working together for mutual benefit. The numbers arriving were large, but in a continent of half a billion people, they were manageable. All that was required was that the burden be shared.

But the nationalists refused. The Visegrád Group flatly rejected any quota system that would see its nations take refugees.

In public, Europe's leaders condemned Orbán. But in private, petrified by the growth of nationalism, they fell in line with his position. They gave up on burden-sharing and instead focused on doing everything they could to stop refugees arriving in the first place.

At the heart of the problem was the war in Syria. The civilians still inside were desperate to escape. Assad and Putin were butchering them in their hundreds of thousands. Many paid smugglers to get them across the country, past the government and various militias, to the Turkish border. Some 247,000 Syrians tried to get to the border area between December 2017 and January 2018 alone. In other cases, Syrians would end up in the vast refugee camps established in neighbouring Lebanon and Jordan. From there, those who could afford it would get a flight into Istanbul and make their way to the coast to take one of the boats to Greece.

It was therefore key to the EU response that the Turkish route into Europe be closed down. In March 2016, it did a deal with Turkish president Recep Tayyip Erdogan to achieve precisely that. Migrants entering Europe would be sent back to Turkey for processing. In return, Turkish visas to the EU would be liberalised and €6 billion contributed for refugee facilities. But in reality, Erdogan gained something far more valuable: leverage. From the moment the joint action plan was signed he was able to bully Europe by threatening to unleash a wave of refugees on it whenever it complained about his human rights record.

Erdogan acted quickly. He returned 315,000 Syrians who had made it into Turkey back into the war zone. He cancelled the visas of those taking flights from Lebanon and Jordan. And he built a wall on the Syrian-Turkish border blocking in those fleeing the bloodshed. Guards manning it shot indiscriminately at people approaching, killing men, women and children.

The deal worked. Almost as soon as the EU-Turkey plan was signed, the number of refugees coming into Europe from the Aegean plummeted. They had created the conditions that would stop people being able to reach the boats.

Europe then went to work on the boats themselves. EU search-and-rescue operations were wound down. Mare Nostrum was downgraded into a new mission called Operation Triton, run by the EU's Frontex border agency, which was far less efficient. This was then replaced by Operation Themis, which was less efficient still.

Between 2015 and 2018, the death rate of those crossing the sea increased more than nine times, from four people per thousand crossings to 37. The numbers themselves were falling, but the likelihood of dying for those who were able to make the journey surged.

Ideally, the EU would have liked to send the migrant boats back to Libya, but it had a problem. The Refugee Convention barred countries from disembarking people in an unsafe country. So instead, it undertook what was effectively a re-flagging operation. It poured money into the Libyan coastguard. As long as the boats finding migrants had a Libyan flag on them, they could be returned to the country without breaking international law. It then helped Libya declare its own search-and-rescue zone, thereby removing EU legal responsibility for patrolling that area of the Mediterranean.

This project was also successful: between 2016 and 2019, 50,000 people intercepted at sea were returned to Libya.

Europe turned a blind eye to what happened next.

No matter how much they wanted to pretend otherwise, Libya was not a functioning state. It had two competing government authorities – the Government of National Accord in the capital Tripoli, which was recognised by the EU, and the rival Interim Government based in the eastern cities of al-Bayda, Tobruk and Benghazi. Both relied on patchwork militia support and struggled to control territory.

The country had no refugee law and no asylum system. The ongoing conflict had led to a complete economic collapse. Smuggling, including of human beings, flourished. This meant that the Libyan coastguard operations were not really rescues at all. They were captures.

In June 2018, Joanna, a migrant from Cameroon, was on a boat with 170 people when they were found by the Libyan coastguard. 'Men on the large Libyan boat threw us a rope and at first we refused to tie it to ours,' she said. 'The Libyans shot into the air and threatened us: "If you don't tie it onto the boat then we will shoot at you."'

Once the migrants were returned to Libyan, they were forced into the country's detention system. Detention was indefinite and not subject to any legal control. Foreigners of any age without authorisation to be Libya could be imprisoned under Gadaffi-era laws that criminalised undocumented stay. When people tried to escape, they were tortured. 'Maybe it was last Thursday,' a detainee told human rights researchers who visited one of the centres, 'a man from Sierra Leone tried to escape but they caught him. They beat him unconscious.'

Detainees were beaten, whipped and subject to electric shock treatment. When the researchers went to one centre, they saw a man sitting in a hallway, rigid, with his knees bent, staring blankly ahead. 'They shocked him with electricity two months ago,' a detainee explained. 'He just sits on the floor. He used to speak normally, now he just stares straight ahead. They took him to the hospital but he came back in the same condition. There are three other men like that here.'

Outside of detention, migrants were exposed to the lawless horror of Libya and in particular its thriving smuggling trade. Kameela, a 23-year-old Somali woman, was held by smugglers in southern Libya for three months between 2017 and 2018. 'A big man there, a Libyan, he raped me,' she said. 'My husband couldn't stop him, they held a gun to his head. Every night he did this to me. If I said "don't touch me," he beat me.' By the time they escaped, she was pregnant with her rapist's child.

Nyala, an unaccompanied 17-year-old from Ethiopia, was held by smugglers in a hanger in the centre of Libya. 'They put a gun to my head and called my parents,' she said. 'They held the phone to my ear and I had to tell my parents to pay for me. The first time they paid $4,000, and the second time they paid $5,500 dollars. I believe I am about four months pregnant. I was raped two, three times.'

Tens of thousands of people had been locked into this hell by the offshoring of the EU's refugee responsibilities. By 2018, there were around 10,000 people in indefinite Libyan detention and another 680,000 outside of detention. No-one knew how many people smugglers and militias were keeping in warehouses and non-official detention centres. It was, in the words of UN High Commissioner for Human Rights Zeid Ra'ad Al Hussein, 'an outrage to the conscience of humanity.'

The EU recognised what was happening. 'We are all conscious of the appalling and degrading conditions in which some migrants are held in Libya,' Dimitris Avramopoulos, the EU migration commissioner, said in November 2017. The EU provided some funding to improve conditions, but the policy stayed in place. The reality was quite simple, no matter how many regretful words politicians uttered. The EU was using Libya as a prison camp to prevent refugee flows. And this was the consequence.

One country in Europe did not even bother paying lip-service to the reality of the Libyan situation and instead pretended it was a perfectly respectable state. That country was Italy.

It had good reason to feel aggrieved. Other European countries had not shared the burden. Populists like Orbán had refused to take any refugees. In a way that was entirely predictable, the nationalists of one country were unable to work with others, even when they shared each other's assessment of what was happening.

The centre-left government in Italy was facing a sustained challenge by a nationalist named Matteo Salvini. He headed what had once been called the Northern League – a regionalist party which blamed Rome for all manner of social and economic evils.

That all changed in December 2013, when Salvini took over. Instead of regional representation, it now sought to appeal to the whole nation. And instead of Rome as the bogeyman, it was the EU. Salvini focused relentlessly on right-wing identity politics, with immigrants and Brussels taking the blame for all of Italy's problems.

In 2017, Salvini called for a 'mass cleansing, street by street' to clear migrants from Italian cities. He embraced the standard nationalist attack on Muslims, saying that Islam was 'incompatible with our values' and adopted the slogan 'Italians first.' As Bannon recognised, 'Trump and Salvini are cut from the same cloth.'

The ruling centre-left party tried desperately to stall Salvini's rise by, in effect, adopting his policy platform. It reduced refugee numbers by offshoring the problem to Libya. It worked. The number of boats crossing the Mediterranean plummeted and between 2016 and 2018 the number of migrants disembarking in Italy fell by 90 per cent. But it made no difference. Accepting the nationalist narrative simply created the conditions for Salvini's success. It provided a political context in which voters might as well vote for the real thing, rather than the watered-down version.

In March 2018, the Democratic party lost badly in national elections. A ragtag coalition of Salvini's Northern League – now renamed the League Party – and the populist Five Star Movement entered government. Five Star dedicated itself to its economic programme and left Salvini in the position of interior minister. From there, he nurtured his power base through social media. He was, in effect if not in technical reality, Italy's prime minister.

By the time he'd secured power, there was little left for him to do. The previous government and the EU had already buckled to his demands. They'd stopped most of the boats and prevented official government rescues. There was only one part of the original compassionate response left to dismantle: the NGO boats.

On 10th June 2018, Salvini declared Italian ports closed to NGO ships saving migrants at sea. There would be no more safe harbour.

The SOS Méditerranée Aquarius, which was carrying 629 people, including 100 children rescued offshore from Libya, was still in the water. It was now barred from disembarking. Spain eventually agreed to take the ship. Then almost immediately a new row broke out over the German ship Mission Lifeline, which was carrying 259 people it had rescued from the sea. Again, the port was closed. It spent a week adrift unable to disembark in Italy before Malta took pity and finally granted it permission.

In summer 2019, just days after a boat carrying migrants capsized in the Mediterranean killing up to 150 people, Salvini passed a new decree giving himself complete legal authority to stop boats docking in Italy. Article two of the decree introduced fines of between €150,000 and €1 million, plus the confiscation and possible destruction of the ship, for any captain who ignored the entry bans. It was a full-scale legal assault on the NGO boats, unparalleled in its financial severity.

Salvini started prosecuting people at the rate of about one case a month. Carola Rackete, the captain of Sea-Watch 3, was put under house arrest after she tried to disembark 40 people she had rescued. Salvini branded her a 'danger to national security.'

In legal terms, the policy was a failure. Most cases closed without ever even going to trial. Others remained open but with no prospect of advancing. And yet in practical terms, it was an unmitigated success. The plan was never really to throw thousands of charity workers in jail. It was to deter them – to make it impossible for them to function under the threat of astronomical fines.

Countless NGOs wrapped up their operations and stopped patrolling the Mediterranean. In 2016, there were still at least a dozen civilian rescue boats. By 2019, only six were operational, one of which had been impounded and another two reduced to monitoring activity.

'We're being forbidden to help people,' charity ship captain Dariush Beigui said. 'It doesn't get more malicious than that. It's one thing to say "people are drowning and I don't want to help them." It's another to then forbid others from helping.'

But that was precisely what happened: the criminalisation of helping migrants. And it did not just happen on the water. It happened on land. Between 2014 and 2019, 250 people in Europe were arrested, charged or investigated for working with migrants.

In the Rhineland-Palatinate region of Germany, where the nationalist Alternative für Deutschland party was polling strongly, five protestant pastors had their phones, legal correspondence and church records seized after they allowed Sudanese refugees to sleep in church buildings.

In Switzerland, an evangelical pastor, Norbert Valley, was arrested in the middle of a church service for helping a Togolese man whose asylum application had been denied. In Denmark, a 70-year-old woman named Lise Ramslog was convicted for offering a lift to a migrant family.

In France, a 72-year-old retired lecturer named Claire Marsol was convicted of facilitating illegal immigration after she gave a boy and a young woman a lift to the train station. Police searched her home, handcuffed her, seized her belongings and put her in custody. A French mountain guide named Benoit Duclos was charged with aiding and abetting illegal immigration for helping a pregnant Nigerian woman across the border in the snow.

It was not enough to leave migrants to die, or to trap them in the torture chambers of Libya or the slaughter house of Syria. Europe, in its petrified fear of nationalism, had gone one step further. It criminalised its own citizens for showing compassion.

A similar culture shift was taking place in Britain. It started well before Brexit, when Theresa May was put in charge of the Home Office in 2010. Over the course of the following six years, she turned the department into her personal fiefdom. A government ministry which had always been known for its indifference to those it affected became more severe and extreme.

In summer 2013, May offered a statement of intent. It ran under the internal codename Operation Vaken. The department sent out billboards, carried on vans, to patrol areas of London with high levels of immigration. 'Go home or face arrest,' they read. Next to the text was a picture of a pair of handcuffs and then the number of immigrants in the local area who had been arrested.

On a superficial level, the vans were a failure. They didn't lead to many arrests and were soon scrapped. But arrests were not their true metric. More than anything, they were intended to be seen – and they were. Extensive reporting in traditional and social media ensured that millions of people came across their grim slogan. The message was not just aimed at undocumented immigrants. It was for anyone who had presumed they might find a warm welcome in Britain. It spread a proposition that would go on to become Home Office policy and eventually the core agenda of the British government. Immigrants were not welcome.

The 2014 Immigration Act expanded the Home Office's system of surveillance, coercion and control so that it was no longer restricted to government departments and instead spread to society itself. Doctors, teachers, landlords and charity workers were turned into outsourced border agents: tasked with discovering and reporting undocumented immigrants for deportation.

This new approach was called the Hostile Environment. Even the name reflected the true intention. Most government initiatives bore euphemistic designations intended to mask their true purpose, like 'quantitative easing' or the 'spare room subsidy.' That wasn't the case here. The phrase Hostile Environment was intended to be heard. It was meant to intimidate.

Britain's National Health Service was ordered to share data on its patients, so that it could be used for 'tracing immigration offenders.' Doctors were told to interrogate patients about their immigration status. A charge was introduced for immigrants to use the NHS. This payment was ostensibly to make up for lost funding due to health tourism – people travelling to Britain to use its free health services. But in fact health tourism was minuscule. The Royal College of GPs estimated that it accounted for just 0.01 per cent of the health service's annual budget. When the European Commission asked Britain for proof of it, officials replied that 'these questions place too much emphasis on quantitative evidence.'

The human cost of this policy was extremely high. One doctor recalled how a man had presented with early stages of lung cancer, but he didn't have the right documentation. He was shipped off to a detention centre for months. When he came back into care his tumour was incurable.

The culture seeped into the police force, with devastating results. In March 2017, a woman walked into a London police station to report that she had been kidnapped and raped. Officers referred her to a sexual assault charity and then promptly arrested her and questioned her over her immigration status.

The demands for papers and proof of status spread everywhere. Landlords had to check the immigration status of potential tenants. Employers had to check papers before offering work. Banks had to run background checks on immigrants trying to open an account. Even driving licence allocation became subject to immigration surveillance.

Groups representing immigrants had tried to warn the Home Office that pursuing this strategy wouldn't just affected undocumented migrants. It would affect people with a legal right to be in Britain.

Many people who were legally living in the UK did not have papers. Among them were the Windrush generation, named after the first boat to arrive from the Caribbean after the war, packed with passengers who had answered Britain's plea for workers to help rebuild the country. They had come as British subjects and did not require papers. The government did not have any records of their arrival or status either. It had destroyed the landing cards in 2010.

The Hostile Environment now reached British citizens themselves and started mutilating their lives. A British man in London who had left Antigua as a child in the 1950s was told he would be deported. A Jamaican-born man was told to pay £58,000 for cancer treatment. Sixty-three people from Windrush families were deported back to countries they hadn't lived in for decades. Others went on holiday and found they weren't allowed back into Britain on their return. Thousands were denied health care. Many were thrown into Britain's immigration detention system.

It was a moment of severe anguish for people who had lived in the UK all their lives and called it their home. Ministers presented it as an error in the system, but it wasn't. It was the system. It had been intentionally designed to cast the widest conceivable net and scoop up as many foreign-born people as possible, regardless of the consequences.

Other British citizens were caught up in the Hostile Environment in the most intimate way imaginable. In 2012, May introduced an income requirement for those in the UK who wanted to bring their non-European husband or wife to live with them from abroad. Until this point, spousal visas were offered without any financial requirements, but now British citizens would need to show six months of income at an annual rate of £18,600 per year, or the partner would remain stranded abroad.

Rebecca, a 30-year-old from Leeds, met her Chinese husband when she was teaching in the country in 2014. He was in a band playing music in the bar she was drinking in and went over to talk to her. Within a year they were married, with a child on the way.

Not long after the birth, she realised her son was having problems with his speech and started to suspect he was autistic. The couple decided he'd get better care back home in England, so she returned to Leeds while her husband saved money in China to pay for his flight to join her.

'After six months I thought my husband would be able to come,' she said. 'Perhaps I was a bit naive. I thought the system was there to support families, not separate them.' The only job she could get was as a teaching assistant, which didn't meet the salary requirements.

She managed to get her son diagnosed and into a decent school which would help with his condition. 'I knew it was the right thing to do,' she said. 'My son is happier, he's doing well at school, he's got all the support he needs. It was the right thing to do as a parent. But I sacrificed two years of the life I was supposed to have with my husband. They basically turned me into a single mum. I can't see my husband. I can't advance in my career.'

The years took their toll. The state had found its way into her most private, personal life and torn it apart. 'It's incredibly lonely. I feel like a teenager. This is the stuff people don't talk about. I've not had sex for two years. You miss that. The physical connection with somebody. The love you share, the conversations.'

The forced separation soon had an impact on her child. 'He gets really anxious when people leave,' she said. 'Especially if I go to the shop. He has a fear I'm not going to come back.'

†

Until 2016, there was at least one group of immigrants who were safe from the Hostile Environment: European citizens. Freedom of movement protected them from the Home Office regime. But once Brexit happened, even that was taken away. The three million Europeans in the UK were suddenly exposed.

Many had come to Britain from Poland following EU expansion in 2004. Others had arrived during Britain's previous 41 years of membership. They lived on the same streets, sent their children to the same schools, paid the same taxes and worked in the same offices as UK citizens. They were as deeply ingrained in British life as any immigrant group could be.

In the weeks and months after the referendum, European families kept asking ever-more urgent questions of the government about their status. They were met with silence. Ministers refused to make any kind of pledge. And then the trade secretary, Liam Fox, gave the game away. Promising to allow Europeans to stay in Britain, he said, would 'hand over one of our main cards' in the negotiations with Brussels. And suddenly it became clear. The millions of continental Europeans in Britain were going to be used as bargaining chips.

The threat of deportation hung in the air for one and a half years. During that time, Europeans were denied any security about their status or confirmation of their rights. They remained that way until December 2017, when May finally confirmed they were safe. 'I greatly value the depth of the contribution you make,' she said. 'You will have your rights written into UK law.' The words were cheap. Europeans knew they had been forced to live in limbo because it had been politically useful.

For those who had a mixed European identity, it came as a shock. The entire context of the debate was about being either British or European but not both. 'That's the first thing I thought,' Jakub said. 'What am I?' He was born in Poland, but arrived in the UK with his parents in 2004, aged 14. 'I always felt that I had this mixed culture. And then one day someone says: "No. It's not yours. Prove it's yours."'

EU citizens were told to register in order to secure their status. Applicants had to provide evidence to a mobile phone app that they had been in the UK for five years. If they had, they were given 'settled status' – if not, they were given 'pre-settled status.' Many people who had been in the UK for decades found themselves being given pre-settled status, despite providing evidence they had been in the country for years. And many chose not to question it on the assumption that it would turn into settled status once the five years were up.

But there was a danger lurking in the system. The upgrade in status was not automatic. If people did not apply for settled status after their five years, they would become undocumented. A time limit was also put on the application process, set for July 2021. Anyone applying after that would not be allowed settled status, unless ministers, in a bit of wriggle-room imposed by the EU, took pity on them. Those who were too late would also become undocumented.

These seemed like details, but the scale of the potential human impact was huge. It would only take one per cent of the three million EU citizens in the UK to fall into difficulty for tens of thousands of people to be affected.

The most vulnerable were at the worst risk: older people who had been in the UK for decades and did not know they needed to apply, farm workers from eastern Europe, the homeless, those with mental health problems, those who couldn't read English. The list of potential victims was endless. But the government did not make any concessions. It remained firm on the system and the timetables. In doing so it created a situation in which tens of thousands of Europeans could fall off the conveyor belt into the Hostile Environment, just like the Windrush generation had before them.

†

Across the Atlantic, the new US president was pursuing an agenda so extreme it overshadowed any of the initiatives in Europe.

Donald Trump began his anti-immigration operation from the moment he took office. It was planned as an onslaught, a machine gun fire of draconian policies which would come so rapidly that no-one would know what hit them.

A working group was appointed, headed by Jeff Sessions' chief legal adviser, Gene Hamilton, and composed of rabidly anti-immigration figures. It put together a bulging programme of executive orders: a wall between the US and Mexico, a ban on Muslims coming to the US, the deportation of non-US citizens who had been in America all their lives.

These battles were not to be fought one by one. They had to be triggered all at once, in a great flurry of activity. Ideally they envisioned Trump signing five executive orders a day. This was Bannon's 'flood the zone with shit' strategy – it would fill the airwaves with so much outrage that the media would be unable to focus on single items and the government bureaucracy would be too confused to block anything. 'Shock and awe' would replace scrutiny.

He went for the Muslims first. On the campaign trail, Trump had demanded a 'total and complete shutdown of Muslims entering the United States.' In office, after lobbying from senior Republicans, that was changed to 'extreme vetting,' so that its obviously unconstitutional discriminatory nature would be harder to demonstrate in court. An executive order was produced banning citizens of Iran, Iraq, Libya, Somalia, Sudan, Syria and Yemen for 90 days.

As a national security argument, it made no sense. The Department of Homeland Security's intelligence office found citizenship of a country was an 'unreliable indicator' of terrorist threat. Out of 82 people convicted of terrorism in the US since the start of the Syrian War in 2011, about half were US-born. The rest came from 26 different countries, most of which were unaffected by Trump's ban, including Bangladesh, Cuba, Ethiopia, Pakistan and Uzbekistan. But the warnings that it would be ineffective were treated as the resistance of the deep state. On 27th January 2017, the executive order went into effect. The result was instant chaos.

Thousands of passengers arriving into the country were detained. Airport workers didn't know what they were doing. Consular officials were desperately looking for guidance. Staff at the White House being asked questions by journalists were reduced to reading the order online.

By the next night, the travel ban had been knocked down by a federal judge. Stephen Miller, Trump's key aide on immigration, went on TV and fired back. 'We have a judiciary that has taken far too much power and become in many cases a supreme branch of government,' he said. 'Our opponents, the media, and the whole world will soon see, as we begin to take further actions, that the power of the president to protect our country are very substantial, and will not be questioned.'

Trump's team had to come up with a new revised order, much to his outrage. 'This is bullshit,' he shouted. 'I don't want a fucking watered-down version.' But he signed it, and then a third, which included the token non-Muslim countries of North Korea and Venezuela, from which there were hardly any arrivals. The third version stuck. It was accepted by the Supreme Court.

People from Iran, Libya, Somalia, Syria and Yemen were now banned from going to the US on almost any visa, even if they had spouses or family members in the country. Thousands of people who had created lives in America, overwhelmingly of Middle

Eastern origin, were trapped. If they visited their home country, they would be unable to return. If they did not, they would never see their family again.

Trump then went after the Dreamers. They were young people who had been brought to the US by their parents when they were children, predominantly from Mexico. They'd gone to American schools, attended American churches, joined the American military. They were remnants of the American Dream – the old pre-Trump American dream – in which everyone was given an opportunity. They were also illegals, according to the anti-immigrant lobby.

While president, Barack Obama had tried to give them protection against immigration enforcement through Congress, but the move had been blocked by the Republican-run Senate, so Obama resorted to an initiative called Deferred Action for Childhood Arrivals (DACA). It was a policy memorandum which gave Dreamers without felonies or serious misdemeanors a renewable two-year period of protection from deportation and eligibility for work permits. Around 800,000 of them enrolled.

For many of them, it was the first time in their young lives they hadn't had to fear immigration officers turning up at the door. 'It meant I can breathe easier knowing I didn't have to look out for every person in uniform,' Dulce, from Mexico, who arrived in the US when she was five, said.

During the election Trump branded DACA an 'illegal amnesty' and promised to repeal it on 'day one' of his presidency. In the end it took until 5th September 2017. Jeff Sessions, now attorney general, announced its repeal, with a six-month suspension on implementation.

The judiciary again sprang into action, ruling that the administration had ended DACA unlawfully. It granted a reprieve, but those on the programme knew that their status was now tenuous. Any day, a court could rule that DACA would end and they would be subject to deportation.

The next target was Temporary Protected Status. These were

stripped-down residency permits for people fleeing war or natural disasters. They didn't offer a road to permanent residency or citizenship. They simply gave people the right to live in the US legally and, if they kept a clean criminal record, a work permit.

They had been handed out over the preceding decades to those most in need – Salvadorians fleeing the civil war, Nicaraguans and Hondurans escaping Hurricane Mitch in 1998, Haitians displaced by the 2010 earthquake. In some cases, the countries came off the list when the situation improved. In others, the country never improved. It would stay flattened, without an effective government to maintain law and order or provide infrastructure. So people started to put down roots. By 2016, there were 195,000 Salvadorians on the programme, alongside 57,000 Haitians, 46,000 Hondurans and 5,300 Nicaraguans.

Trump attempted to close it down. It amounted to a plan for mass deportations of around 800,000 people – one of the largest forced removals in American history.

Intense pressure was put on officials to sign off on the plan, regardless of their independent assessment of conditions in the country. And one by one they gave way. It was terminated for Nicaragua, then Haiti, then El Salvador, and finally Honduras.

As before, the institutions held firm. Multiple court cases sprang up. In 2018, a federal court judge imposed a nationwide injunction, forcing the administration to put the termination on hold. Again, the system of checks and balances worked. But again, for the people themselves, it meant life on stand-by, relying on a safety net which could be cut away at any moment.

Trump's main problem centred on the tens of thousands of Central Americans arriving at the border through Mexico. They were desperate. Many countries in Central America had fallen apart altogether. Poverty was endemic. Political violence was commonplace.

Gang warfare had turned whole swatches of countries like Guatemala and El Salvador into no-go zones, with rape, kidnapping, assault and murder becoming day-to-day occurrences.

Things were particularly brutal for indigenous Mayan populations, who were especially prevalent in Guatemala. They lived in grinding poverty, typically in houses with tin roofs and earthen floor. Since a genocide against them in the 1980s by a far-right military government, they had faced endemic discrimination and racism from the rest of the population.

The journey to the US was brutal and dangerous. Those who undertook it were considered the lowest of the low. No-one cared about them – not their government, or the governments of the states they passed through, or the government of the country they were trying to get to. They had no protection and no security. Predators could do whatever they liked with them.

While on the migrant trail they were routinely kidnapped and forced at gunpoint to call their families for money for their release. Women were raped with impunity. Children were often subject to sexual and physical abuse. One girl discovered by American investigators in one of their detention camps had been held in captivity for months, during which time she was tortured, raped and became pregnant. Another child had been held for ransom by a gang in a compound while attempting to cross from Guatemala into Mexico. He had watched as the gang executed another individual in the camp. The woman who helped him escape was shot.

Others died on the trail. Trump's increased enforcement at the border did little to stem numbers, but it did force migrants into ever more treacherous territory in order to try and enter into the US.

In June 2019, a photo emerged of Óscar Alberto Martínez Ramírez, a 25-year-old man from El Salvador, and his 23-month-old daughter Angie Valeria. They were dead, face down in the mud, washed up with the beer cans and rubbish onto the banks of the Rio Grande. The girl's arm was draped around her father's neck. His shirt had been stretched to cover them both. Her waterlogged nappy bulged from underneath her red pants. Four years later and half the world away, nothing had changed. The photo was almost identical to the one taken of Alan Kurdi.

Trump was unconcerned by the deaths but he was obsessed with stopping the border crossings. 'We're toughening up at the border,' he insisted. 'We cannot let people enter our country – we have no idea who they are, what they do, where they came from. We don't know if they're murderers, if they're killers.'

His team debated all sorts of strategies. They proposed entering into a tariff war with Mexico to make them stem the numbers, violating direct judicial orders to keep families for longer periods of time, stripping children of protection so they could be sent back, and sending the military to secure the border. Eventually they settled on separating children from their family. This would send a message to migrants: if you come, we'll take your kids. And that might scare them so badly they would not make the journey.

In July 2017, Justice Department and Border Patrol officials began a secret five-month pilot project in the El Paso sector, covering New Mexico to western Texas. Customs and Border Protection had previously exempted migrants with children from criminal prosecution, unless they were unrelated to the children or suspected of another crime. Now they reversed that approach. Families with children would be criminally prosecuted. And that entailed removing their children.

After a few months, the number of families crossing the border illegally in that sector was down 64 per cent. The White House hailed the pilot as a success.

Plans started being formulated. A document raising 'policy options' for the border circulated around the Department of Homeland Security with a plan for prosecuting family units. 'The parents would be prosecuted for illegal entry (misdemeanour) or illegal entry (felony) and the minors present with them would be placed in Department of Health & Human Services custody,' it suggested. 'The increase in prosecutions would be reported by the media and it would have a substantial deterrent effect.'

In May 2018, family separation became official US government policy. Families crossing the border without authorisation were forcibly separated from their children and jailed ahead of prosecution. Children were designated as unaccompanied minors and sent to detention facilities.

'Today we are here to send a message to the world,' Sessions announced triumphantly along a section of border fence. 'We are not going to let this country be overwhelmed. The Department of Homeland Security is now referring 100 per cent of illegal south-west border crossings to the Department of Justice for prosecution. If you are smuggling a child, then we will prosecute you, and that child will be separated from you as required by law.'

Marco Antonio Muñoz, from Honduras, was taken into custody with his wife and three-year-old son five days after the separation policy came into effect. They were transported to a nearby processing centre, where they said they wanted to claim asylum. Border Patrol informed him that the family would be separated. 'The guy lost his shit,' one of the agents said. 'They had to use physical force to take the child out of his hands.' He was taken to Starr County Jail in Rio Grande City and placed in a padded isolation cell. By the next morning he had committed suicide.

Across the country, thousands of families were torn apart. Evelyn, from Guatemala, had fled an abusive relationship and made it to America with her daughter. She was taken to a detention centre. 'Look miss, you know what's going to happen now?' an officer said to her. 'We're going to take your child away.'

The same thing happened to Angelica and her seven-year-old. 'They told me to sign a consent form to take my daughter, but that it did not matter whether or not I signed, because they were going to take her either way,' she said. 'One of the officers asked me: "In Guatemala do they celebrate Mother's Day?" When I answered yes, he said: "Then happy Mother's Day."'

Even veterans of the asylum regime were astonished by what they were seeing. Taylor Levy, the legal coordinator for Annunciation House, a religious organisation which helped people at the border, had nine years experience of the US immigration and detention system. 'I have borne witness to countless stories of rape, torture and murder,' he said. 'Despite all of this, I have never been as emotionally impacted by anything as intensely as I have been working with these mothers and fathers.'

Dutch Ruppersberger, a Democratic congressman for Maryland, visited a detention center in Glen Burnie, Maryland, to interview two detainees about their separation from their children. 'Both men visibly struggled to maintain their composure while recounting the trauma that they experienced since coming to the United States and ultimately broke down into tears,' he said. 'Our interpreter too broke down into tears, finding their stories too painful to bear.'

Mothers were placed in detention centres, where the incarceration and emotional trauma created outbreaks of collective delusion. People in one centre told researchers that several detainees swore they could hear the sound of children crying inside the jail.

Fathers were packed into standing-room-only cells. An internal Department of Homeland Security investigative team took photos of them, crammed together, many of them topless, pressed up against a glass separation wall. One held up a scrap of paper on which he'd scrawled the word 'help.'

The children were kept in separate detention facilities, which quickly became overrun. They slept under metallic blankets behind chain-linked fences. Democrat Senator Jeff Merkley visited a border detention facility in Texas. 'What you have is cyclone fencing and fence posts that look like cages,' he said. 'They look like the way you would construct a dog kennel.'

Children, some as young as toddlers, were stuffed inside, caked in dirt and tears and snot, with no soap, diapers, showers or hot food. The guards called them 'animals.'

One person visiting a centre was so distressed by what they saw that they surreptitiously took an audio recording of what was going on around them. It was given to a civil rights attorney who passed it to the website ProPublica. On the tape, you could only hear wailing. Ten Central American children were crying incessantly. It was a constant noise, which never let up. Some were crying so hard they could barely breathe. They said 'mami' and 'papa' over and over again. 'We have an orchestra here,' a border patrol agent said. 'What's missing is a conductor.'

The Department of Health and Human Services' inspector general found that the children separated from their parents were undergoing severe trauma. Many thought they had been abandoned. Some were suffering post-traumatic stress from the separation. Acute grief was causing them to cry inconsolably.

In an interview, Stephen Miller showed no regret at all. Instead he read out a series of documents listing crimes by immigrants. 'We arrested an illegal alien who conducted lewd and lascivious acts with a minor,' he said. 'We arrested someone who had been convicted of murder, child neglect. Negligent manslaughter, stolen vehicle. Prostitution, racketeering, rape.'

But the outrage was growing. Hundreds of thousands of people demonstrated in over 700 locations. The pope called the policy 'immoral.' The UN's top human rights official called it 'unconscionable.' Even Trump's wife, Melania, and his daughter, Ivanka, voiced their concern.

On Capital Hill, Democrat Ted Lieu stood at the lectern on the floor of the House, took an audio device out of his pocket and pressed play. It was the ProPublica recording. The sound of weeping children filled the chamber.

'The gentleman will suspend,' the speaker said. He refused to do so. 'Rule 17 prohibits the use of an electronic device to make sounds in the Chamber,' he was told. 'We have 2,300 babies and kids in detention facilities who were ripped from their parents,' Lieu replied. 'I think the American people need to hear this.'

In fact, the number was higher. Some 2,500 children had been separated from their parents since the policy became official. Thousands more had been separated when it was run as a secret pilot.

Eventually Trump decided he'd had enough. 'The crying babies,' he decided, 'doesn't look good politically.' He issued an executive order reversing the policy.

The children who were eventually returned to their parents had changed from the ones pulled from their grasp. 'My son is not the same since we were reunited,' Olivia, who was separated from her one-year-old son for three months, said. 'I thought that, because he is so young he would not be traumatised by this experience, but he does not separate from me. He cries when he does not see me. He cries for fear of being alone.'

Trump's assault on immigrants had become so depraved that even he had to change course. But it was the only reversal he made. Every other policy continued.

TOMORROW

Nationalism is marching across the world. Wherever it establishes a position, it transmits its narrative, which consists of a series of lies.

Behind those lies is a grim reality. It is most obvious in immigration policy. The members of the supposed elite are not put in camps. The banking executives or finance ministers are not separated from their children. Instead, it is the most vulnerable: the marginalised, the dispossessed.

Nationalism claims that liberalism represents the powerful. In fact, liberalism is the shield that protects the powerless. It is the safeguard for those who have no other defences. When it fails, there is nothing left. We've seen this in the past. And we're seeing it again now.

Different societies, at different times, in different ways, target different minorities. In our society presently, it is immigrants: from Brazil to the US, and from Hungary to Italy. In the Mediterranean, and in the Hostile Environment. In Trump's detention facilities, populated by weeping children. And the things which have been done to immigrants, which have been inflicted on them by nationalist and non-nationalist governments alike, are the result of liberal failure.

Some people have developed a fatalistic approach to politics as we've watched these events play out. They have begun to speak as if this deterioration is inevitable, as if the great tectonic plates of political change have shifted and nothing can be done to halt their movement.

That overstates the scale of the defeat. Many societies have fought off a nationalist surge. Many institutions and individuals have held firm. Liberalism is not dead, as much as some people would like it to be. But it is in a battle for its life.

What happens next is not set. It will hinge on what liberals do.

That response will be based on two things: Confidence and humility. We will require the confidence to stand up for our values and the humility to understand what has gone wrong, so that we can address it.

There is nothing unusual in that. Many of the greatest moments of liberal development have followed from a recognition of the fragility of freedom. The great liberal project after the war was based not just on moral insight, but also on the chastening experience of watching liberalism totter on the brink of extinction.

Things are not as bad today. But if liberalism continues to falter, if it does not regain control over events, there is no limit to how badly wrong they can go.

The liberal values which we have to rediscover were constructed over centuries. They were based on an idea, a beautiful and world-changing idea, of individual freedom.

René Descartes inadvertently demonstrated the existential truth of the individual at the dawn of the age of science and gave it its language, in the form of reason. Early English radicalism, through the Levellers and John Locke, started to process that idea into religious and political thought. The individual's consent was the foundation of the legitimacy of government and the actions of that government were restrained by the rights of the individual.

The American revolution constrained that state power still further, working to splinter it and hold it in different places. The importance of that work was demonstrated by the French Revolution, which began with unparalleled radicalism and sophistication but descended into barbarism when the principle of consent turned into the will of the people and the separation of powers collapsed, taking individual rights along with it.

Benjamin Constant took the right lesson from that disaster. He recognised that the Terror did not result from too much freedom, but too little. He then reformulated liberal thought on the basis of individual freedom, and argued that the threats to it did not exist solely from the state, but from society itself, which would seek to mould its members into whichever majority characteristics were dominant at the time. The particular minority being targeted would change, but a system that protected the individual could defend whoever it turned out to be.

Harriet Taylor and John Stuart Mill refined Constant's work, creating the harm principle to test interference in individual sovereignty. They established the notion of half-truth, of there being elements of validity across political debate, which stood both as a testament to the need for free speech and also as a rejection of the idea that any one solution could address all problems. Most importantly of all, they developed an understanding of what was required for reason to thrive. It was autonomy: the need to be present in your decisions, to stand apart from the crushing weight of convention and choose your own life.

Many years later, Isaiah Berlin added a final principle to those which had already been established. He focused his work on the values made possible by freedom and recognised that they often come into conflict with each other. Moderation was therefore required, in the pursuit of government and the practice of politics, in order to soften these conflicts wherever possible.

Over the centuries, that long storyline established liberal values: the freedom of the individual, reason, consent in government, individual rights, the separation of powers, protection of minorities, autonomy and moderation.

Instinctively, liberals look for compromise. Our system of thought is based on managing the competing interests and rights of individuals, which entails a form of balance – of giving a bit here, a bit there, in the pursuit of coexistence. But that compromise does not extend to our founding principles. The pillars of liberalism are non-negotiable. To undermine them does not enhance freedom. It destroys it.

For many years now, liberals have failed to argue for our values. We have apologised for them, or seemed embarrassed by them, or not even mentioned them at all.

The case for immigration was made reluctantly by civil servants and business people, well away from the public eye, but it was not made in trade union meetings, or town halls, or news programmes. The defence of human rights was heard in the courtroom, but not by the water cooler. The argument for countries pooling their sovereignty echoed along the corridors of the EU and the WTO, but it was not made on the street or in the pub.

For a while, the reason for that failure was complacency. It felt as if the wind of history – a destiny myth which seduced liberals in the late Victorian period and again after the collapse of the Soviet Union – was blowing in our direction. There was no longer any need to argue for principles. We could tinker around the edges instead – through policy, through legal cases, away from the public debate.

But political debates do not take place in isolation. They have a frame, a set of assumptions that dictate the manner in which they are conducted.

The rise of nationalism did not start with the electoral success of its political parties. It started with the assertion of nationalist framing. Its assumptions and values slowly became the assumptions of the mainstream conversation. Immigration was a problem so the question was how to address it. International institutions were useless and undemocratic so the question was how to manage them.

This was the basis on which the eventual nationalist victory was won. It lay not with the discussion itself, but in the way that nationalist values shifted the parameters of political debate.

For years liberals asked themselves why they kept losing individual battles, blind to the fact that they had already conceded the war. They handed over the narrative and then wondered why it kept leading to dismal plotlines.

After Brexit and Trump, liberal complacency turned into liberal fear: fear of being branded an elitist, fear of being targeted by online mobs, fear of seeming out of touch with one's own country.

Complacency allowed liberalism to fossilise. Fear left it exposed. And nationalism could then, with shocking ease, shatter it into pieces.

Liberalism's history does not just provide an insight into its values. It also indicates what went wrong in our own period. And it's by understanding that process that we can start to repair the damage.

Liberalism had an internal tension from the very beginning. It first emerged in the Putney debates and John Locke's writing. Eventually, this tension fissured liberalism into two wings – laissez-faire on the one hand and egalitarianism on the other. The philosophy of let-things-be and the philosophy of shake-things-up.

This applied predominantly to economics, but as time passed it became clear that it also had a more general application as part of liberalism's attitude to the wider world. Would it content itself with securing freedom for society as it was – or use freedom as an ideal to aggressively remake society?

Constant was one of the first to position himself firmly on the laissez-faire side, basing his thinking on the economics of Adam Smith. He argued against state restrictions on the market, both because of the impact on individual property rights and also because property increased the material benefits of society at large. He was followed by Friedrich von Hayek, who considered any state interference to be the start of a slippery slope that led to tyranny.

Mill took a different approach. He emphasised areas where the market did not succeed, where the profit motive failed, or private monopolies developed. He resisted the idea that there would ever be a solution to the question of state versus market. Instead, cases should be dealt with individually, with an assessment of whether they were improving conditions for most people. The state and the market were both a potential source of progress and a potential threat to freedom. Each should be admired for what it could do and prevented from what it could not.

John Maynard Keynes took up that challenge in the 20th Century, showing how state employment in public works could help prevent suffering, give people jobs and stimulate a shrinking economy. Like Mill, his vision was not of state intervention in all cases, but only where the market failed.

From the late 1970s, the laissez-faire wing took control. It did a few welcome things. In some areas, the market was a better provider of services than the state, in others a certain degree of deregulation was welcome. But it did not limit itself to those areas and in fact did not show any real interest in assessing the matter in individual cases. It was akin to a religious mission, a deep-seated belief that the market was always best. It was the reverse face of communism: a zealous commitment to the market in all things, as the solution to all problems. This proposition was simplistic and the consequences were catastrophic.

The financial crash and austerity which followed ushered in the age of nationalism. They made people poorer and less secure – in their work, their income and their access to public services. They created the sense of an untouchable financial elite which would be unaffected by the consequences of its actions, while others suffered. And they cast doubt on the opinions of experts in general, by providing a case study in how political and business complacency masked a complete failure to assess the reality of the world.

But the principle of let-things-be was not restricted to economics. Historically, the hands-off approach to society often translated into an indifference towards social oppression. It was this instinct that had tolerated slavery, which had excluded people without property from democracy, which had subjected women to domestic servitude, which ignored the routine abuse of racial minorities, gay men and lesbians.

Laissez-faire failed. And it failed for a reason. It did not speak to people's lives. It did not offer them protections. It did not provide real freedom, because the restrictions they faced – discrimination, insecure work, educational disadvantage, lack of social respect, absence of representation – were not addressed or even recognised. It was cold, distant and ineffective. It was a form of liberalism with nothing to say.

Its approach to economics left struggling communities behind. Its approach to society trapped marginalised groups in a state of oppression.

Many of the people discarded by this form of liberalism then abandoned liberalism in turn – not just laissez-faire, but as a whole. And in its place, other voices emerged, with an age old story to tell, in which people could find meaning through an authentic collective consciousness – by placing the group identity over that of the individual.

This idea began with Jean-Jacques Rousseau, whose argument for the general will served to diminish and eradicate individuals. It continued with Karl Marx and was then given full practical form by the horrors of communism and fascism. Today it is put forward by nationalism on the right and identity politics on the left.

Sometimes it is expressed by people who are well meaning. Sometimes it is expressed by people who are not. The end result is nevertheless the same. Authority is handed to the group instead of the individual. Its members are homogenised and robbed of their individuality. The misfortunes of the group are blamed on an outside force – either as a form of pollution, or an enemy conspiracy. Leaders emerge who claim to speak on behalf of the group, by virtue of a mythical association.

Those left behind by laissez faire and those oppressed by discrimination often face very similar struggles. Many ethnic minorities experience the same grim economic realities as the white working class, for instance. Many in the white working class are discriminated against by their accent or their education. These are not really distinct groups.

But in the new world of brute categories, they have been cast into a culture war with each other. That war now takes place every day: a zero-sum game which permits no solution, and would only end if one set were able to gain permanent dominance over the other. In all likelihood that set would be the one representing dominant cultural groups, because of numerical superiority. And indeed, that is typically what has happened electorally, for instance through Brexit or Trump.

The identity war provides no answers. It is the politics of division and resentment over mutual advancement and debate. It helps no-one, except for its self-proclaimed leaders and the commentators who make careers off the back of it. It solves no problems, except those it invents. It has no agenda for how to improve the world, except the continued degeneration of human life into warring tribes. It is a betrayal of those it claims to represent. And it is false as a description of human life or political society.

For years now, liberalism's enemies on left and right have claimed that we are a spent force, a relic of an age of distant managerialism, consigned to the dustbin of history.

That is a fiction. In fact, there is another form of liberalism, one which has agitated for justice and equality throughout liberal history. It is egalitarian liberalism: the philosophy of shake-things-up.

It was this form of liberalism which rejected the false choice between communism and laissez-faire. It was this form which delivered the material plenty of capitalism with the protections of the state and made some of the great advances in social progress, from Britain's National Health Service to America's tight regulation of finance.

It worked to uncover discrimination and domination. It led the fight against the subjugation of women. It provided the tools in the great battles against racism and homophobia. It did the hard work of recognising people's sense of group identity while protecting the individuals within it. It did not settle for accepting how life is now, but asked itself instead how life could be if the logic of individual freedom was followed to its proper conclusion.

That is the liberalism of the future. If there was ever a time for liberalism to let things be, it has passed. Liberalism is no longer in charge. Its task is not to maintain the world, but to change it. It must show the people who are targeted by nationalism and identity politics that there is a better way. We are not homogeneous with those like us, nor at war with those who are not.

The new liberalism must be radical, or it will be nothing.

Many now suggest the battle is already lost. Emotion and tribalism have replaced reason and the individual has been subsumed into the whole.

But they are wrong. This is not an analysis. It is a propaganda effort. It is designed to suck the confidence and sense of mission from those who aspire to a better society.

If you ignore the noise for a moment, the constant drumbeat of mandated despair, there are signs of hope all around us.

The period of liberal complacency is over. It is rediscovering its values. The period of fear must now end too. Fear does not save immigrants' lives. It does not protect the open society. It cannot preserve moderation.

Around the world, people are committing to the fight against nationalism. It is happening today. It is happening all around you. It is in the protests that spring up in America against Trump's policies, in the enormous movement for EU membership which emerged in Britain during the Brexit period, in the work of brave journalists in

Hungary who continue to report independently despite harassment and abuse, in the voters across Europe who go out on election day and reject nationalist parties.

The struggle is everywhere. In the courts and parliaments and newspapers, within the political parties and campaign groups, on protests in the street, conversations across the office and arguments at the dinner table. No matter how small or frustrating they seem at the time, they all matter. They are all a battle in the greater war, a demonstration that the fight is still very much alive. Our values will prosper, as long as there are people willing to fight for them.

Some of these battles will be lost. Some will be won. Regardless, we keep fighting. We organise. We plot. We make the case. We stand firm when others turn away.

At the heart of all these encounters stands one single thing: a liberal who speaks up for their principles. Who refuses to move with the crowd, no matter how difficult it is, or how unpopular. Who resists the pressure of convention, the passing winds of consensus, and commits themself to the principles that liberated humankind four hundred years ago – and will do the same today.

This struggle could have happened at any time, to anyone. But it has happened now. It has happened to us.

That is a burden. But in the right light, it is also a privilege. We are the next page in the liberal story.

It starts with the individual.

SORRY & THANK YOU

Apologies first, appreciation later. First and foremost, sorry to the liberals I left out. You're mostly dead of course, so are unlikely to be too fussed by it, but I did spend rather a lot of time feeling guilty about it nonetheless.

Liberalism is an enormous, boisterous, confounding bloody thing. This book is not a universal description of all its various schools and tendencies. It is an account of the liberalism I embrace and why. You could quite easily write a book on the subject that didn't mention any of the figures I've used here and had a quite different emphasis, or even one that shared the same emphasis but included different figures. But that being said, I'm particularly sorry that I missed out Ronald Dworkin, TH Green, François Guizot, Leonard Hobhouse, Wilhelm von Humboldt, Immanuel Kant, Robert Nozick, Martha Nussbaum, Karl Popper, John Rawls, Friedrich Schiller and Alexis de Tocqueville. I would also like to apologise to myself for researching and writing about at least two of these figures only to realise they didn't fit the narrative. That time could have been better spent in the pub, or indeed on almost anything.

A quick note on quotations. 'If I write an article,' Christopher Hitchens once said, 'and I quote somebody and for space reasons put in an ellipsis like this (...), I swear on my children that I am not leaving out anything that, if quoted in full, would alter the original meaning or its significance.' He was asking for a bond of trust between writer and reader. I've adopted the same approach, but left out the ellipses. They slow things down and make it all too academic and stodgy for a book with this kind of tone. The language has also been updated if it was in old English. But in every case, the principle is the same: nothing has been misrepresented or had its meaning changed in any way whatsoever. Where something added nuance to the statement, but didn't contribute to the argument, I kept it anyway, to guard against any suggestion of misdirection.

A further apology is required for any mistakes in this book, of which there will invariably be a few. If you spot an error, or a logical, philosophical, political or factual problem with the argument, send me an email at howtobealiberalinfo@gmail.com or contact me on Twitter at @iandunt using the hashtag #howtobealiberal. I'll address any substantial objections or mistakes on my blog at iandunt.com. I've avoided footnotes in the text because this book is meant to appeal to the broadest possible audience, but my blog will have a space where I delve further into the decisions I've made here if people are interested.

Thanks go first to you, the reader, for giving me your time. I hope I did something useful with it. Thank you also in advance for the things you will do and the arguments you will make which will help arrest and then reverse the nationalist advance.

Many individuals took time out of their lives to read through chapters, sometimes several times, to make sure I wasn't making a complete arse of myself. They're all busy people, experts in their field, and they gained nothing from helping except for this thank you. They did it because someone was asking if something was right, and they were the kind of person who wanted to make sure that it was. Their appearance on this list does not mean they agree with me, either in the section which pertains to their specialism, or the general arguments. All errors are my own.

They were: Ruth Abbey, Anne Applebaum, Charles Arthur, Angus Armstrong, Roger Backhouse, Jamie Bartlett, David Blanchflower, Michael Braddick, Toby Buckle, Tom Chivers, Ed Conway, Robert Cook, Roger Crisp, George Crowder, Richard Davies, Richard Disney, William Doyle, John Dunn, Richard J. Evans, Alison Finch,

James Forder, Iain Gadd, Zoe Gardner, Conor Gearty, Chris Giles, Ilka Gleibs, Craig Grannell, Dmitry Grozoubinski, Ruth Harris, Timothy Harris, Kilian Huber, Robert Jackson, Heather Jones, Patrick Kingsley, Brian Klaas, David Leopold, Marisa Linton, Dorian Lynskey, Paul McNamara, Anand Menon, Michael Molcher, Cas Muddie, Ben Myring, Colm O'Cinneide, Stuart Ormy, Brian Parkinson, Pal Daniel Rényi, Emma Rothschild, Valeria Rueda, Viktória Serdült, Catriona Seth, Frank Sharry, John Skorupski, Kurt Smith, David Stevenson, Ronald Grigor Suny, Jim Tomlinson, Peter Ungphakorn, Edward Vallance, Shahin Vallée, Natacha Postel-Vinay, Jo Wolff, and Colin Yeo.

I also want to thank the people who sat with me, often for hours at a time, on the phone or in a cafe somewhere, or sometimes admittedly in a pub with me paying, and lent me their brain. I have made my career listening to experts, working to understand them, and then translating their expertise into something which is hopefully easy to understand while you're on the bus and worrying about whether you'll be late for your next meeting. I have developed a kind of reverence for them, to be honest, and for their eagerness to share knowledge.

They were: David Aaronovitch, Madeline Abbas, Angus Armstrong, Timothy Garton Ash, Alex Barber, Jamie Bartlett, Meghan Benton, Christopher Bertram, Julie Bindel, Chad Bown, Guillaume Chaslot, Tom Chivers, Chris Cook, Frances Coppola, George Crowder, Karen Douglas, Daniel Drezner, Robin Dunbar, Martin Marix Evans, Mónica Moreno Figueroa, Marc Fisher, Rob Ford, Ian Fraser, Ian Gadd, David Galloway, Julia Gelatt, Ilka Gleibs, AC Grayling, Dmitry Grozoubinski, Tim Naor Hilton, Ian Harris, Keith Kahn-Harris, Jonathan Healey, Stephen Hodkinson, Valerie Hopkins, Kevin Hylton, Robert Jackson, Nina Jankowicz, Schona Jolly, Sunder Katwala, Daniel Kelemen, Patrick Kingsley, Sarah L. de Lange, David Leopold, Marisa Linton, Steve Lukes, George Magnus, Kenan Malik, Richard Mash, Paul McNamara, Cas Mudde, Maria Norris, Anne Phillips, Jonathan Portas, John Rees, Pal Daniel

Rényi, Alasdair Richmond, Jay Rosen, Alan Ryan, Cliff Schecter, Viktória Serdült, Jo Shah, Punit Shah, Alasdair Smith, David Sneath, Nikos Sotirakopoulos, Margaret Sullivan, Kurt Sylvan, Robert Tombs, Peter Ungphakorn, Shahin Vallee, Matteo Villa, Natacha Postel-Vinay and Jo Wolff.

Thanks as well to Refugee Action, the JCWI, the3million, the Migration Policy Institute, Migrant Voice, Reunite Families, Satbir Singh and Sonia L, who helped me with the chapter on immigration, including helping me find people in the immigration system to tell their story. Also thanks to the British Library – if it wasn't for that extraordinary resource, of being able to secure any book in the history of the world for free with a few hours' notice, this book would not have been possible.

I'm grateful to my publisher, Martin Hickman, for getting me to write this book, supporting me while I did it, and never once using euphemisms when he was trying to communicate that something was crap and should be rewritten. Twice in my life, Martin has said a single sentence which defined the next period of my work. In the first case it was the title of my first book and in the second case it was the title of my second book. As soon as he did that, all the disparate thoughts in my head slotted into place and I could see a through-line of an argument which would carry the project through. If you find someone like that, who clarifies what you already want to do, work closely with them.

Thanks also to Alice Marwick, who designed the extraordinary cover of the book, Paula Clarke Bain, who proofed, fact-checked and indexed it, to Sarah Anderson, Kate Woodruff and their colleagues in the sales team at Simon & Schuster UK, and to their counterparts at Casemate in the US and Booktopia in Australia.

Thanks also to my agent, Lisa Moylett, from Coombs Moylett Maclean, and Zoe Apostolides, who looked over the first version of the manuscript. Publishing is a weird world, of people who I frankly do not understand. Lisa has been there in my corner, standing up for me, egging me forward, providing sensible advice, and generally being a cheerleader for my work. The whole process would be unutterably more dreadful without her.

Thanks to Nathan Coyne, my director at Politics.co.uk, who understood what writing a book entailed and made the flexibility it required possible without making a fuss over it, because he is resolutely unflappable in seemingly all things. Also thanks to the team and the listeners at Remainiacs and the Bunker who shifted things around when required and generally kept my spirits up by being lovely. Special thanks to Dorian Lynskey, for all the walks and conversation around Soho. It's lonely writing a book and a great bit of luck to have someone to talk to who is in the same business.

Thanks to all the friends and family who made sure to always ask me about the book during those seemingly endless bloody years that I was writing it and almost never fell asleep when I started warbling on about it. You know who you are. You can only ever really do anything when you have friends who will take you for a pint. It's the precondition of all intellectual and moral accomplishments. So thank you for making it possible.

And finally thank you to Menissa Saleem – the person who stuck with me throughout, who makes me laugh every day, who sits and listens and then lightly provides suggestions when I am having an emotional meltdown, who challenges me to be better, and who supports me when I need someone to say that it'll be alright in the end. None of this would be possible if you weren't there next to me. And even if it were, it would not be worth doing.

FURTHER READING

The best comprehensive overview of liberalism is *Liberalism: The Life of an Idea*, by Edmund Fawcett. Very few books encompass the whole history and various offshoots of liberalism, but this partially makes up for it by providing a sweeping, readable guide.

The Stanford Encyclopedia of Philosophy, available for free online, is an extraordinary resource – very thorough and reliable, with entries on almost any element of philosophy you could ask for. If there is a topic which interests you, this is the best springboard for further reading.

Toby Buckle's *Political Philosophy* podcast is an excellent listen on liberal issues. Toby is extremely well read and eloquent, and, more importantly, humane and generous.

Many academic articles mentioned in this section will be available on jstor.org. Readers outside of academia are entitled to a set number of free articles a month.

Descartes' work – particularly *The Discourse* and *The Meditations* – is lively and can be read on its own. It's not exactly easy going, but it's a lot more pleasant than you might expect. Everyman does a decent collected edition of *The Discourse*, *The Meditations* and *Principles of Philosophy*.

For a thorough and illuminating account of Descartes' life read *Descartes: A Biography* by Desmond Clarke. The philosopher's ideas are more thoroughly explored in *Descartes: An Intellectual Biography*, by Stephen Gaukroger. For an extensive look at the Cogito read Joseph Almog's two books: *Cogito? Descartes and Thinking the World*, which looks at the 'I think,' and *What Am I? Descartes and the Mind-Body Problem*, which looks at the 'I am.' *The Cambridge Companion to Descartes*, edited by John Cottingham, gives a broader overview of his life's work.

Alice Browne's article *Descartes's Dreams* in volume 40 of the Journal of the Warburg and Courtauld Institutes is a good overview of what, if anything, was going on when Descartes had those dreams. If you'd prefer an account of their impact on Descartes' work try Michael Keevak's article *Descartes's Dreams and Their Address for Philosophy*, in volume 53 issue 3 of the Journal of the History of Ideas.

The most gripping English Civil War history, with a real sense of detail and narrative thrust is Michael Braddick's *God's Fury, England's Fire*. Blair Worden's *The English Civil Wars: 1640–1660* carries you through to the Restoration. Diane Purkiss' widely admired *The English Civil War: A People's History* covers the period up to the regicide through individual stories.

The World Turned Upside Down: Radical Ideas During the English Revolution, by Christopher Hill, looks at the radicalism of the period, including not only the Levellers but also the Diggers, the Ranters, the Muggletonians and the early Quakers. John Rees' *The Leveller Revolution*, focuses on the Levellers alone and is highly readable. Andy Wood's *Riots, Rebellion and Popular Politics in Early Modern England* provides a useful but dense account of how diverse the social and political make-up of the country was, together with an extended analysis of the phrase 'middling sort.'

Milton's *Areopagitica* can be read on its own, and deserves to be. The Online Library of Liberty is undertaking the extraordinary project of putting the entire collection of Leveller tracts on the internet, including a transcript of the Putney debates. You can access it at https://oll.libertyfund.org/pages/leveller-tracts-summary.

Anthony Milton provides a brilliant overall exploration of the printing press through the period in *Licensing, Censorship, and Religious Orthodoxy in Early Stuart England*, found in volume 41 issue 3 of the Historical Journal. David R. Como's *Secret Printing, the Crisis of 1640, and the Origins of Civil War Radicalism*, in volume 196 issue 1 of Past & Present, is excellent on blackmarket printing culture. His book, *Radical Parliamentarians and the English Civil War*, is pricey but authoritative.

John Miller's *The Glorious Revolution* is arguably the standard introduction to the Glorious Revolution. For a more popular, page-turning approach, the three best books on the period are Edward Vallance's *The Glorious Revolution: 1688, Britain's Fight for Liberty*, Tim Harris' *Revolution: The Great Crisis of the British Monarchy, 1685-1720* and Steve Pincus' *1688: The First Modern Revolution*.

For a comprehensive history of the American Revolution, try *The Creation of the American Republic, 1776–1787* by Gordon S. Wood. If you fancy a shorter encapsulation, opt for his *The American Revolution: A History*, although I always find that the longer a history book is, the easier it is to read for some reason. *The Glorious Cause: The American Revolution, 1763-1789* by Robert Middlekauff is also very highly regarded, as is *Angel in the Whirlwind: The Triumph of the American Revolution* by Benson Bobrick. David J. Bodenhamer's *The U.S. Constitution: A Very Short Introduction* gives an extremely quick and efficient overview of the document and the debates that took place over it in the centuries after it was written.

For the French Revolution, William Doyle's *The Oxford History of the French Revolution* is encyclopedic in its scope and yet somehow still compelling and pacey. I relied on it extensively for this section. Simon Schama's *Citizens: A Chronicle of the French Revolution* is controversial but colourful. *The French Revolution: From Enlightenment to Tyranny* by Ian Davidson has its detractors, but it is swift and especially perceptive on the economics of the assignats.

John Locke's *Two Treatises on Government* can be read on its own, as can *A Letter Concerning Toleration*, which I didn't have time to go into here but is extremely valuable. As with all philosophers from this period, or frankly later ones, it can be difficult to read the original text, but you get used to it after a few pages if you persevere. It's like getting into *A Clockwork Orange* for the first time – you get the hang of it fairly quickly. If you're going to get into this stuff – and you should, because it holds the key to personal and political liberation – it is best to go back to the original source.

Locke: A Biography by Roger Woolhouse provides the most recent account of the philosopher's life and times, although the older *John Locke, A Biography* by Maurice Cranston is also available. For an overview of his ideas, including the non-political work, read the *Cambridge Companion to Locke*, edited by Vere Chappell. Ruth W Grant's *John Locke's Liberalism* is good if you can find a copy, as is *The Lockean Theory of Rights* by A John Simmons.

Jean-Jacques Rousseau's *The Social Contract* is actually a delight to read on its own. He might not be right, and he may indeed have provided the basis for centuries of political tyranny and bloodshed, but he had a wonderful turn of phrase.

Jean-Jacques Rousseau: Restless Genius, by Leo Damrosch, gives the best account of his rather extraordinary life. *Rousseau*, by Nicholas Dent, is a decent introduction to his thoughts. You really do need to take Rousseau's work as a whole to grasp what he's saying – especially the sections on education, but even arguably the approach towards nature, which I think helps inform the romanticism of the mystical process in the general will.

The Cambridge Companion to Rousseau, edited by Patrick Riley, is an overview of his general philosophy as well as the political elements. *Rousseau, the Age of Enlightenment, and Their Legacies*, edited by Bryan Garsten, collects essays by Robert Wokler, the leading Rousseau scholar of the 20th Century. For a brief, laugh-out-loud funny, bitterly critical assessment of Rousseau, read the short chapter on him in Bertrand Russell's *History of Western Philosophy*, which you should read anyway, because it is very good.

Benjamin Constant tends to attract the worst biographers. Works on him are typically written in the arrogant biographic style of the mid-20th Century, although that form of writing does have its own strange pleasures. Harold Nicolson's *Benjamin Constant* is a case in point. Leonard Tancock's introduction to the Penguin edition of *Adolphe* is along the same lines, but it's still a decent version of the novel. William W Holdheim's assessment of Constant's life and work, *Benjamin Constant*, is far superior and properly discusses his ideas. Dennis Wood's *Benjamin Constant: A Biography*, is by distance the best single book on the subject, although it's tempered by the author's regular baffling forays into Freudian psychoanalysis. Renee Winegarten's *Germaine de Staël and Benjamin Constant: A Dual Biography* is much more recent and well regarded. Constant's *Principles of Politics Applicable to All Governments* has been translated by Dennis O'Keeffe and reads very well on its own. It is also available online at the Online Library of Liberty, which you can access here: https://oll. libertyfund.org/titles/constant-principles-of-politics-applicable-to-all-governments

Adam Smith's *The Wealth of Nations and The Theory of Moral Sentiments* are worth reading on their own terms. Jerry Muller's *Adam Smith in His Time and Ours* is a very good introduction to his life and work. It's also well worth reading the sections on Smith in *A History of Economic Thought: The LSE Lectures*, by Lionel Robbins. Robbins was Hayek's patron and ally at LSE, but then later moved towards Keynesianism. He is like an embodiment of the perfect Platonic form of an academic. The lectures are witty, vivid, informative: an absolute joy.

There's also a good description of Smith and classical economics in Ha-Joon Chang's *Economics: The User's Guide*. He explains the distinctions between classical and neoclassical economics, as well as pretty much every other aspect of the subject you could hope for, in a breezy, easy to understand style. Along the same lines, *The Penguin History of Economics* by Roger Backhouse provides a brilliant introduction to economic thinking. It's one of those books economists regularly recommend to non-economists. Joyce Appleby's *The Relentless Revolution: A History of Capitalism* runs through the ideas and events which constitute free market history.

As stated in the text, there are no biographies of Harriet Taylor. Instead, we have to rely on the invaluable *Complete Works of Harriet Taylor Mill*, painstakingly put together and edited by Jo Ellen Jacobs. Her book *The Voice of Harriet Taylor Mill*, corrals the historical evidence into a made-up first-person diary which her subject could have written. It's thanks to Friedrich Hayek that we have the historical documents that allow us to put Harriet Taylor in the proper intellectual context and his *John Stuart Mill and Harriet Taylor: Their Correspondence and Subsequent Marriage* is still required reading.

Richard Reeves' *John Stuart Mill: Victorian Firebrand* gives an authoritative, thorough, and compelling account of his life. *John Stuart Mill: A Biography*, by Nicholas Capaldi, is also worth checking out. For a broader approach to his work try *The Cambridge Companion to Mill*, edited by John Skorupski.

Mill's *Autobiography* is a difficult read, but if you're going for it, which really isn't advisable, the Oxford World Classics edition comes with a very useful introduction by Mark Philp that supplies the proper emotional context. *Essays on Sex Equality*, edited with a very good introductory essay by Alice S. Rossi, collects the pair's main writings on women's rights, including the *Enfranchisement of Women* and *The Subjection of Women*. The latter in particular is a masterclass in how to present an argument.

You owe it to yourself to read *On Liberty*. It's not always easy. There's no point pretending it is. But it contains treasures beyond my capacity to describe in words. If you read just one work of liberal philosophy, make it this.

The Marxist historian Eric Hobsbawm's *Age of Empire: 1875–1914*, part of his masterly series of world histories, is probably the best account of the period between John Stuart Mill's death and the First World War. Hannah Arendt's *Origins of Totalitarianism* is still one of the dominant books on the subject of what came afterwards. Her insights are very striking and occasionally unforgettable, but it is an idiosyncratic work and on some matters her judgement is disturbing. It includes an account of the Dreyfus Affair, of which there is another in Robert Rapley's interesting and worthwhile *Witch Hunts: From Salem to Guantanamo Bay*. *The Dreyfus Affair: J'Accuse and Other Writings* is a collection of Zola's articles, letters and interviews during the period. For something more thorough, the best single book on the subject is *Dreyfus: Politics, Emotion, and the Scandal of the Century*, by Ruth Harris. Pierre Birnbaum's *The Anti-Semitic Moment: A Tour of*

France in 1898, puts together newspaper, police and local government reports from the period to map out the eruption of anti-semitism that shook the country.

Marx's *Communist Manifesto* can be read on its own. It remains a supremely readable, and often unexpectedly funny, piece of political propaganda. His *Critique of the Gotha Programme*, which is also short and highly readable, contains the section on individual rights and the best indications of how he expected the transition from capitalism to communism to work. For his more encouraging comments – although they're not exactly definitive – on the requirement of elections under socialism, see *The Civil War in France*. Marxists.org is an amazing online resource which contains all his writings. *Statism and Anarchy* by Mikhail Bakunin is arguably the best contemporaneous critique of Marx's writings, which is all the more powerful for having been conceived by a fellow traveller. The best biographies of Marx are *Karl Marx: A Biography* by David McLellan, *Karl Marx: A Nineteenth-Century Life*, by Jonathan Sperber, *Karl Marx* by Francis Wheen, and *A World to Win: The Life and Thought of Karl Marx*, by Sven-Eric Liedman.

For the full account of the famine in Ukraine, read Anne Applebaum's brilliant *Red Famine: Stalin's War on Ukraine*, on which much of that section is based. It is a profoundly moral and well-researched book. Her work on the Soviet camp system – *Gulag: A History* – is also one of the best works on that topic. It's still worth reading Aleksandr Solzhenitsyn's *Gulag Archipelago*, which is full of raw horror, outrage and some seriously dark humour. Orlando Figes' *The Whisperers: Private Life in Stalin's Russia* is a profoundly moving and incredibly well-researched account of how ordinary people lived under the Soviet regime, from which many of the examples in the text were taken.

Robert O Paxton's *The Anatomy of Fascism* is a masterful assessment of Mussolini and Hitler's regimes and how exactly we can try to define a concept as slippery and vapid as fascism. Robert Gellately's *Backing Hitler: Consent and Coercion in Nazi Germany* gives a good assessment of the degree of social conformity and tacit assistance of the regime. But the definitive work on Nazi Germany, and the one on which those sections were predominantly based, is Richard J Evans' masterly and comprehensive *Third Reich Trilogy: The Coming of the Third Reich*, *The Third Reich in Power*, and *The Third Reich at War*.

Nicholas Wapshott's *Keynes/Hayek* offers an account of the friendship and arguments between John Maynard Keynes and Friedrich Hayek. It's readable and intriguing, although some of the economics is hard to grasp without some background knowledge. For the full treatment on Keynes, read Robert Skidelsky's immense three-volume biography of *Keynes: Hopes Betrayed, The Economist as Saviour and Fighting for Britain*, or, if you're feeling rushed, the one-volume condensed version, *John Maynard Keynes 1883-1946*, which is very highly regarded. The Penguin Classics *Essential Keynes*, also edited by Robert Skidelsky, provides a single-volume edition of Keynes' writings on economics, philosophy, social policy. For books on Hayek, try *Hayek: His Contribution to the Political and Economic Thought of Our Time*, by Eamonn Butler or *Friedrich Hayek: A Biography*, by Alan Ebenstein. To get a sense of his own writing, read *The Constitution of Liberty* and *The Road to Serfdom*.

The negotiations over the establishment of the world trading system outlined in the book were much more intense and fragile than there was space to describe. The WTO's own resource on the talks is very useful and can be found at https://www.wto.org/english/thewto_e/history_e/history_e.htm. It's worth paying particular attention to the article on the *Atlantic Charter* and the blogs by Roy Santana, an expert on tariffs and customs issues. The WTO's own *The History and Future of the World Trade Organization*, by Craig VanGrasstek, gives an overview of the institution. It also has resources available online at https://www.wto.org/english/thewto_e/whatis_e/tif_e/tif_e.htm. Peter Ungphakorn's *Trade Beta* blog is a useful resource for level-headed thinking and explainers on how the WTO operates and what it's going through. It can be found at https://tradebetablog.wordpress.com/.

For a look at how the EU works, try *The European Union: A Citizen's Guide*, by Chris Bickerton, *Understanding the European Union: A Concise Introduction*, by John McCormick, or *The Oxford Handbook of the European Union*, edited by Erik Jones, Anand Menon and Stephen Weatherill.

Books on human rights that are suitable for the general reader are hard to find, but there are three strong examples in *On Human Rights* by James Griffin, *On Fantasy Island: Britain, Europe, and Human Rights* by Conor Gearty, and *Universal Human Rights in Theory and Practice*, by Jack Donnelly.

You can find many of George Orwell's thoughts on a variety of topics in *Essays*, published by Penguin, which is an absolute treasure house. The Penguin Modern Classics edition of *Nineteen Eighty-Four* is still required reading too and should be followed up with *The Ministry of Truth*, by Dorian Lynskey. *Orwell: The Life*, by DJ Taylor is a very good biography.

Liberty by Isaiah Berlin incorporates many of the philosopher's writings on the subject. It's also worth reading *The Crooked Timber of Humanity: Chapters in the History of Ideas*, *The Power of Ideas*, and *Three Critics of the Enlightenment: Vico, Hamann, Herder*. The best biography, without question, is *Isaiah Berlin: A Life*, by Michael Ignatieff. It is a beautiful work in its own right – the biography as art form.

The best single work on Berlin's philosophy is George Crowder's masterful *Isaiah Berlin: Liberty and Pluralism*. For a different take read John Gray's influential, but I think wrong, *Isaiah Berlin: An Interpretation of his Thoughts*.

On Milton Friedman, Paul Krugman's article *Who Was Milton Friedman?* in volume 54 issue 2 of the *New York Review of Books* is very good. You can find further discussion of some of the issues in this section in *A Companion to the History of Economic Thought*, edited by Warren J Samuels, Jeff E Biddle, and John B Davis. Chapters 26 and 27 are particularly good, but the book is also recommended for its discussion of Adam Smith and John Maynard Keynes. For a different, and more critical look at Friedman's legacy, including his reputation on inflation, read *Macroeconomics and the Phillips Curve Myth*, by James Forder.

The best work on the 2008 financial crash and the eurozone crisis, by some distance, is *Crashed: How a Decade of Financial Crises Changed the World*, by Adam Tooze. People tend to stay away from official reports, but the *Final Report of the National Commission on the Causes of the Financial and Economic Crisis in the United States*, by the Financial Crisis Inquiry Commission, is a truly majestic work – as readable as any popular economics book and freely available online at https://www.govinfo.gov/content/pkg/GPO-FCIC/pdf/GPO-FCIC.pdf. The section on the crash leant on those two sources. For an account of the moves against Papandreou and Berlusconi read the eye-opening FT series *How the Euro Was Saved* at https://www.ft.com/content/f6f4d6b4-ca2e-11e3-ac05-00144feabdc0.

It's very much worth reading EM Forster's *Maurice*, which is a supremely beautiful piece of early gay literature. Whatever you do, do not watch the film. Forster's views on politics and culture are in *Two Cheers for Democracy*, which is infuriatingly difficult to get hold of – but well worth it.

Estelle B Freedman's *No Turning Back: The History of Feminism and the Future of Women*, is a passionate and under-recognised history of feminism and outline of its principles. There's an excellent introduction to identity politics by James Tully in *The Cambridge History of Twentieth-Century Political Thought*, edited by Terence Ball. Mary Bernstein's article on *Identity Politics* in Vol 31 of the Annual Review of Sociology is also informative. Stuart Hall's article *Cultural Identity and Diaspora*, published in issue 36 of Framework, grapples with matters of identity through the lens of the cinematic representation of Afro-Caribbeans and provides an evocative account not just of how people approach these issues but why. The Combahee River Collective statement is available online at https://americanstudies.yale.edu/sites/default/files/files/Keyword%20Coalition_Readings.pdf. Kimberlé Crenshaw's *Mapping the Margins* is available at https://pdfs.semanticscholar.org/734f/8b582b7d7bb375415d2975cb783c839e5e3c.pdf?_ga=2.35438689.1124182733.1592412974-645344686.1592412974 and *Demarginalizing the Intersection of Race and Sex* is available at

https://chicagounbound.uchicago.edu/cgi/viewcontent.
cgi?article=1052&context=uclf. Some of her best writing is collected
in *On Intersectionality: The Essential Writings of Kimberlé Crenshaw*. *Intersectionality*
by Patricia Hill Collins and Sirma Bilge is probably the best one-
stop-shop guide to the theory. It's also worth reading the classic *Justice
and the Politics of Difference*, by Iris Marion Young.

One of the best and most comprehensive academic accounts
of the approaches to cultural appropriation can be found in *From
Cultural Exchange to Transculturation: A Review and Reconceptualization of Cultural
Appropriation*, by Richard A Rogers, published in volume 16 issue 4 of
Communication Theory. The best critique of its effect on literature
comes from Zadie Smith, in her article *Fascinated to Presume: In Defense
of Fiction*, in volume 66 issue 16 of the *New York Review of Books*.

Cas Mudde's *The Far Right Today* provides an excellent account of
the new nationalist movement, alongside its fellow travellers. *The
People*, by Margaret Canovan, one of the foundational theorists of
what's typically called populism, takes a broad look at the concept
of 'the people.' *What is Populism?*, by Jan-Werner Müller, explores the
ideas further and with clarity. *The Populist Explosion: How the Great Recession
Transformed American and European Politics*, by John B Judis, looks at the
explosions in 2016 and provides a good introduction, although it
is overly reductive on the causes being economic.

Angela Nagle's *Kill All Normies* – a quick, entertaining tour of the
online left and right culture wars – will make you feel quite dirty by
the time you've turned the last page. Douglas Murray's *The Madness of
Crowds* provides useful examples of left-wing identity politics online
and on campus, although it is fatally weakened by a complete lack
of interest in similar behaviour from the right.

Kenan Malik's *From Fatwa to Jihad* is fascinating and way ahead
of its time on the notion of identity politics and liberalism. The
sections on local government policy in England relied heavily on
it. For the liberal debate over multiculturalism and group rights,
try Charles Taylor's *Politics of Recognition*, in *Multiculturalism*, edited
by Amy Gutmann. Will Kymlicka's *Liberalism, Community, and Culture*

and *Multicultural Citizenship: A Liberal Theory of Minority Rights* provided the jumping off point for the ensuing arguments. Brian Barry's views are in *Culture and Equality*, as well as *Second Thoughts — and Some First Thoughts Revived*, in *Multiculturalism Reconsidered: Culture and Equality and its Critics*, edited by Paul Kelly. Ronald Dworkin's are in *Taking Rights Seriously*. Chandran Kukathas' are in *Liberal Archipelago*. Susan Okin's are in *Is Multiculturalism Bad for Women?*, edited by J Cohen, M Howard and M Nussbaum, and *'Mistresses of Their Own Destiny': Group Rights, Gender, and Realistic Rights of Exit*, in volume 112 issue 2 of Ethics. To get a much easier grasp of the debate, read George Crowder's brilliant summary, with his own take on how it can be resolved, in *Theories of Multiculturalism: An Introduction*.

For more on the Robbers Cave experiment check out *The Robbers Cave Experiment: Intergroup Conflict and Cooperation*, by Muzafer Sherif, OJ Harvey et al. Other accounts of group identity and prejudice without competitive circumstances can be found in Henri Tajfel's *Experiments in Intergroup Discrimination*, in volume 223 issue 5 of Scientific American or *Social Categorisation and Intergroup Behaviour*, by Henri Tajfel, MG Billig, RP Bundy and Claude Flament, in volume 1 issue 2 of the European Journal of Social Psychology. For a general modern appraisal of these studies read *Social Psychology: Revisiting the Classic Studies*, edited by Joanne R. Smith and S. Alexander Haslam.

The potentials and dangers, but mostly dangers, of new technology are laid out in *The People Vs Tech*, by Jamie Bartlett, which is very cogent and well judged, and *Stand Out of Our Light* by James Williams, which is the best account of the attention economy and a poetic, melancholic description of what it is doing to the quality of human life. *Auditing Radicalization Pathways* on YouTube, by Manoel Horta Ribeiro, Raphael Ottoni, Robert West, Virgílio AF Almeida and Wagner Meira Jr looks at the relationship between YouTube recommendations and extremism.

The IRA, Social Media and Political Polarization in the United States, 2012-2018 by Philip N. Howard, Bharath Ganesh, Dimitra Liotsiou, John Kelly and Camille François, is the first major analysis of the

Russian disinformation attack on the US, based on data provided by social media firms to the Senate Select Committee on Intelligence. *The Global Disinformation Order 2019 Global Inventory of Organised Social Media Manipulation*, by Samantha Bradshaw and Philip N Howard, gives information on how extensively these techniques are now being used around the world.

For accounts of disinformation in the digital age see David Patrikarakos' lively and important *War in 140 Characters: How Social Media is Reshaping Conflict in the 21st Century*, from which the account of the Russian disinformation building is taken, and *How to Lose the Information War: Russia, Fake News, and the Future of Conflict*, by Nina Jankowicz.

Useful books on what's happening in Hungary include *Orbán: Hungary's Strongman*, by Paul Lendvai and the more academic *The Rise of Hungarian Populism: State Autocracy and the Orbán Regime*, by Attila Antal.

On Brexit, it would remiss of me not to mention *Brexit: What the Hell Happens Now?*, by me, which wasn't bad at all frankly. *All Out War: The Full Story of How Brexit Sank Britain's Political Class*, by Tim Shipman, provides an overview of the campaign. *Heroic Failure: Brexit and the Politics of Pain*, by Fintan O'Toole, dissects the project's psychological and political failures. *Nine Lessons in Brexit*, by Ivan Rogers, authoritatively describes the dangers and inadequacies involved.

The Despot's Apprentice, by Brian Klaas provides a lucid, principled and breezy overview of Trump's authoritarian tendencies. The best account of Trump's immigration policy comes from *Border Wars: Inside Trump's Assault on Immigration*, by Julie Hirschfeld Davis and Michael D Shear, which is forensic and absolutely crammed with detail. I borrowed from it extensively.

The two best books on the last few decades of British immigration policy are *Hostile Environment: How Immigrants Became Scapegoats*, by Maya Goodfellow, and *Drawbridge Britain: Love and Hostility in Immigration Policy from Windrush to the Present*, by Russell Hargrave. Goodfellow is purposeful, detailed and highly knowledgeable. Hargrave has a breezy, conversational style, a humane instinct and gives really lucid moral insight.

INDEX

Quality contemporary non-fiction.
See the world more clearly.

We're committed to finding talented writers and getting their accounts into the hands of the right people: people like you. This sometimes includes crowdfunding campaigns, like the one that has allowed us to publish *99 Immigrants Who Made Britain Great*. We will continue to experiment with innovative ways to publish these important and true stories. If you'd like to be kept updated about our new projects, please sign up to our email newsletter – you'll get 10 per cent off all titles you order direct from our website – or consider our new subscription service.

By subscribing, you allow us to invest in important new works of non-fiction. For £55* for 12 months, you'll receive:

- Five mystery titles, tailored to you, sent as soon as they are printed, with a total RRP of £59.95 or more
- Free postage and packing
- At least one signed or special edition, or a free gift
- A 20% discount code for use in our online shop
- Advance notice and priority booking for author events.

If you're interested in becoming a subscriber, or giving a subscription as a gift, visit:

www.canburypress.com/subscriptions
@canburypress

*Offer only available in the UK. All information stated is correct at time of printing